Advances in Computer Vision and Pattern Recognition

For further volumes:
www.springer.com/series/4205

Andrea Fossati · Juergen Gall · Helmut Grabner ·
Xiaofeng Ren · Kurt Konolige
Editors

Consumer Depth Cameras for Computer Vision

Research Topics and Applications

Springer

Editors
Andrea Fossati
Computer Vision Laboratory
ETH Zürich
Zürich, Switzerland

Juergen Gall
Perceiving Systems Department
Max Planck Inst. for Intelligent Systems
Tübingen, Germany

Helmut Grabner
Computer Vision Laboratory
ETH Zürich
Zürich, Switzerland

Xiaofeng Ren
Intel Science and Technology Center
Seattle, WA, USA

Kurt Konolige
Industrial Perception
Palo Alto, CA, USA

Series Editors
Prof. Sameer Singh
Research School of Informatics
Loughborough University
Loughborough, UK

Dr. Sing Bing Kang
Microsoft Research
Microsoft Corporation
Redmond, WA, USA

ISSN 2191-6586 ISSN 2191-6594 (electronic)
Advances in Computer Vision and Pattern Recognition
ISBN 978-1-4471-4639-1 ISBN 978-1-4471-4640-7 (eBook)
DOI 10.1007/978-1-4471-4640-7
Springer London Heidelberg New York Dordrecht

Library of Congress Control Number: 2012950032

© Springer-Verlag London 2013
This work is subject to copyright. All rights are reserved by the Publisher, whether the whole or part of the material is concerned, specifically the rights of translation, reprinting, reuse of illustrations, recitation, broadcasting, reproduction on microfilms or in any other physical way, and transmission or information storage and retrieval, electronic adaptation, computer software, or by similar or dissimilar methodology now known or hereafter developed. Exempted from this legal reservation are brief excerpts in connection with reviews or scholarly analysis or material supplied specifically for the purpose of being entered and executed on a computer system, for exclusive use by the purchaser of the work. Duplication of this publication or parts thereof is permitted only under the provisions of the Copyright Law of the Publisher's location, in its current version, and permission for use must always be obtained from Springer. Permissions for use may be obtained through RightsLink at the Copyright Clearance Center. Violations are liable to prosecution under the respective Copyright Law.
The use of general descriptive names, registered names, trademarks, service marks, etc. in this publication does not imply, even in the absence of a specific statement, that such names are exempt from the relevant protective laws and regulations and therefore free for general use.
While the advice and information in this book are believed to be true and accurate at the date of publication, neither the authors nor the editors nor the publisher can accept any legal responsibility for any errors or omissions that may be made. The publisher makes no warranty, express or implied, with respect to the material contained herein.

Printed on acid-free paper

Springer is part of Springer Science+Business Media (www.springer.com)

Foreword

Kinect for Xbox 360 launched worldwide in November 2010. This was a groundbreaking moment: for the first time you could control your entertainment devices with voice and full-body markerless motion capture; for the first time, computer vision had played a pivotal role in a mass-market and highly publicized consumer product. But perhaps Kinect will come to be remembered most for this: for the first time you could buy a high-resolution depth-sensing camera at a consumer price point. As the examples in this book testify, Kinect, as the first consumer depth camera, has excited thousands of people around the world, both enthusiasts and academics, to start tinkering away and creating an incredible variety of amazing experiences.

Why is depth sensing important? It bypasses many of the traditional problems that have plagued practical applications of computer vision for decades: widely varying foreground and background colors and textures, unknown object scales, and variable lighting conditions. Depth cameras overcome these obstacles by design, and are starting to allow real-world applications of computer vision that work robustly outside the lab.

Several varieties of depth sensing technology have been in development for many years. Dense stereo is a "passive" technique that uses two or more standard RGB cameras, and attempts to find correspondences between image points in order to triangulate depth. Stereo has advanced considerably, though still struggles with large textureless surfaces and in low light levels. "Active" approaches for measuring depth instead have their own light sources and thus can potentially overcome the limitations of passive stereo. There are two main varieties of active depth sensing: time of flight, and structured light. Time of flight cameras send out a pulse of light and measure the time taken for the light to bounce back to the sensor. Structured light sensors instead use a pattern projector to emit a known spatially (and sometimes temporally) varying pattern of light, and triangulate based on the image of the reflected light to find the depth.

Working on Human Pose Estimation for Kinect

The Kinect sensor is a structured light device. Bringing it to market at a consumer price point involved substantial advances in structured light pattern projection, calibration, and manufacturing technologies. But for all these advances in the hardware, we would not have had a viable commercial product without a compelling reason for consumers to buy it. So far, the most compelling consumer scenario for Kinect is that you can play games without holding a controller. I was lucky enough to have been involved with the research and development of the pose estimation software that makes this possible. I would like to take this opportunity to briefly share my behind-the-scenes story and thank a few people along the way.

Any history of Kinect must begin with Alex Kipman, the leader of the Kinect project within Xbox. Alex had the bold vision of making an immersive experience in which technology disappears. Like many people before, he could foresee the fantastic value in interacting with games without a hand-held controller. But unlike anyone else, he had the ambition and tenacity to actually bring the right people together to build the hardware and software platforms needed to turn Kinect for Xbox 360 into a real product and to make it such a success.

It was mid-summer 2008, when Mark Finocchio, one of Alex's team approached me and my colleagues Andrew Fitzgibbon and Andrew Blake, to help with the human pose estimation software for Kinect. We were, as you might expect, initially rather skeptical. Not only did Alex want us to solve human pose estimation, he wanted us to do it in under two years, and for the whole system to consume less than 10 % of the Xbox 360's resources leaving enough room for the games themselves to run concurrently. How could we hope to succeed with such an ambitious goal where so many others had failed?

But two things got us very excited: firstly the depth camera itself, which produced depth images of a quality that far surpassed anything that we had seen before in a consumer device; and secondly a prototype skeletal tracking algorithm, called Bones, that Alex's team had put together. In fact, Bones was so good that we were unsure initially why they needed our help at all! But the limitations of Bones soon became apparent: it relied on frame-to-frame tracking of a fixed-size model. We needed Kinect to be robust—never to lose track of the player catastrophically—and we also wanted to avoid any calibration step, so that any user could just jump in and play. Bones could not quite meet these requirements, and so the challenge was clear.

The first thing we realized was that we would need to look at a single frame at a time in order to avoid potential loss of track. This idea went somewhat against the grain of the established human pose estimation literature which had largely focused on frame-to-frame tracking. Of course, a considerable concern with a single frame at a time approach was that the search space of human poses is enormous, and without an estimate of where to start looking, search might be slow.

Our second decision was to have the algorithm try to learn invariance to body shape and size. If this worked, then we could hope to avoid the calibration step. We realized that, because simulating depth images is considerably easier than simulating real photographs, we could get the large quantities of training images we would need relatively cheaply by using computer graphics. As long as these images matched real camera images closely enough, and the data contained sufficiently varied poses, shapes and sizes, we should be able to achieve invariance to all these factors.

Now, what to do with these training data? We prototyped a template matching approach, but this did not look like it would scale to the accuracy and speed we needed. We brainstormed various other ideas, and then one morning it hit me that we could revisit some of the semantic segmentation work from my Ph.D. Instead of inferring at each pixel a distribution over object categories (sheep, grass, sky, etc.), we could infer instead a distribution over parts of the body (left hand, right hand, head, etc.) based on a local window in the depth image. I put together a quick implementation trained from around 100 images. This gave remarkably encouraging results, and some considerable hope that this body parts approach might be able to reach our goals.

My conviction was that "all" we really needed to do next was to scale up: to design a pattern of body parts that would allow us to localize the body joints of interest; to improve the realism, variety, and number of training images; to build software that could train from millions of images in a reasonable period of time; to speed up the inference to super real-time; and to integrate this per-pixel machine learning algorithm with the Bones algorithm to get a final output skeleton that enforced kinematic and temporal constraints. This we did, with substantial help, notably from Toby Sharp, Mat Cook, Mihai Budiu, Mark Finocchio, and Richard Moore, among many others too numerous to thank individually. And we were perhaps a little too successful! Robert Craig, who led the team in Redmond that was now in charge of the end-to-end tracking pipeline, decided the signal from the body parts classifier was so reliable that the original Bones algorithm could be replaced with a much lighter-weight alternative which became known as "ST" (Skeletal Tracking). ST is now what Kinect uses to track your body, both for Xbox 360 and for Windows.

Beyond Entertainment

Entertainment and gaming turned out to be the "killer app" that took depth cameras out of the lab. But entertainment is really just a first stride. Soon after the launch of Kinect, an amazing thing happened. A host of enthusiast "Kinect hacks" started to appear, including many we had not envisioned. Some were simple but useful, such as measuring the distance between two points in space; others built impressive interaction scenarios, such as virtual pianos and browsing the web. Depth cameras have also opened up wide-ranging opportunities for scientific research in vision, robotics, interaction, and several other fields. The academic community has thus been quick to get involved, for example using Kinect to reconstruct detailed 3D models of indoor environments, to navigate quadcopters autonomously, or even (something that we are investigating at Microsoft Research Cambridge) to allow surgeons to navigate through a patient's CT and MRI scans mid-surgery without touching a potentially non-sterile keyboard or mouse. The chapters in this book, based on the eponymous workshop at ICCV 2011 in Barcelona, contain a fascinating cross-section of this research. Finally, with the launch of Kinect for Windows and the Kinect Accelerator initiative, real-world commercial applications are being developed, including virtual fitting rooms, training for athletes, and assistance for the elderly.

Looking to the Future

Depth camera technology is maturing, yet has a long way to go to reach the frame rates and resolutions possible with traditional sensors, and as yet does not work well outdoors. Camera technology is sure to advance in these respects, while also dropping in price, weight and power consumption. Just imagine the applications that small, lightweight, wireless depth sensors could enable. But even with today's depth sensors, I believe we are just scratching the surface of a world of new applications. I hope that this book gives you some inspiration, and I for one cannot wait to see what you come up with next.

Microsoft Research Jamie Shotton
Cambridge

Preface

The Workshop on Consumer Depth Cameras for Computer Vision (CDC4CV) brought together researchers from around the world, to explore the latest ideas about using a revolutionary consumer-priced depth camera, Microsoft's Kinect. This book is an outgrowth of that workshop, with the workshop organizers (Andrea Fossati, Juergen Gall, and Helmut Grabner from ETH Zürich; Xiaofeng Ren from Intel Labs Seattle; and Kurt Konolige from Willow Garage) inviting expanded contributions from the workshop participants.

The Kinect appeared as a consumer device in late 2010, and developer versions of the PrimeSense technology were available to some researchers up to a year earlier, Kurt Konolige at Willow Garage, and Xiaofeng Ren at Intel Labs in Seattle among them. Prior to this, Kurt Konolige had pursued a stereo system at Willow Garage that projected a texture onto a scene, and so allowed stereo to work on untextured objects. It worked great, and the limitation of "stereo dropouts", the lack of depth information on untextured surfaces, could finally be overcome. This system was incorporated into Willow Garage's PR2 robot platform, and was a primary enabler for many robot tasks. Along with colleagues Gary Bradski in vision, Sachin Chitta in manipulation, and many others both at Willow Garage and elsewhere, he implemented applications such as obstacle avoidance for robot arms, segmentation of planes, simple object recognition and pickup, discovery and modeling of articulated objects, and automatic plug-in to standard sockets, to name a few. With the advent of PrimeSense devices, however, he realized that the Willow Garage development of textured projection stereo could not compete in price, robustness, or convenience, and quickly abandoned it in favor of the former.

The Intel Seattle lab actively pursued the use of prototype PrimeSense devices as a major research thrust between 2010–2011, in collaboration with the University of Washington. The Intel-UW team promoted the name *RGB-D*, to emphasize the synergy of jointly using depth and color, and completed a number of successful projects on 3D mapping and modeling, object and gesture recognition, as well as interactive toy playing using projected display. Much of the RGB-D research transitioned to the newly founded Intel Science and Technology Center for Pervasive Computing.

Due to its low cost, once the sensor became publicly available, many research groups around the world began to exploit it. In the early 2011, the team at ETH Zürich started exploring several potential applications for RGB-D cameras, including action recognition, head pose estimation, physics-based tracking and human-computer interfaces. In fact it turned out that many very challenging vision tasks had great benefits from the addition of real-time reliable depth data.

Since that time, the field has progressed rapidly, to the point where it made sense to have a workshop in the autumn of 2011, to exchange ideas on the now widely available Kinect device, both its functioning and applications. The response to the call for participation was overwhelming—over 60 submissions, with 10 accepted oral presentations, and an equal number of posters. This book contains a selection of papers originating from the workshop, expanded and revised to full-length expositions, taking advantage of the book format to present results in more detail. It is divided into three main categories.

Part I, 3D Registration and Reconstruction, addresses the classic vision problem of multi-view geometry: how to correlate images from different viewpoints to simultaneously estimate camera poses and world points. The addition of depth information, as well as the constraint of real-time performance on a video stream, offer opportunities as well as difficulties that are addressed in these contributions.

Part 2, Human Body Analysis, offers a set of studies on human pose estimation, perhaps the most-researched area using video-rate depth images. The studies range from pose estimation for gaming and motion capture, through 3D human body scans for individuals, to recognition of hand pose and its application to sign language parsing.

Part 3, RGB-D Datasets, gives an overview of approaches to various recognition problems: category and instance learning of objects, human activity recognition. In computer vision, much progress has been made in these areas by having commonly available databases to test against; here we see the first steps towards the same approach using depth information as well.

As Jamie Shotton so aptly explained in the Forward, the Kinect, based on structured-light technology developed by PrimeSense, Ltd., has extraordinary depth quality, especially considering its cost. In the 1990s, Kurt Konolige witnessed and participated in amazing advances in mapping and navigation for robotics that were made possible by accurate depth information in a single plane from scanning laser rangefinders; we can only expect that PrimeSense-class devices, with precise depth over a full-field view, at video rates, will similarly help to advance applications in a much larger variety of fields.

We would like to thank all our collaborators at our respective institutions—at the Computer Vision Laboratory of the Swiss Federal Institute of Technology in Zürich, at the Computer Science and Engineering Department of the University of Washington, and at Willow Garage, Inc. in Menlo Park. Further thanks go to the heads of our groups for providing financial support and setting up constructive and fruitful working environments. To the workshop participants and presenters, as well as Gary Bradski and Jamie Shotton, the invited speakers, we extend our gratitude for their efforts at making it a great experience. Finally we would like to acknowledge

Preface

all the contributors of this book, especially Pushmeet Kohli and Jamie Shotton for preparing a very interesting invited chapter.

Zürich, Switzerland   Andrea Fossati
                                       Juergen Gall
                                       Helmut Grabner
Seattle, USA   Xiaofeng Ren
Menlo Park, USA   Kurt Konolige

Contents

Part I 3D Registration and Reconstruction

1   **3D with Kinect**   3
    Jan Smisek, Michal Jancosek, and Tomas Pajdla

2   **Real-Time RGB-D Mapping and 3-D Modeling on the GPU Using
    the Random Ball Cover** 27
    Sebastian Bauer, Jakob Wasza, Felix Lugauer, Dominik Neumann, and
    Joachim Hornegger

3   **A Brute Force Approach to Depth Camera Odometry** 49
    Jonathan Israël and Aurélien Plyer

Part II Human Body Analysis

4   **Key Developments in Human Pose Estimation for Kinect** 63
    Pushmeet Kohli and Jamie Shotton

5   **A Data-Driven Approach for Real-Time Full Body Pose
    Reconstruction from a Depth Camera** 71
    Andreas Baak, Meinard Müller, Gaurav Bharaj, Hans-Peter Seidel, and
    Christian Theobalt

6   **Home 3D Body Scans from a Single Kinect** 99
    Alexander Weiss, David Hirshberg, and Michael J. Black

7   **Real Time Hand Pose Estimation Using Depth Sensors** 119
    Cem Keskin, Furkan Kıraç, Yunus Emre Kara, and Lale Akarun

Part III RGB-D Datasets

8   **A Category-Level 3D Object Dataset: Putting the Kinect to Work** . . 141
    Allison Janoch, Sergey Karayev, Yangqing Jia, Jonathan T. Barron,
    Mario Fritz, Kate Saenko, and Trevor Darrell

9 **RGB-D Object Recognition: Features, Algorithms, and a Large Scale Benchmark** 167
   Kevin Lai, Liefeng Bo, Xiaofeng Ren, and Dieter Fox

10 **RGBD-HuDaAct: A Color-Depth Video Database for Human Daily Activity Recognition** 193
   Bingbing Ni, Gang Wang, and Pierre Moulin

Index 209

Acronyms

AMT	Amazon Mechanical Turk
ANN	Artificial Neural Network
AP	Average Precision
ASL	American Sign Language
BA	Bundle Adjustment
BF	Brute Force
CPU	Central Processing Unit
CUDA	Compute Unified Device Architecture
EMK	Efficient Match Kernels
EM-ICP	Expectation-Maximization Iterative Closest Point
GPU	Graphics Processing Unit
HIT	Human Intelligence Task
HOC	Histogram Of Curvature
HOG	Histogram Of Gradients
ICP	Iterative Closest Point
IR	InfraRed
FOV	Field Of View
fps	Frames per second
LIDAR	Light Detection And Ranging
LR	Landmark-to-Representative
MEI	Motion Energy Image
MHI	Motion History Image
MRF	Markov Random Field
NN	Nearest Neighbor
PCA	Principal Component Analysis
PR	Precision-Recall
RANSAC	Random Sample Consensus
RBC	Random Ball Cover
RDF	Random Decision Forest
RDT	Random Decision Tree
RGB	Red, Green and Blue. It is the standard input provided by regular cameras

RGB-D	Red, Green, Blue and Depth. It is the standard input provided by consumer depth cameras
ROS	Robot Operating System
SCAPE	Shape Completion and Animation of People
SDK	Software Development Kit
SfM	Structure from Motion
SIFT	Scale-Invariant Feature Transform
SLAM	Simultaneous Localization And Mapping
SLR	Single-lens Reflex
STIP	Spatio-Temporal Interest Point
SVM	Support Vector Machine
ToF	Time-of-Flight
USB	Universal Serial Bus
VFH	Viewpoint Feature Histograms
VGA	Video Graphics Array

Part I
3D Registration and Reconstruction

Depth cameras are, first and foremost, 3D measuring devices. A lot of early research efforts using consumer depth cameras have been devoted to 3D registration and reconstruction: (1) to quantify the 3D measuring capabilities of Kinect and PrimeSense cameras; and (2) to register continuous streams of RGB-D (color+depth) frames in real-time and to model objects and environments in 3D.

The chapter on *3D with Kinect* from Smisek et al. presents an in-depth study of Kinect cameras as 3D measuring devices. They develop a geometric for Kinect as a multi-view system with IR, RGB and depth channels. They analyze optical centers, distortions, and effective resolutions of the Kinect sensor. Accordingly, they propose a calibration technique for Kinect that outperforms methods in open source software. Depth data from Kinect are compared to a stereo system (using high-quality SLR cameras) and a time-of-flight system (SwissRanger SR-4000), where Kinect performs similar to SLR stereo on a calibration pattern and much better than the SwissRanger. Depth data from Kinect are combined with RGB-based Structure-from-Motion to greatly improve the quality of 3D surface reconstruction.

Once we have a solid understanding of the data captured in a single Kinect frame, the next step is to compute 3D registrations of multiple frames so that they can be aligned in a global coordinate system. The RGB-D mapping work of Henry et al. (RGB-D Mapping: Using Depth Cameras for Dense 3D Modeling of Indoor Environments, IJRR, 2012) shows that established algorithms for 3D registration, including both the *Iterative Closest Point* (ICP) and the *Bundle Adjustment* (BA) algorithms, can adapt to and play an important role in the alignment of RGB-D data. One interesting aspect of Kinect data is the frame rate (30 Hz): as shown in the KinectFusion work of Newcombe et al. (KinectFusion: Real-Time Dense Surface Mapping and Tracking, ISMAR, 2011), 3D registration can run in real-time, utilizing all the data coming in, when using modern hardware such as GPUs.

The two following chapters both address real-time 3D registration on GPUs: the use of random ball cover (RBC) for correspondence in ICP matching, and the use of semi-sparse features. The work of Bauer et al. adapts the RBC data structure, typically used for high dimensional data, to the Kinect case. This allows a direct nearest-neighbor search in 6-dimensional RGB-D data, avoiding the approximations needed in projective data association schemes. The RBC algorithm is extensively evaluated, qualitatively and quantitatively, on scene and object reconstruction scenarios. An efficient implementation of RBC on the GPU leads to frame-to-frame registrations of less than 20 ms. On the other hand, the work of Israël and Plyer develops a registration approach using semi-sparse features: instead of using point clouds or sparse features (e.g. SIFT), they pursue a middle path where depth edges are extracted and registered in 3D. Their approach reduces the number of points to be registered by orders of magnitude, enabling a brute-force approach where incoming Kinect frames can be matched in real-time on a GPU to a large number of stored exemplars.

3D reconstruction is an area where consumer depth cameras are making a breakthrough. With a consumer price tag and a compact form factor, Kinect-style cameras make 3D modeling feasible for large environments and accessible to a large community of enthusiasts. It is conceivable that compact, portable systems can be built soon to robustly and interactively scan everyday environments into accurate 3D models.

Chapter 1
3D with Kinect

Jan Smisek, Michal Jancosek, and Tomas Pajdla

Abstract We analyze Kinect as a 3D measuring device, experimentally investigate depth measurement resolution and error properties, and make a quantitative comparison of Kinect accuracy with stereo reconstruction from SLR cameras and a 3D-TOF camera. We propose a Kinect geometrical model and its calibration procedure providing an accurate calibration of Kinect 3D measurement and Kinect cameras. We compare our Kinect calibration procedure with its alternatives available on Internet, and integrate it into an SfM pipeline where 3D measurements from a moving Kinect are transformed into a common coordinate system, by computing relative poses from matches in its color camera.

1.1 Introduction

Kinect [4, 14, 22] has become an important 3D sensor. It has received a lot of attention thanks to the rapid human pose recognition system developed on top of 3D measurement [17]. Its low cost, reliability and speed of the measurement promise to make Kinect the primary 3D measuring device in indoor robotics [25], 3D scene reconstruction [7], and object recognition [12].

In this chapter we provide a geometrical analysis of Kinect, design its geometrical model, propose a calibration procedure and demonstrate its performance. We extend here our preliminary results presented in [18].

Approaches to modeling Kinect geometry, which have appeared recently, provide a good basis for understanding the sensor. There exists the following most relevant work: The authors of [2] combined OpenCV camera calibration [24] with Kinect

---

J. Smisek (✉) · M. Jancosek · T. Pajdla
Center for Machine Perception, Dept. of Cybernetics, FEE, Czech Technical University in Prague, Prague, Czech Republic
e-mail: smisek.jan@gmail.com

M. Jancosek
e-mail: jancom1@cmp.felk.cvut.cz

T. Pajdla
e-mail: pajdla@fel.cvut.cz

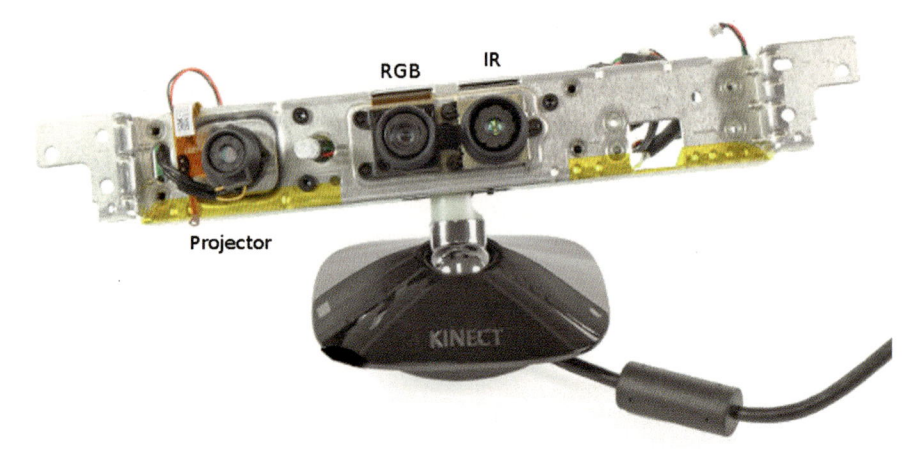

Fig. 1.1 Kinect consists of infrared (IR) projector, IR camera and RGB camera (illustration from [11])

inverse disparity measurement model [3] to obtain the basic Kinect calibration procedure. The project did not study particular features of Kinect sensors and did not correct for them. An almost identical procedure [11] is implemented in ROS, where an apparent shift between the infrared and depth images is corrected. Another variation of that approach appeared in [8], where OpenCV calibration is replaced by Bouguet's [1] calibration toolbox. We build on top of previous work and design an accurate calibration procedure based on considering geometrical models as well as on "learning" of an additional correction procedure accounting for remaining non-modeled errors. We use the full camera models and their calibration procedures as implemented in [1], the relationship between Kinect inverse disparity and depth as in [3], correct for depth and infrared image displacement as in [11], and add additional corrections trained on examples of calibration boards. We demonstrate that a calibrated Kinect can be combined with Structure from Motion to get 3D data in a consistent coordinate system allowing to construct the surface of the observed scene by Multiview Stereo. Our comparison shows that Kinect is superior in accuracy to SwissRanger SR-4000 3D-TOF camera and close to a medium resolution SLR Stereo rig. Our results are in accordance with [10] that mentions compatible observations about the Kinect depth quantization.

1.2 Kinect as a 3D Measuring Device

Kinect is a composite device consisting of a near-infrared laser pattern projector, an IR camera and a color (RGB) camera, Fig. 1.1. The IR camera and projector are used as a stereo pair to triangulate points in 3D space. The RGB camera can be then used to texture the 3D points or to recognize the image content. As a measuring device Kinect delivers three outputs: IR image, RGB image, and an (inverse) depth image.

1 3D with Kinect

Fig. 1.2 A rig with a Kinect and two Nikon D60 SLR cameras

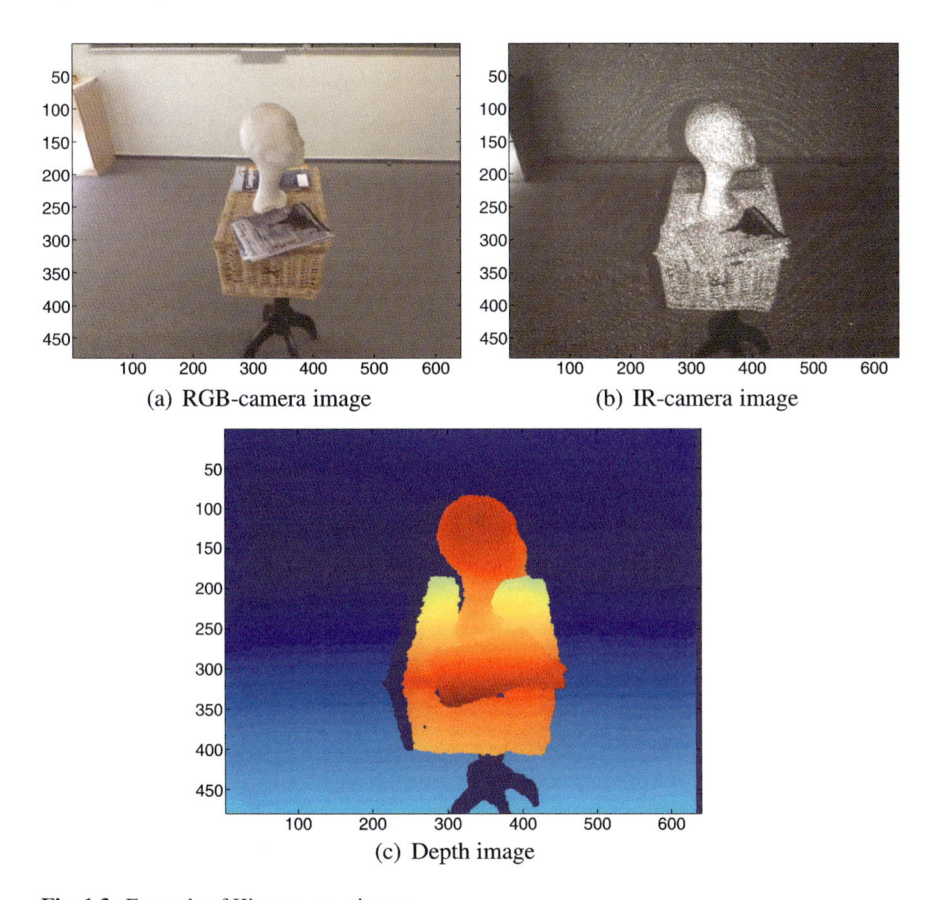

Fig. 1.3 Example of Kinect output images

1.2.1 IR Image

The IR camera, Fig. 1.3(b), (1280 × 1024 pixels for 57 × 45 degrees FOV, 6.1 mm focal length, 5.2 μm pixel size) is used to observe and decode the IR projection pattern to triangulate the 3D scene. If suitably illuminated by a halogen lamp [19, 23] and with the IR projector blocked, Fig. 1.7(c, d), it can be reliably calibrated by [1] using the same checkerboard pattern used for the RGB camera calibration. The camera exhibits non-negligible radial and tangential distortions, see Sect. 1.4.

1.2.2 RGB Image

The RGB camera, Fig. 1.3(a), (1280 × 1024 pixels for 63 × 50 degrees FOV, 2.9 mm focal length, 2.8 μm pixel size) delivers medium quality images. It can be calibrated by [1] and used to track relative poses between subsequent images by using an SfM system, e.g. [6, 20].

1.2.3 Depth Image

The main raw output of Kinect is an 11-bit image, Fig. 1.3(c), which corresponds to the depth in the scene. Rather than providing the actual depth z, Kinect returns "inverse depth" $1/z$, as shown in Fig. 1.4(a). Taking into account the depth resolution achievable with a Kinect (Sect. 1.2.4), we adopted the model suggested in [11]. The depth image is constructed by triangulation from the IR image and the projector and hence it is "carried" by the IR image, as shown in Eq. 1.5.

The depth image has a vertical stripe of pixels on the right (8 pixels wide) where no depth is calculated, see Fig. 1.3(c). This is probably due the windowing effect of block correlation used in calculating the disparity [11]. We have estimated the size of the correlation window (see Sect. 1.3.1) to be 9 × 7 pixels.

1.2.4 Depth Resolution

Figure 1.4(b, c) shows the resolution of the measured depth as a function of the true depth. The depth resolution was measured by moving Kinect away (0.5 m–15 m) from a planar target in sufficiently fine steps to record all the values returned in a view field of approximately 5° around the image center.

The size of the quantization step q [mm], which is the distance between two consecutive recorded values, was found to be the following function of the depth z [m]:

$$q(z) = 2.73\, z^2 + 0.74\, z - 0.58. \tag{1.1}$$

This is in accordance with the expected quadratic depth resolution for triangulation-based devices. The values of q at the beginning, resp. at the end, of the operational range were $q(0.50\text{ m}) = 0.65$ mm, resp. $q(15.7\text{ m}) = 685$ mm. These findings are in accordance with [10].

1 3D with Kinect

Fig. 1.4 The estimated size of the Kinect quantization step q as a function of target distance for 0–5 m

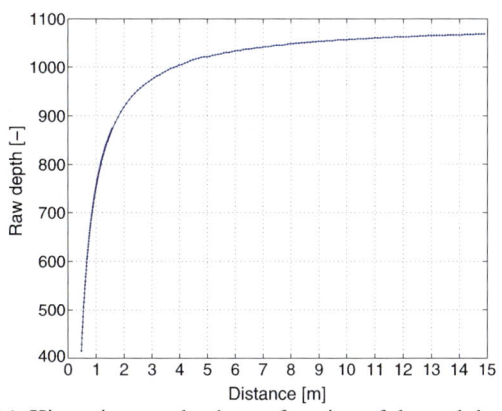

(a) Kinect inverse depth as a function of the real depth.

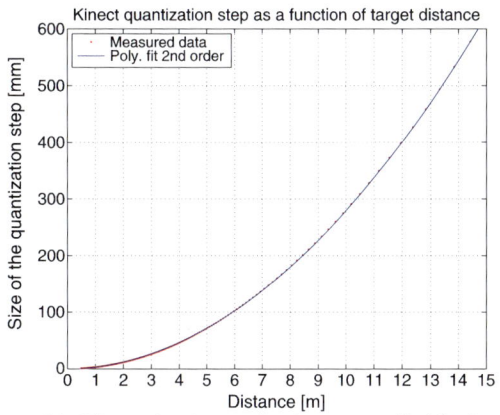

(b) Kinect depth quantization step q (0-15 m).

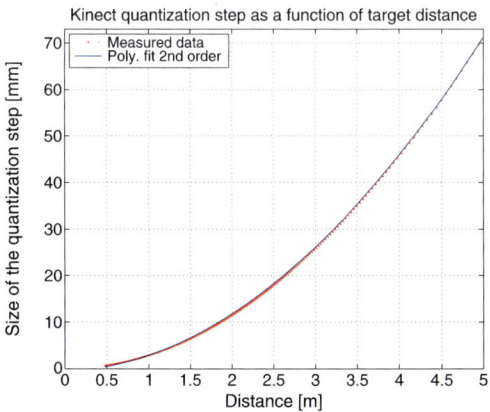

(c) Kinect depth quantization step (0-5 m detail).

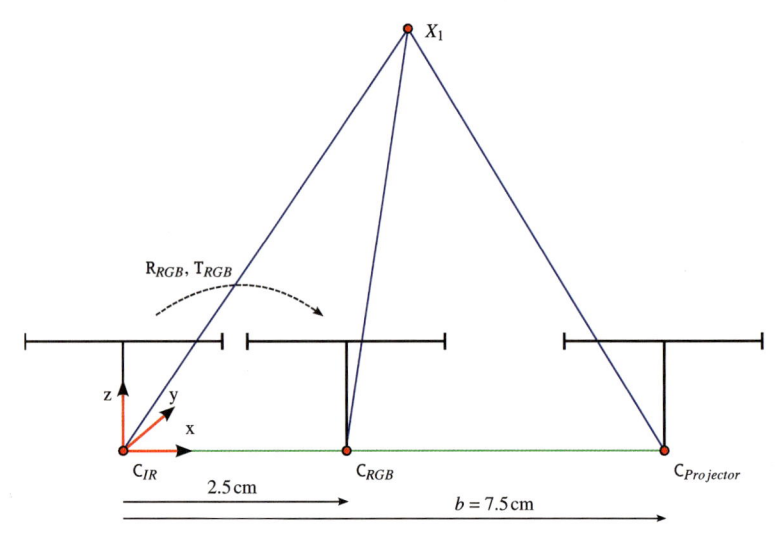

Fig. 1.5 Geometrical model of Kinect

1.3 Kinect Geometrical Model

We model Kinect as a multi-view system consisting of RGB, IR and Depth cameras. A Geometrical model of RGB and IR cameras, which project a 3D point X into an image point $[u, v]^\top$, is given by [1]:

$$\begin{bmatrix} u \\ v \\ 1 \end{bmatrix} = \mathrm{K} \begin{bmatrix} s \\ t \\ 1 \end{bmatrix} \quad (1.2)$$

$$\begin{bmatrix} s \\ t \\ 1 \end{bmatrix} = \underbrace{\left(1 + k_1 r^2 + k_2 r^4 + k_5 r^6\right) \begin{bmatrix} p \\ q \\ 0 \end{bmatrix}}_{\text{radial distortion}} + \underbrace{\begin{bmatrix} 2 k_3\, p\, q + k_4\, (r^2 + 2\, p^2) \\ 2 k_4\, p\, q + k_3\, (r^2 + 2 q^2) \\ 1 \end{bmatrix}}_{\text{tangential distortion}} \quad (1.3)$$

$$r^2 = p^2 + q^2, \qquad \begin{bmatrix} p\,z \\ q\,z \\ z \end{bmatrix} = \mathrm{R}\,(\mathrm{X} - \mathrm{C}) \quad (1.4)$$

with distortion parameters $\mathrm{k} = [k_1, k_2, \ldots, k_5]$, camera calibration matrix K, rotation R and camera center C [5].

The Depth camera of Kinect is associated to the geometry of the IR camera. It returns the inverse depth d along the z-axis, as visible in Fig. 1.5, for every pixel

Table 1.1 IR to Depth-camera pixel position shift

Circle	1	2	3	4	5	6	7	Mean
u_0	4.1	4.3	4.0	4.0	3.9	4.2	4.1	4.1
v_0	3.0	2.9	3.5	3.1	3.0	3.3	2.8	3.1

$[u, v]^\top$ of the IR cameras as

$$\begin{bmatrix} x \\ y \\ d \end{bmatrix} = \begin{bmatrix} u - u_0 \\ v - v_0 \\ \frac{1}{c_1} \frac{1}{z} - \frac{c_0}{c_1} \end{bmatrix}, \quad (1.5)$$

where u, v are given by Eq. 1.3, true depth z by Eq. 1.4, $[u_0, v_0]^\top$ by Table 1.1, X stands for 3D coordinates of a 3D point, and c_1, c_0 are parameters of the model. We associate the Kinect coordinate system with the IR camera and hence get $R_{IR} = I$ and $C_{IR} = 0$. A 3D point X_{IR} is constructed from the measurement $[x, y, d]$ in the depth image by

$$X_{IR} = \frac{1}{c_1 d + c_0} \, \text{dis}^{-1}\left(K_{IR}^{-1} \begin{bmatrix} x + u_0 \\ y + v_0 \\ 1 \end{bmatrix}, k_{IR} \right) \quad (1.6)$$

and projected to the RGB images as

$$u_{RGB} = K_{RGB} \, \text{dis}\left(R_{RGB}(X_{IR} - C_{RGB}), k_{RGB} \right) \quad (1.7)$$

where dis is the distortion function given by Eq. 1.3, k_{IR}, k_{RGB} are the respective distortion parameters of the IR and RGB cameras, K_{IR} is the IR camera calibration matrix and K_{RGB}, R_{RGB}, C_{RGB} are the calibration matrix, the rotation matrix and the center of the RGB camera, respectively.

1.3.1 Shift Between IR Image and Depth Image

IR and Depth images were found to be shifted. To determine the shift $[u_0, v_0]^\top$, circular targets spanning the field of view were captured from different distances in the IR and Depth images, Fig. 1.8(a). Edges of the targets were computed in the IR and Depth images using the Sobel edge detector. In order to mitigate the effect of the unstable Depth image edges, reconstruction circles were fit to the measured data, Fig. 1.8(b). The pixel distances between centers of the fitted circles are shown in Table 1.1. The shift was estimated as the mean value of the distances over all the experiments. We conclude that there is a shift of about 4 pixels in the u direction and of 3 pixels in the v direction.

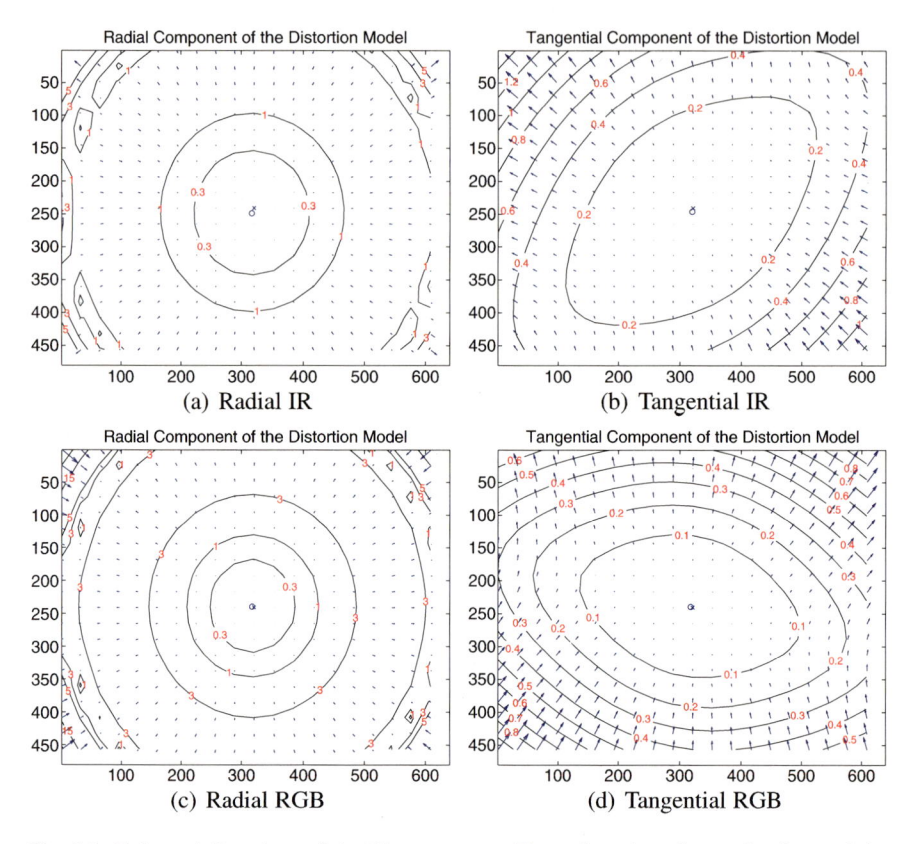

Fig. 1.6 Estimated distortions of the Kinect cameras. The *red numbers* denote the sizes and the *arrows* denote the directions of pixel displacements induced by the lens distortion. The *cross* indicates the image center, the *circle* marks the location of the principal point

1.3.2 Identification of the IR Projector Geometrical Center

We have first acquired seven IR and Depth images of a plane positioned at different distances. The projected pattern contains nine brighter and easily identifiable speckle dots, Fig. 1.9(a). These points were formed by $r = 1, \ldots, 9$ rays l_r transmitted from the IR projector. Each point was reconstructed in the 3D space and grouped by its ray of origin $X_{IR_{i,r}}$. The IR projector center C_P is located in the common intersection of the nine rays. We formulated a nonlinear optimization problem to find the projector center C_P by minimizing the perpendicular distances of the reconstructed points $X_{IR_{i,r}}$ from a bundle of rays passing through C_P. Figure 1.9(b) shows the resulting ray bundle next to the IR cameras frame. Figure 1.9(c) shows the residual distances from the points $X_{IR_{i,r}}$ to their corresponding rays of the optimal ray bundle. All residual distances are smaller than 2 mm. The estimated projector center has coordinates $C_P = [74.6, 1.1, 1.3]^\top$ [mm] in the IR camera reference frame.

1 3D with Kinect   11

(a) IR image of a calibration checkerboard illuminated by the IR pattern.

(b) IR image of the calibration checkerboard illuminated by a halogen lamp with the IR projection blocked.

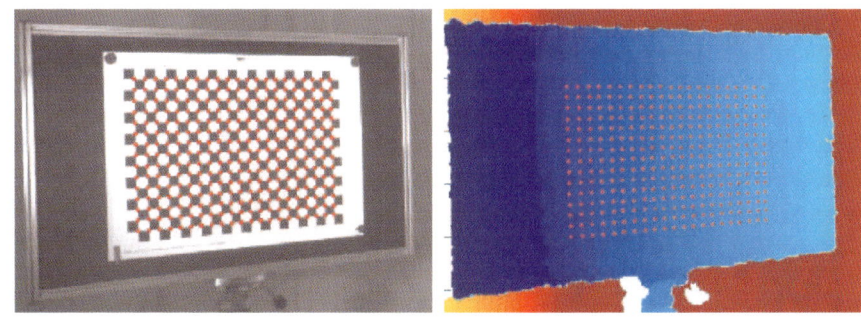

(c) Calibration points extracted in the RGB image.

(d) Calibration points in the Depth image.

Fig. 1.7 The calibration board in the IR, RGB and Depth images

(a) IR image with Depth data

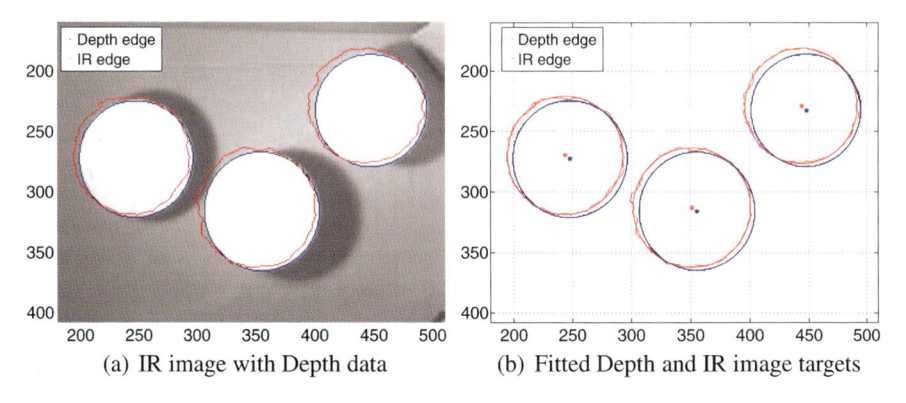

(b) Fitted Depth and IR image targets

Fig. 1.8 Illustration of the IR to Depth image shift

Fig. 1.9 Identification of the geometrical model

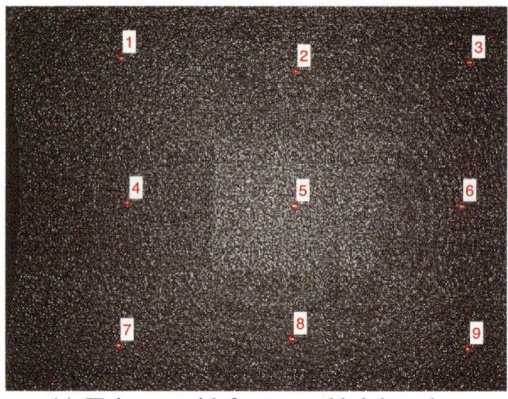

(a) IR image with 9 extracted brighter dots

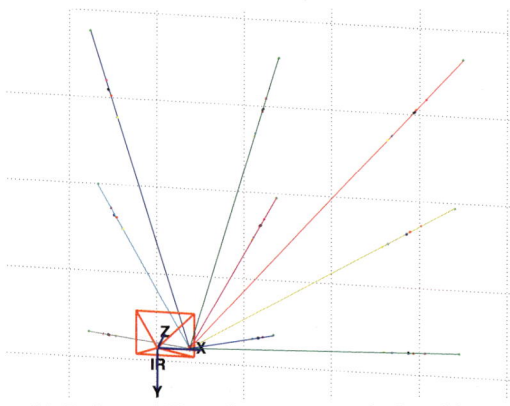

(b) Estimated IR projector geometrical position

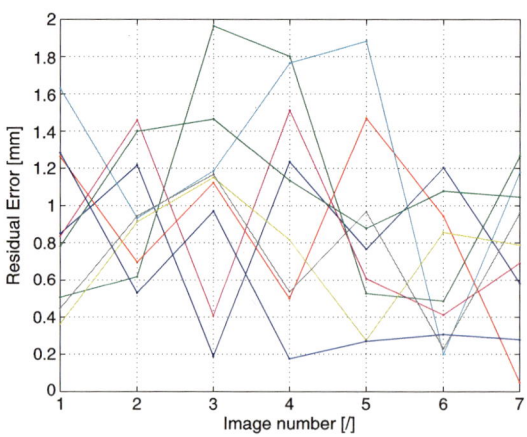

(c) Residual error between reconstructed points and rays passing through them to estimated projector position

1 3D with Kinect

Fig. 1.10 Kinect IR camera (*blue*) and projector (*green*) view fields and ray distribution in the x–y plane estimated in Sect. 1.3.3. For clarity, we plot only every 64th camera ray, i.e. there are 11 rays for the IR camera, and every 150th projector ray, i.e. there are 32 projector rays. *Red dots* illustrate the sampling of the space by points that can be reconstructed. The *bold blue line* marks the center ray of the IR camera where the distance resolution shown in Fig. 1.11 was estimated. Note that the closest point, which is actually measured by the real device, is at a depth of about 40 cm

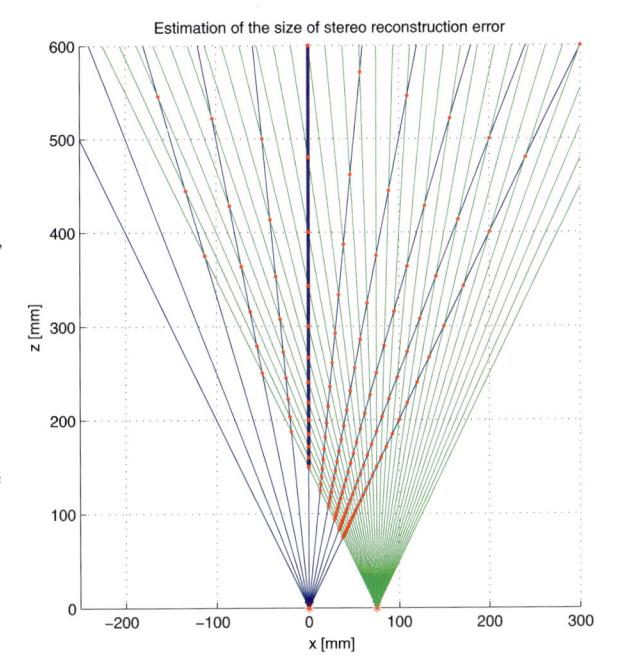

1.3.3 Identification of Effective Depth Resolutions of the IR Camera and Projector Stereo Pair

In this section the view fields of the Kinect IR camera and of the Kinect projector and their effective resolution, which determines the distribution of the resolution in 3D measurement, will be investigated.

The size of the IR image and of the depth image is known to be 640 × 480 pixels with 10.4 μm pixel size, spanning approx. 60° × 45° view angle. This gives an angular resolution of 0.0938°/pixel in the IR camera.

Counting the speckle dots on the projected pattern yields about 800 dots along the central horizontal line across the projector field of view. Projector FOV and IR camera FOV are approximately the same. Hence we get 800 dots per 60° and an angular resolution of 0.0750°/ray for the projector rays. The green curve in Fig. 1.11 shows the simulated depth quantization along the central IR camera ray (the blue line in Fig. 1.10) for the camera and projector resolution described above. It clearly does not correspond to the red curve measured on a real Kinect.

To get our simulation closer to reality, we assume that ray detection is done with higher accuracy by interpolating rays from the projected patterns. The blue curve in Fig. 1.11 corresponds to detecting rays with 1/8 pixel accuracy, as was hypothesized in [11]. Hence we get the effective resolution of $5120 = 640 \times 8$ rays per 60°, i.e. 0.00938°/ray, in the projector. This corresponds to our measurement on a real Kinect.

Fig. 1.11 Comparison of stereo reconstruction uncertainty measured with Kinect and simulated using identified parameters of the stereo system

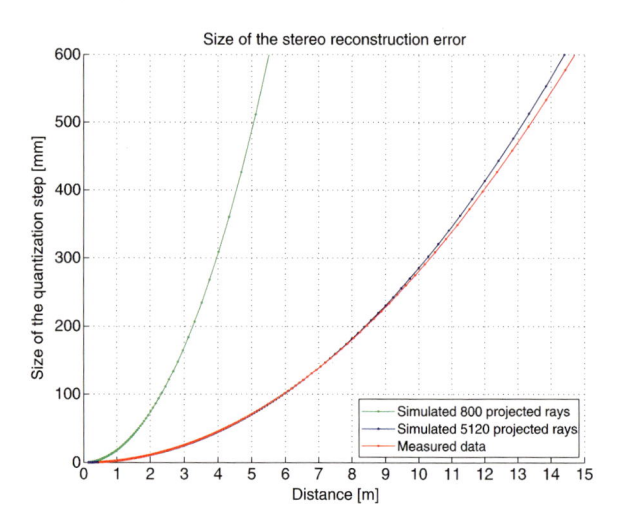

Figure 1.10 illustrates view fields and ray arrangements for Kinect IR camera (blue) and projector (green). The bold blue line marks the center of the IR camera view where the distance resolution was evaluated. For clarity, we show only every 64th camera ray and every 150th projector ray and their intersections as red dots.

1.4 Kinect Calibration

We calibrate, as proposed in [1], Kinect cameras together by showing the same calibration target to the IR and RGB cameras, Fig. 1.7(c). This allows to calibrate both cameras w.r.t. the same 3D points and hence the poses of the cameras w.r.t. the points can be chained to give their relative pose, Fig. 1.12. Taking the Cartesian coordinate system of the IR camera as the global Kinect coordinate system makes the camera relative pose equal to R_{RGB}, C_{RGB}.

Tables 1.2 and 1.3 show the internal parameters and Fig. 1.6 shows the effect of distortions in the cameras. We included the tangential distortion since it non-negligibly increased the overall accuracy of 3D measurements. Figure 1.7(a) shows the IR image of the calibration board under the normal Kinect operation when it is illuminated by its IR projector. A better image is obtained by blocking the IR projector and illuminating the target by a halogen lamp Fig. 1.7(b).

Parameters c_0, c_1 of the Depth camera are calibrated as follows: We get n measurements $X_{D_i} = [x_i, y_i, d_i]^\top$, $i = 1, \ldots, n$, of all the calibration points from the depth images, Fig. 1.7(d). The Cartesian coordinates X_{IR_i} of the same calibration points were measured in the IR Cartesian system by intersecting the rays projecting the points into IR images with the best plane fits to the reconstructed calibration points. Parameters c_0, c_1 were optimized to best fit X_{D_i} to X_{IR_i} using Eq. 1.6.

1 3D with Kinect

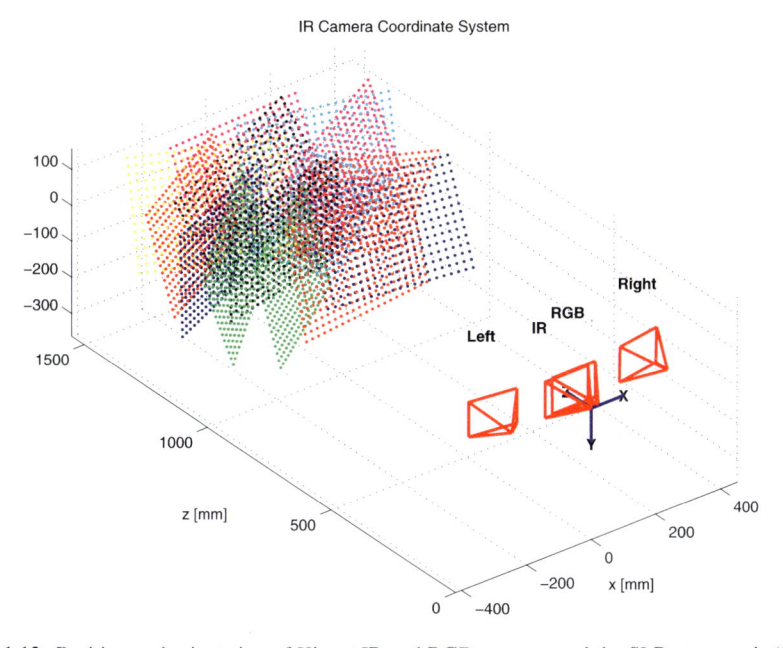

Fig. 1.12 Position and orientation of Kinect IR and RGB cameras and the SLR stereo pair (*Left*, *Right*) altogether with 3D calibration points reconstructed on planar calibration targets

Table 1.2 Intrinsic parameters of the Kinect IR camera

Focal length		Principal point		Distortion coefficients			
f [px]	f [mm]	x_0 [px]	y_0 [px]	k_{c_1}	k_{c_2}	k_{c_3}	k_{c_4}
585.6	6.1	316	247.6	−0.1296	0.45	−0.0005	−0.002

Table 1.3 Intrinsic parameters of the Kinect RGB camera

Focal length		Principal point		Distortion coefficients			
f [px]	f [mm]	x_0 [px]	y_0 [px]	k_{c_1}	k_{c_2}	k_{c_3}	k_{c_4}
524	2.9	316.7	238.5	0.2402	−0.6861	−0.0015	0.0003

1.4.1 Learning Complex Residual Errors

It has been observed that a Kinect calibrated with the above procedure still exhibited small but relatively complex residual errors for the close range measurements. Figure 1.13 shows residuals after fitting the plane to the calibrated Kinect measurement of a plane spanning the field of view. The target has been captured from 18 different distances ranging from 0.7 to 1.3 meters. Highly correlated residuals were accounted.

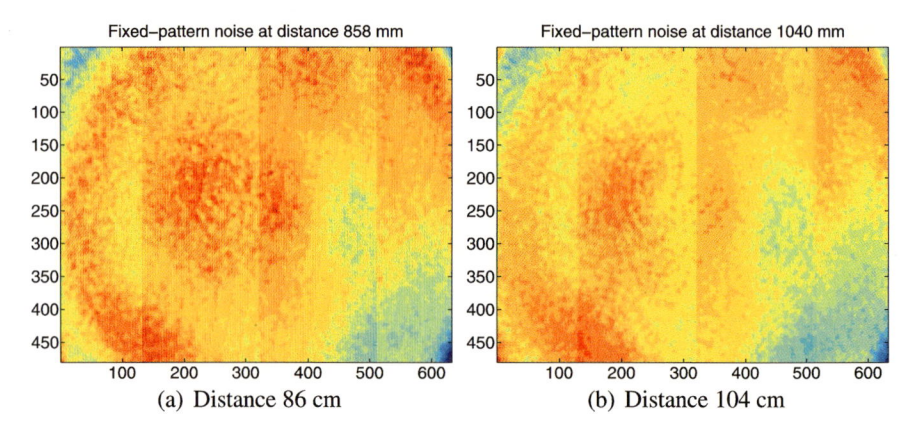

Fig. 1.13 Residuals of the plane fitting showing the fixed-pattern noise on depth images from different distances

Table 1.4 Evaluation of the z-correction. The standard deviation of the residuals of the plane fit to the measurement of a planar target has been reduced

Data-set	Standard deviation [mm]	
	Original σ	Corrected σ
Even images	2.18	1.54
Odd images	1.98	1.34

Residuals along the 250th horizontal Depth image row are shown in Fig. 1.14(a). Note that the residual values do not depend on the actual distance to the target plane (in this limited range). The values are consistently positive in the center and negative at the periphery. To compensate for this residual error, we form a z-correction image of z values constructed as the pixel-wise mean of all residual images. The z-correction image is subtracted from the z coordinate of X_{IR} computed by Eq. 1.6.

To evaluate this correction method, the z-correction image was constructed from residuals of even images and then applied to odd (the first row of Table 1.4) and to even (the second row of Table 1.4) depth images. The standard deviation of residuals decreased.

After applying the z-correction to Kinect measurements from the experiment described in Sect. 1.5.2, the mean of the residual errors decreased by approximately 0.25 mm, Fig. 1.14(b). The residuals were evaluated on 4410 points spanning the field of view.

1.5 Validation

In this section, different publicly available Kinect depth models are tested and compared to our method on a 3D calibration object. Furthermore, we provide a com-

1 3D with Kinect

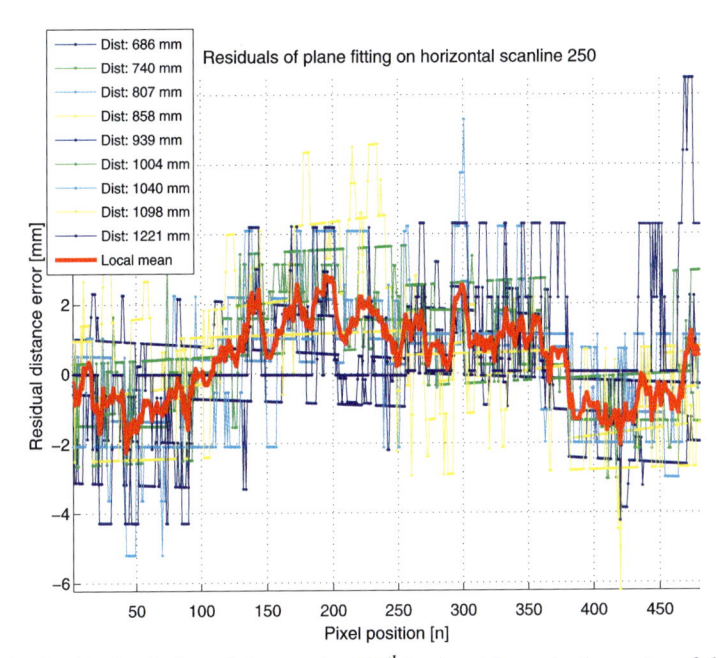

(a) Residuals of plane fitting on the 250th horizontal row in the center of the Depth image. The local mean is shown as a solid red line.

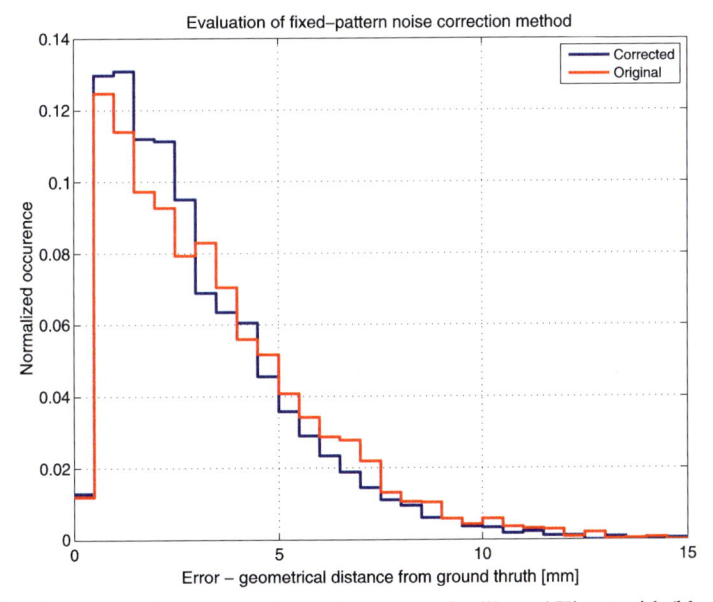

(b) Normalized histogram of the residual errors of calibrated Kinect with (blue) and without (red) complex error correction.

Fig. 1.14 Correcting complex residual errors

Fig. 1.15 Kinect accuracy evaluation on a 3D reference object with five flat targets mounted on a rigid bench

(a) IR image

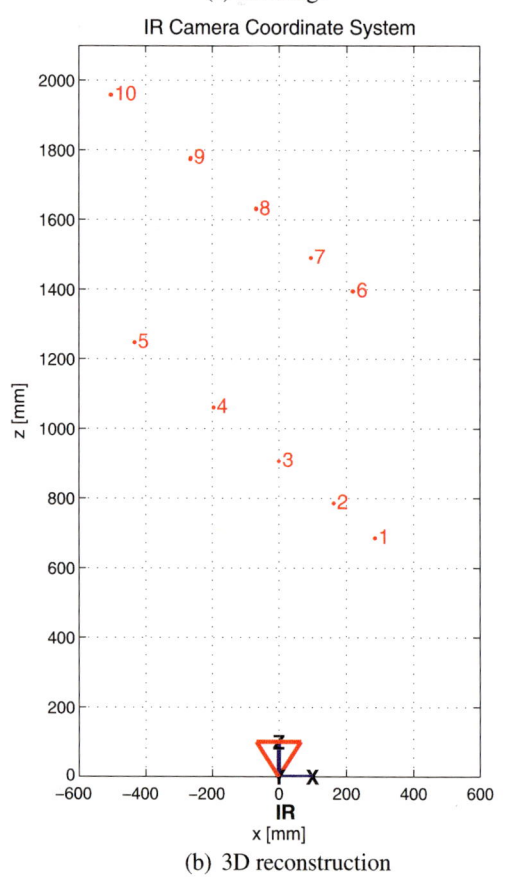

(b) 3D reconstruction

parison of the accuracy of Kinect measurements against stereo triangulation and 3D measurements based on Time-of-Flight. Finally, we demonstrate the functionality of our Kinect calibration procedure by integrating it into an SfM pipeline.

1 3D with Kinect

Table 1.5 Accuracy evaluation of different reconstruction methods on a reference 3D object. Kinect 1 is the device for which we made complete calibration as described in this chapter. Kinect 2 was evaluated with the calibration from Kinect 1

Device	Method	Distance difference d [mm]								$\mu(d)$	$\sigma(d)$
Kinect 1	Our	1.17	3.52	−1.98	−2.56	1.73	−7.09	−1.31	5.21	**−0.16**	**3.89**
	ROS	2.69	5.69	1.22	1.91	4.21	−3.33	3.44	11.33	3.39	4.17
	Burrus	10.64	15.29	12.03	13.41	9.84	3.28	10.49	18.28	11.66	4.41
	Tangent	3.15	6.19	1.95	3.35	5.30	−1.45	6.02	15.00	4.94	4.78
	OpenNI	−3.08	9.37	−0.69	−12.12	2.55	−5.85	0.59	11.99	0.34	7.82
	Kinect SDK	N.A.[a]	N.A.	−2.62	−6.98	7.10	−12.22	5.98	1.99	−1.12	7.58
Kinect 2	Our	2.09	9.90	−6.49	−11.82	2.81	2.58	0.47	−7.31	−0.97	7.02
	ROS	3.16	11.32	−4.32	−8.82	4.38	4.73	3.37	−3.38	1.30	6.38
	Burrus	10.97	20.56	6.33	2.38	9.68	11.04	9.85	2.86	9.21	5.75
	Tangent	3.47	11.77	−3.58	−7.10	5.58	6.55	6.19	0.96	2.98	**6.05**
	OpenNI	−1.14	12.22	−9.12	−11.45	5.24	6.09	−7.40	2.68	**−0.36**	8.37
	Kinect SDK	N.A.	N.A.	−2.36	−7.83	7.00	−0.47	−2.97	12.22	0.93	7.34

[a] Kinect SDK currently limits the measurement range to 0.8–4 m

1.5.1 Kinect Depth Models Evaluation on a 3D Calibration Object

We evaluate the accuracy of the calibration by measuring a reference 3D object. The 3D object consisted of five flat targets that were rigidly mounted together along a straight line on a rigid bench, Fig. 1.15(a). As ground truth, the distances between centers of the targets were carefully measured by a measure tape with accuracy better than 1 mm.

The object was then captured using Kinect from two different distances to get measurements in the range between 0.7 m to 2 m, Fig. 1.15(b). After extracting the central points of the targets in the IR image, Fig. 1.15(a), several different reconstruction methods were used to get their 3-dimensional positions, Fig. 1.15(b).

Our Kinect calibration model, which was described in Sect. 1.4, was compared to the ROS calibration [11], Burrus calibration [2], Magnenat calibration [21], OpenNi calibration [16] and Microsoft Kinect SDK calibration [15].

Distances between the reconstructed target points were compared to the ground truth measurements in Table 1.5 and in Fig. 1.16. The experiment was performed on two Kinect devices. Kinect 1 is the device for which the complete calibration, as described in this chapter, was made. Kinect 2 was evaluated with the calibration from Kinect 1, to determine whether it is possible to transfer calibration parameters of one device to another. We see that our method is the best for Kinect 1 and among the best three for Kinect 2.

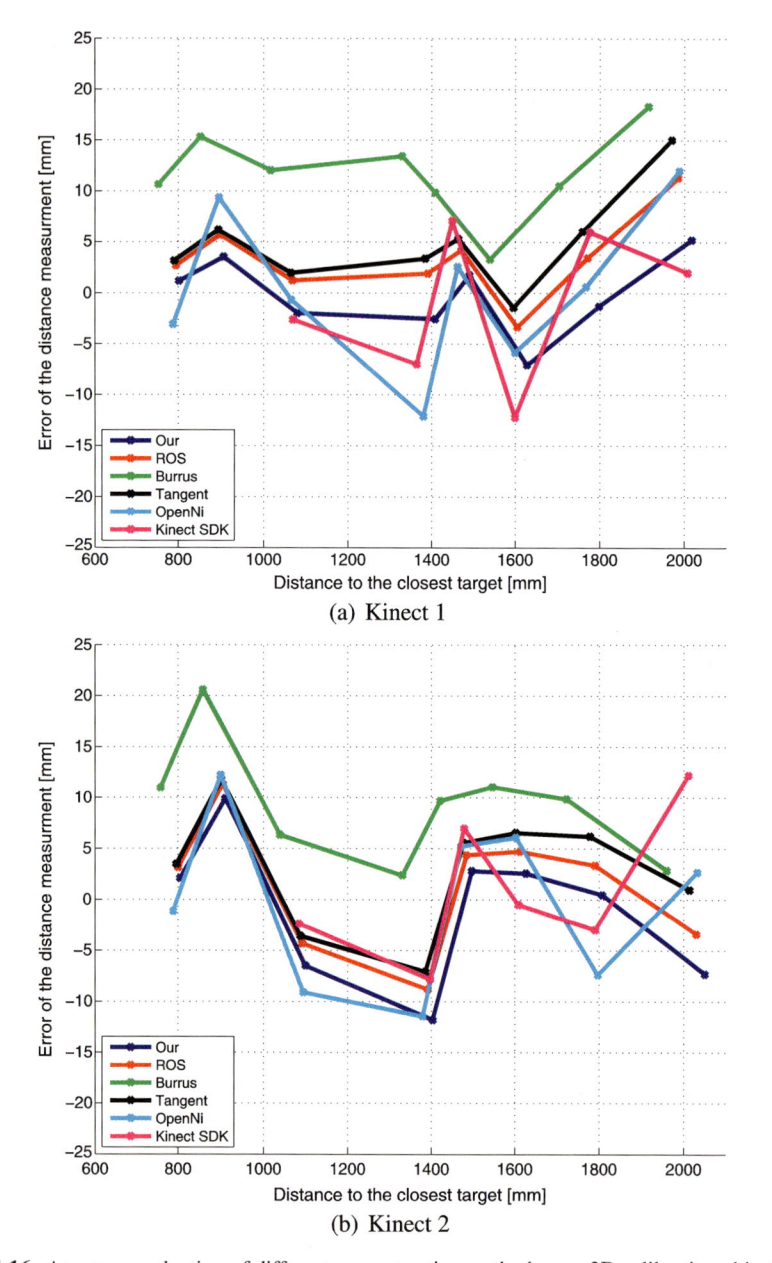

Fig. 1.16 Accuracy evaluation of different reconstruction methods on a 3D calibration object

1.5.2 Comparison of Kinect, SLR Stereo and 3D TOF

We have compared the accuracy of Kinect, SLR Stereo and 3D TOF cameras on the measurements of planar targets: Kinect and SLR Stereo (image size 2304 × 1536

1 3D with Kinect

Table 1.6 Comparison of SLR Stereo triangulation, Kinect and SR-4000 3D TOF depth sensing

Method	Geometrical error e [mm]		
	$\mu(e)$	$\sigma(e)$	$\max(e)$
SLR Stereo	1.57	1.15	7.38
Kinect	2.39	1.67	8.64
SR-4000	27.62	18.20	133.85

(a) RGB image (b) Depth image

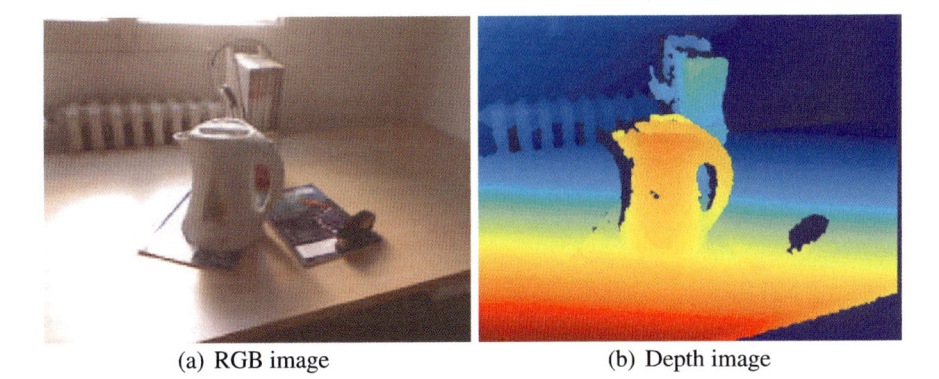

Fig. 1.17 Example of images from Kinect RGB cameras and the corresponding depth that were used for scene reconstruction

pixels) were rigidly mounted (Fig. 1.2) and calibrated (Fig. 1.12) together. SLR Stereo was performed by reconstructing calibration points extracted by [1] and triangulated by the linear least squares triangulation [5]. They measured the same planar targets in 315 control calibration points on each of the 14 targets. SR-4000 3D TOF [13] measured different planar targets but in a comparable range of distances 0.9–1.4 meters from the sensor in 88 control calibration points on each of the 11 calibration targets. The error e, Table 1.6, corresponds to the Euclidean distance between the points returned by the sensors and points reconstructed in the process of calibration of the cameras of the sensors. SLR Stereo is the most accurate, Kinect follows and SR-4000 is the least accurate.

1.5.3 Combining Kinect and Structure from Motion

Figure 1.17 shows a pair of 1/2-resolution (640 × 480) Kinect RGB and depth images (where the original depth image was reprojected using Eq. 1.7 to correspond with the RGB image pixels). A sequence of 50 RGB-Depth image pairs has been acquired and the relative poses of the RGB cameras have been computed by a SfM pipeline [6, 20]. Figure 1.18(a) shows a surface reconstructed from 3D points obtained by mere Multiview stereo [9] using only Kinect RGB images. Utilizing

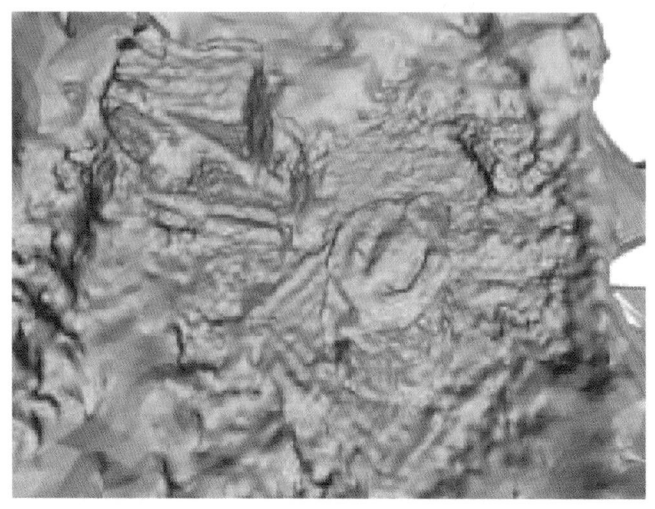

(a) Only visual data were used to reconstruct the scene by [10].

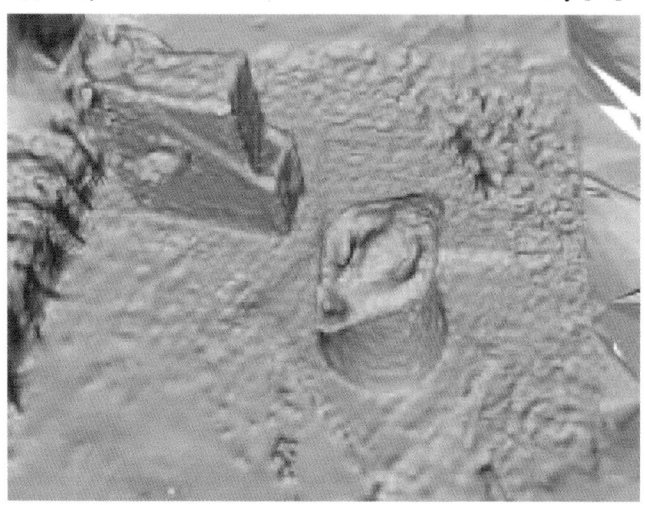

(b) Improved reconstruction using Kinect depth data registered by SfM applied to Kinect RGB images.

Fig. 1.18 Scene reconstruction from Kinect RGB camera. The figure shows a comparison of reconstruction quality when the scene is reconstructed only using *Multiview stereo* and the case when the 3D data from Kinect are also available

retrieved relative poses, depth data were registered together and used in the same method to provide improved reconstruction, Fig. 1.18(b).

Figure 1.19 compares a 3D surface reconstruction from point cloud computed by plane sweeping [9] with 70 Kinect 3D data processed by surface reconstruction of [9] (2304 × 1536 pixels). Kinect 3D data were registered into a common coordinate system via SfM [6, 20] applied to Kinect image data. We see that when multiple

1   3D with Kinect

(a) Left SLR image.   (b) Kinect true depth.   (c) Right SLR image.

(d) Multiview reconstruction [10].

(e) Reconstruction from registered Kinect 3D data.

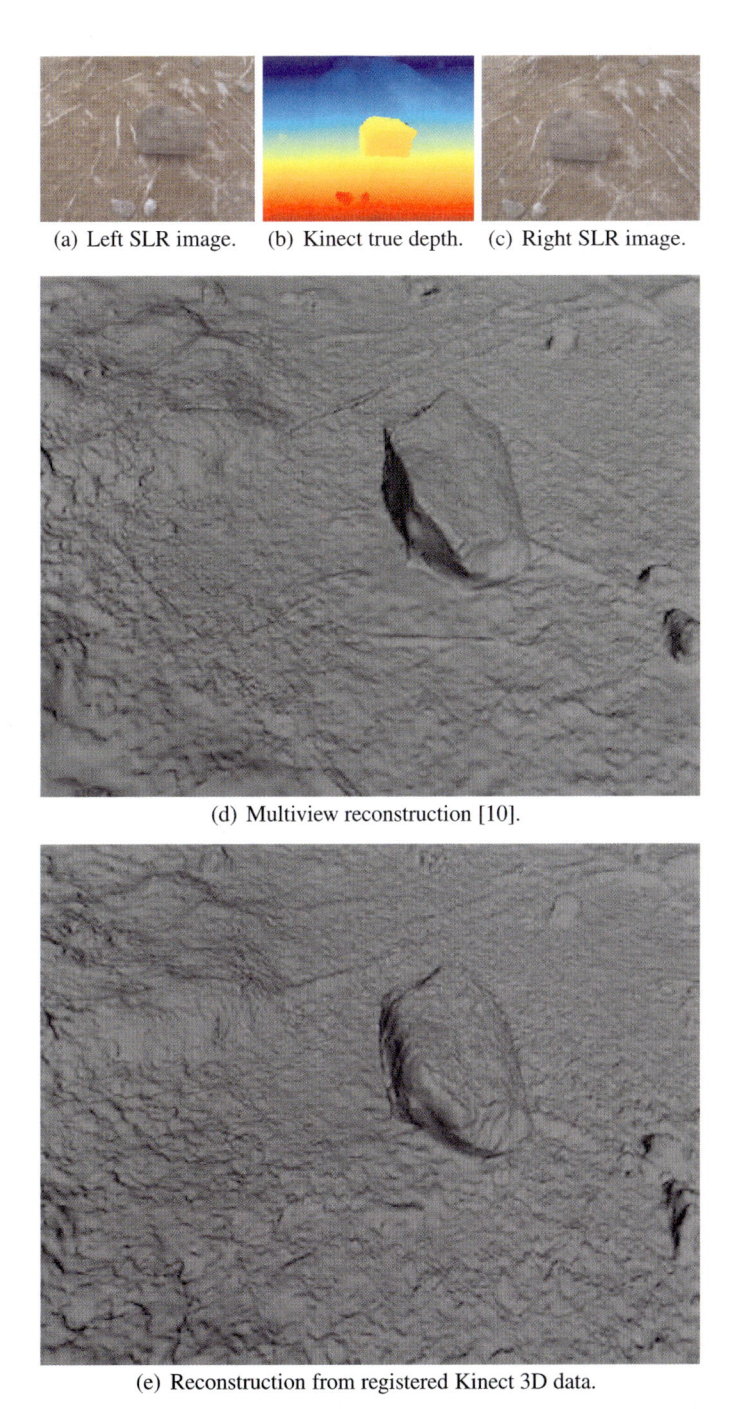

Fig. 1.19 Comparison of Kinect with Multiview reconstruction [9]

measurements are used, the Kinect result is quite comparable to more accurate Multiview stereo reconstruction.

1.6 Conclusion

We have provided an analysis of Kinect 3D measurement capabilities and its calibration procedure allowing to combine Kinect with SfM and Multiview Stereo, which opens a new area of applications for Kinect. It was interesting to observe that in the quality of the multi-view reconstruction, Kinect over-performed SwissRanger SR-4000 and was close to 3.5 M pixel SLR Stereo.

Acknowledgements This research was supported by TA02011275—ATOM—Automatic Three-dimensional Terrain Monitoring and FP7-SPACE-241523 ProViScout grants.

References

1. Bouguet, J.Y.: Camera calibration toolbox. http://www.vision.caltech.edu/bouguetj/calib_doc/ (2010)
2. Burrus, N.: Kinect calibration. http://nicolas.burrus.name/index.php/Research/KinectCalibration (2010)
3. Dryanovski, I., Morris, W., Magnenat, S.: kinect_node. http://www.ros.org/wiki/kinect_node (2010)
4. Freedman, B., Shpunt, A., Machline, M., Arieli, Y.: Depth mapping using projected patterns. US Patent (2010)
5. Hartley, R., Zisserman, A.: Multiple View Geometry in Computer Vision, 2nd edn. Cambridge University Press, Cambridge (2003)
6. Havlena, M., Torii, A., Pajdla, T.: Efficient structure from motion by graph optimization. doi:10.1007/978-3-642-15552-9_8
7. Henry, P., Krainin, M., Herbst, E., Ren, X., Fox, D.: RGB-D mapping: using Kinect-style depth cameras for dense 3d modeling of indoor environments. Int. J. Robot. Res. (2012). doi:10.1177/0278364911434148
8. Herrera, D.C., Kannala, J., Heikkila, J.: Accurate and practical calibration of a depth and color camera pair. http://www.ee.oulu.fi/~dherrera/kinect/2011-depth_calibration.pdf (2011)
9. Jancosek, M., Pajdla, T.: Multi-view reconstruction preserving weakly-supported surfaces. In: IEEE Conference on Computer Vision and Pattern Recognition (2011)
10. Khoshelham, K.: Accuracy analysis of Kinect depth data. In: ISPRS Workshop Laser Scanning, vol. XXXVIII (2011)
11. Konolige, K., Mihelich, P.: Technical description of Kinect calibration. http://www.ros.org/wiki/kinect_calibration/technical (2011)
12. Lai, K., Bo, L., Ren, X., Fox, D.: Sparse distance learning for object recognition combining RGB and depth information. In: IEEE International Conference on Robotics and Automation (2011)
13. MESA Imaging: SwissRanger SR-4000. http://www.mesa-imaging.ch/ (2011)
14. Microsoft: Kinect for X-BOX 360. http://www.xbox.com/en-US/kinect (2010)
15. Microsoft: Kinect for Windows. http://www.kinectforwindows.org/ (2012)
16. Openni: http://openni.org/ (2011)

17. Shotton, J., Fitzgibbon, A., Cook, M., Sharp, T., Finocchio, M., Moore, R., Kipman, A., Blake, A.: Real-time human pose recognition in parts from a single depth image. In: IEEE Conference on Computer Vision and Pattern Recognition (2011)
18. Smisek, J., Jancosek, M., Pajdla, T.: 3D with Kinect. In: International Conference on Computer Vision—Workshop on Consumer Depth Cameras for Computer Vision (2011)
19. Smisek, J., Pajdla, T.: 3D camera calibration. M.Sc. thesis, Czech Technical University in Prague (2011)
20. Snavely, N., Seitz, S., Szeliski, R.: Modeling the world from internet photo collections. Int. J. Comput. Vis. (2007)
21. Magnenat, S.: Stéphane Magnenat's distance model. http://groups.google.com/group/openkinect/browse_thread/thread/31351846fd33c78/e98a94ac605b9f21 (2011)
22. Wikipedia: Kinect. http://en.wikipedia.org/wiki/Kinect
23. Willow Garage: ROS—Kinect calibration: code complete. http://www.ros.org/news/2010/12/kinect-calibration-code-complete.html (2010)
24. Willow Garage: Camera calibration and 3D reconstruction. http://opencv.willowgarage.com/documentation/cpp/camera_calibration_and_3d_reconstruction.html (2011)
25. Willow Garage: Turtlebot. http://www.willowgarage.com/turtlebot (2011)

Chapter 2
Real-Time RGB-D Mapping and 3-D Modeling on the GPU Using the Random Ball Cover

Sebastian Bauer, Jakob Wasza, Felix Lugauer, Dominik Neumann, and Joachim Hornegger

Abstract In this chapter, we present a system for real-time point cloud mapping and scene reconstruction based on an efficient implementation of the iterative closest point (ICP) algorithm on the graphics processing unit (GPU). Compared to state-of-the-art approaches that achieve real-time performance using projective data association schemes which operate on the 3-D scene geometry solely, our method allows to incorporate additional complementary information to guide the registration process. In this work, the ICP's nearest neighbor search evaluates both geometric and photometric information in a direct manner, achieving robust mappings in real-time. In order to overcome the performance bottleneck in nearest neighbor search space traversal, we exploit the inherent computation parallelism of GPUs. In particular, we have adapted the random ball cover (RBC) data structure and search algorithm, originally proposed for high-dimensional problems, to low-dimensional RGB-D data. The system is validated on scene and object reconstruction scenarios. Our implementation achieves frame-to-frame registration runtimes of less than 20 ms on an off-the-shelf consumer GPU.

S. Bauer (✉) · J. Wasza · F. Lugauer · D. Neumann
Pattern Recognition Lab, Department of Computer Science, Friedrich-Alexander-Universität Erlangen-Nürnberg, Martensstr. 3, 91058 Erlangen, Germany
e-mail: sebastian.bauer@cs.fau.de

J. Wasza
e-mail: jakob.wasza@cs.fau.de

F. Lugauer
e-mail: felix.lugauer@gmail.com

D. Neumann
e-mail: dominik.neumann@gmail.com

J. Hornegger
Erlangen Graduate School in Advanced Optical Technologies (SAOT) & Pattern Recognition Lab, Department of Computer Science, Friedrich-Alexander-Universität Erlangen-Nürnberg, Martensstr. 3, 91058 Erlangen, Germany
e-mail: joachim.hornegger@cs.fau.de

2.1 Introduction

In the past, the acquisition of dense 3-D range data was both tedious, time consuming and expensive. Lately, advances in RGB-D sensor design have rendered metric 3-D surface acquisition at convenient resolutions (up to 300k points) and framerates (up to 40 Hz) possible, holding potential for a variety of applications where real-time demands form a key aspect. The advent of Microsoft's Kinect [14], with more than 10 million sales within a few months, has caused a furor in the field of consumer electronics. In fact, the device has attracted the attention of various research communities.

This chapter addresses the field of 3-D scene and model reconstruction that provides the basis for many practical applications. Among others, 3-D modeling is a key component for the acquisition of virtual 3-D models from real objects, the digitalization of archaeological buildings or sculptures for restoration planning or archival storage [11], and the construction of environment maps in robot or vehicle navigation [19, 28]. In particular, in the field of robotics, there is an increasing interest in both 3-D environment reconstruction and simultaneous localization and mapping (SLAM) solutions [2, 6, 32].

We present a framework that is capable of mapping RGB-D point cloud data streams on-the-fly, enabling real-time 3-D scene modeling. We have implemented a hybrid 6-D ICP variant that performs the alignment by considering both photometric appearance and geometric shape [24]. Photometric (color) data may be an essential source of information to guide the registration process in cases when geometric surface information is not discriminative enough to achieve a correct alignment, see Fig. 2.1 for an example. Without loss of generality, we have designed the framework in a manner that allows to incorporate further complementary information into an n-dimensional point signature. In order to enable on-the-fly processing, the corpus of the framework is implemented on the GPU. For the nearest neighbor search, being the performance bottleneck in the majority of previous ICP implementations, we use a data structure that is specifically designed to benefit from the parallel architecture of modern GPUs. In this work, we investigated the fitness of the random ball cover (RBC) data structure and search algorithm [7, 8] for low-dimensional 6-D data. Trading accuracy against runtime, we propose a modified approximate RBC variant that is optimized in terms of performance. Please note that this chapter is a substantial extension of previous work by the authors [30]. In particular, we further enhanced the GPU implementation and achieved significant speedups.

The remainder of this chapter is organized as follows. In Sect. 2.2, we review relevant literature. We present our method for RGB-D mapping and 3-D modeling in Sect. 2.3. Implementation details are given in Sect. 2.4. In Sect. 2.5, we evaluate the proposed framework and discuss experimental results. Eventually, we draw a conclusion in Sect. 2.6.

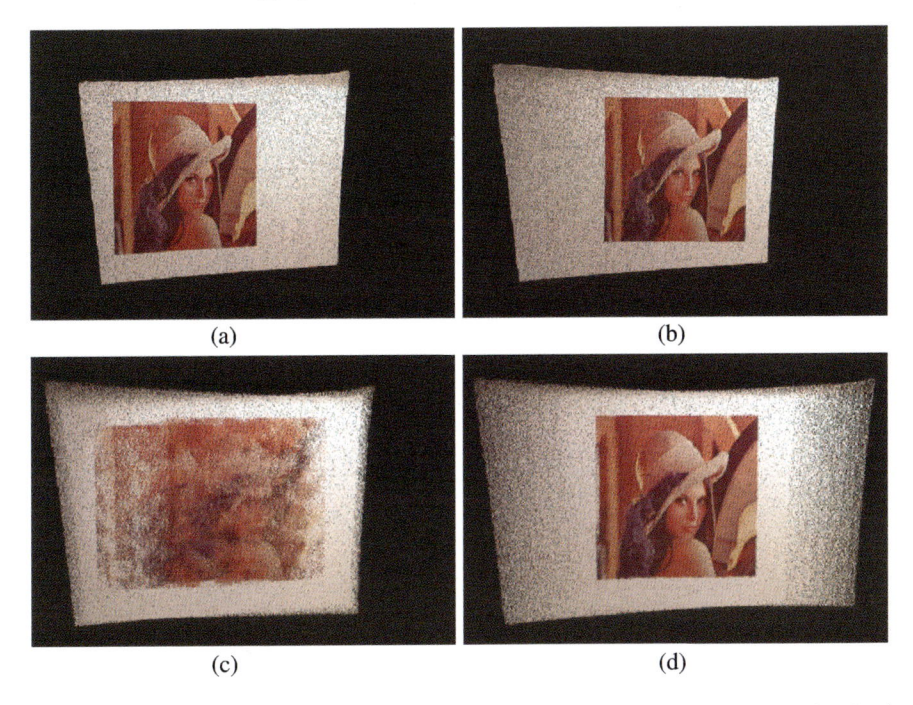

Fig. 2.1 Illustration of the benefit of incorporating photometric information into the point cloud alignment process in situations of non-salient surface geometry. The *top row* (**a**, **b**) depicts the first and last frame of an RGB-D sequence capturing a colored poster stuck to a plane wall from changing perspectives. Using scene geometry as the only source of information for the registration algorithm results in an erroneous alignment (**c**). Instead, by considering both geometric and photometric information, the correct alignment is found using the proposed framework (**d**)

2.2 Related Work

The iterative closest point (ICP) algorithm is state-of-the-art for the rigid alignment of 3-D point clouds [4, 9, 36], and the vast majority of related work builds upon this established scheme. However, in the field of 3-D environment and model reconstruction, only few existing approaches have achieved interactive frame-rates so far [12, 13, 19, 22]. Huhle et al. proposed a system for on-the-fly 3-D scene modeling using a low resolution Time-of-Flight camera (160 × 120 px), typically achieving per-frame runtimes of >2 s [22]. Engelhard et al. presented similar runtimes on Microsoft Kinect data (640 × 480 px) for an ICP-based RGB-D SLAM framework [12]. The RGB-D mapping framework of Henry et al. performs ICP registration in an average of 500 ms [19].

Only recently, real-time frame-rates were reported for geometric ICP variants [13, 23, 31]. In particular, the *KinectFusion* framework [23, 31] has gained popularity in the field of 3-D reconstruction. The fundamental core of this framework is based on the work of Rusinkiewicz et al. [35], combining projective data association [5] and a point-to-plane metric [9] for rigid ICP surface registration and sensor pose estimation, respectively. While the original work was limited to a frame-to-frame alignment [35], KinectFusion tracks the depth frame against a globally fused implicit surface model of the observed scene [10]. This limits the drift behavior and results in an increased robustness and reconstruction accuracy, respectively. Real-time capability is achieved using a parallelized implementation on the GPU.

Compared to related methods based on projective data association [5] that primarily consider the surface geometry for finding corresponding points, our approach allows to incorporate multiple complementary sources of information (in our case geometry and photometry) into the nearest neighbor search. Furthermore, explicitly performing a nearest neighbor search according to a point signature potentially allows one to extend the framework to handle large misalignments by a feature-based initial pre-alignment [3].

More than a decade ago, Johnson and Kang presented the first approach to incorporate photometric information into the ICP framework (*Color-ICP*) in order to improve its robustness [24]. The basic idea is that photometric information can compensate for regions with non-salient topologies, whereas geometric information can guide the pose estimation for faintly textured regions. In experiments, Johnson and Kang observed that the additional use of color information decreased the registration error by one order of magnitude. Recently, modifications have been proposed that try to accelerate the color ICP's nearest neighbor search by pruning the search space w.r.t. photometrically dissimilar points [11, 25]. However, this reduction typically comes with a loss in robustness.

Since modern RGB-D devices produce and propagate an immense data stream, efficient implementations are inevitable in order to fulfill real-time constraints. For the ICP algorithm in general, a comprehensive survey of efficient implementation variants was given by Rusinkiewicz and Levoy [36]. However, their survey did not include hardware acceleration techniques.

For the nearest neighbor search, being a major bottleneck in terms of runtime, CPU architectures have shown to benefit from space-partitioning data structures like k-d trees [1]. In contrast to algorithmic improvements, hardware acceleration techniques are increasingly attracting the attention of the community. Garcia et al. have shown that a GPU-based brute-force implementation outperforms a CPU-based k-d tree [15]. The reason for this lies in the fact that the brute-force primitive can be implemented efficiently using techniques known from the well understood problem of GPU-based matrix–matrix multiplication. Implementations of traditional nearest neighbor search acceleration strategies on the GPU are challenging due to the non-parallel and recursive nature of construction and/or traversal of the underlying data structures. For instance, Qiu et al. [33] achieved excellent frame-rates for GPU-based k-d tree queries. However, the construction of the tree is performed on the CPU, thus limiting performance when the tree must be constructed on a per-frame basis as in the application scenarios considered in this chapter. Recently, space-partitioning strategies that are specifically designed for GPU architectures have been addressed. A promising approach is the random ball cover (RBC) proposed by Cayton [7, 8]. The basic principle behind the RBC is a two-tier nearest neighbor search,

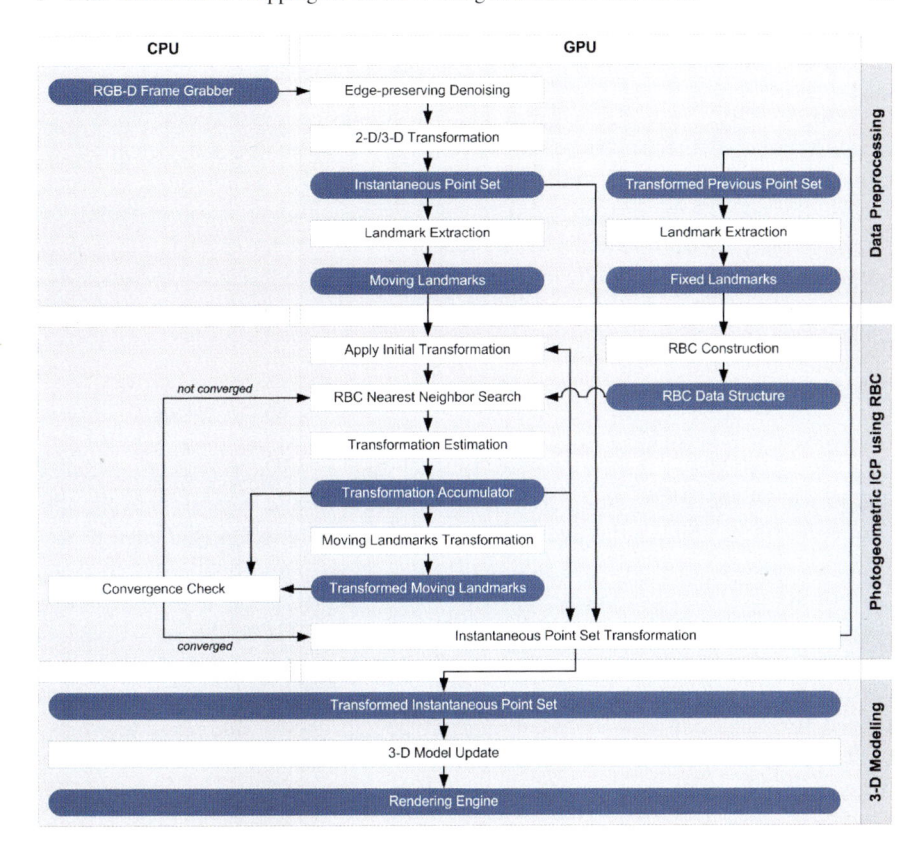

Fig. 2.2 Flowchart of the proposed 3-D scene reconstruction framework. Apart from the camera hardware interface and the ICP control flow management, the corpus of the computational load of both data preprocessing and photogeometric ICP alignment using RBC is outsourced to the GPU

building on the brute-force primitive, to prune the search space. In this work, we adapted the random ball cover data structure and search algorithm, originally proposed for high-dimensional problems, to low-dimensional RGB-D data for accelerating the ICP alignment.

2.3 Methods

The proposed RGB-D mapping and modeling framework is composed of three stages, as depicted in Fig. 2.2. In an initial stage, the sensor data consisting of orthogonal distance measurements and photometric color information are transferred to the GPU where the corpus of the pipeline is executed. On the GPU, first, data preprocessing and the transformation from orthogonal range measurements in the 2-D sensor domain to 3-D world coordinates are performed (Sect. 2.3.1). Second, based on a set of extracted landmarks, the proposed color ICP variant is applied

(Sect. 2.3.2). Our method exploits the arithmetic power of modern GPUs for efficient nearest neighbor search with an inherently parallel data structure and query framework (RBC, Sect. 2.3.3). Third and last, the instantaneous point cloud is attached to the global reconstructed model based on the estimated transformation. We point out that the rigid body transformation is estimated in a frame-to-frame manner, i.e. the pose of the instantaneous frame is estimated by registration against the previous frame. In the remainder of this section, we outline the essential steps of the proposed ICP framework. GPU implementation details are discussed in Sect. 2.4.

2.3.1 Data Preprocessing on the GPU

The Microsoft Kinect device acquires RGB-D data with VGA resolution (640 × 480 px) at 30 Hz. With respect to real-time constraints and regardless of the specific application, this spatial and temporal data density poses a challenge to data processing solutions. Hence, in addition to the actual point cloud alignment, we perform RGB-D data preprocessing on-the-fly on the GPU. First, we apply edge-preserving denoising (e.g. guided image filtering [18, 37]) on the raw depth and RGB data, respectively, as acquired by the Microsoft Kinect sensors. Next, the enhanced depth measurements are transformed to the 3-D world coordinate system. Indeed, for each point $\mathbf{x}_c \in \mathbb{R}^2$ in the camera plane, its depth value $z(\mathbf{x}_c)$ describes a world coordinate position vector $\mathbf{x}_w \in \mathbb{R}^3$. The transformation can be computed independently for each pixel, thus fitting perfectly for parallel processing on the GPU (see Sect. 2.5.2).

Nomenclature Let us introduce the notation for this chapter. Let $\tilde{\mathcal{M}}$ denote a *moving* set of template points $\tilde{\mathcal{M}} = \{\mathbf{m}\}$, where $\mathbf{m} \in \mathbb{R}^6$ concatenates a point's geometric and photometric information $\mathbf{m}_g \in \mathbb{R}^3$ and $\mathbf{m}_p \in \mathbb{R}^3$:

$$\mathbf{m} = \begin{pmatrix} \mathbf{m}_g \\ \mathbf{m}_p \end{pmatrix}. \tag{2.1}$$

The indices g and p denote that only the geometric and photometric part is considered, respectively. In order to compensate for inconsistencies due to changes in illumination and viewpoint direction, the photometric information is transformed to the normalized RGB space [16]:

$$\mathbf{m}_p = (i_r + i_g + i_b)^{-1} \begin{pmatrix} i_r \\ i_g \\ i_b \end{pmatrix}, \tag{2.2}$$

where i_r, i_g, i_b denote the intensities of the red, green and blue photometric channel.

In analogy to the moving set of template points $\tilde{\mathcal{M}}$, let $\tilde{\mathcal{F}} = \{\mathbf{f}\}$ denote a *fixed* set of $|\tilde{\mathcal{F}}|$ reference points $\mathbf{f} \in \mathbb{R}^6$, where $\mathbf{f}^\top = (\mathbf{f}_g^\top, \mathbf{f}_p^\top)$.

Landmark Extraction Considering the application of 3-D scene or object modeling using a real-time, hand-held and steadily moved RGB-D device implies that a portion of the scene that was captured in the previous frame $\tilde{\mathcal{F}}$ is no longer visible in the instantaneous data $\tilde{\mathcal{M}}$ and vice versa. Facing these issues, we heuristically discard the set of points that correspond to range measurements at the edge of the 2-D sensor domain in order to improve the robustness of ICP alignment. This clipping is performed in conjunction with the extraction of the sparse sets of ICP landmarks, denoted by $\mathcal{M} \subset \tilde{\mathcal{M}}$ and $\mathcal{F} \subset \tilde{\mathcal{F}}$. In practice, the landmark extraction is performed by sub-sampling the clipped point set.

For the case of 3-D object reconstruction, we apply a dedicated scheme for landmark extraction. Instead of considering the entire scene, we segment the foreground using a depth threshold. From the set of foreground pixels, we then select a set of landmarks.

2.3.2 Photogeometric ICP Framework

Being the state-of-the-art in rigid point cloud alignment [4, 9, 36], the ICP estimates the optimal rigid transformation $(\mathbf{R}, \mathbf{t})$ that brings $\mathcal{M}$ in congruence with $\mathcal{F}$, where $\mathbf{R} \in \mathbb{R}^{3 \times 3}$ denotes a rotation matrix with $\mathbf{R}^\top = \mathbf{R}^{-1}$, $\det(\mathbf{R}) = 1$ and $\mathbf{t} \in \mathbb{R}^3$ denotes a translation vector. Based on an initial guess $(\mathbf{R}^0, \mathbf{t}^0)$, the ICP scheme iteratively estimates this transformation by minimizing an error metric assigned to repeatedly generated pairs of corresponding landmarks $(\mathbf{m}, \mathbf{y})$ where $\mathbf{m} \in \mathcal{M}$ and $\mathbf{y} \in \mathcal{F}$. In terms of correspondence search, our *photogeometric* ICP variant incorporates both geometric and photometric information. Let us note that competing strategies, including projective data association, typically rely on the pure geometry and cannot incorporate additional information in a straightforward manner. We now outline the essential steps of our photogeometric ICP variant.

In the geometric case, the distance d between an individual moving landmark $\mathbf{m}_g$ and the set of reference landmarks $\mathcal{F}_g = \{\mathbf{f}_g\}$ is defined as

$$d(\mathbf{m}_g, \mathcal{F}_g) = \min_{\mathbf{f}_g \in \mathcal{F}_g} \|\mathbf{f}_g - \mathbf{m}_g\|_2^2, \qquad (2.3)$$

where $\|\cdot\|_2$ denotes the Euclidean norm. In order to incorporate the additional photometric information available with modern RGB-D sensors, let us modify the distance metric d:

$$d(\mathbf{m}, \mathcal{F}) = \min_{\mathbf{f} \in \mathcal{F}} \left((1-\alpha) \|\mathbf{f}_g - \mathbf{m}_g\|_2^2 + \alpha \|\mathbf{f}_p - \mathbf{m}_p\|_2^2 \right), \qquad (2.4)$$

where $\alpha \in [0, 1]$ is a non-negative constant weighting the influence of the photometric information. The benefit of this hybrid approach is that photometric information compensates for regions with non-salient surface topology, and geometric information compensates for faintly textured regions or photometric inconsistencies due to changes in illumination and viewpoint direction. The landmark $\mathbf{y} \in \mathcal{F}$ yielding the minimum distance to $\mathbf{m}$ is then given by

$$\mathbf{y} = \arg\min_{\mathbf{f} \in \mathcal{F}} \left((1-\alpha)\|\mathbf{f}_g - \mathbf{m}_g\|_2^2 + \alpha\|\mathbf{f}_p - \mathbf{m}_p\|_2^2\right). \quad (2.5)$$

By assigning a nearest neighbor $\mathbf{y}$ to all $\mathbf{m} \in \mathcal{M}$, a set of nearest neighbors $\mathcal{Y}$ is given as $\mathcal{Y} = \{\mathbf{y}\}$, $\mathbf{y} \in \mathcal{F}$, $|\mathcal{Y}| = |\mathcal{M}|$, and the landmark correspondences can be denoted by $(\mathcal{M}, \mathcal{Y})$. The GPU-based nearest neighbor search framework that we use to establish these landmark correspondences is described in Sect. 2.3.3. Next, based on the landmark correspondences $(\mathcal{M}^k, \mathcal{Y}^k)$ found in the kth ICP iteration, the transformation $(\hat{\mathbf{R}}^k, \hat{\mathbf{t}}^k)$ is estimated by either minimizing a point-to-point error metric in a least-squares sense using a unit quaternion optimizer [21],

$$(\hat{\mathbf{R}}^k, \hat{\mathbf{t}}^k) = \arg\min_{\mathbf{R}^k, \mathbf{t}^k} \frac{1}{|\mathcal{M}_g^k|} \sum_{\mathcal{M}_g^k, \mathcal{Y}_g^k} \|(\mathbf{R}^k \mathbf{m}_g^k + \mathbf{t}^k) - \mathbf{y}_g^k\|_2^2, \quad (2.6)$$

or by minimizing a point-to-plane distance metric [9] using a nonlinear solver,

$$(\hat{\mathbf{R}}^k, \hat{\mathbf{t}}^k) = \arg\min_{\mathbf{R}^k, \mathbf{t}^k} \frac{1}{|\mathcal{M}_g^k|} \sum_{\mathcal{M}_g^k, \mathcal{Y}_g^k} \left(((\mathbf{R}^k \mathbf{m}_g^k + \mathbf{t}^k) - \mathbf{y}_g^k)^\top \mathbf{n}_{\mathbf{y}_g^k}\right)^2. \quad (2.7)$$

Here, $\mathbf{n}_{\mathbf{y}_g^k}$ denotes the surface normal associated with the point $\mathbf{y}_g^k \in \mathcal{F}$. After each iteration, the global solution $(\mathbf{R}, \mathbf{t})$ is accumulated:

$$\mathbf{R} = \hat{\mathbf{R}}^k \mathbf{R}, \qquad \mathbf{t} = \hat{\mathbf{R}}^k \mathbf{t} + \hat{\mathbf{t}}^k, \quad (2.8)$$

and $\mathcal{M}_g^k$ is updated according to $\mathbf{m}_g^k = \mathbf{R}\mathbf{m}_g + \mathbf{t}$. The two stages of first finding the set of nearest neighbors $\mathcal{Y}^k$ and then estimating the optimal transformation for the correspondences $(\mathcal{M}^k, \mathcal{Y}^k)$ are repeated iteratively until a convergence criterion is fulfilled, see Fig. 2.2 and Sect. 2.4.1.

2.3.3 6-D Nearest Neighbor Search Using RBC

The Random Ball Cover (RBC) is a novel data structure for efficient nearest neighbor (NN) search on the GPU proposed by Cayton [7, 8]. By design, it exploits the parallel architecture of modern graphics cards hardware. In particular, both the construction of the RBC and dataset queries are performed using brute-force (BF) primitives. Using techniques known from matrix–matrix multiplication, the BF search can be performed in a highly efficient manner on the GPU. The RBC data structure relies on randomly selected points $\mathbf{r} \in \mathcal{F}$, called *representatives*. Each of them manages a local subset of $\mathcal{F}$. This indirection creates a hierarchy in the database such that a nearest neighbor query is processed by (i) searching the nearest neighbor $\mathbf{r}$ among the set of representatives and (ii) performing another search for the subset of

RBC Construction Scheme

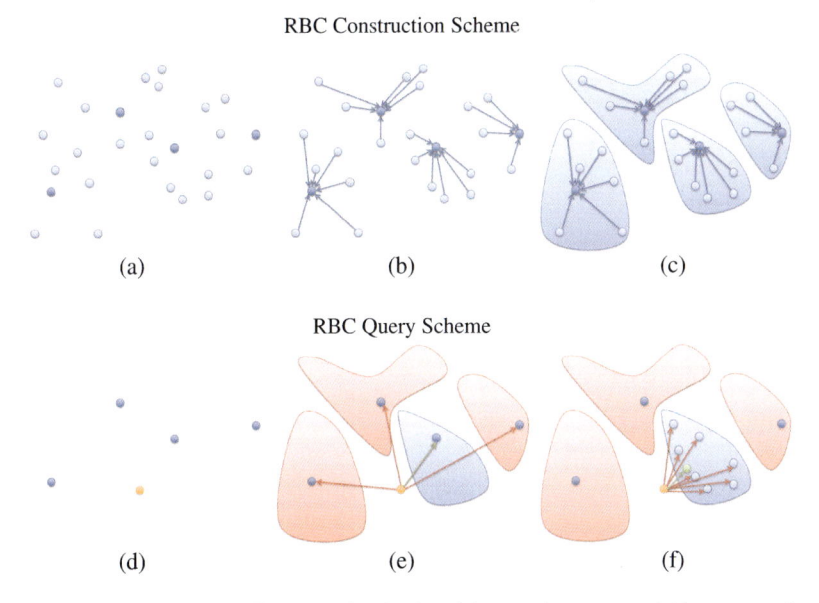

(a) (b) (c)

RBC Query Scheme

(d) (e) (f)

Fig. 2.3 Illustration of the RBC construction (**a–c**) and the two-tier nearest neighbor query scheme (**d–f**) for the simplified case of 2-D data. (**a**) Selection of a set of representatives $\mathcal{R}$ (*labeled in dark blue*) out of the set of database entries $\mathcal{F}$ (*light blue*). (**b**) Nearest representative search over the set of database entries, to establish a landmark-to-representative mapping. (**c**) Nearest neighbor set of each representative (*shaded in blue*). (**d**) Query data (*orange*) and set of representatives $\mathcal{R}$ (*dark blue*). (**e**) Identification of the closest representative **r**, in a first brute-force (BF) run. (**f**) Identification of the nearest neighbor (*green*) in the subset of entries managed by **r** (*shaded in blue*), in a second BF run

entries managed by **r**. This two-tier approach outperforms a global BF search due to the fact that each of the two successive stages explore a heavily pruned search space.

In this work, we have investigated the fitness of the RBC for acceleration of the 6-D nearest neighbor search of our photogeometric ICP. Optimizing this particular ICP stage is motivated by the fact that it is a major performance bottleneck—see Sect. 2.5.2 and [30].

Cayton proposed two alternative RBC search strategies [8]. The *exact* search is the appropriate choice when the exact nearest neighbor is required. Otherwise, if a small error may be tolerated, the approximate *one-shot* search is typically faster. Originally, in order to set up the *one-shot* data structure, the representatives are chosen at random, and each **r** manages its s closest database elements. Depending on s, points typically belong to more than one representative. However, this implies a sorting of all database entries for each representative—hindering a high degree of parallelization for implementation on the GPU—or the need for multiple BF runs [7]. Hence, we introduce a modified version of the *one-shot* approach that is even further optimized in terms of performance. In particular, we simplified the RBC construction, trading off accuracy against runtime, see Fig. 2.3 (a–c). First, we select a random set of representatives $\mathcal{R} = \{\mathbf{r}\}$ out of the set of fixed points $\mathcal{F}$. Second, each representative **r** is assigned a local subset of $\mathcal{F}$. This is done in an inverse manner by simply computing the nearest representative **r** for each point $\mathbf{f} \in \mathcal{F}$. The query scheme of our modified *one-shot* RBC variant is basically consistent with the original approach and can be performed efficiently using two subsequent BF runs [8], see Fig. 2.3 (d–f). First, the closest representative is identified among $\mathcal{R}$. Second, based on the associated subset of entries managed by **r**, the nearest neighbor is located.

Please note that this modified RBC construction scheme results in an approximate nearest neighbor search being error-prone from a theoretical point of view. In practice, facing the trade-off between accuracy and runtime, we tolerate this approximation, cf. Sect. 2.5.2. Let us further remark that the scheme is not limited to 6-D data but can be applied to data of any dimension. For application in 3-D reconstruction, this potentially allows us to extend the point signature from 6-D to higher dimensions, e.g. appending additional complementary information or local feature descriptors to the raw geometric and photometric measurements acquired by the sensor, cf. [19].

2.4 Implementation Details

In this section, we discuss implementation details and comment on practical issues. In particular, we address the RBC implementation on the GPU.

2.4.1 Details Regarding the ICP Framework

Regarding the quality and robustness of point cloud alignment, we observed a strong impact of outliers that occur in RGB-D data particularly due to sensor noise, quantization, occlusion, and changes in viewpoint direction. Sensor noise and quantization issues are reduced using edge-preserving denoising filters in the preprocessing stage of the framework, recall Fig. 2.2. We typically apply the concept of guided image filtering [18] or median filtering that both can be parallelized in an efficient manner on the GPU [29, 37].

The remaining set of outliers arise from a change in viewpoint direction or occlusion and cannot be eliminated by denoising. To take them into account, we optionally reject low-grade correspondences in the transformation estimation stage. The term *low-grade* is quantified by comparing the distance of a corresponding pair of landmarks (Eq. 2.4) w.r.t. an empirically set threshold δ. The set of low-grade correspondences is re-computed for each ICP iteration and discarded in the subsequent transformation estimation step.

As initialization for the ICP alignment, we incorporate the estimated global transformation $(\mathbf{R}^0, \mathbf{t}^0)$ from the previously aligned frame, see Fig. 2.2, assuming a smooth trajectory of the hand-guided acquisition device. In practice, this speeds up convergence and reconstruction, respectively.

In our implementation, the ICP transformation is estimated by minimizing the point-to-point distance metric (Eq. 2.6). The estimation of the transformation matrix according to Horn [21] is performed on the GPU. Both the computation of the centroids of $\mathcal{F}$ and $\mathcal{M}$ and the summation of the intermediate M-matrix are implemented using the established parallel reduction technique [17]. For details on Horn's scheme we refer to [21]. Note that low-grade correspondences may have been removed from $\mathcal{F}$ and $\mathcal{M}$ at this stage. The resulting eigenvalue problem is solved using the iterative Jacobi scheme on the GPU. This is motivated by practical experience: on the one hand, using a CPU-based implementation of Jacobi's scheme would result in notable host-device and device-host transfer times, depending on the number of ICP iterations. On the other hand, solving the eigenvalue problem on the GPU using Ferrari's closed form solution [26] as proposed by Loop and Blinn [27] would imply a non-negligible number of branches and root calculations that are also performed iteratively in hardware [34].

As ICP convergence criterion we analyze the variation of the estimated transformation over the iterations. In particular, we evaluate the change in translation magnitude and rotation angle w.r.t. heuristically set thresholds of 0.01 mm and 0.001°, respectively.

2.4.2 RBC Construction and Queries on the GPU

Originally designed for offline and high-dimensional data queries, utilizing the RBC for real-time low-dimensional RGB-D mapping requires certain adaptations. We found that the originally proposed RBC construction routine does not satisfy runtime constraints imposed by the frame-rate of modern RGB-D imaging devices. We therefore employ a different RBC construction routine as introduced in Sect. 2.3.3. As a consequence, this implies a query approach that slightly differs from the original proposal. Below, we describe the details and hardware related considerations of our RBC implementation. An illustration of the workflow for RBC construction and query, as well as data interaction, is depicted in Fig. 2.4.

RBC Construction   As a first step in the RBC construction, we extract the set of representatives $\mathcal{R} = \{\mathbf{r}\}$ from the given fixed landmarks $\mathcal{F}$. For each landmark $\mathbf{f} \in \mathcal{F}$, we then compute the nearest representative $\mathbf{r}$ by a brute-force search strategy. This can be done efficiently in parallel over the landmarks using block-decomposition techniques known from matrix–matrix multiplication on the GPU. These landmark-to-representative (LR) mappings are subsequently used to (i) set up the RBC *meta information* and (ii) to generate a compact and cache friendly *permuted database* of the original landmarks $\mathcal{F}$ for RBC queries. An illustration is given in Fig. 2.5. For meta information generation, let us note that the number of managed landmarks for each representative can be derived in the LR mapping computation directly by using synchronized counters employing atomic operations. We found this approach more performant compared to a separate approach. Next,

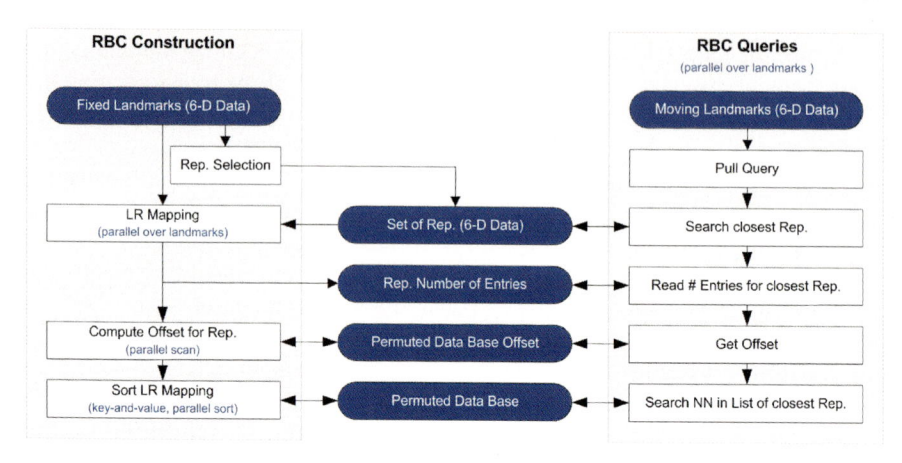

Fig. 2.4 Flowchart describing the GPU workflow and data interaction for RBC construction (*left*) and queries (*right*). Note the high degree of parallelism for both construction and queries. For details on the landmark-to-representative (LR) mapping see Fig. 2.5

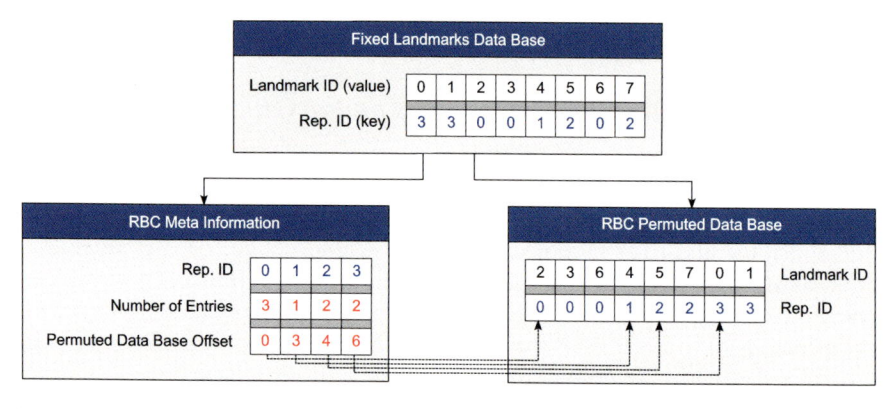

Fig. 2.5 Data structures for RBC construction and queries. Note the differentiation between meta information (*left*) and the permuted database (*right*) to improve cache hit ratio for queries

we compute an offset table by performing a parallel scan [17] on the number of managed entries. This offset table ultimately defines the unique position for each representative's first managed entry in the permuted database. To re-arrange the original data into a cache friendly layout for RBC queries, we perform a key-and-value sort [20] on the LR mappings. Here, a landmark ID denotes the value and the associated representative ID defines the key. By using such a database layout, a representative's managed entries are located in contiguous memory regions, improving cache hit ratio for RBC queries. We note that our approach still requires sorting, however, sorting breaks down to $|\mathcal{F}|$ elements in contrast to $|\mathcal{F}| \cdot |\mathcal{R}|$ entries as originally described [8].

RBC Nearest Neighbor Queries As described in Sect. 2.3.3, RBC queries rely on a two-tier approach—each employing a brute-force search—to prune the search space. The first tier consists of finding the nearest representative **r** for each query element by a BF search. This is basically the same procedure as for deriving the LR mappings during RBC construction and can be performed efficiently in parallel over the query elements by using a block-decomposition scheme. The second tier consists of finding the nearest entry managed by the representative **r** identified in the first tier. Again, this is done by utilizing a BF search, however, an efficient block-decomposition scheme is not a performant option here. In the first tier this scheme is efficient and possible due to the prior knowledge that all query elements have to visit exactly the same representatives. However, in the second tier, each query element must examine (i) different entries and/or (ii) a different number of entries. Both are given by the entry's nearest representative which in general is not consistent across different query elements. Though sophisticated techniques to implement a block-decomposition-like scheme can be used, in most cases they are counterproductive. We found that due to the computational overhead a potential performance gain is lost. Instead, we employ a simple BF search over a representative's contiguous memory region in the *permuted database* which allows to increase the cache hit ratio and results in lower runtimes.

2.5 Experiments and Results

We have evaluated the proposed framework for on-the-fly 3-D reconstruction and modeling of real data (640 × 480 px, 30 Hz) from a hand-held Microsoft Kinect sensor. Below, first, we present qualitative results for both indoor scene mapping and object reconstruction scenarios, and investigate the influence of the parameter settings (Sect. 2.5.1). Second, being a major focus of this system, we demonstrate its real-time capability in a comprehensive performance study (Sect. 2.5.2). Third, we compare our approximate RBC variant to an exact nearest neighbor search in terms of accuracy (Sect. 2.5.3). For all experiments, the number of representatives was set to $|\mathcal{R}| = \sqrt{|\mathcal{F}|}$ according to Cayton's rule of thumb [8], if not stated otherwise. The ICP transformation was estimated by minimizing the point-to-point distance metric, see Eq. 2.6. The performance study was conducted on an off-the-shelf consumer desktop computer equipped with an NVIDIA GeForce GTX 460 GPU and a 2.8 GHz Intel Core 2 Quad Q9550 CPU. The GPU framework is implemented using CUDA.

2.5.1 Qualitative Results

Qualitative results for a scene reconstruction scenario in indoor environments are depicted in Fig. 2.6. The three point cloud sequences were acquired from a static

Fig. 2.6 On-the-fly 3-D scene reconstruction for different types of room. *First row*: bedroom (295 frames). *Second row*: lounge (526 frames). *Third row*: family room (380 frames). For each sequence, the *left column* depicts a bird-eye view of the respective room layout. The *remaining columns* provide a zoom-in for selected regions. All reconstructions were performed using our default parameter settings as stated in Sect. 2.5.1. Note that for visualization of the reconstructed scenes, we rendered a subset of the global model point cloud

observer location by rotating the hand-held sensor around the observer's body axis. RGB-D data were aligned on-the-fly. The different rooms were reconstructed using identical preprocessing pipeline and ICP/RBC parameter settings (default configuration): Edge-preserving denoising (geometric median, geometric and photometric guided image filter), $|\mathcal{F}| = |\mathcal{M}| = 16{,}384$ ICP landmarks, 10 % edge clipping, photogeometric weight $\alpha = 0.8$, no elimination of low-grade correspondences ($\delta \to \infty$).

In order to demonstrate the effectiveness of our system for reconstruction of scenes with non-salient 3-D geometry, we refer to Fig. 2.1. Facing a colored poster stuck to a plane wall, the reconstruction could benefit significantly from incorporating the photometric domain as a complementary source of information.

In addition to scene reconstruction, the proposed framework can also be employed for 3-D model digitalization scenarios. Here, the hand-held acquisition device is moved around an object to acquire RGB-D data from different perspectives while continuously merging the data into a global model using the proposed framework. As stated in Sect. 2.3.1, for the case of 3-D object reconstruction, we select the set of landmarks from a defined foreground region only. Background data points

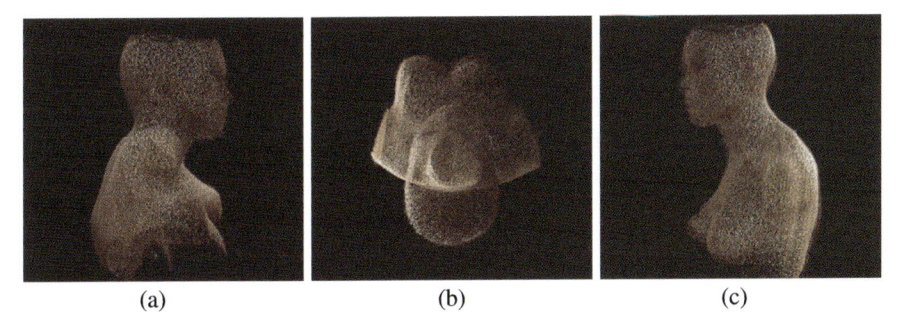

Fig. 2.7 3-D reconstruction of a female torso model, where the hand-held acquisition device was moved around the model in a 360°-fashion in order to cover the entire object. RGB-D data from different perspectives (525 frames) were merged into a global model on-the-fly. For visualization of the reconstructed model, we rendered a subset of the global model point cloud

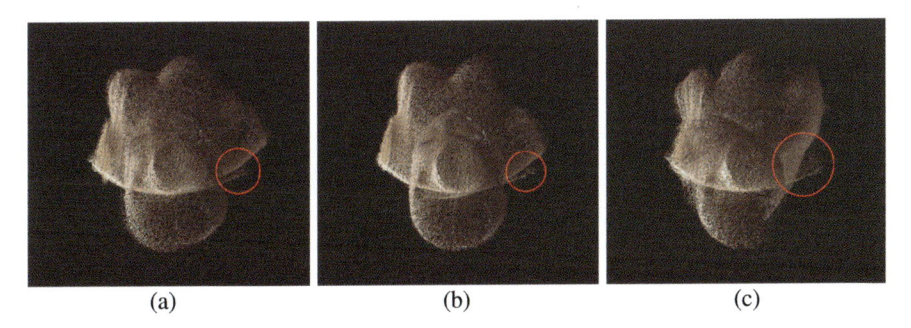

Fig. 2.8 Influence of parameter settings, again for the reconstruction of the female torso model, cf. Fig. 2.7(**b**). Subfigure (**a**) depicts the reconstruction result when edge-preserving denoising was disabled. In subfigures (**b**, **c**), we increased the low-grade correspondence threshold to $\delta = 10$ mm (**b**) and $\delta \to \infty$ (**c**), leading to decreasing reconstruction quality. For instance, please note the labeled issues regarding loop closure

that are located beyond a certain depth level are ignored within the ICP alignment procedure. For object reconstruction, our default settings are: Edge-preserving denoising (geometric guided image filter), $|\mathcal{F}| = |\mathcal{M}| = 16{,}384$ ICP landmarks, $\alpha = 0$ (invariance to illumination issues), $\delta = 3$ mm.

Qualitative results for model reconstruction are depicted in Fig. 2.7. Note that by setting a rather rigorous threshold for discarding low-grade correspondences ($\delta = 3$ mm), our framework is able to achieve a sufficient degree of loop closure although it relies on a frame-to-frame alignment.

The influence of different parameter settings is investigated in Fig. 2.8. As a baseline, we refer to the reconstruction results in Fig. 2.7(b) using our default settings (guided image filter denoising, $\delta = 3$ mm). Disabling edge-preserving denoising increases issues regarding loop closure, see Fig. 2.8(a). Relaxing the low-grade correspondence threshold δ results in similar effects (Fig. 2.8(b), $\delta = 10$ mm) and can eventually lead to model reconstruction failures (Fig. 2.8(c), $\delta \to \infty$).

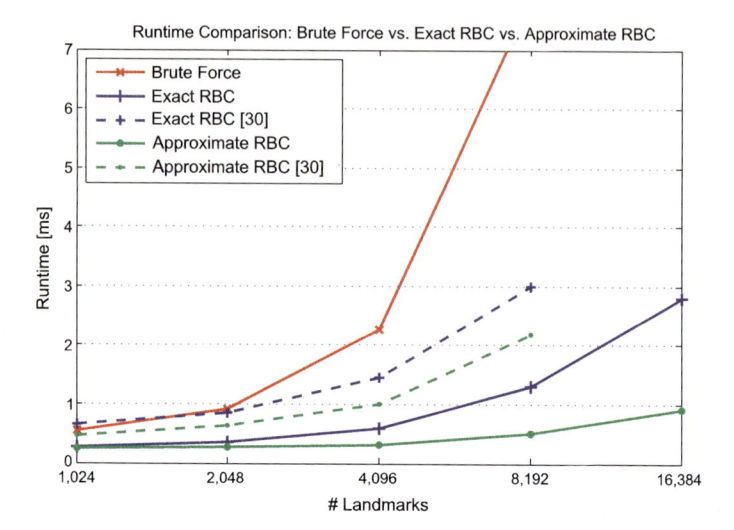

Fig. 2.9 Comparison of the average runtime for a single ICP iteration based on a GPU brute-force primitive, the exact RBC and our optimized approximate RBC variant as described in Sect. 2.3.3, for increasing number of landmarks. The number of representatives is chosen according to Cayton's rule of thumb, $|\mathcal{R}| = \sqrt{|\mathcal{F}|}$. Note that our modified approximate RBC approach outperforms the exact RBC up to a factor of 3. The BF primitive scales quadratically w.r.t. the number of landmarks

2.5.2 Performance Study

The corpus of the proposed framework including both preprocessing and RGB-D mapping is executed on the GPU, recall Fig. 2.2. This section presents quantitative results for individual modules of the framework.

Preprocessing Pipeline Edge-preserving image filtering is parallelized in an efficient manner on the GPU [29, 37]. The computation of 3-D world coordinates from the measured depth values requires less than 1 ms for Microsoft Kinect data of VGA resolution, including CPU-GPU memory transfer of the RGB-D data. The subsequent edge clipping and landmark extraction for $\mathcal{M}$ and $\mathcal{F}$ in scene reconstruction scenarios depends on $|\mathcal{M}| = |\mathcal{F}|$, denoting the number of landmarks (LMs), with typical runtimes of less than 0.3 ms. Let us conclude that runtimes for data preprocessing assume a minor role. As we target scene reconstruction in the first place, landmark extraction for object reconstruction scenarios including foreground segmentation and random landmark selection was implemented on the CPU with a runtime of about 5 ms, as proof-of-concept.

ICP Using RBC Being the cornerstone of our framework, we have investigated the performance of our GPU-based ICP/RBC implementation in detail. A single ICP iteration consists of three steps: (i) nearest neighbor search using RBC, (ii) transformation estimation and (iii) application of the transformation. With an increasing

Table 2.1 Runtimes [ms] for the construction of the RBC data structure ($t_{RBC,C}$) and ICP execution for reconstructing a typical indoor scene, for varying number of landmarks. In the *first rows*, average runtimes for our default setting $|\mathcal{R}| = \sqrt{|\mathcal{F}|}$ are given. In the *second rows*, we state performance numbers for $|\mathcal{R}|$ being optimized in terms of runtime. Note that optimizing runtime comes with a loss in accuracy, cf. Fig. 2.10. We state both the runtime for a single ICP iteration (t_{ICP}) and typical total ICP runtimes t_{tot} (including RBC construction) for 10 and 20 iterations, respectively

# Landmarks	$|\mathcal{R}|$	$t_{RBC,C}$ [ms]	t_{ICP} [ms]	t_{tot} (10 its) [ms]	t_{tot} (20 its) [ms]
1,024	$\sqrt{|\mathcal{F}|} = 32$	0.58	0.25	3.13	5.68
1,024	128	0.59	0.12	1.79	3.00
2,048	$\sqrt{|\mathcal{F}|} = 45$	0.60	0.27	3.31	6.03
2,048	128	0.60	0.14	2.02	3.44
4,096	$\sqrt{|\mathcal{F}|} = 64$	0.63	0.32	3.80	6.97
4,096	128	0.67	0.21	2.76	4.86
8,192	$\sqrt{|\mathcal{F}|} = 91$	0.76	0.50	5.80	10.82
8,192	256	1.22	0.40	5.22	9.22
16,384	$\sqrt{|\mathcal{F}|} = 128$	0.90	0.91	9.96	19.07
16,384	256	1.49	0.78	9.25	17.04

number of landmarks, the nearest neighbor search dominates the runtime considerably [30]. Hence, we have put emphasis on optimizing the RBC construction and query performance. Note that for all subsequent performance evaluations, runtimes where averaged over several successive runs.

A comparison of absolute runtimes for a single ICP iteration is presented in Fig. 2.9. Our modified approximate RBC outperforms both a BF search and our reference implementation of Cayton's exact RBC. Note that the BF search scales quadratically with the number of landmarks. Our approximate RBC variant outperforms the exact RBC implementation up to a factor of 3. Compared to previous work by the authors [30], significant runtime speedups were achieved using the permuted database and its cache friendly layout as detailed in Sect. 2.4.2.

Typical scene reconstruction runtimes of the method are given in Table 2.1. From our experiments in indoor scene mapping, we observed the ICP to converge after 10–20 iterations using the stopping criterion described in Sect. 2.4.1. Hence, as an overall performance indicator, let us refer to the runtime of 19.1 ms for 16,384 landmarks, $|\mathcal{R}| = \sqrt{|\mathcal{F}|}$, for 20 iterations.

2.5.3 Approximate RBC

As motivated in Sect. 2.3.3, our approximate RBC construction and nearest neighbor search trades exactness for runtime speedup. We quantitatively investigated the error

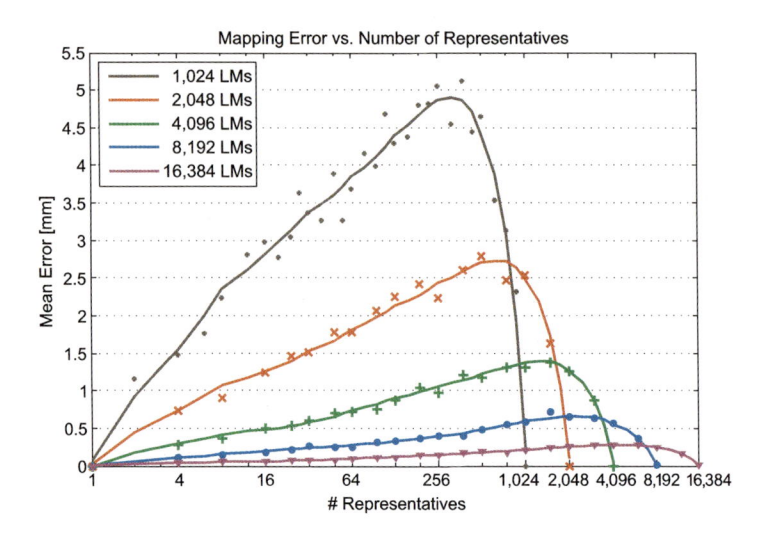

Fig. 2.10 Evaluation of the influence of $|\mathcal{R}|$ on mapping accuracy, compared to an exact BF search, for varying number of landmarks. Given is the mean Euclidean distance [mm] between the mapped points $\hat{\mathbf{m}}_{\text{RBC}}$ and $\hat{\mathbf{m}}_{\text{BF}}$. Increasing the number of landmarks decreases the error. The graph shows both discretized measurements and a trendline for each setting. Note the semi-log scale

that results from our approximate nearest neighbor search compared to an exact BF scheme, considering the aligned point clouds $\hat{\mathcal{M}}_{\text{RBC}}$ and $\hat{\mathcal{M}}_{\text{BF}}$, see Fig. 2.10. The error measures the mean pointwise Euclidean distance [mm] between the points $\hat{\mathbf{m}}_{\text{RBC}}$ and $\hat{\mathbf{m}}_{\text{BF}}$, being transformed w.r.t. different estimations for $(\mathbf{R}, \mathbf{t})$. With an increasing number of representatives $|\mathcal{R}|$, the mapping error rises increasingly until dropping sharply when approaching $|\mathcal{R}| = |\mathcal{F}|$. In general, increasing the number of landmarks decreases the error. Please note that both situations of $|\mathcal{R}| = 1$ and $|\mathcal{R}| = |\mathcal{F}|$ correspond to a BF search, hence yielding an identical transformation/mapping estimate and a mean error of zero.

In order to further illustrate the impact of the relation between the number of landmarks and representatives on reconstruction accuracy, we refer to Fig. 2.11. For $|\mathcal{R}| \ll |\mathcal{F}|$, decreasing $|\mathcal{R}|$ with a fixed number of landmarks reduces the error. This results from our approximate RBC construction scheme, where the probability of erroneous nearest neighbor assignments increases with the number of representatives. Again, increasing the number of landmarks decreases the error. We remark that by using our default configuration (16,384 LMs, $|\mathcal{R}| = \sqrt{|\mathcal{F}|}$), the mapping error is less than 0.25 mm. This is an acceptable scale for the applications considered in this work.

Furthermore, we have related the runtime per ICP iteration to $|\mathcal{R}|$, see Fig. 2.12. Apart from the runtime minimum that is located around $|\mathcal{R}| = 2\sqrt{|\mathcal{F}|}$, the computational load rises when increasing or decreasing the number of representatives. Simultaneously, the error decreases, recall Fig. 2.10. Hence, the application-related requirements in terms of runtime and accuracy motivates the choice of $|\mathcal{R}|$. Together, Figs. 2.10–2.12 illustrate the trade-off between error and runtime.

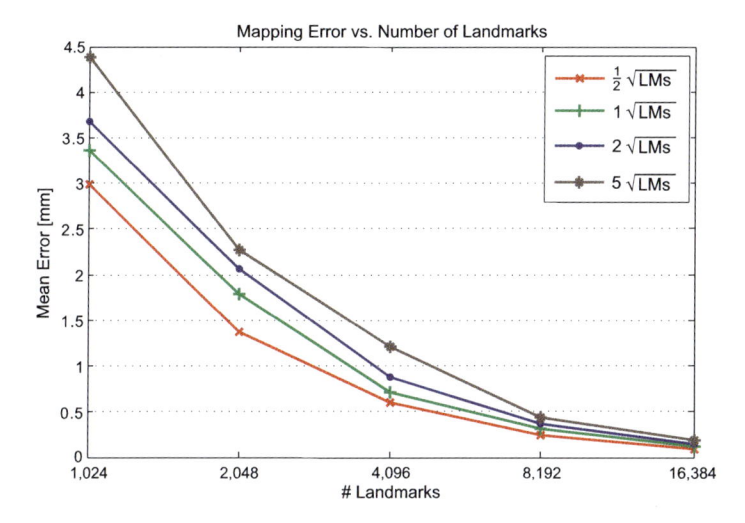

Fig. 2.11 Investigation of the mean mapping error vs. number of landmarks, for varying $|\mathcal{R}|$. Here, the analysis is restricted to $|\mathcal{R}| \ll |\mathcal{F}|$. Note that decreasing $|\mathcal{R}|$ with a fixed number of landmarks reduces the error

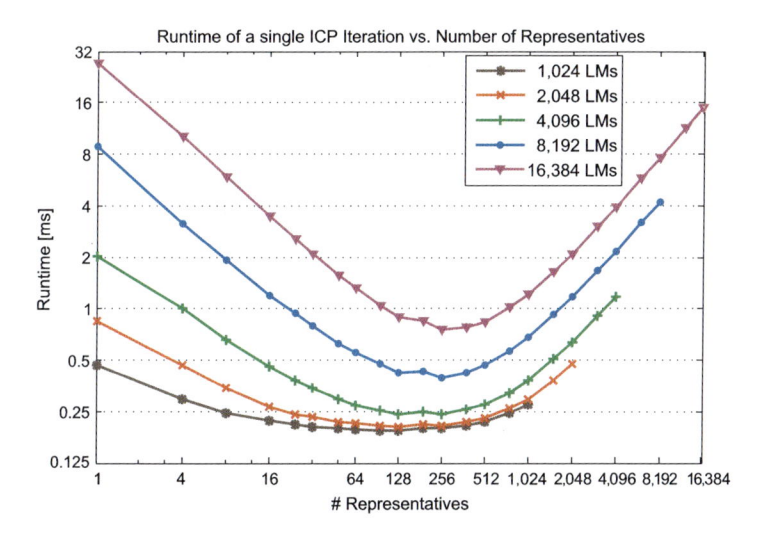

Fig. 2.12 Runtimes of a single ICP iteration, for varying number of landmarks and representatives. The runtime minimum is located around $|\mathcal{R}| = 2\sqrt{|\mathcal{F}|}$. Note the logarithmic scale

2.6 Discussion and Conclusions

In this chapter, we have proposed a GPU framework for real-time mapping and modeling of textured point cloud streams enabling on-the-fly 3-D reconstruction with modern RGB-D imaging devices. Our quantitative RBC experiments demonstrate that using a data structure which is specifically designed to exploit the parallel computing power of GPUs is beneficial even for low-dimensional (6-D) data. Using our optimized approximate RBC for the photogeometric nearest neighbor search, our system achieves reconstruction runtimes of less than 20 ms on an off-the-shelf consumer GPU in a frame-to-frame scenario.

The proposed framework was evaluated using a point-to-point metric for estimating the transformation within ICP. In general, minimizing a point-to-plane distance metric holds advantages over the point-to-point approach as it allows the surfaces described by $\mathcal{M}$ and $\mathcal{F}$ to slide over each other [9], avoiding snap-to-grid effects. However, solving the corresponding optimization problem as denoted in Eq. 2.7 would require an iterative scheme. We did not observe a negative impact on the reconstruction results using the point-to-point approach in our experiments.

Compared to a conventional ICP that relies on the pure 3-D geometry [4, 9], incorporating photometric appearance as a complementary source of information is advantageous in cases of non-salient surface topology, recall Fig. 2.1 and the experimental results in related work [24]. Approaches that combine dense geometric point associations with a sparse set of correspondences derived from local photometric features are limited to interactive frame-rates, as feature extraction is computationally expensive even if performed on the GPU [19]. In contrast, our approach evaluates both geometric and photometric information in a direct and dense manner, cf. [11, 24, 25]. We found that incorporating photometric appearance in such an elementary manner gives the best compromise between reconstruction robustness and runtime performance. Nonetheless, the proposed scheme using the RBC for efficient nearest neighbor queries on the GPU can be potentially extended to higher-dimensional point signatures.

Ongoing work includes the implementation of a multi-resolution ICP alignment scheme in order to improve the convergence behavior, and the transition from frame-to-frame to frame-to-model registration using an implicit surface model [10]. Furthermore, an automatic scene-dependent weighting of the photogeometric weight α by low-level analysis of the depth image as part of the preprocessing stage will be subject of our upcoming research.

Acknowledgements S. Bauer and J. Wasza gratefully acknowledge the support by the European Regional Development Fund (ERDF) and the Bayerisches Staatsministerium für Wirtschaft, Infrastruktur, Verkehr und Technologie (StMWIVT), in the context of the R&D program IuK Bayern under Grant No. IUK338. Furthermore, this research was supported by the Graduate School of Information Science in Health (GSISH) and the TUM Graduate School.

References

1. Akenine-Möller, T., Haines, E., Hoffman, N.: Real-Time Rendering, 3rd edn. AK Peters, Natick, MA (2008)
2. Bailey, T., Durrant-Whyte, H.: Simultaneous localization and mapping (SLAM): part II. IEEE Robot. Autom. Mag. **13**(3), 108–117 (2006)
3. Bauer, S., Wasza, J., Haase, S., Marosi, N., Hornegger, J.: Multi-modal surface registration for markerless initial patient setup in radiation therapy using Microsoft's Kinect sensor. In:

International Conference on Computer Vision—Workshop on Consumer Depth Cameras for Computer Vision, pp. 1175–1181 (2011)
4. Besl, P., McKay, N.: A method for registration of 3-D shapes. IEEE Trans. Pattern Anal. Mach. Intell. **14**(2), 239–256 (1992)
5. Blais, G., Levine, D.M.: Registering multiview range data to create 3-D computer objects. IEEE Trans. Pattern Anal. Mach. Intell. **17**(8), 820–824 (1995)
6. Castaneda, V., Mateus, D., Navab, N.: SLAM combining ToF and high-resolution cameras. In: IEEE Workshop on Applications of Computer Vision, pp. 672–678 (2011)
7. Cayton, L.: A nearest neighbor data structure for graphics hardware. In: International Workshop on Accelerating Data Management Systems Using Modern Processor and Storage Architectures (2010)
8. Cayton, L.: Accelerating nearest neighbor search on manycore systems. CoRR arXiv: 1103.2635 (2011)
9. Chen, Y., Medioni, G.: Object modelling by registration of multiple range images. Image Vis. Comput. **10**(3), 145–155 (1992)
10. Curless, B., Levoy, M.: A volumetric method for building complex models from range images. In: Conference on Computer Graphics and Interactive Techniques, SIGGRAPH, pp. 303–312. ACM, New York (1996)
11. Druon, S., Aldon, M., Crosnier, A.: Color constrained ICP for registration of large unstructured 3D color data sets. In: IEEE International Conference on Information Acquisition, pp. 249–255 (2006)
12. Engelhard, N., Endres, F., Hess, J., Sturm, J., Burgard, W.: Real-time 3D visual SLAM with a hand-held RGB-D camera. In: RGB-D Workshop on 3D Perception in Robotics, European Robotics Forum (2011)
13. Fioraio, N., Konolige, K.: Realtime visual and point cloud SLAM. In: RGB-D Workshop: Advanced Reasoning with Depth Cameras, Robotics Science and Systems Conference (2011)
14. Garcia, J., Zalevsky, Z.: Range mapping using speckle decorrelation. US Patent No. 7433024 (2008)
15. Garcia, V., Debreuve, E., Barlaud, M.: Fast k nearest neighbor search using GPU. In: IEEE Conference on Computer Vision and Pattern Recognition—Workshop on Computer Vision on GPU (2008)
16. Gevers, T., Smeulders, A.W.: Color-based object recognition. Pattern Recognit. **32**(3), 453–464 (1999)
17. Harris, M., Sengupta, S., Owens, J.D.: Parallel prefix sum (scan) with CUDA. In: GPU Gems 3, pp. 851–876. Addison-Wesley, Reading (2007)
18. He, K., Sun, J., Tang, X.: Guided image filtering. In: European Conference on Computer Vision, pp. 1–14 (2010)
19. Henry, P., Krainin, M., Herbst, E., Ren, X., Fox, D.: RGB-D mapping: using depth cameras for dense 3D modeling of indoor environments. In: International Symposium on Experimental Robotics (2010)
20. Hoberock, J., Bell, N.: Thrust: a parallel template library (2010). URL http://code.google.com/p/thrust/. Version 1.3.0
21. Horn, B.: Closed-form solution of absolute orientation using unit quaternions. J. Opt. Soc. Am. **4**(4), 629–642 (1987)
22. Huhle, B., Jenke, P., Strasser, W.: On-the-fly scene acquisition with a handy multi-sensor system. Int. J. Intell. Syst. Technol. Appl. **5**, 255–263 (2008)
23. Izadi, S., Newcombe, R.A., Kim, D., Hilliges, O., Molyneaux, D., Hodges, S., Kohli, P., Shotton, J., Davison, A.J., Fitzgibbon, A.W.: KinectFusion: real-time dynamic 3D surface reconstruction and interaction. In: ACM Symposium on User Interface Software and Technology, p. 23 (2011)
24. Johnson, A., Kang, S.B.: Registration and integration of textured 3-D data. In: International Conference on Recent Advances in 3-D Digital Imaging and Modeling, pp. 234–241 (1997)

25. Joung, J.H., An, K.H., Kang, J.W., Chung, M.J., Yu, W.: 3D environment reconstruction using modified color ICP algorithm by fusion of a camera and a 3D laser range finder. In: IEEE/RSJ International Conference on Intelligent Robots and Systems, pp. 3082–3088 (2009)
26. Korn, G.A., Korn, T.M.: Mathematical Handbook for Scientists and Engineers: Definitions, Theorems, and Formulas for Reference and Review. Dover, New York (2000)
27. Loop, C., Blinn, J.: Real-time GPU rendering of piecewise algebraic surfaces. ACM Trans. Graph. **25**(3), 664–670 (2006)
28. May, S., Droeschel, D., Holz, D., Fuchs, S., Malis, E., Nüchter, A., Hertzberg, J.: Three-dimensional mapping with time-of-flight cameras. J. Field Robot. **26**, 934–965 (2009)
29. McGuire, M.: A fast, small-radius GPU median filter. In: ShaderX6, pp. 165–173. Charles River Media (2008)
30. Neumann, D., Lugauer, F., Bauer, S., Wasza, J., Hornegger, J.: Real-time RGB-D mapping and 3-D modeling on the GPU using the random ball cover data structure. In: International Conference on Computer Vision—Workshop on Consumer Depth Cameras for Computer Vision, pp. 1161–1167 (2011)
31. Newcombe, R.A., Izadi, S., Hilliges, O., Molyneaux, D., Kim, D., Davison, A.J., Kohli, P., Shotton, J., Hodges, S., Fitzgibbon, A.W.: KinectFusion: real-time dense surface mapping and tracking. In: IEEE International Symposium on Mixed and Augmented Reality, pp. 127–136 (2011)
32. Nüchter, A., Surmann, H., Lingemann, K., Hertzberg, J., Thrun, S.: 6D SLAM with an application in autonomous mine mapping. In: IEEE International Conference on Robotics and Automation, vol. 2, pp. 1998–2003 (2004)
33. Qiu, D., May, S., Nüchter, A.: GPU-accelerated nearest neighbor search for 3D registration. In: International Conference on Computer Vision Systems, pp. 194–203. Springer, Berlin (2009)
34. Reis, G., Zeilfelder, F., Hering-Bertram, M., Farin, G.E., Hagen, H.: High-quality rendering of quartic spline surfaces on the GPU. IEEE Trans. Vis. Comput. Graph. **14**(5), 1126–1139 (2008)
35. Rusinkiewicz, S., Hall-Holt, O., Levoy, M.: Real-time 3D model acquisition. ACM Trans. Graph. **21**(3), 438–446 (2002)
36. Rusinkiewicz, S., Levoy, M.: Efficient variants of the ICP algorithm. In: International Conference on 3-D Digital Imaging and Modeling, pp. 145–152 (2001)
37. Wasza, J., Bauer, S., Haase, S., Hornegger, J.: Real-time preprocessing for dense 3-D range imaging on the GPU: defect interpolation, bilateral temporal averaging and guided filtering. In: International Conference on Computer Vision—Workshop on Consumer Depth Cameras for Computer Vision, pp. 1221–1227 (2011)

Chapter 3
A Brute Force Approach to Depth Camera Odometry

Jonathan Israël and Aurélien Plyer

Abstract By providing direct access to 3D information of the environment, depth cameras are particularly useful for perception applications such as Simultaneous Localization And Mapping or object recognition. With the introduction of the Kinect in 2010, Microsoft released a low cost depth camera that is now intensively used by researchers, especially in the field of indoor robotics. This chapter introduces a new 3D registration algorithm that can deal with considerable sensor motion. The proposed approach is designed to take advantage of the powerful computational scalability of Graphics Processing Units (GPUs).

3.1 Introduction

Frame registration is one of the primary processing stages that requires to be executed in many 3D video applications. When a 3D sensor such as the Kinect is robot-mounted or hand-moved, its attitude variation can show significant movements, especially large rotations, which may lead a local registration method such as Iterative Closest Point (ICP) to fail. Furthermore, in the case of the Kinect, the temporal registration of the huge amount of data captured by the sensor (640×480 16-bits pixels at 30 Hz) can hardly be fully processed in real-time applications. The method presented in this chapter relies on a probabilistic framework where a global matching criterion applied to extracted features can be evaluated in parallel in the projective plane defined by the sensor camera. We show that most steps of this algorithm are particularly well suitable for a real-time GPU-based implementation since they rely mostly on vector and matrix multiplications or element-wise operations.

This chapter is organized as follows. We give a brief overview of 3D registration methods in Sect. 3.2. The general framework and the key steps of the proposed

---

J. Israël (✉)
ONERA—The French Aerospace Lab, Chemin de la Hunière BP 80100, 91123 Palaiseau Cedex, France
e-mail: jonathan.israel@onera.fr

A. Plyer
LAGA—Paris 13, 99 Avenue Jean-Baptiste Clément, 93430 Villetaneuse, France
e-mail: aurelien.plyer@gmail.com

method are described in Sect. 3.3. We demonstrate experimentally in Sect. 3.4 the suitability of our approach for real-time processing. Conclusions and perspectives are given in Sect. 3.5.

3.2 Related Work

The objective of 3D registration is to find the Euclidean motion between two 3D data sets such as range images or point clouds. When a good estimate of the relative transformation is available, the registration problem can be efficiently solved using local registration methods. Since its introduction by Besl and McKay [2], the ICP technique has been widely used by the community. As they are based on the underlying assumption that a good initialization is known, ICP-like techniques can easily get trapped in a local minimum. Even in the presence of small displacements, the Euclidean distance used in ICP suffers from its difficulty to capture the sensor rotation. In [1], the authors overcome this limitation by introducing a new metric that can be used for point-to-surface distance estimation in the matching phase. The robustness of this modified ICP comes at a cost of a higher computational complexity, which is already another drawback of local and iterative registration methods. For instance, the most time-consuming stage of the ICP is the determination of the closest point, which is basically of $\mathcal{O}(n^2)$ for 3D scans containing n points. Optimized search structures like $k-d$ trees or box decomposition trees are used in numerous publications such as [8] or [16] to reach a complexity of $\mathcal{O}(n \log n)$.

Reduced search spaces can also be used during the correspondence stage. For instance, approximation of the nearest neighbor search can be done directly on the GPU using the Random Ball Cover Data Structure, [14], as also proposed in the previous chapter. In [1] the authors use a sliding window which limits candidates for each point within an angular window. In [10], the neighborhood relationships in both frames are used to restrict recursively the nearest neighbor search. Several approximation techniques such as the latter allow us to reach $\mathcal{O}(n)$ complexity but are not necessarily convenient for a massively parallel implementation, mainly due to their recursive nature.

In order to further decrease the computational complexity of the registration, several authors reduce directly the number of points that are processed. In [15], the authors perform point reduction and generate approximate $k-d$ trees by subsampling the data depending on their distance to the sensor. A Frustrum ICP is used in [13] to remove iteratively 3D points from non-overlapping areas. The registration precision of subsampling techniques that dismiss or approximate some of the original data depend strongly on the subsampling scheme. Nevertheless, those techniques remain fast and efficient and real-time processing has even been recently reported on subsampled RGB-D data [7]. Finally, reduction of the computational payload can also be achieved while preserving efficiency with estimations based on feature matching. Registration is then performed directly on selected points with low-dimension features [5, 20] or on extracted 3D contours [9, 17]. Those kinds of approach can be extended to a multi-resolution framework where details are introduced incrementally to increase the solution resolution while controlling the computational payload [21].

While optimization techniques tried mostly to reduce the data size or to approximate the nearest neighbor search stage, several implementations of recent algorithms were adapted to take advantage of the computational power of the GPU. Different variants of the ICP such as Modified Iterative Closest Point [11], Expectation-Maximization ICP and soft-assign [22] or ICP based on $k - d$ tree priority search [19] allowed a huge reduction of the processing time while preserving robustness and precision. [18] presents a CUDA-based implementation of a point-to-plane 3D registration technique where the costly corresponding point search is replaced with a direct estimation based on a point to plane projection. In [6], exhaustive search in a reduced dimension space is performed.

By computing in a projective space a matching criterion based on extracted 3D features, the method proposed in this chapter allows a fast and exhaustive search through the full 6 degree-of-freedom space. As opposed to most ICP-derived techniques, it does not rely on any one-to-one point correspondence assumption or any reweighting scheme whose parameters are often hard to tune automatically.

3.3 Proposed Method

We propose in this chapter an approach that takes advantage of the particular geometry of the depth image, contrary to many ICP-like techniques that are designed for the general registration of two unstructured 3D point clouds. In our case, a 3D point cloud computed from a depth image is associated with the inverse projection of pixel depth measurements. This implies that the sensor depth image plane has a coherent projective geometry that can be used to compute approximate neighborhoods and distances. A matching criterion can be computed very efficiently in this projective space and thus evaluated in parallel in the full 6D transformation space. To achieve fast computation on recent and massively parallel processors, we comply with the two following rules:

- the algorithm will have a Single Process, Multiple Data scheme for parallel scalability,
- the criterion and projective operations will rely as much as possible on vector and matrix multiplications or element-wise operations.

Sparse structures (3D contours corresponding to a list of edges) are extracted from the depth image and used in a pose score evaluation for different movement hypotheses. A likelihood function is defined on the set of all possible transformations and used in the final decision process. In the following section, we will develop our approach from the abstract mathematical framework to the implementation details.

Fig. 3.1 Global decomposition of the algorithm. The processing which is executed at each data acquisition from a video stream is encircled in orange

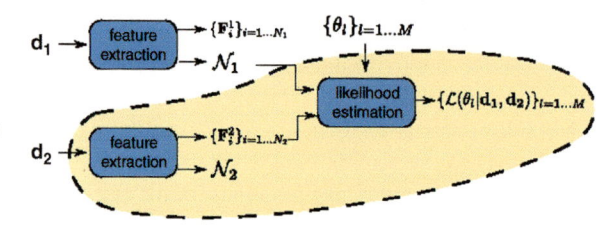

3.3.1 Algorithm Overview

The proposed algorithm includes two main stages, see Fig. 3.1. In a first step, a set of features $\mathcal{F}^1 = \{\mathbf{F}_i^1\}_{i=1...N_1}$ (resp. $\mathcal{F}^2 = \{\mathbf{F}_i^2\}_{i=1...N_2}$) is extracted from the reference depth image $\mathbf{d}_1$ (resp. the current depth image $\mathbf{d}_2$). These 3D features are derived from a 2D criterion map which is defined on the projective plane of each depth image. In our experiment, we choose the depth image gradient to obtain 3D contours as shown in Fig. 3.4(b). In a second step, we evaluate simultaneously the likelihood function $\mathcal{L}(\theta|\mathbf{d}_1, \mathbf{d}_2)$ over a large set of hypotheses with displacement parameters belonging to the 6D space $\Theta = \{\theta_l\}_{l=1...M}$. This likelihood is defined as a normalized score function computed on the set of features extracted from both frames under the hypothesis θ:

$$\mathcal{L}(\theta|\mathbf{d}_1, \mathbf{d}_2) = \frac{1}{L} \sum_{i=1}^{N_2} g\left(\mathbf{F}_i^2, S_\theta\left(\mathbf{F}_i^2, \mathcal{F}^1\right)\right), \tag{3.1}$$

where L is a normalization factor and g is a score functional. The score function S_θ is the average value of the integrated pseudo-distance from a feature $\mathbf{F}_i^2$ extracted from the current frame to the *nearest* features of the reference frame under the transformation hypothesis θ:

$$S_\theta\left(\mathbf{F}_i^2, \mathcal{F}^1\right) = \frac{1}{\|\mathbf{F}_i^2\|} \int_{\mathbf{F}_i^2} \|\mathcal{N}_1(\mathcal{P}_1(\phi_\theta(\mathbf{X}))) - \phi_\theta(\mathbf{X})\| \, d\mathbf{X}. \tag{3.2}$$

In Eq. 3.2, $\mathbf{X} \in \mathbb{R}^3$ belongs to the feature $\mathbf{F}_i^2$ and $\phi_\theta : \mathbb{R}^3 \to \mathbb{R}^3$ is the 3D Euclidean transformation corresponding to the current parameter θ. $\|\mathbf{F}_i^2\|$ is the arc length of the 3D contour $\mathbf{F}_i^2$. $\mathcal{P}_1 : \mathbb{R}^3 \to \mathbb{R}^2$ is the projection from $\mathbb{R}^3$ to the reference depth image plane. Its computation supposes that the sensor calibration has been done previously. $\mathcal{N}_1 : \mathbb{R}^2 \to \mathbb{R}^3$ is the function that gives for every 3D point projected in the reference depth image plane the *nearest* 3D point that belongs to a feature extracted from the reference data. In the score evaluation, the *nearest* point is not found directly in $\mathbb{R}^3$. Instead, its approximation is given by the $\mathcal{N}_1$ function applied to the projection of the feature $\mathbf{F}_i^2$ in the reference plane under the current hypothesis with transformation parameter θ. This allows a very fast processing as we will see in the implementation details of Sect. 3.3.3.

3.3.2 Practical Issues

In this section we present the chosen instantiations of the feature extraction and the score evaluation used in the proposed approach.

Feature Extraction The depth image gradient is computed with a Sobel mask. We use a classical edge linking scheme based on the thresholded gradient norm image and the gradient orientation. The features are 3D contours corresponding to the reprojection in $\mathbb{R}^3$ of the detected edges (see Fig. 3.4). This approach can be easily extended to any kind of features such as segments, curvature-based salient keypoints for instance or even any kind of RGB-D features like textured spin images [4] could be used.

Score Evaluation In order to favor long edges that are projected close to edges from the reference frame, we will choose a functional g defined by

$$g(\mathbf{F}_i^k, S_\theta) = \|\mathbf{F}_i^k\| e^{-\alpha S_\theta} \qquad (3.3)$$

In all our experiments, α was set to 1.

3.3.3 Implementation Details

The proposed approach is tightly linked with implementation possibilities given on recent computer architectures.

Two important processing blocks are detailed here:

- the computing of the $\mathcal{N}_k$ function based on extracted features,
- the evaluation of the likelihood $\mathcal{L}(\theta|\mathbf{d}_1, \mathbf{d}_2)$.

The $\mathcal{N}_1$ function aims at providing a fast access to the *nearest* 3D points belonging to a feature in the reference image projective plane. First, a gradient convolution algorithm is used to compute the norm gradient image. Then, based on two successive scans of the thresholded gradient image, we compute a Chebyshev distance map that keeps track of the coordinates of the *nearest* feature. The first scan (resp. the second scan) is a direct scan (resp. an inverse scan) of the thresholded gradient image where the computation of each block is performed after the computation of the up and left (resp. down and right) blocks. This stage is the main sequential part of our implementation but remains very fast for our depth images (taking around 20 ms in practice). As we show in Fig. 3.2, this algorithm can be easily parallelized with a tiled strategy. For instance, a theoretical speed-up factor of 3 (which corresponds roughly to the $\frac{36}{11}$ gain factor) can be reached on the basis of a 6 processor core working on 36 tiles of a binary contour image. For access efficiency, $\mathcal{N}_1$ has been put in texture memory.

The likelihood hypothesis test has been totally implemented in CUDA and performed on the GPU. Special attention has been paid to the mapping between data

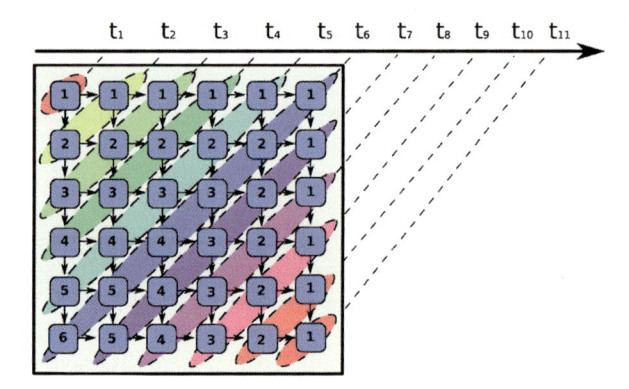

Fig. 3.2 Tiled parallel version of the causal filter used during the first scan in the distance map computation. The processor ID associated with each tile is indicated. Time dependencies between tile processing are represented by *arrows*. Since the *blocks in each diagonal* can be executed simultaneously, the basic execution time will be dominated by the time corresponding to 11 block executions instead of 36 in a fully sequential approach

Fig. 3.3 CUDA implementation of the likelihood function. *Green blocks* are CUDA computation blocks and *red circles* are CUDA threads

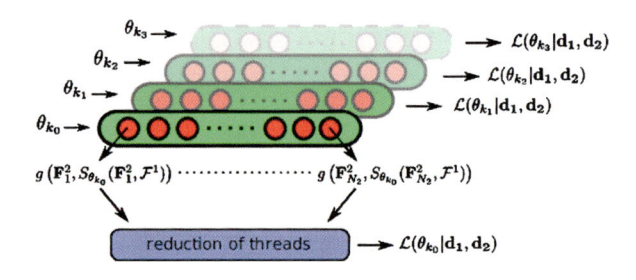

and the computing hierarchy (grid, blocks, threads). We assigned one hypothesis to each CUDA block and map the different threads of each block to features, as illustrated in Fig. 3.3.

Each thread computes a feature score $g(\mathbf{F}_i^2, S_{\theta_k}(\mathbf{F}_i^2, \mathcal{F}^1))$ with the help of a fast Bresenham line-drawing algorithm [3]. After the reduction of threads, each block computes the likelihood $\mathcal{L}(\theta_k|\mathbf{d}_1, \mathbf{d}_2)$ under the hypothesis θ_k.

3.4 Experimental Results

3.4.1 Qualitative Evaluation

We tested our approach on a depth image sequence of several minutes that was captured with a hand-moved Kinect. Several tests have been conducted, with a time separation ranging from 0.1 s to 1 s between the reference frame and the current one. The search space parameters $\{T_x, T_y, T_z, \theta, \phi, \psi\}$ were defined accordingly, ranging from $\{0.1\,\text{m}, 0.1\,\text{m}, 0.1\,\text{m}, 5°, 5°, 5°\}$ to $\{0.5\,\text{m}, 0.5\,\text{m}, 0.5\,\text{m}, 15°, 15°, 15°\}$.

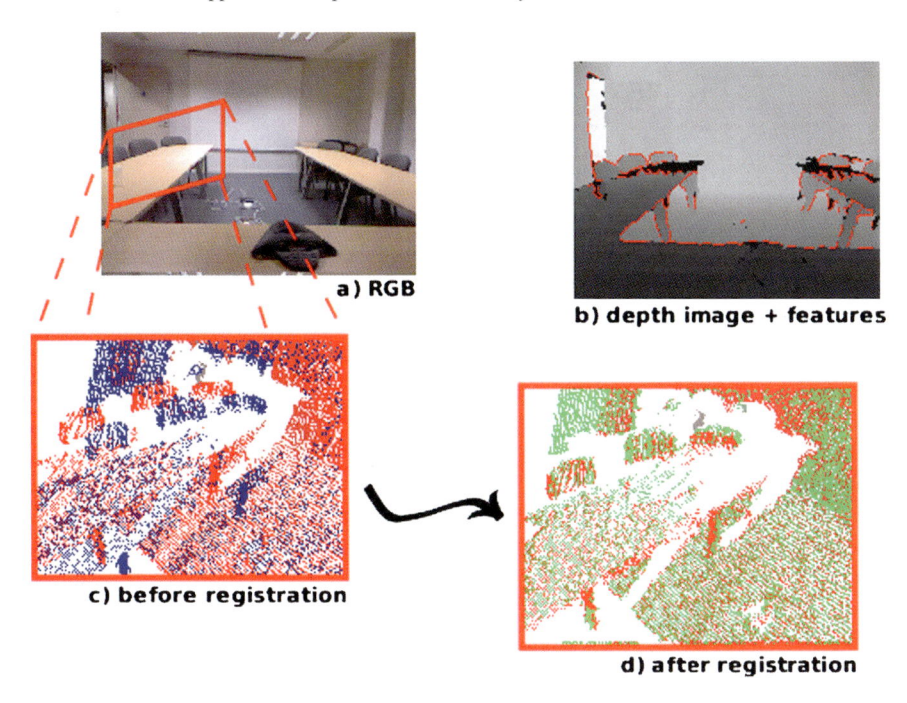

Fig. 3.4 (**a**) The RGB image of a conference room. (**b**) The Kinect depth image. Extracted features are superimposed in *red*. (**c**) A view of the reference frame (*red*) and the current frame before registration (*blue*). (**d**) The reference frame (*red*) and the current frame after registration (*green*)

The number of steps in each dimension was chosen from 6 to 13, thus the computation time ranged from a few dozen ms to a few seconds. As can be seen in Fig. 3.4 and in Fig. 3.5, good results were obtained on structured environments. As expected, results are insensitive to large sensor motions as long as the search space bounds are large enough to include the solution.

3.4.2 Precision Analysis

We followed the methodology proposed in [1] to evaluate the precision of our method. We matched each of 30 scans against itself with random initial sensor location. All the scans were taken in the conference room shown in Fig. 3.4(a). The sensor initial translation varied from 0 m to 0.5 m while its rotation on all axes (roll, pitch, yaw) varied from 0° to 15°. We evaluated separately the translation and rotation effects.

The residual rotations and translations are given in Fig. 3.6. Since rotation residuals are mostly related to roll angles, we represent only roll angle residuals w.r.t. initial roll angles. The mean registration error remains quite low even if it shows a significant quantization effect (due to the search space quantization and to approx-

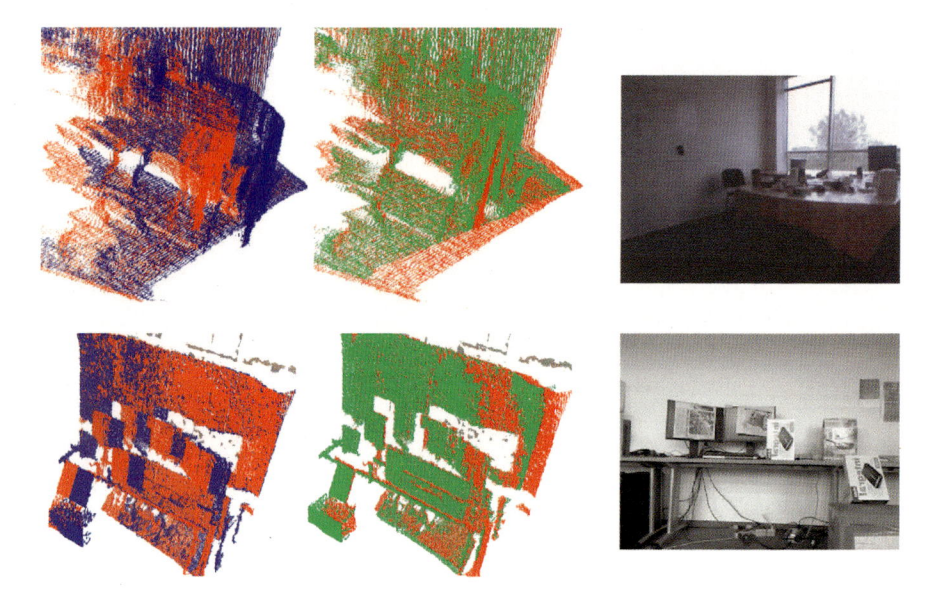

Fig. 3.5 (*Left*) A view of the reference frame (*red*) and the current frame before registration (*blue*). (*Middle*) The reference frame (*red*) and the current frame after registration (*green*). (*Right*) The corresponding RGB image

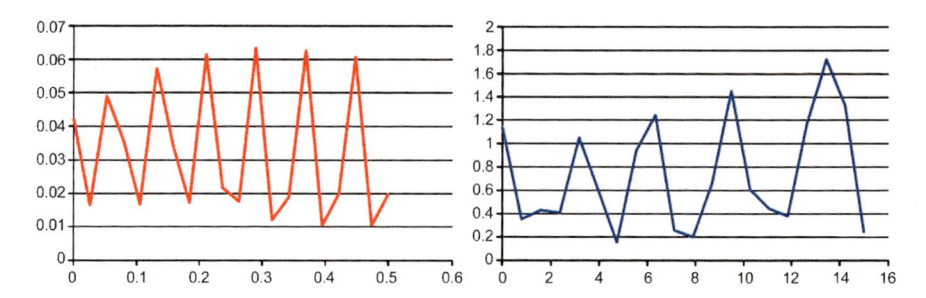

Fig. 3.6 (*Left*) Translation residuals w.r.t. the initial translation (in meters). (*Right*) Rotation residuals w.r.t. initial rotation (in degrees)

imations in the nearest neighbor search). In practice, the quantization step should be chosen accordingly with the desired precision. The average processing time per hypothesis ranged from 0.5 µs to 1.5 µs depending on the total number of hypotheses. Evaluation was performed on a computer whose specifications are given in Table 3.1. We emphasize the fact that in practice and due to prior constraints or pose prediction, the search space will never be isotropic and will focus around specific values.

The quantization step has a direct effect on the precision, as can be seen in Fig. 3.7. As we reduce the quantization steps, the precision is increased and tends to be comparable with the sensor precision. The computation time grows almost lin-

Table 3.1 Hardware specifications

CPU	Intel Core i7 @ 2.67 GHz
Memory	8 Go
GPU	nVidia GeForce GTX 460
OS	Linux 2.6

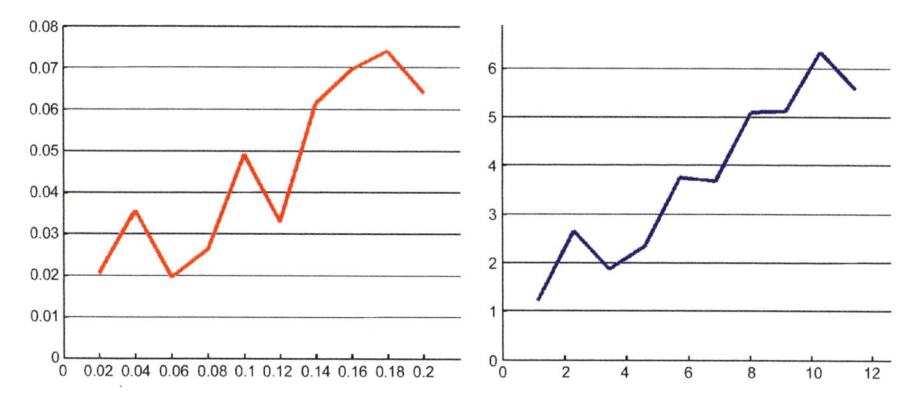

Fig. 3.7 (*Left*) Translation residuals w.r.t. the quantization step (in meters). (*Right*) Rotation residuals w.r.t. the quantization step (in degrees)

Fig. 3.8 Computing time (in s) w.r.t. the number of hypotheses (in millions)

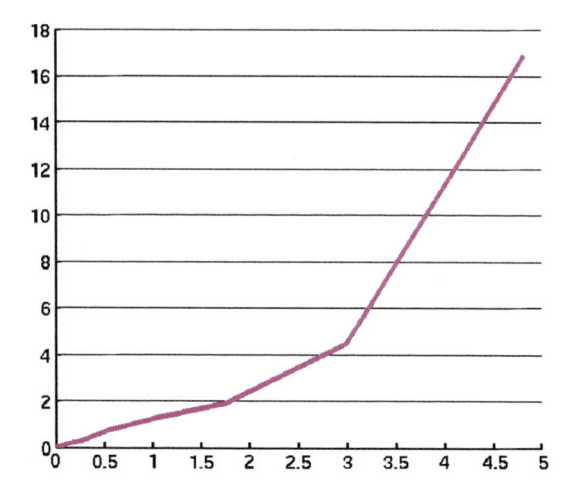

early with the number of hypotheses (see Fig. 3.8). Ultimately, the computation will be limited by the CPU-GPU bandwidth and by memory restrictions.

Except for the limitations mentioned previously, related to the quantization effects, the registration showed heterogeneous quality in "3D textureless" environments with low geometric saliency like corridors.

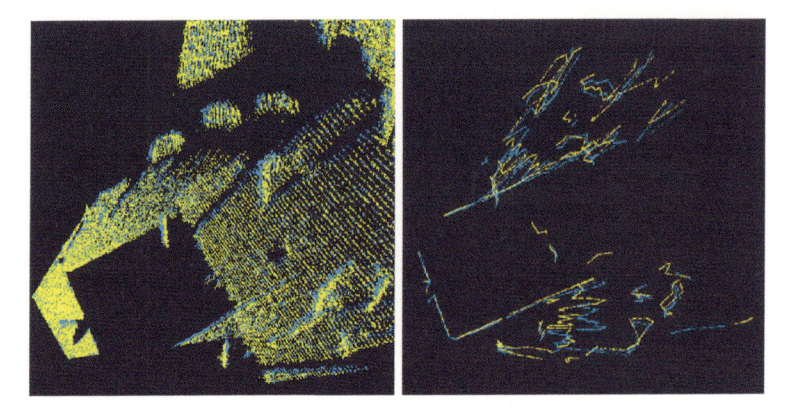

Fig. 3.9 *Left*: EM-ICP matching in the conference room. *Right*: EMICP applied to edges extracted from the conference room

3.4.3 Comparison with the ICP Method

The CUDA-based implementation of EM-ICP, described in [22] and available at home.hiroshimau.ac.jp/tamaki/study/cuda_softassign_emicp/ has been tested on our conference room data set, in order to provide a qualitative comparison with our method. EM-ICP is a variant of the classical Iterative Closest Point algorithm where soft correspondences are used instead of hard ones in order to prevent convergence to local minima. Given two point sets **X** and **Y**, it aims at finding the rotation R and the translation t that minimize the error function:

$$\mathbf{E} = \sum_{j=1}^{n_x} \sum_{i=1}^{n_y} \alpha_{ij} d_{ij}^2, \quad \text{where } d_{ij} = \left\| x_j - (R y_i + t) \right\|. \quad (3.4)$$

α_{ij} are the parameters of the soft correspondence. The iterative procedure depends on four parameters. Three of them are related to the annealing scheme and the fourth one is an outliers control parameter.

Due to memory and time constraints, we have applied the EM-ICP procedure to decimated point clouds (10 % of the total amount of 3D data). We have also applied the EM-ICP to points sampled from the extracted features. Generally, the result precision is good and residuals are linked to noise due to the sensor or to the sampling process (see Fig. 3.9).

Since we have not tried to finely tune the EM-ICP parameters, no performance assessment on our data set has been done and we indicate only in Table 3.2 the computing time w.r.t. the number of points to be registered.

Even with this GPU-based approach, several dozens of iterations are necessary and lead to a non negligible processing time. We believe that our approach could be used as a preliminary step in order to reduce the computation payload of a fine matching procedure such as this EM-ICP algorithm.

Table 3.2 Computation time

Data set	Number of points per data set	Time (EM-ICP, in s)	Time (our approach, in s)
10 % downsampled	30,720	27	6.4
Points from features	2,120	1.9	0.7

3.5 Conclusion and Future Work

In this chapter, we described and presented an experimental validation of a new registration method based on a similarity metric defined in the camera projective plane. The focus was on the derivation of the likelihood used in the matching process. Experimental results have shown that this brute force algorithm can be used to provide real-time registration of depth camera data. The computational payload could be significantly reduced by avoiding the likelihood estimation near areas with low scores (see [12]) and that are unlikely to give high scores due to the continuity of the likelihood function. Future work will focus on coupling the pose estimation with a particle filtering approach and its embedding in a global and multi-scale SLAM framework.

References

1. Armesto, L., Minguez, J., Montesano, L.: A generalization of the metric-based iterative closest point technique for 3D scan matching. In: IEEE International Conference on Robotics and Automation, pp. 1367–1372 (2010)
2. Besl, P., McKay, H.: A method for registration of 3-d shapes. IEEE Trans. Pattern Anal. Mach. Intell. **14**(2), 239–256 (1992)
3. Bresenham, J.E.: Algorithm for computer control of a digital plotter. IBM Syst. J. **4**, 25–30 (1965)
4. Brusco, M., Andreetto, M., Giorgi, A., Cortelazzo, G.: 3D registration by textured spin-images. In: International Conference on 3-D Digital Imaging and Modeling, pp. 262–269 (2005)
5. Chu, J., Mei Nie, C.: Multi-view point clouds registration and stitching based on sift feature. In: International Conference on Computer Research and Development, vol. 1, pp. 274–278. (2011)
6. Enqvist, O., Jiang, F., Kahl, F.: A brute-force algorithm for reconstructing a scene from two projections. In: IEEE Conference on Computer Vision and Pattern Recognition (2011)
7. Fioraio, N., Konolige, K.: Realtime visual and point cloud slam. In: Robotics Science and Systems Conference (2011)
8. Greenspan, M., Yurick, M.: Approximate K-d tree search for efficient ICP. In: International Conference on 3-D Digital Imaging and Modeling, pp. 442–448 (2003)
9. Hu, S., Zha, H., Zhang, A.: Registration of multiple laser scans based on 3d contour features. In: International Conference on Information Visualization, pp. 725–730 (2006)
10. Jost, T., Hugli, H.: A multi-resolution ICP with heuristic closest point search for fast and robust 3D registration of range images. In: International Conference on 3-D Digital Imaging and Modeling, pp. 427–433 (2003)

11. Kitaaki, Y., Okuda, H., Kage, H., Sumi, K.: High speed 3-d registration using gpu. In: SICE Annual Conference, pp. 3055–3059 (2008)
12. Li, H., Hartley, R.: The 3D–3D registration problem revisited. In: International Conference on Computer Vision (2007)
13. May, S., Droeschel, D., Fuchs, S., Holz, D., Nuchter, A.: Robust 3D-mapping with time-of-flight cameras. In: IEEE/RSJ International Conference on Intelligent Robots and Systems, pp. 1673–1678 (2009)
14. Neumann, D., Lugauer, F., Bauer, S., Wasza, J., Hornegger, J.: Real-time RGB-d mapping and 3-D modeling on the GPU using the random ball cover data structure. In: International Conference on Computer Vision—Workshop on Consumer Depth Cameras for Computer Vision, pp. 1161–1167 (2011)
15. Nuchter, A., Lingemann, K., Hertzberg, J., Surmann, H.: 6D SLAM with approximate data association. In: International Conference on Advanced Robotics, pp. 242–249 (2005)
16. Nuchter, A., Lingemann, K., Hertzberg, J.: Cached K-d tree search for ICP algorithms. In: International Conference on 3-D Digital Imaging and Modeling, pp. 419–426 (2007)
17. Ohno, K., Nomura, T., Tadokoro, S.: Real-time robot trajectory estimation and 3d map construction using 3d camera. In: IEEE/RSJ International Conference on Intelligent Robots and Systems, pp. 5279–5285 (2006)
18. Park, S.-Y., Choi, S.-I., Moon, J., Kim, J., Park, Y.W.: Real-time 3D registration of stereo-vision based range images using GPU. In: Workshop on Applications of Computer Vision (2009)
19. Qiu, D., May, S., Nüchter, A.: GPU-accelerated nearest neighbor search for 3D registration. In: International Conference on Computer Vision Systems, pp. 194–203 (2009)
20. Rusu, R., Blodow, N., Marton, Z., Beetz, M.: Aligning point cloud views using persistent feature histograms. In: IEEE/RSJ International Conference on Intelligent Robots and Systems, pp. 3384–3391 (2008)
21. Strand, M., Erb, F., Dillmann, R.: Range image registration using an octree based matching strategy. In: International Conference on Mechatronics and Automation, pp. 1622–1627 (2007)
22. Tamaki, T., Abe, M., Raytchev, B., Kaneda, K.: Softassign and EM-ICP on GPU. In: International Conference on Networking and Computing, pp. 179–183 (2010)

Part II
Human Body Analysis

The commercial breakthrough of depth cameras required a killer application. This application came with the launch of Kinect that allows to control computer games by body movements without additional controllers. This has been achieved by estimating the human skeleton of a user from the depth data in a fraction of time. Human body analysis, however, is more than body pose estimation. It also includes the analysis of body shapes, facial expressions, gestures, and much more.

While, as shown by Moeslund et al. (Visual Analysis of Humans, Springer, 2011), human body analysis from image data has been studied thoroughly, depth sensors changed the game in two ways: (1) depth is a very important perception cue that resolves many pose ambiguities present in image data; and (2) it is relatively easy to synthesize millions of depth images for training. While the Foreword by Shotton describes the story behind the development of the pose estimation algorithm for Kinect, *Human Body Analysis* contains four chapters and looks at the development on human body analysis with depth sensors after the launch of Kinect.

The chapter of Kohli and Shotton summarizes the key ideas of the original body part classification system (Real-time human pose recognition in parts from single depth images, CVPR, 2011) and presents further improvements. For instance, instead of estimating which body part each pixel in the depth image belongs to, and then using this information to reason about the location of the body joints, the joint locations can be directly estimated from the depth data by a voting approach. An approach for real-time human pose tracking is presented in the chapter by Baak et al. Instead of all body parts, the approach only detects the body parts that can be easily localized, namely hands, feet, and head. The localized body parts are then matched against a large motion capture dataset using an efficient retrieval technique. Both approaches have in common that they rely on a large motion capture dataset. However, Shotton et al. use the data to synthesize depth images of humans with various poses and shapes, whereas Baak et al. require a person specific body model and map the motion capture data to the skeleton of the body model. How such a person specific body model can be acquired is shown in the chapter of Weiss et al. They describe an inexpensive body scanning system. Such a system could be used for remote health care services or help customers of online shops to find the apparel that fits. The fourth chapter by Keskin et al. shows how the approach of Shotton et al. can be applied to hand pose estimation. The hand pose is then used to recognize hand gestures, which is demonstrated for digit recognition of the American Sign Language (ASL).

Although the presented approaches already achieve impressive results, they scratch only the surface of human body analysis. While more works are appearing, for instance, the work on face analysis by Fanelli et al. (Random Forests for Real Time 3D Face Analysis, IJCV, 2012) or the work on face animation by Weise et al. (Realtime Performance-based Facial Animation, SIGGRAPH, 2011), many aspects of the human body like hair, apparel, emotions, or gestures are still widely unexplored.

Chapter 4
Key Developments in Human Pose Estimation for Kinect

Pushmeet Kohli and Jamie Shotton

Abstract The last few years have seen a surge in the development of natural user interfaces. These interfaces do not require devices such as keyboards and mice that have been the dominant modes of interaction over the last few decades. An important milestone in the progress of natural user interfaces was the recent launch of Kinect with its unique ability to reliably estimate the pose of the human user in real time. Human pose estimation has been the subject of much research in Computer Vision, but only recently with the introduction of depth cameras and algorithmic advances has pose estimation made it out of the lab and into the living room. In this chapter we briefly summarize the work on human pose estimation for Kinect that has been undertaken at Microsoft Research Cambridge, and discuss some of the remaining open challenges. Due to the summary nature of this chapter, we limit our description to the key insights and refer the reader to the original publications for the technical details.

4.1 Introduction: The Challenge

In the summer of 2008, computer vision researchers at Microsoft Research Cambridge received a call from an Xbox team who were working on a top-secret project code-named Project Natal.[1] The Xbox team, headed by Alex Kipman, told researchers that they were building a system for human pose estimation that would work using the output of a depth sensor. The team demonstrated a tracking-based system for pose estimation which, once initialized to the correct pose, could track the pose of the human from one frame to the next. However, the system suffered from two critical problems: (i) it required the user to adopt an initialization pose, and (ii) it would typically lose track after a few frames. The Xbox team wanted the researchers to help build a system that avoided the initialization pose, that looked at a

---

[1] This project would eventually be launched as Kinect.

P. Kohli (✉) · J. Shotton
Microsoft Research, Cambridge, UK
e-mail: pkohli@microsoft.com

J. Shotton
e-mail: jamiesho@microsoft.com

single frame at a time to avoid possible loss-of-track, and that was super efficient—it had to use just a fraction of the computational power of the Xbox 360.[2]

In this chapter, we summarize the publications that have resulted from working on this challenge of efficient pose estimation from single depth images. We start in Sect. 4.2 by describing the key ideas and intuitions that led to the development of the body part classification system as described fully in Shotton et al. [13]. This system works by first estimating which body part each pixel in the depth image belongs to, and then using this information to reason about the location of different body joints. We then move in Sect. 4.3 to discuss the offset vote regression approach [6] where instead of predicting their own body part labels, pixels vote for where they think the different body joints are located in 3D. In Sect. 4.4 we discuss [15], which shows how pose estimates can be improved by using a conditional random forest model that uses a latent variable to incorporate dependencies between joint positions. This latent variable encodes some global property of the image, such as the person's height or the direction they are facing. Section 4.5 gives an overview of the recently proposed Vitruvian Manifold model [16] that predicts at each pixel an estimate of the correspondence to an articulated mesh model. An energy function can then be optimized to efficiently fit the model to the observed data. Finally in Sect. 4.6 we briefly discuss some of the remaining open challenges.

4.2 Body Part Classification—The Natural Markers Approach

Human pose estimation is a well studied problem in the computer vision community (see [8, 10] for a survey of the literature). Certain variants of the problem, for instance, estimation of the pose of a human from a single RGB image remain unsolved. Early commercial systems for human pose estimation worked by tracking easily localizable markers that were pre-attached on the body of the human subject. Marker-based systems for human pose estimation are usually quite reliable and highly accurate, but suffer from the limitation that markers need to be worn. Further, the approach also requires a calibration step where the relationship between the position of the markers and that of the body parts needs to be defined.

A natural approach motivated by the success of the marker-based pose estimation systems is to use classifiers that are be able to identify and thus localize different parts of the body. Variants of this approach have been explored in a number of research studies [1, 17]. For instance, a prominent approach for recognition and pose estimation is the Pictorial Structures model [4] that tries to estimate the location of different human body parts while maintaining certain spatial relationships between them. In light of these observations, Shotton et al. [13] decided to formulate the pose estimation problem as a body part labeling problem where the human body is divided into 31 body parts that were naturally associated with certain skeletal joint positions that needed to be estimated.

---

[2]For more detail on the story behind Kinect, please see the Foreword.

4.2.1 Generating the Training Data

The datasets used for training machine learning systems need to cover the variations the system would observe when it is deployed. Creating such a dataset is an expensive and time consuming process. Researchers have used computer graphics to overcome this problem [11] but this approach has its own set of problems. Synthetic body pose renderers use, out of necessity, real motion capture (mocap) data. Although techniques exist to simulate human motion they do not yet produce a full range of volitional poses or motions of a human subject that the system may encounter in the real world. The team at Microsoft overcame this problem by collecting a very large and diverse set of motion capture [13]. Rendering realistic intensity images is also hampered by the huge color and texture variability induced by clothing, hair, and skin. However, as the Kinect skeletal tracking system works with depth images, which are invariant to factors such as color or texture, this issue does not create a problem. Other factors which do affect the depth image, such as body shape, were varied as much as possible when creating the dataset. The result was a dataset of a million synthetic pairs of images of people of varied shapes in varied poses. Each image pair contained the depth image expected from the camera, and the body part label image that we were to train the system to recognize.

4.2.2 Randomized Forests for Classification

The body part classification problem is similar to many image labeling problems encountered in computer vision. These problems are generally formulated using Markov random field (MRF) models that have produced impressive results for various problems [3]. However, MRFs are currently too computationally expensive for real time human pose estimation. Shotton et al.[14] had proposed a decision forest-based method to overcome this problem which avoided the need for sophisticated and computationally expensive inference algorithms. This decision forest framework is not only simple and efficient but also allows for parallelization and could be implemented on a GPU [12]. These properties made decision forests a natural choice for solving the body part classification problem.

Shotton et al. [13] used a family of features that involved computing the differences between just a few depth image pixels. These were thus very inexpensive to compute. The decision trees were learned by employing the standard entropy minimization based objective and greedy tree learning schedule. The final processing pipeline involved computing features on every pixel and depending on the response traversing down the left or right side of the decision tree. This process is repeated until a leaf node is reached which contained a learned histogram. This histogram represents the posterior distribution over the body part label that the pixel should be assigned. These per-pixel body part distributions could then be clustered together to produce reliable hypotheses about the positions of the various joints in the body.

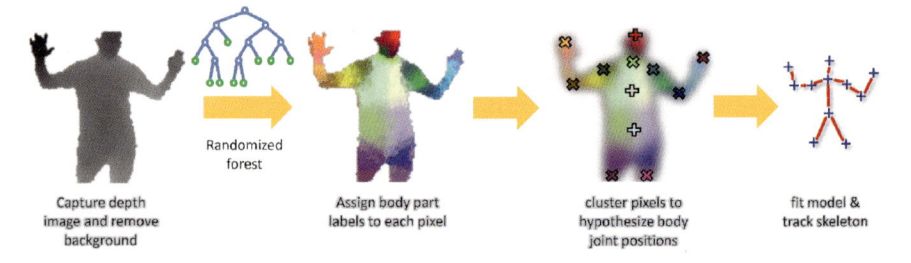

Fig. 4.1 The basic pipeline of the Kinect skeletal tracking system

Figure 4.1 illustrates the full skeleton tracking pipeline as used for Kinect. This pipeline takes the depth image, removes the background, applies the body part recognition and clustering algorithm described above, and finally applies a model fitting stage which exploits kinematic and temporal constraints to output a full skeleton.

4.3 Random Forest Regression—The Voting Approach

The body part classification algorithm allowed us to solve the hard challenges we needed to ship Kinect. However, it of course did not work perfectly in all scenarios, and so we set out to fix some of its limitations. Because body part classification works by labeling pixels, it cannot estimate the location of joints whose surrounding body parts are not visible in the image due to occlusion or field of view of the sensor. Furthermore, its two-step procedure comprising of pixel labeling followed by clustering may introduce errors. To overcome these problems we decided to investigate an offset regression approach [6] where pixels vote directly for the position of the different body joints, without going through the intermediate body part representation.

Similar voting approaches have been used in the literature for solving object localization problems. For example, in the implicit shape model (ISM) [7], visual words are used to learn voting offsets to predict 2D object centers. In an extension, Müller et al. [9] apply ISM to body tracking by learning separate offsets for each body joint.

In [6], we use a random regression forest to learn to predict how pixels vote for 3D locations of the various joints in the body. The regression forest shares the same structure and features as the body part classification approach [13]. However, as illustrated in Fig. 4.2, at each leaf node of a regression tree we instead store a distribution over the relative 3D offset from the re-projected 3D pixel coordinate to each body joint of interest. Representing these leaf node distributions efficiently is very important given the large size of our decision trees. Approximating the distribution over offsets as a Gaussian would be inappropriate, because even for fairly deep trees, we have observed highly multi-modal empirical offset distributions at

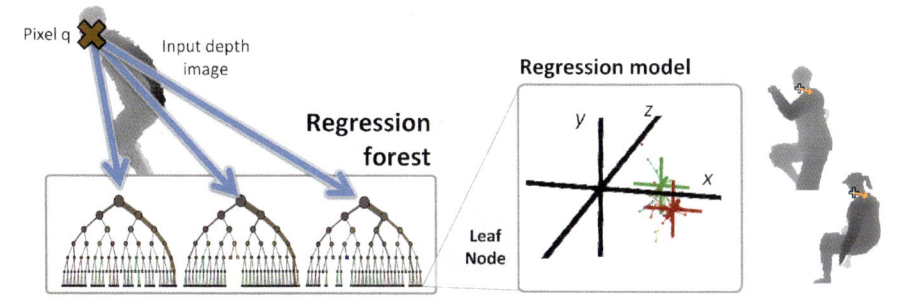

Fig. 4.2 The regression forest model for body joint position estimation

the leaves. One alternative, Hough forests [5], is to represent the distribution non-parametrically as the set of all offsets seen at training time. However, Hough forests trained on our large training sets would require vast amounts of memory and be prohibitively slow for a realtime system. Therefore, we instead represent the distribution using a compact set of 3D relative vote vectors learned by clustering the training offsets. The result is a system that can, in super real time, cast votes from each pixel to potentially all joints in the body, whether they are visible or not. Furthermore, these votes can directly predict interior body joint positions rather than the positions on the body surface predicted by [13]. Overall this was seen to improve body joint prediction accuracy significantly over [13].

4.4 Context-Sensitive Pose Estimation—Conditional Regression Forests

Even with the improvements in [6], there are some remaining limitations. The model does not encode dependency relationships between positions of different joint positions explicitly; the predictions for each body joint are made independently. Further, the model is not able to exploit prior knowledge that might be available during prediction in certain application scenarios. For instance, while estimating the pose of a person playing a golf game, information about the player's height or torso orientation might be available and potentially useful. Similarly, in a surveillance application, we might know the walking directions of pedestrians.

In [15], we show how both these limitations can be simultaneously overcome by incorporating a latent variable in the regression forest prediction model that encodes some global property of the image. In particular, we show that by conditioning on the players height or torso orientation, we can outperform [6] in terms of joint prediction accuracy, and as a by-product, make predictions about the conditioned-upon properties. The relationships encoded by different models are depicted in Fig. 4.3.

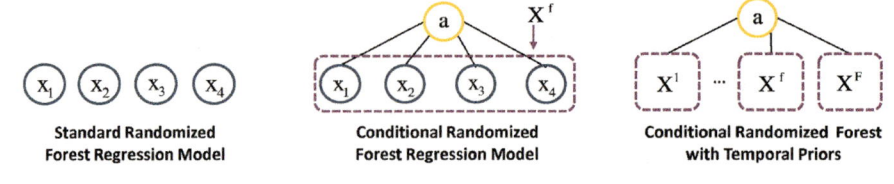

Fig. 4.3 The figure shows the relationships encoded by different regression forest models. The basic model (*left*) makes predictions for each body joint independently. The conditional model (*center*) encodes dependency relationships between the body joint positions and a global variable. The temporal conditional regression forest model (*right*) incorporates the prior that the value of the global variables associated with multiple image frames should be consistent. For instance, the height of a human subject remains constant through the video sequence

4.5 One-Shot Model Fitting: The Vitruvian Manifold

All the work presented above estimates zero, one, or more hypotheses for the positions of each body joint. However, the work above cannot enforce kinematic constraints such as limb lengths, and is not able to disambiguate which hypotheses to stitch together into a coherent skeleton. In the Vitruvian Manifold paper [16] we attempt to address these concerns by fitting an articulated skeleton model to the observed data. A standard way to represent such an articulated skeleton is a global transformation (rotation, translation, scale) and then a hierarchical kinematic tree of relative transformations. In these transformations, the translation relative to the parent might be fixed (representing fixed limb lengths) but the rotation is parameterized (representing bending joints). Given the kinematic hierarchy of transformations, one can use, for example, linear blend skinning to generate a surface mesh of the body.

A standard way to fit the parameters of such a mesh model to the data is called Iterated Closest Point (ICP) [2]. Starting from an initialization, ICP alternates between finding the closest corresponding point on the model for each observed data point, and optimizing the parameters of the model (e.g. joint rotations) to minimize the sum of squared distances between the corresponding model and observed points. Unfortunately, ICP requires a good initialization, and can take many iterations to converge. In the Vitruvian Manifold paper [16] we decided to address 'One-Shot' pose estimation: we could achieve a good model fit by inferring these correspondences directly from the test image, and then performing only a single optimization of the model parameters. To investigate this, we took our body part classification forests from [13] and extended them to predict at each pixel the corresponding vertex on the surface of the mesh model in a canonical pose (the so-called Vitruvian Manifold). The forests effectively become regression forests over this manifold, and allow a dense estimate of correspondence across the test image, without any initialization. Taking these correspondences and optimizing the model parameters resulted in most cases in a very accurate fit of the articulated skeleton to the observed data at low computational cost. An illustration of the algorithm is given in Fig. 4.4.

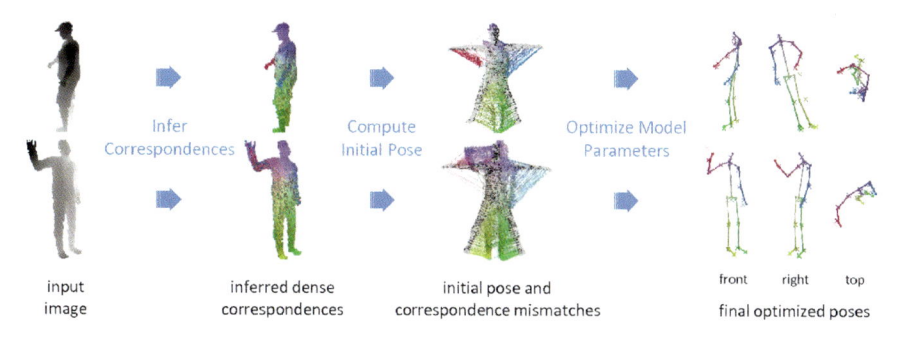

Fig. 4.4 The pose estimation pipeline in the Vitruvian Manifold algorithm

4.6 Directions for Future Work

The contributions summarized above represent a considerable advance in the state of the art in single image human pose estimation. But there remain open questions. How can we fix the remaining inaccuracies to achieve a reliable pose estimation for everyone, all the time, no matter what pose they adopt and no matter their body shape? How can we make such a system work from standard RGB cameras as well as depth cameras? How can we reliably map out the fine detail of the body, face, clothing, hair, etc.? How can we achieve a level of detail that means that instrumenting the body for motion capture becomes redundant? We believe that these and many other questions will mean that human pose estimation remains an active area of research for years to come.

Acknowledgements This chapter is a summary of existing published work, and we would like to highlight the contributions of all the original authors.

References

1. Anguelov, D., Taskar, B., Chatalbashev, V., Koller, D., Gupta, D., Ng, A.: Discriminative learning of Markov random fields for segmentation of 3D scan data. In: IEEE Conference on Computer Vision and Pattern Recognition (2005)
2. Besl, P., McKay, N.: A method for registration of 3-D shapes. IEEE Trans. Pattern Anal. Mach. Intell. (1992). doi:10.1109/34.121791
3. Blake, A., Kohli, P.: Introduction to Markov Random Fields. Markov Random Fields for Vision and Image Processing. MIT Press, Cambridge (2011)
4. Felzenszwalb, P., Huttenlocher, D.: Pictorial structures for object recognition. Int. J. Comput. Vis. **61**(1), 55–79 (2005)
5. Gall, J., Lempitsky, V.: Class-specific Hough forests for object detection. In: IEEE Conference on Computer Vision and Pattern Recognition (2009)
6. Girshick, R., Shotton, J., Kohli, P., Criminisi, A., Fitzgibbon, A.: Efficient regression of general-activity human poses from depth images. In: International Conference on Computer Vision (2011)
7. Leibe, B., Leonardis, A., Schiele, B.: Robust object detection with interleaved categorization and segmentation. Int. J. Comput. Vis. **77**(1–3), 259–289 (2008)

8. Moeslund, T., Hilton, A., Krüger, V.: A survey of advances in vision-based human motion capture and analysis. Comput. Vis. Image Underst. (2006). doi:10.1016/j.cviu.2006.08.002
9. Müller, J., Arens, M.: Human pose estimation with implicit shape models. In: ARTEMIS (2010)
10. Poppe, R.: Vision-based human motion analysis: an overview. Comput. Vis. Image Underst. **108** (2007). doi:10.1016/j.cviu.2006.10.016
11. Shakhnarovich, G., Viola, P., Darrell, T.: Fast pose estimation with parameter sensitive hashing. In: International Conference on Computer Vision (2003)
12. Sharp, T.: Implementing decision trees and forests on a GPU. In: European Conference on Computer Vision (2008)
13. Shotton, J., Fitzgibbon, A.W., Cook, M., Sharp, T., Finocchio, M., Moore, R., Kipman, A., Blake, A.: Real-time human pose recognition in parts from single depth images. In: IEEE Conference on Computer Vision and Pattern Recognition (2011)
14. Shotton, J., Johnson, M., Cipolla, R.: Semantic texton forests for image categorization and segmentation. In: IEEE Conference on Computer Vision and Pattern Recognition (2008)
15. Sun, M., Kohli, P., Shotton, J.: Conditional regression forests for human pose estimation. In: IEEE Conference on Computer Vision and Pattern Recognition (2012)
16. Taylor, J., Shotton, J., Sharp, T., Fitzgibbon, A.: The Vitruvian Manifold: inferring dense correspondences for one-shot human pose estimation. In: IEEE Conference on Computer Vision and Pattern Recognition (2012)
17. Tu, Z.: Auto-context and its application to high-level vision tasks. In: IEEE Conference on Computer Vision and Pattern Recognition (2008)

Chapter 5
A Data-Driven Approach for Real-Time Full Body Pose Reconstruction from a Depth Camera

Andreas Baak, Meinard Müller, Gaurav Bharaj, Hans-Peter Seidel, and Christian Theobalt

Abstract The 3D reconstruction of complex human motions from 2D color images is a challenging and sometimes intractable problem. The pose estimation problem becomes more feasible when using streams of 2.5D monocular depth images as provided by a depth camera. However, due to low resolution of and challenging noise characteristics in depth camera images as well as self-occlusions in the movements, the pose estimation task is still far from being simple. Furthermore, in real-time scenarios, the reconstruction task becomes even more challenging since global optimization strategies are prohibitive. To facilitate tracking of full-body human motions from a single depth-image stream, we introduce a data-driven hybrid strategy that combines local pose optimization with global retrieval techniques. Here, the final pose estimate at each frame is determined from the tracked and retrieved pose hypotheses which are fused using a fast selection scheme. Our algorithm reconstructs complex full-body poses in real time and effectively prevents temporal drifting, thus making it suitable for various real-time interaction scenarios.

A. Baak (✉)
MPI Informatik & Saarland University, Campus E1.4, 66123 Saarbrücken, Germany
e-mail: abaak@mpi-inf.mpg.de

M. Müller
Bonn University & MPI Informatik, Römerstraße 164, 53117 Bonn, Germany
e-mail: meinard@mpi-inf.mpg.de

G. Bharaj · H.-P. Seidel · C. Theobalt
MPI Informatik, Campus E1.4, 66123 Saarbrücken, Germany

G. Bharaj
e-mail: gbharaj@mpi-inf.mpg.de

H.-P. Seidel
e-mail: hpseidel@mpi-inf.mpg.de

C. Theobalt
e-mail: theobalt@mpi-inf.mpg.de

5.1 Introduction

In recent years, several approaches for marker-less human pose estimation from multiple video streams have been presented [5, 9, 13, 17, 51]. While multi-view tracking already requires solving challenging non-linear optimization problems, monocular pose estimation puts current technology to its limits since, with intensity images alone, the problem is considerably underconstrained [8, 31, 37]. In order to have a chance to reconstruct human movements, non-trivial inference or optimization steps are needed in combination with strong priors. In general, real-time reconstruction of complex human motions from monocular intensity-image sequences can still be considered an open problem.

New depth sensors, such as time-of-flight (ToF) cameras or the Microsoft Kinect sensor, provide depth images at video frame rates. In such images, each pixel stores a depth value instead of a color value. Since this representation of a scene stands somewhere in the middle between a pure 2D color-based representation and full 3D scene geometry, depth images are also referred to as 2.5D data [25]. It turns out that with depth cameras the 3D pose reconstruction of human poses from a single viewpoint becomes more feasible as shown in [7, 15, 18, 24, 35, 48, 56], see also Sect. 5.2. In this chapter, we present a tracking framework that yields robust pose estimates from monocular depth-image sequences. Moreover, our framework enables significant speed-ups of an order of magnitude compared to most of the previous approaches. In fact, we reach similar run time behavior as the algorithm implemented in the Microsoft Kinect [48], whereas we do not need multicore or GPU implementations.

Our procedure follows a hybrid strategy combining generative and discriminative methods, which is an established paradigm for pose estimation and tracking problems. While local optimization strategies [24] have proven to yield high frame rates, such techniques tend to fail for fast motions. Algorithms using global optimization provide more reliable pose estimates, but are typically slow and prohibitive for real-time scenarios. Various data-driven approaches have also been suggested to overcome some of these issues, enabling fast yet robust tracking from intensity-image streams, see [34, 40, 46, 52]. These approaches rely on databases that densely cover the range of poses to be tracked, and fail on poses that are not contained in the database. Moreover, due to the high variability of general human motion, constructing such a database might become intractable. Hybrid strategies that combine generative and discriminative methods have proven to be a suitable methodology for pose estimation and tracking procedures, see [4, 12, 18, 41, 43, 50, 55]. In this work, the main idea is to stabilize generative optimization algorithms by a discriminative component based on a database lookup or a classification scheme. Using this strategy, the risk of getting stuck in local minima is significantly reduced, while time-consuming global optimization methods are avoided.

In our approach, we employ a data-driven hybrid strategy conceptually similar to [12], where local optimization is combined with global retrieval techniques, see Fig. 5.1 for an overview. In our scenario, an actor may perform even complex and fast motions in a natural environment facing a single depth camera at a reasonable

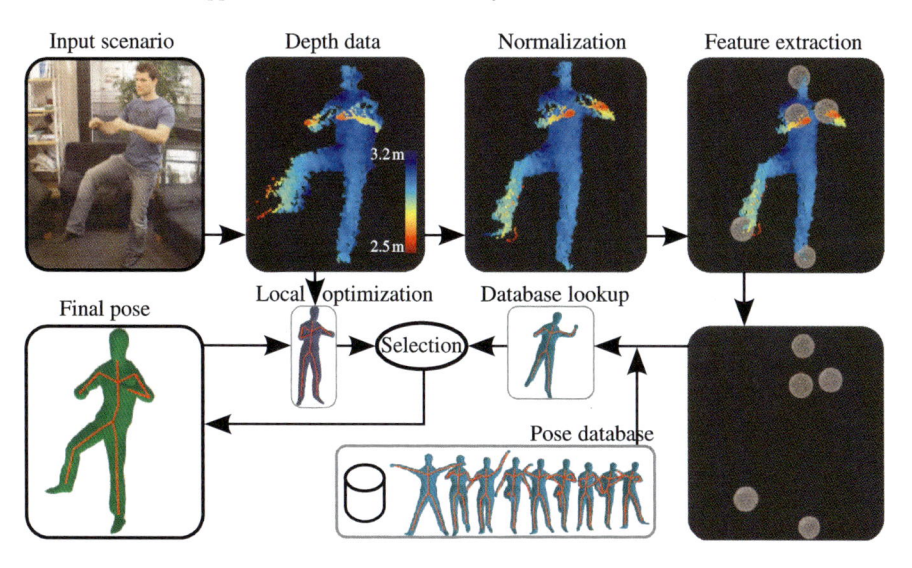

Fig. 5.1 Overview of our proposed pose estimation framework. Using features extracted from the depth data, we retrieve a pose candidate using a database lookup scheme. An additional candidate is obtained by running a local optimization algorithm that is initialized with the final pose of the previous frame. Then, a hypothesis selection decides for the either of the candidates

distance. Similar to [12], we retrieve a pose hypothesis from a large database of 3D poses using sparse features extracted from the depth input data. Additionally, a further hypothesis is generated based on the previously tracked frame. After a local optimization of both hypotheses, a late-fusion selection approach combines the hypotheses to yield the final pose. While the overall procedure is inspired by previous work [12, 18], we explain a number of novel techniques which add robustness and significantly speed up computations at various stages including efficient feature computation, efficient database lookup, and efficient hypothesis selection. In our experiments, we also compare our pose estimation results to previous work using the publicly available benchmark data set [18]. We gain significant improvements in accuracy and robustness (even for noisy ToF data and fast motions) while achieving frame rates of up to 100 fps (as opposed to 4 fps reported in [18]).

Contributions In this chapter, we present a system for full-body pose estimation from monocular depth images that requires only 10 to 16 milliseconds per frame on a standard single-core desktop PC, while being able to track even fast and complex full-body motions. Following a data-driven hybrid strategy that combines local pose estimation with global retrieval techniques, we introduce several technical improvements. Firstly, in the feature extraction step, we introduce a variant of Dijkstra's algorithm that allows for efficiently computing a large number of geodesic extrema. Secondly, in the retrieval step, we employ an efficient database lookup scheme where semantic labels of the extrema are not required. Thirdly, we describe a novel late-fusion scheme based on an efficiently computable sparse and symmetric distance measure. It is the combination of all these techniques that avoids computational bottlenecks while providing robust tracking results.

The remainder of this chapter is organized as follows. After giving an overview about related work in Sect. 5.2, we describe the input data and preprocessing steps in Sect. 5.3. The steps of the pose reconstruction framework are defined in Sect. 5.4. We describe our extensive experiments in Sect. 5.5, before we conclude in Sect. 5.6.

5.2 Related Work

Intensity-Image-Based Tracking Monocular 3D human pose tracking from intensity images has become an important research topic. In order to deal with challenges coming from occlusions and missing 3D information, different approaches have been pursued making use of statistical body models [21], physical constraints [53], object interaction [39], or motion capture data [41]. For example, Guan et al. [21] fit a statistical model of human body pose and shape to a single image using cues such as silhouettes, edges, and smooth shading. In a similar vein, Hasler et al. [22] present a method for estimating human body pose and shape from single images using a bilinear statistical model. Physics-based constraints are used in Brubaker et al. [10], where a physically based modeling of the lower body helps to track walking motions from monocular images. In [53], the authors propose to annotate parts of image sequences with 2D joint positions, bone directions, and environmental contacts. From such annotations and the image data, they compute physically realistic human motion. As a different type of constraint, the interaction with objects can be exploited as demonstrated in [39]. Having a database of admissible poses, approaches such as [33, 34, 40, 46, 52] compute a mapping from image features to database poses. With such discriminative approaches, poses that are not contained in the database are difficult to recover. By combining generative and discriminative approaches, robust and smooth pose estimates from a single view can be achieved [14, 41, 43, 50].

Depth-Image-Based Tracking 3D human pose tracking based on a single depth-image stream has received increasing attention in the last years. While it appears like a simpler problem at first sight, one still has to deal with noise in the input data, low resolution sensors, lack of color information, and occlusion problems. Nowadays, commercial packages [7] or software libraries exist that can compute joint positions from depth images for multiple people in real time (Microsoft Kinect SDK [30], Primesense NITE middleware [38]). While the algorithm behind the NITE middleware is not revealed to the public, Microsoft published the approach that is implemented in the Kinect SDK in [48]. As explained in the previous chapter, the authors use randomized decision forests trained on a huge set of various body poses and shapes in order to hypothesize joint locations from features on the raw depth input data. The approach was recently combined with a regression scheme to predict joint locations more accurately [19]. Also, positions of occluded joints can be estimated.

Some pose reconstruction approaches use *global optimization* methods in order to solve the pose reconstruction task. For example, Friborg et al. [15] use a GPU-accelerated particle filter to fit a surface mesh consisting of rigidly connected generalized cylinders to stereo depth data. However, even with GPU implementations, such approaches are often not real-time capable. Pure *local optimization* strategies have also been explored, which are implemented as variants of the iterative closest points (ICP) method [6]. For example, Pekelny and Gotsman [35] simultaneously track and reconstruct the shape of limbs through depth images. Knoop et al. [24] show that a combination of ToF and stereo data enables full-body pose estimation at real-time frame rates. Also using ICP, Grest et al. [20] combine depth and silhouette data to capture articulated motion with ten degrees of freedom in real time. Although yielding high frame rates, such methods often fail due to noise and motion blur present in the depth data. In particular with fast motions, local optimization easily gets stuck in erroneous poses which are hard to recover from.

In order to yield a more robust tracking, many approaches stabilize the optimization algorithms using additional *prior knowledge*. For example, Schwarz et al. [44] include a database of motions as prior knowledge for a particle filter optimization method. However, motions not present in the database cannot be tracked. As a complementary technique for stabilization, many approaches *detect features in a bottom-up fashion* directly from the depth input data. Here, geodesic distances are used in some work in order to detect anatomic landmarks. Following such a scheme, Ganapathi et al. [18] classify geodesic extrema features extracted from depth images according to the class labels 'hand', 'foot', and 'head'. With these detections, the search space of a particle filter is constrained. Integrating constraints into similar optimization techniques, anatomical landmarks are identified using feature tracking or heuristics in [1, 28, 49]. Using object detectors to estimate the position of the head and the hands, Gall et al. [16] stabilize a local optimization-based algorithm for tracking the upper body from depth data. Also, constrained inverse kinematics has been used on anatomical landmarks in [45, 57]. In our approach, we also make use of bottom-up detected features in order to stabilize a local optimization approach. As for the feature extraction, we build on the idea of accumulative geodesic extrema [36] and contribute with an efficient feature computation strategy.

Depth cameras seem to be an ideal type of sensor to facilitate intuitive human computer interaction based on full-body motion input. Therefore, many approaches focus on achieving *real-time* performance and try to find efficient algorithms for the pose reconstruction task. Although efficiency is clearly one of the key aspects to make pose estimation applicable for home use, most approaches with a focus on robustness reach only interactive run times around 10 fps [18, 20, 57]. Only recently, methods have been published that perform robust pose estimation within just a couple of milliseconds per frame [19, 48], see also the previous chapter. Such approaches for pose estimation are interesting from a practical point of view since they leave enough CPU cycles free for applications or games that use the reconstructed pose as input. Exceeding the performance of most published methods, we can report nearly 100 fps for full body pose estimation. Apart from the methodology of combining discriminative and generative models, the key to our efficient and stable

Fig. 5.2 Point cloud obtained by a ToF camera (**a**) without and (**b**) including a method for removing lens distortion effects. Note the straightening effect on the left edge of the door

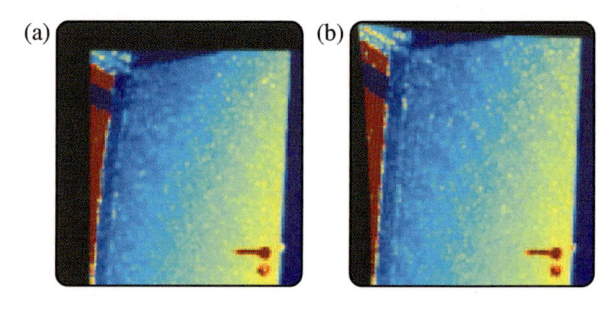

pose estimation procedure is a compound of efficient feature computation, efficient database lookup, and an efficient selection strategy.

5.3 Acquisition and Data Preparation

5.3.1 Depth Data

Before ToF cameras and the Kinect sensor became popular, stereo cameras were predominantly used to obtain depth data in real time. In order to compute depth values, such passive stereo systems need to identify corresponding features in the two images captured at every time step. However, computing and matching such features is computationally expensive and often fails for objects without texture.

Current depth cameras based on active illumination with infrared light overcome these limitations. Moreover, current ToF cameras are robust to background illumination and yield stable distance values independent of the observed textures. In principle, ToF cameras capture depth/distance data at video frame rates by measuring the round trip time of infrared light emitted into and reflected from the scene. Several successive measurements have to be made in order to estimate the phase shift of the infrared light from which the round trip time is derived [25]. Moreover, further measurements are taken over a longer period of time in order to reduce the amount of noise. For static scenes, this process leads to measurements with high accuracies in the range of millimeters. For dynamic scenes with moving objects, however, this process can lead to errors in the estimation of depth values. Problematic are edges that separate an object from another, more distant object, resulting in strongly corrupted depth measurements, also called *mixed pixels*. Furthermore, low resolution, strong random noise and a systematic bias [25] lead to data that is difficult to handle.

A depth camera returns a distance image $I := \mathbb{Z}^2 \to \mathbb{R}$ with $\mathbb{Z}^2$ being the pixel domain. Since the camera also produces an amplitude image in the infrared domain, we use a standard pattern-based camera calibration [29] to recover the camera matrix and parameters for the lens distortion. To remove lens distortion effects, we apply the method of [23] which yields stable and accurate metric distance values, see Fig. 5.2 as an example. We do not calibrate for systematic bias of the camera,

Fig. 5.3 (**a**) Original depth point cloud. (**b**) Point cloud after background subtraction and filtering. Some mixed pixel artifacts remain, see, e.g., the left leg

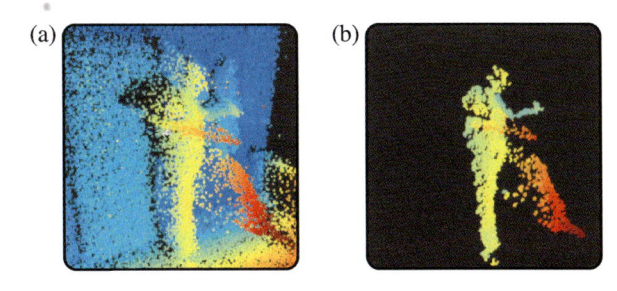

since for full-body pose estimation slight constant deviations in the measurements do not play an important role. For a recent method that calibrates for systematic bias using an intensity-based approach we refer to [27]. Using the calibration information, we transform the per-pixel distances into a metric 3D point cloud $\mathcal{M}_I \subseteq \mathbb{R}^3$ for every input frame of our online pose estimation framework, see Fig. 5.3(a). We then perform background subtraction using a static prerecorded background model and delete contour pixels to remove the influence of mixed pixels. Finally, a 3×3 median filter is used to reduce noise in the measurements, see Fig. 5.3(b).

In contrast to a ToF camera, the Microsoft Kinect depth sensor uses an active stereo approach. More specifically, a camera records an image of a projected structured light pattern in the infrared domain. Then, from the recorded pattern, a depth map is derived. In contrast to a ToF camera, only one image is analyzed in every time step. Thus, the Kinect camera is less susceptible to mixed pixels in dynamic scenes. However, the data also exhibits significant noise. In particular, artifacts like holes in the data appear when the projected pattern cannot be recognized. Moreover, the coarse depth quantization limits the accuracy in the far field from the camera, where, for example, a 2.5 cm quantization gap occurs at 3 meters distance to the camera. The presented algorithms in this chapter have been applied to depth data coming from ToF cameras as well as data coming from the Microsoft Kinect. Without changing or tuning the proposed algorithms, the final pose estimates with each of the cameras are qualitatively very similar as shown in the accompanying video [2].

5.3.2 Model of the Actor

The body of the actor is modeled as a kinematic chain [32]. We use $J = 20$ joints that are connected by rigid bones, where one distinguished joint is defined as the root of the kinematic chain, see Fig. 5.4(a). A pose is fully determined by the configuration of a kinematic chain specified by a pose parameter vector χ containing the position and orientation of the root joint as well as a set of joint angles. Through forward kinematics [32] using χ, 3D joint positions represented by a stacked vector $P_\chi \in \mathbb{R}^{3J \times 1}$ can be computed. Using linear blend skinning [26], we attach a surface mesh with a set of 1170 vertices $\mathcal{M}_\chi$ to the kinematic chain to model the deforming body geometry, see Fig. 5.4(b). Initializing the body model to the shape of a specific actor is beyond the scope of this chapter. Methods exist to solve this task using

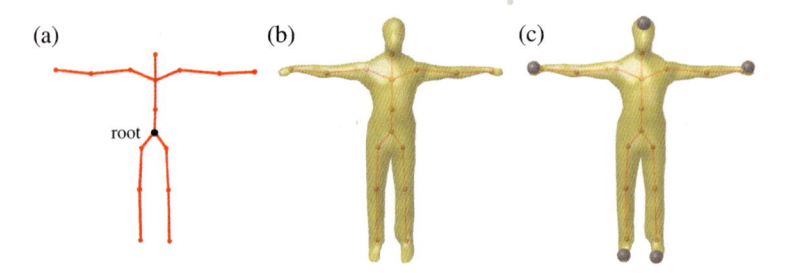

Fig. 5.4 (**a**) Skeletal kinematic chain. (**b**) Rigged mesh. (**c**) Highlighted end effectors (hands, feet, and head)

image data and a large database of scanned humans, see, e.g., [21, 22]. Recently, Weiss et al. [54] have shown that the body shape of a person can be determined using depth images from four different views, see also the following chapter for details. As shown in our experiments (Sect. 5.5), even with a fixed body model we can track people for a range of different body sizes.

5.3.3 Pose Database

Pose reconstruction approaches based on local optimization update the model parameters (in our case the joint angles) by optimizing a specified cost function, where convergence only to a near local minimum can be guaranteed. Although such methods typically run very fast, they fail when the initialization is too far away from the actual pose. For such a failure case we say that the algorithm loses track. This is often the case for fast motions where body parts can move far from frame to frame. One strategy to overcome such limitations is to reinitialize the local optimization when the track is lost. In the proposed algorithm, we use global pose estimates derived from database knowledge for such reinitializations. To this end, we create a database of human full body poses obtained with a marker-based motion capture system. The actor performs a variety of motions including hand gestures and foot motions to span a large range of different poses. To enable invariance under global transformations, the obtained poses χ_i are then normalized according to the positions of the root joint and the viewing direction. Furthermore, to maximize the variety and minimize the number of poses in the database, we select a subset of the recorded poses using a greedy sampling algorithm [52]. In this algorithm, the distance of two poses specified by χ_1 and χ_2 is measured by taking the distance of the corresponding joint positions into account:

$$d_P(\chi_1, \chi_2) := \frac{1}{J} \cdot \|P_{\chi_1} - P_{\chi_2}\|_2. \tag{5.1}$$

In contrast to [52], we truncate the sampling as soon as the minimal distance between all pairs of selected poses reaches a certain threshold. Using the truncated sampling, we obtain roughly 25 000 poses in which any two selected poses have a pose distance d_P larger than 1.8 cm. For each selected pose, we then consider end effector positions of the left/right hand, the left/right foot, and the head, modeled as $E_\chi^5 := (e_\chi^1, \ldots, e_\chi^5) \in (\mathcal{M}_\chi)^5$, see Fig. 5.4(c).

The following three reasons motivate the use of end effector positions as features. Firstly, end effector positions can be efficiently estimated for a large set of different poses even from depth data alone, see Sect. 5.4.2. Secondly, for many poses these positions are characteristic, thus yielding a suitable representation for cutting down the search space. Thirdly, they lead to low-dimensional feature vectors which facilitates the usage of efficient indexing methods. Thus, end effector positions constitute a suitable mid-level representation for full-body poses that on the one hand abstract away most of the details of the noisy input data, yet on the other hand retain the discriminative power needed to cut down the search space in the pose estimation procedure.

For indexing, we use a kd-tree [11] on the 15-dimensional stacked vectors E_χ^5 since they provide logarithmic search time in the size of the database and have turned out to be an efficient search structure for low-dimensional feature vectors. Since the size of the skeleton (e.g., body height or arm span) varies with different actors, the pose database has to be adapted to the actor. While not implemented in the presented system, this task can be solved using a retargeting framework. Even without retargeting, by manipulating the depth input point cloud $\mathcal{M}_I$ we are able to track motions of people if body proportions are not too far off the database skeleton, see Sect. 5.5.

5.3.4 Normalization

In the proposed tracking framework, we allow the actor to move freely within the field of view of the camera, while we restrict variations of the viewing direction to the range of about ±45° rotation around the vertical axis with respect to the frontal viewing direction. Recall that in our database all poses have been normalized with regard to the position of the root joint and the viewing direction. Thus, in order to query the database in a semantically meaningful way, we need to cope with variations in global position and orientation of the actor. We normalize $\mathcal{M}_I$ with respect to global position by means of a 3D ellipsoid fit around $\mathcal{M}_I$ using a mean-shift algorithm similar to [52]. To cope with global rotations, one could augment the database to contain pose representations from several viewing directions [12, 46, 52]. In this case, the retrieval time as well as the risk of obtaining unwanted poses would increase. Instead, in our framework, we normalize the depth input point cloud according to an estimated viewing direction. To this end, we compute a least-squares plane fit to points corresponding to the torso, which we assume to be the points that are closer than 0.15 m to the center of $\mathcal{M}_I$, see Fig. 5.5. The normal to the plane, as indicated by the cyan arrow in Fig. 5.5, corresponds to the eigenvector with the smallest eigen-value of the covariance matrix of the points. The

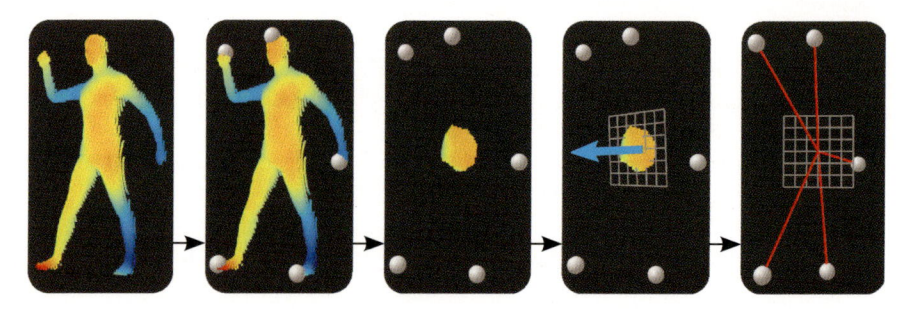

Fig. 5.5 Normalization of the geodesic extrema with respect to a computed viewing direction

viewing direction is its projection onto an imagined horizontal ground plane. We then rotate the positions of the geodesic extrema about the vertical axis through the center such that the normal of the rotated plane points to front. To cope with frames in which the viewing direction cannot be estimated because, e.g., the torso is occluded, we adaptively smooth the estimated directions over time. We detect whether the torso is occluded by inspecting the eigen-values of the above mentioned covariance matrix. Here, occluding body parts often lead to a stronger curvature in the regarded points (smallest eigen-value is relatively large) or a less circular fit (largest eigen-values are not similar). Then, we minimize the influence of the estimated normal. As a consequence, the detected viewing direction remains stable even if the arms occlude the torso or the center of $\mathcal{M}_I$ does not correspond to the torso. The proposed strategy might yield inaccurate viewing directions for persons with a very roundish belly, where the regarded points might always posses a strong curvature and thus the influence of the estimated normals might be continuously down-weighted. Moreover, the depth data of a side view of such a belly might appear similar to the depth data of a front view which could lead to invalid normals.

5.4 Pose Reconstruction Framework

As explained in the previous section, in the offline preprocessing phase, the camera matrix is obtained and the background model is created. We now describe our proposed online framework, see also Fig. 5.1. At a given frame t, the first steps are to compute the point cloud $\mathcal{M}_I$ from the distance image I, to perform background subtraction, to filter out noise and to normalize according to the viewing direction. Let χ_{t-1}^* be the final pose estimate of the previous frame $t-1$. From χ_{t-1}^*, we obtain a pose hypothesis χ_t^{LocOpt} by refining χ_{t-1}^* with a local optimization procedure that takes the input depth data into account (Sect. 5.4.1). A second pose hypothesis is obtained as follows. We extract a 15-dimensional feature vector from $\mathcal{M}_I$, representing the 3D coordinates of the first five geodesic extrema (Sect. 5.4.2). Being a low-dimensional yet characteristic pose representation, the features permit rapid retrieval of similar full-body poses from a large pose database (Sect. 5.4.3). From the set of retrieved poses we choose a single pose hypothesis χ_t^{DB} using a distance

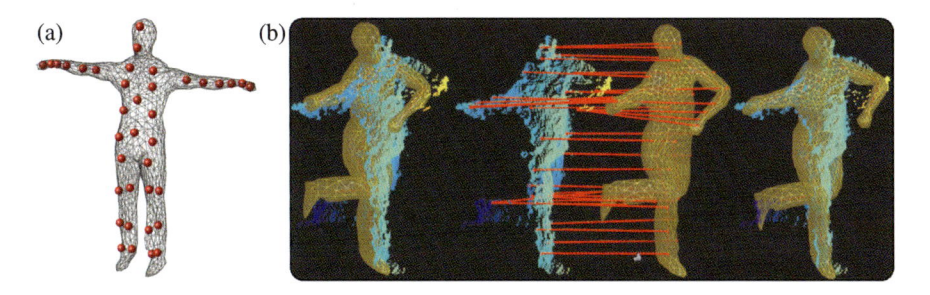

Fig. 5.6 (**a**) Subset of vertices $\mathcal{C}_\chi \subseteq \mathcal{M}_\chi$. (**b**) From pose χ (*left*), correspondences for mesh vertices in $\mathcal{C}_\chi$ are estimated (*middle*). Local optimization using the correspondences yields an updated pose χ' (*right*)

function which takes the influence of the estimated pose of the previous frame χ^*_{t-1} into account. Based on a late-fusion selection scheme that combines two sparse distances measures, our algorithm decides between χ_t^{DB} and χ_t^{LocOpt} to find the final pose χ_t^*, see Sect. 5.4.4.

5.4.1 Local Optimization

In our local pose optimization, we follow a standard procedure as described in, e.g., [42]. Here, the goal is to modify an initial pose χ such that the modified pose χ' fits to the point cloud $\mathcal{M}_I$ more accurately. To this end, we seek correspondences between vertices in $\mathcal{M}_\chi$ and points in $\mathcal{M}_I$.

Finding correspondences for all $v \in \mathcal{M}_\chi$ is not meaningful for three reasons. Firstly, many vertices do not have semantically meaningful correspondences in $\mathcal{M}_I$, e.g., the vertices of the back of the person. Secondly, the number of correspondences for the torso would be much higher than the number of correspondences in the limbs, which would disregard the importance of the limbs for pose estimation. Thirdly, the computation time of local optimization increases with the number of correspondences.

Therefore, we use a predefined set $\mathcal{C}_\chi \subseteq \mathcal{M}_\chi$ of mesh vertices as defined in Fig. 5.6(a). Here, we make sure that we select a couple of vertices for each body part. Using a local kd-tree built up in every frame, we efficiently obtain the ℓ nearest neighbors in $\mathcal{M}_I$ of each vertex $v \in \mathcal{C}_\chi$ and claim correspondence of v to the median of its ℓ nearest neighbors to reduce the influence of noise. Using these correspondences, we obtain updated pose parameters χ' by applying an optimization framework similar to the one in [42].

5.4.2 Feature Computation

To obtain a sparse yet expressive feature representation for the input point cloud $\mathcal{M}_I$, we revert to the concept of geodesic extrema as introduced in [36]. Such ex-

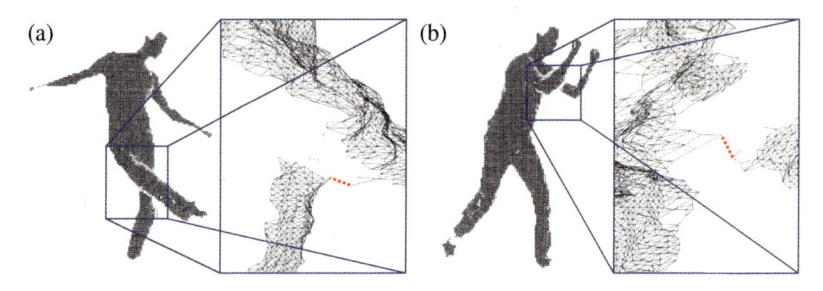

Fig. 5.7 Graph obtained from the depth image (*black lines*) and a zoom-in from a more lateral viewpoint for two poses with self-occlusions. The initially disconnected graph is automatically connected using edges indicated by the *red dashed lines*, respectively

trema often correspond to end effector positions, yielding characteristic features for many poses as indicated by Fig. 5.10. Following [36], we now summarize how one obtains such features. Furthermore, we introduce a novel variant of Dijkstra's algorithm that allows for efficiently computing a large number of geodesic extrema. We model the tuple of the first n geodesic extremal points as

$$E_I^n := (e_I^1, \ldots, e_I^n) \in (\mathcal{M}_I)^n. \tag{5.2}$$

To compute E_I^n, the point cloud data is modeled as a weighted graph where each point in $\{p_1, \ldots, p_L\} := \mathcal{M}_I$ represents a node in the graph. We refer to a node by its index $\ell \in [1:L]$. To efficiently build up the edge structure of the graph, we exploit the neighborhood structure in the pixel domain $\mathbb{Z}^2$ of the underlying distance image. For a given $p_\ell \in \mathcal{M}_I$, we consider the 8-neighborhood in the domain of the underlying image. For each such neighboring pixel $p_m \in \mathcal{M}_I$, we add an edge between m and ℓ of weight $w = \|p_m - p_\ell\|_2$ if w is less than a distance threshold τ. This way, we obtain a weighted edge structure in form of an adjacency list

$$\mathcal{E}(\ell) := \{(m, w) \in [1:L] \times \mathbb{R}_+ \mid p_m \text{ and } p_\ell \text{ share an edge of weight } w\} \tag{5.3}$$

for $\ell \in [1:L]$. Here, note that when building up the edge structure, the distance between any two points in $\mathcal{M}_I$ has to be evaluated only once.

In our approach, in contrast to the method in [36], we need to obtain a fully connected graph with only one connected component in order to obtain meaningful geodesic extrema. In practice, however, the graph computed as described above is not fully connected if, for example, the depth sensor misses parts of the thin limbs, or due to occlusions, see Fig. 5.7. To cope with such situations, we use an efficient union-find algorithm [47] in order to compute the connected components. To reduce small artifacts and noise pixels, we discard all components that occupy a low number of nodes. Furthermore, we assume that the torso is the component with the largest number of nodes. All remaining components are then connected to the torso by adding an edge between the respective closest pair of pixels if the edge weight is less than 0.5 m, see the red dotted lines in Fig. 5.7. This allows us to find meaningful geodesic extrema even if the initial graph splits into separate connected

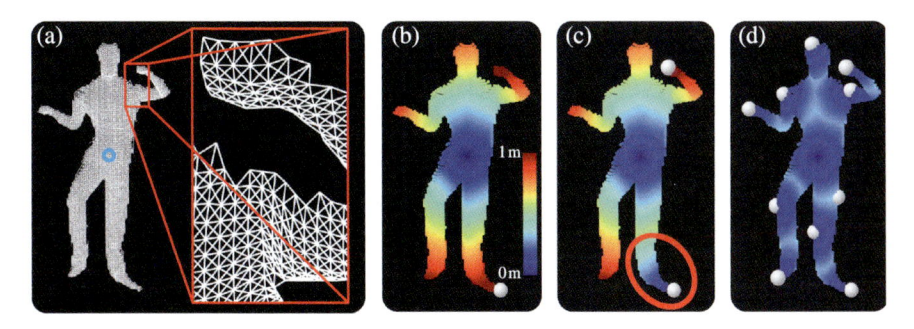

Fig. 5.8 Computation of geodesic extrema using a variant of Dijkstra's algorithm. (**a**) Graph structure and source node (*cyan circle*). (**b**) Geodesic distances and first geodesic extremum. (**c**) Updated geodesic distances and second geodesic extremum. (**d**) The first ten geodesic extrema

components, see Fig. 5.10(b)–(h) for the resulting geodesic extrema of the graphs shown in Fig. 5.7. Still, the estimated connections might lead to unwanted geodesic extrema in some poses. In this case, the database lookup (as will be explained in Sect. 5.4.3) might yield an inaccurate pose hypothesis. However, the influence of such a pose on the final pose estimate will be minimized by means of a hypothesis selection, as will be explained in Sect. 5.4.4.

We now show how a large number of extrema can be computed efficiently. Basically, we follow an iterative computation strategy. In each iteration, we use Dijkstra's algorithm [11] to compute the geodesic distances from a centroid node ℓ_0 (referred to as *source node*) to all other nodes in the graph. We then pick the node with the maximal distance as the corresponding extremal point. The efficiency of our algorithm is based on the observation that only in the first iteration of our algorithm, a full pass of Dijkstra has to be computed. In all remaining iterations one needs to consider only a small fraction of the nodes. As another observation, we only need to obtain the geodesic distances of each node and do not need to store the actual shortest path information which is usually saved in a predecessor array in Dijkstra's algorithm [11]. Therefore, we save additional time in each iteration by omitting the predecessor array.

As input to Algorithm 1, we use the graph structure with nodes, edges, and the designated source node ℓ_0, see Fig. 5.8(a). Additionally, we use a priority queue Q that stores tuples $(m, w) \in [1 : L] \times \mathbb{R}_+$ of nodes and weights sorted by increasing weight. The priority queue allows us to extract the tuple with the minimal weight by the Q.getMin() operation. To keep track of the distance values of each node, we use an auxiliary array Δ having L entries.

We start the algorithm by initializing Δ, see Lines 1–3. Then, we insert the source node into the previously empty priority queue Q in Line 4. We then iterate over all geodesic extrema to be computed. The first pass of Dijkstra (Lines 6 to 13) stores the shortest geodesic distances from the source node to any other node in the graph in the array Δ, see Fig. 5.8(b). Then, the point corresponding to the node ℓ^* with the largest distance in Δ is taken as the first geodesic extremum e_I^1 (Lines 14 to 15). Note that if there are still nodes which are not reachable from the source node ℓ_0,

Algorithm 1 Geodesic Extrema Computation

Input: $\{p_1 \ldots p_L\} := \mathcal{M}_I$: 3D point cloud with points $p_\ell \in \mathbb{R}^3$ and nodes $\ell \in [1:L]$
$\mathcal{E}(\ell) := \{(m, w) \in [1:L] \times \mathbb{R} | p_m \text{ and } p_\ell \text{ share an edge of weight } w\}$:
edge adjacency list defined on $\mathcal{M}_I$
$\ell_0 \in [1:L]$: index of the designated source node
Q: priority queue for elements $(m, w) \in [1:L] \times \mathbb{R}$
n: number of geodesic extrema to be computed
Output: $(e_I^1, \ldots, e_I^n) \in (\mathcal{M}_I)^n$: the n first geodesic extrema of G

1: **for** $\ell \leftarrow 1$ **to** L **do**
2:     $\Delta[\ell] \leftarrow \infty$ ▷ Initialize distance array
3:     $\Delta[\ell_0] \leftarrow 0$ ▷ Distance to source
4:     $Q.\text{insert}((\ell_0, 0))$
5: **for** $i \leftarrow 1$ **to** n **do**   ▷ Compute the first n extrema
6:     **while** $Q \neq \emptyset$ **do**
7:        $\ell \leftarrow Q.\text{getMin}()$ ▷ Get entry with minimal weight
8:        $Q.\text{removeMin}()$ ▷ Remove the entry from Q
9:        **for each** $(m, w) \in \mathcal{E}(\ell)$ **do**   ▷ For all nodes connected by an edge to p_ℓ
10:           **if** $\Delta[\ell] + w < \Delta[m]$ **then**
11:              $\Delta[m] = \Delta[\ell] + w$ ▷ A shorter path has been found
12:              $Q.\text{insert}((m, \Delta[m]))$
13:     **end while**   ▷ Δ now contains the geodesic distances
14:     $\ell^* \leftarrow \arg\max_{\ell \in [1:L]} \Delta[\ell]$ ▷ Note: the arg max must ignore nodes that were not reached
15:     $e_I^i \leftarrow p_{\ell^*}$ ▷ Store ith extremum
16:     $\Delta[\ell^*] \leftarrow 0$ ▷ Simulates edge insertion between p_{ℓ_0} and p_{ℓ^*}
17:     $Q.\text{insert}((\ell^*, 0))$ ▷ Let ℓ^* act as new source
18: **end for**

they bear the same distance values ∞ as set in the initialization. Of course, such unreachable nodes should not be considered as geodesic extrema. Therefore, the arg max operator in Line 14 must ignore these nodes in order to recover the true geodesic extremum. In Fig. 5.8(b), the detected extremum e_I^1 is indicated by the gray sphere on the left foot. According to [36], the next step is to add a zero-cost edge between ℓ_0 and ℓ^* and then to restart Dijkstra's algorithm to find e_I^2, and so on. This leads to a run time of $O(n \cdot D)$ for n extrema with D being the run time of Dijkstra's algorithm for the full graph.

Note that the second run of Dijkstra's algorithm shows a high amount of redundancy: the entries in the array Δ corresponding to all nodes in the graph that are geodesically closer to ℓ_0 than to the node of e_I^1 will not change in the second run. For example, in Fig. 5.8(c), only the distance values of the nodes within the highlighted area have changed.

Therefore, to compute the second pass, we keep the distance values of the first pass and let the node ℓ^* corresponding to e_I^1 act as the new source, see Lines 16 and 17. This way, the second iteration will be by an order of magnitude faster than

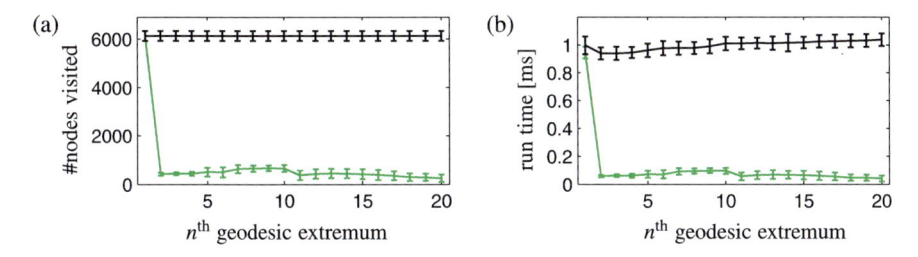

Fig. 5.9 (a) Number of nodes visited and (b) run time in milliseconds to find the nth geodesic extremal point for the baseline (*black*) and our optimized algorithm (*green*). Average values and standard deviation bars for a sequence of 400 frames from the data set of [18] are reported

the first iteration, as also confirmed by our experiments described in the subsequent paragraphs. Using ℓ^* as the new source, we update Δ with a pass of Dijkstra's algorithm and pick e_I^2 as the point with the maximal distance in the updated Δ, see Fig. 5.8(c). For the third pass we let the node corresponding to e_I^2 act as the new source by setting the corresponding value in Δ to 0, and run Dijkstra again. This way, in the third pass, only nodes in the graph that are closer to the node of e_I^2 than to all other previously used source nodes are touched. We proceed iteratively to compute the subsequent extremal points, see Fig. 5.8(d) for the resulting distance values and extrema after 10 iterations.

Our computational strategy leads to drastic improvements in the run time for each pass. To experimentally verify this, we evaluated the algorithm on a depth input sequence of 400 frames taken from the data set of [18]. We computed the first 20 geodesic extrema for each of the 400 frames using both a baseline algorithm that runs a full Dijkstra pass in each iteration and our optimized algorithm. We traced the number of nodes visited in each iteration as well as the actual run time for each iteration. Figure 5.9 shows that in the first iteration all reachable nodes in $\mathcal{M}_I$ (on average there were more than 6000 nodes in the graph) were visited. In the second iteration, only 413 ± 61 nodes (average $\pm$ standard deviation over all frames) were visited. This substantial reduction is also reflected by the run time of the algorithm, which drops from 1 millisecond in the first iteration to about 0.058 ± 0.0085 milliseconds in the second iteration, see Fig. 5.9(b). As a result, the overall run time for computing the first 20 geodesic extrema is only slightly higher than the run time of the original Dijkstra algorithm for computing the first geodesic extremum. Thus, the algorithm allows us to efficiently compute a large number of geodesic extrema.

The overall approach enables the detection of semantically meaningful end effector positions even in difficult scenarios. Figure 5.10 shows a number of challenging examples, where legs occlude each other (b)–(c), multiple body parts occlude each other (d)–(f), a fast punching motion with occlusions is performed (g)–(k), a leg is bent to the back (l), and the hands are outstretched to the camera (m). However, in poses where the end effectors are very close to other parts of the body, the topology of the graph may change and the detected extrema may differ from the actual set of end effectors, see Fig. 5.11(a)–(c). In these poses, the left elbow, the left shoulder,

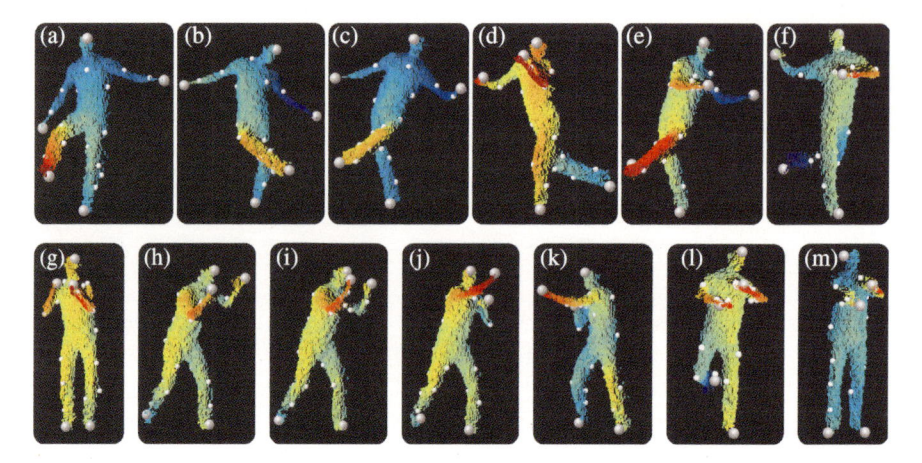

Fig. 5.10 Example poses with the first five geodesic extrema drawn as big spheres, and extrema 6 to 20 drawn as smaller blobs. For many poses, the first five extrema correspond to the end effectors, even when self-occlusions are present.

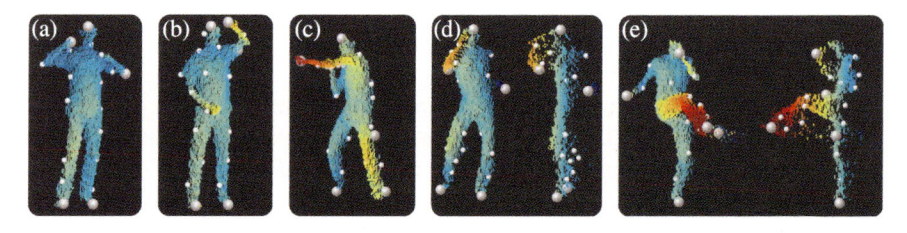

Fig. 5.11 (**a**)–(**c**) Problematic example poses. In particular when the hands come close to the body, end effector detection becomes difficult. (**d**)–(**e**) Flying mixed pixels lead to deviations in the end effector detection

and the left hip are selected as e_I^5, respectively. Also, flying mixed pixels can cause the topology of the graph to change, as depicted in Fig. 5.11(d), where we show a pose once from a frontal view and once from a side view. Note that although the left hand keeps a reasonable distance from the head, mixed pixels build a bridge in the graph from the hand to the head. Thus, the fifth extremum is located at the elbow. Figure 5.11(e) shows a similar situation in which the head is not detected due to mixed pixels. Instead, the fifth extremum is located at the hip.

In the subsequent section, we will explain the discriminative component of our framework, where pose candidates are obtained from the database by using the positions of the first five geodesic extrema as a query. If the end effectors are not revealed by these extrema, however, the obtained pose candidates are often meaningless. As will be explained later, the influence of such meaningless poses on the final pose estimates can be minimized with our combined generative and discriminative framework.

5.4.3 Database Lookup

As for the database lookup component, the goal is to identify a suitable full-body pose χ_t^{DB} from our pose database using the extracted geodesic extrema E_I^5 as the query input. However, as opposed to the database motions where the semantics of the end effector positions are known, the semantic labels of the extrema on the query side are not known. To partially solve for missing semantics, the method [18] uses a classifier trained on 'hand', 'head', and 'foot' patches of distance images. This process, however, is relatively expensive (taking 60 ms per frame according to [36]) and is thus not directly suitable in real-time scenarios. Also, when using depth data alone, misclassification of patches might occur because of missing color information, strong noise, and the low resolution of the measurements. In order to circumvent the classification problem, we propose a query strategy that does not rely on having a-priori semantic labels for the extracted geodesic extrema. Intuitively speaking, we use different queries that reflect different label assignments. As explained in the following, from the retrieved poses, we then choose a candidate pose that most likely corresponds to the correct labeling.

Let $\mathbb{S}_5$ be the symmetric group of all five-permutations. For a permutation σ and a five-tuple E, we denote the permuted tuple by σE. Now, let $\mathcal{S} \subseteq \mathbb{S}_5$ be a subset containing permutations σ such that the positions in σE_I^5 are close to the end effectors of the previous frame χ_{t-1}^*. More specifically, we define

$$\mathcal{S} := \left\{ \sigma \in \mathbb{S}_5 \mid \forall n \in [1:5] : \left\| e_I^{\sigma(n)} - e_{\chi_{t-1}^*}^n \right\| < \mu \right\}. \tag{5.4}$$

In our experiments, we use a distance threshold of $\mu = 0.5$ meters to effectively and conservatively prune the search space while still allowing for large jumps in the end effector positions which may be present in fast motions. In frames with clear geodesic extrema, the number of considered permutations $|\mathcal{S}|$ typically drops to one. To further increase robustness to false estimations in the previous frame, we add additional permutations to $\mathcal{S}$ if we detect jumps in the positions of the geodesic extrema. To compute the additional permutations, we assume that the two lowest extrema w.r.t. the vertical axis, say e_I^1 and e_I^2, correspond to the feet. This leads to two possible label assignments where the label 'left foot' is assigned to either e_I^1 or e_I^2. For each of the two assignments, the remaining three extrema can receive $3! = 6$ different labellings. This leads to $2 \cdot 6 = 12$ additional permutations added to $\mathcal{S}$.

By querying the kd-tree of the pose database for K nearest neighbors for each permutation in $\mathcal{S}$, we obtain $K \cdot |\mathcal{S}|$ pose candidates $\chi_{k,\sigma}$ with $k \in [1:K]$ and $\sigma \in \mathcal{S}$. For each (k, σ), we define a distance value between the pose candidate $\chi_{k,\sigma}$ and the permuted E_I^5 by

$$\delta\left(\chi_{k,\sigma}, E_I^5\right) := \frac{1}{5} \cdot \| E_{\chi_{k,\sigma}} - \sigma E_I^5 \|_2. \tag{5.5}$$

Note that to compute the distance $\delta(\chi_{k,\sigma}, E_I^5)$, we stack the tuples $E_{\chi_{k,\sigma}}$ and σE_I^5 into 15-dimensional vectors, respectively. The result of the database lookup χ_{k^*,σ^*}

for frame t is then chosen by also considering temporal consistency using

$$(k^*, \sigma^*) = \underset{(k,\sigma)}{\arg\min}\, \lambda \cdot \delta(\chi_{k,\sigma}, E_I^5) + (1-\lambda) \cdot d_P(\chi_{k,\sigma}, \chi_{t-1}^*) \qquad (5.6)$$

with a weighting factor λ that balances out the influence of d_P (defined in Eq. 5.1) and δ. In our experiments, we use $\lambda = 0.5$. Finally, we refine χ_{k^*,σ^*} to the hypothesis χ_t^{DB} using local optimization as described in Sect. 5.4.1.

5.4.4 Hypothesis Selection

At this stage, two alternative pose hypotheses have been derived, namely χ_t^{LocOpt} from the generative and χ_t^{DB} from the discriminative component. In the next step, we need to create a single, final pose χ_t^* taking both hypotheses into account. Recall that the pose hypothesis χ_t^{DB} might be inaccurate when the end effectors are not revealed. Therefore, it is not meaningful to take the average pose of χ_t^{LocOpt} and χ_t^{DB} as final pose. Instead, for this late-fusion step, we propose a novel selection scheme that decides for either χ_t^{LocOpt} or χ_t^{DB} as the final pose χ_t^* based on an efficiently computable sparse and symmetric distance measure. With the proposed selection strategy, the local optimization and database lookup schemes benefit from each other. On the one hand, if the database lookup component fails, then the local optimization component can continue to track the motion. On the other hand, the local optimization might fail to track fast and abrupt motions. In such situations, the database lookup can reinitialize the tracking.

In the proposed selection scheme, we want to avoid a dominant influence of potential errors coming from the feature extraction or from the database lookup. Therefore, we use distance measures that revert to the original input point cloud $\mathcal{M}_I$ rather than to derived data. One possible distance measure could be defined by projecting $\mathcal{M}_\chi$ into a synthetic distance image and comparing it to I. In practice, however, because of the relatively low number of pixels in the thin limbs, such a distance measure is dominated by the torso. For this reason, we propose a novel distance metric that can be computed efficiently and accounts for the importance of the limbs for pose estimation.

To this end, we combine two sparse distances measures. The first distance expresses how well the mesh is explained by the input data:

$$d_{\mathcal{M}_\chi \to \mathcal{M}_I} := \frac{1}{|\mathcal{C}_\chi|} \sum_{v \in \mathcal{C}_\chi} \min_{p \in \mathcal{M}_I} \|p - v\|_2. \qquad (5.7)$$

Here, we revert to only the subset $\mathcal{C}_\chi \subseteq \mathcal{M}_\chi$ of vertices as defined in Sect. 5.4.1. Likewise, the second distance measure expresses how well $\mathcal{M}_I$ is explained by $\mathcal{M}_\chi$:

$$d_{\mathcal{M}_I \to \mathcal{M}_\chi} := \frac{1}{20} \sum_{n \in [1:20]} \min_{v \in \mathcal{M}_\chi} \|e_I^n - v\|_2. \qquad (5.8)$$

To emphasize the importance of the limbs, we take only the first 20 geodesic extrema of the input depth data, which largely correspond to points on the limbs rather than the torso, see Fig. 5.10. Since also for the mesh we take only a subset of vertices, see Fig. 5.6(a), the distance measures are sparse. Both distance measures can be computed efficiently because firstly, geodesic extrema can be extracted very efficiently (Sect. 5.4.2), and secondly, only a small number of points are taken into account. The final pose χ_t^* is then given through

$$\chi_t^* := \underset{\chi \in \{\chi_t^{DB}, \chi_t^{LocOpt}\}}{\arg\min} (d_{\mathcal{M}_\chi \to \mathcal{M}_I} + d_{\mathcal{M}_I \to \mathcal{M}_\chi}). \qquad (5.9)$$

5.5 Experiments

We implemented the proposed hybrid tracking strategy in C++ and ran our experiments on a standard off-the-shelf desktop PC with a 2.6 GHz CPU. To numerically evaluate and to compare our hybrid strategy with previous work, we used the publicly available benchmark data set of [18]. In this data set, 28 sequences of ToF data (obtained from a Mesa Imaging SwissRanger SR 4000 ToF camera) aligned with ground truth marker positions (obtained from a marker-based motion capture system) are provided. This data set comprises 7900 frames in total. In addition to numerically evaluating on this data set, we demonstrate the effectiveness of the proposed algorithm in a real-time scenario with fast and complex motions captured from a PMD Camcube 2 in a natural and unconstrained environment, see Fig. 5.13 and Fig. 5.14. In the accompanying video [2], we show that the same framework also works with the Microsoft Kinect depth sensor without any further adjustments.

5.5.1 Feature Extraction

First, we evaluate the effectiveness of the proposed feature extractor on the benchmark data set. Not all ground truth markers in all frames are visible, thus, for this evaluation, we use only the 3992 frames in which all five end effector markers are visible. A good recognition performance of the feature extractor is needed for a successful subsequent database lookup. In 86.1 % of the 3992 frames, each of the found five geodesic extrema E_I^5 is less than 0.2 meters away from its corresponding ground truth marker position. This shows that we can effectively detect the end effector positions for most motions contained in the test data set.

5.5.2 Quantitative Evaluation

We run our pose reconstruction algorithm on the benchmark data set. Since the surface mesh of the actor is not part of that data set, we scale the input point cloud data

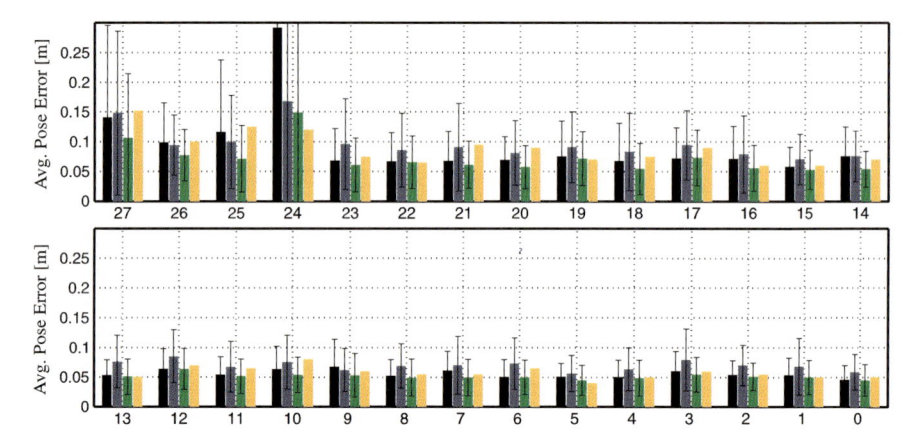

Fig. 5.12 Average pose error and standard deviation of sequences 27 to 0 of the data set of [18]. *Bars left to right*: Using only local optimization, using only the database lookup, results using the proposed fusion scheme, and values reported by [18] (without std. dev.)

so that it roughly fits the proportions of our actor. We manually fix correspondences between each motion capture marker and a mesh vertex. For a test sequence with T frames, let M_t be the number of visible motion capture markers in frame t, let $m_{t,i}$ be the 3D position of the ith visible marker in frame t and $\tilde{m}_{t,i}$ the position of the corresponding mesh vertex of the reconstructed pose. As also used in [18], the average pose error for a sequence is computed as

$$\bar{\epsilon}_{\text{avg}} := \frac{1}{\sum_{t=1}^{T} M_t} \sum_{t=1}^{T} \sum_{i=1}^{M_t} \|m_{t,i} - \tilde{m}_{t,i}\|_2. \tag{5.10}$$

Whereas the overall accuracy of the tracking algorithm is expressed by means of Eq. 5.10, potential local tracking errors can be averaged out. Therefore, we use this evaluation measure to show tendencies in the accuracy by comparing different pose estimation strategies for all benchmark sequences, see Fig. 5.12. To this end, we report how the local optimization component (Sect. 5.4.1) and the database lookup component (Sect. 5.4.3) perform individually, without being combined with the late-fusion hypothesis selection. When using only local optimization (first bar) the method often gets stuck in local minima and loses track. When using only a database lookup (second bar), poses where the end effectors are not revealed by the first five geodesic extrema may cause a false lookup result. Thus, in terms of the average pose error, both methods in isolation do not perform well on all sequences. The third bar shows the result of the proposed hybrid strategy which leads to substantial improvements. Also in comparison to [18] (last bar, std. dev. values were not available), we achieve comparable results for basic motions and perform significantly better in the more complex sequences 20 to 27. Only for sequence 24, the method [18] performs better than our approach. The reason for this is that this sequence contains a 360° rotation around the vertical axis, which cannot be han-

Table 5.1 Average run times in milliseconds over all frames of the benchmark data set

	Total	Preparation	Local optim.	E_I^{20}	Lookup	Selection
Full resolution	16.6 ms	1.2 ms	5.7 ms	6.2 ms	1.2 ms	0.9 ms
	100 %	7 %	34 %	37 %	7 %	5 %
Half resolution	10.0 ms	1.1 ms	4.6 ms	1.5 ms	1.2 ms	0.9 ms
	100 %	11 %	46 %	15 %	12 %	9 %

dled by our framework. However, our system can cope with rotations in the range of ±45° since we normalize the input data based on the estimated viewing direction. For the benchmark data set, the hypothesis selection component decided in 22.5 % of the frames for the retrieval component, and in 77.5 % for the local optimization from the previous frame. With our hypothesis selection, we significantly reduced the average pose error of the final pose estimate in comparison to either method ran individually.

5.5.3 Run Time

In Table 5.1, we report the average run time of our pose estimation framework in milliseconds per frame. In [18], the authors report a performance of 4 fps on downsampled input data. By contrast, with our proposed algorithm, we achieve 60.4 fps (16.6 ms per frame) on average on the full resolution input data, and 100 fps (10.0 ms per frame) with half of the resolution which we track with nearly the same accuracy. The run times are in the same order of magnitude than other state-of-the-art approaches like [48] where the authors report 200 fps on a different dataset and "at least 10×" speedup with respect to [18]. As for a more detailed analysis, we also give the run time of each algorithmic component, namely the data preparation phase (Sect. 5.3), the local optimization component (Sect. 5.4.1), the feature extraction (Sect. 5.4.2), the database lookup (Sect. 5.4.3), and the selection (Sect. 5.4.4). Note that our efficient algorithms lead to run times that are well distributed among the different components, such that no clear bottleneck is present. For the full resolution, the run time of local optimization and the feature extraction are approximately the same. The latter benefits most from downsampling the data.

5.5.4 Qualitative Evaluation

In Fig. 5.13, we show example results of fast and complex motions captured in an unconstrained environment. The considered motions are much faster and contain more challenging poses than the ones used in [18]. The leftmost image in each subfigure shows a video frame of the pose captured from a separate video camera

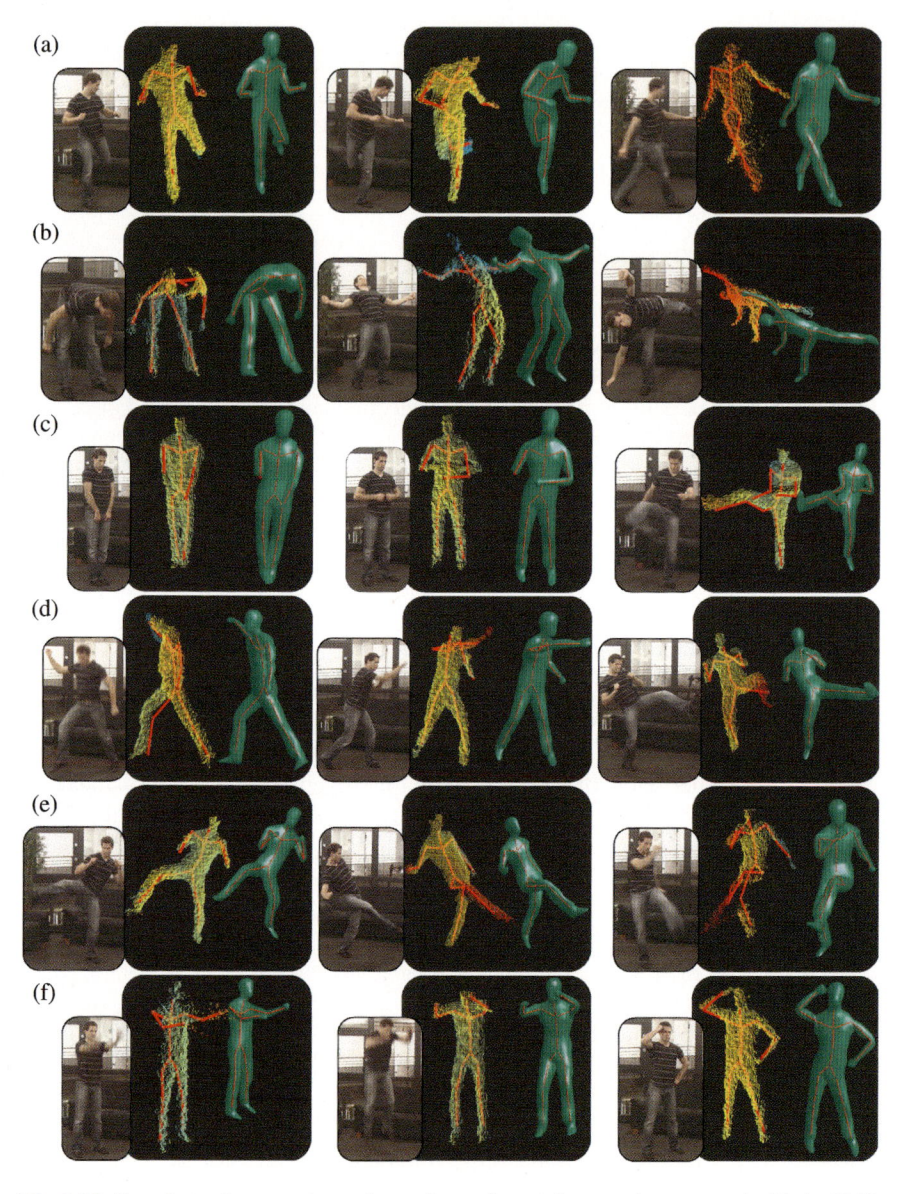

Fig. 5.13 Snapshots of our results on fast and complex motions on data captured with the PMD camera. For every motion we show a video frame of the actor (not used for tracking), ToF data overlaid with the reconstructed skeleton, and a rendering of the corresponding mesh

not used for tracking. In the room where we recorded the data, the video camera was standing to the left of the depth camera. The middle image shows the depth data overlaid with the estimated skeleton of the pose χ_t^*. The rightmost image depicts a rendering of the surface mesh in the corresponding pose.

The first row (Fig. 5.13(a)) shows some frames of a successfully tracked motion sequence. Even though the left foot is bent to the back and is nearly hidden from the depth camera, the 3D geometry of the legs has been recovered correctly. Figure 5.13(b) depicts difficult bending motions. Despite the fact that such poses were not part of our pose database, the motions were tracked successfully. For such motions, the result χ_t^{DB} of the lookup step does not reflect the true pose of the actor. Thus, our selection scheme decided in each frame correctly for the local optimization component which successfully tracked the motions. Figure 5.13(c) contains typical failure cases. The first two images show poses with severe self-occlusion which are still a challenge for pose reconstruction. Nonetheless, the overall pose is reliably captured and arm tracking quickly recovered once the occlusion was resolved. The rightmost image shows a case where the right arm was not visible in the depth input data. Since the proposed method assumes that at least parts of all limbs are still visible in the depth data, the pose of the right arm is not correctly recovered. Figure 5.13(d) shows examples of fast jumping, punching, and kicking motions where the first two motions are additionally rotated to more than $\pm 45°$ around the vertical axis with respect to the frontal viewing direction. The poses in this row are roughly recovered. However, small misalignments of some limbs might occur as visible in the right leg and the right arm, respectively. Also note the inaccuracy in the left leg (third pose). Such minor inaccuracies can locally occur and are typically resolved after a few frames. Figure 5.13(e) shows some poses of a successful tracking of a sequence with fast and complex kicking motions. Note that in the second pose of Fig. 5.13(e) it is difficult to distinguish the left leg from the right leg when having only the depth data of a single frame. However, since the local optimization and the database lookup components use temporal continuity priors, the legs can be tracked successfully. Finally, Fig. 5.13(f) contains a very fast arm rotation motion in a pose where the arms are close to being outstretched to the camera (first image), and a jumping motion in a similar pose (second image). Although only a small part of the arm is visible to the depth camera due to self-occlusions, the 3D geometry of the arm is successfully recovered. The last image shows a pose where the hands touch different parts of the body. Despite the fact that in such poses not all geodesic extrema in E_I^5 correspond to the end effectors, the motion has been tracked successfully since the hypothesis selection decided for the local optimization component. In the accompanying video [2] we show the performance of our prototype implementation also with the Microsoft Kinect depth camera.

First experiments showed that actors with different body proportions can be tracked if they are not too different from our body model. Therefore, we scaled the input data to roughly match the proportions of the model, see Fig. 5.14 and the accompanying video for examples. By scaling the input data, we avoid the recomputation of the pose database for a different model.

Fig. 5.14 Experimental results with a different person (ToF data from a PMD camera)

5.5.5 Limitations

In the proposed framework, we rely on certain model assumptions in several stages of the framework. For example, we use a rigged surface mesh that is assumed to fit the respective actor to be tracked. Therefore, we cannot directly track persons with substantially different body proportions than the ones reflected by the surface mesh. However, as shown in [54], the depth input can be used to estimate the body shape of the actual person. First experiments have shown that one can use the same tracking pipeline after applying a preprocessing step where the pose database is retargeted to correspond to the estimated body shape.

A second limitation arises in situations where only parts of the actor are visible in the field of view of the depth camera. Two assumptions within our framework lead to false pose estimates in these situations. Firstly, in the local optimization component, correspondences between the mesh and the depth data for all body parts of the mesh are established. If some limbs are not visible in the depth data, then the correspondences will inherently be semantically incorrect. Secondly, the geodesic extrema will not correspond to the limbs anymore and retrieved database poses can no longer stabilize the pose estimation. Therefore, the full body of the actor should always be visible in the depth data.

Another problematic situation can occur when the end effectors are not revealed for a longer period of time. Although we run two pose estimation components in parallel, each component in isolation does not give satisfying pose estimates as shown in the accompanying video—it is the combination that facilitates stable and accurate results. Therefore, if one of the components fails for an extended period of time, the results might become unstable. For example, if the end effectors are not revealed by the geodesic extrema for many successive frames, our algorithm continues to track using only local optimization. Then, fast motions lead to unstable pose estimation results, which are resolved as soon as the end effectors are detected again. To overcome this limitation, additional techniques for detecting end effectors could be employed. For example, a fast method for detecting body parts similar to [48] could be used to identify the end effectors and supplement the geodesic extrema detections.

Finally, we expect the user to face the camera and rotate the body only within a typical range for interaction ($\pm 45°$). We make use of this assumption in the normalization step in Sect. 5.3.4. By normalizing the depth data with respect to the estimated viewing direction, we can use a comparatively small pose database that contains each pose only in one normalized orientation. However, with our proposed method, the estimates for the viewing direction become unstable once the user leaves the admissible range of rotations. Since the database lookup component relies on a correct normalization of the input data, the retrieved pose hypotheses will not reflect the true pose in such cases. Another problem with strong rotations of the body is that then limbs are more likely hidden behind the body. To meliorate pose estimates in these situations, one could employ a dynamic model for simulating hidden limbs.

5.6 Conclusions

In this chapter, we introduced a combined generative and discriminative framework that facilitates robust as well as efficient full-body pose estimation from noisy depth-image streams. As one main ingredient, we described an efficient algorithm for computing robust and characteristic features based on geodesic extrema. These extracted geodesic extrema are used as query to retrieve semantically meaningful pose candidates from a 3D pose database, where no a-priori semantic labels of the extrema are necessary. Finally, a stable fusion of local optimization and global database lookup is achieved with a novel sparse distance measure that also accounts for the importance of the limbs. For all components of the pipeline, we have described efficient algorithms that facilitate real-time performance of the whole framework. In our experiments we improved on the results of previous work, both in terms of efficiency and robustness of the algorithm, as well as complexity of the tracked motions. As for future work, we plan to integrate a dynamic model for achieving stable pose estimates also for $360°$-rotations and for occluded limbs. Furthermore, the fast run time of our method is one main ingredient that could spur further research for capturing several interacting people. Finally, we aim to integrate a method for automatically estimating the surface mesh of the person from depth data only.

Acknowledgements This work was supported by the German Research Foundation (DFG CL 64/5-1) and by the Intel Visual Computing Institute. Meinard Müller has been funded by the Cluster of Excellence on Multimodal Computing and Interaction (MMCI) and is now with the University of Bonn.

References

1. Azad, P., Asfour, T., Dillmann, R.: Robust real-time stereo-based markerless human motion capture. In: IEEE/RAS International Conference on Humanoid Robots, pp. 700–707 (2008)

2. Baak, A., Müller, M., Bharaj, G., Seidel, H.P., Theobalt, C.: Accompanied video to [3]. http://www.youtube.com/watch?v=QWNn01FWUkk (2011)
3. Baak, A., Müller, M., Bharaj, G., Seidel, H.P., Theobalt, C.: A data-driven approach for real-time full body pose reconstruction from a depth camera. In: IEEE International Conference on Computer Vision, pp. 1092–1099 (2011)
4. Baak, A., Rosenhahn, B., Müller, M., Seidel, H.P.: Stabilizing motion tracking using retrieved motion priors. In: IEEE International Conference on Computer Vision, pp. 1428–1435 (2009)
5. Bălan, A.O., Sigal, L., Black, M.J., Davis, J.E., Haussecker, H.W.: Detailed human shape and pose from images. In: IEEE Conference on Computer Vision and Pattern Recognition (2007)
6. Besl, P.J., McKay, N.D.: A method for registration of 3-D shapes. IEEE Trans. Pattern Anal. Mach. Intell. **14**(2), 239–256 (1992)
7. Bleiweiss, A., Kutliroff, E., Eilat, G.: Markerless motion capture using a single depth sensor. In: SIGGRAPH ASIA Sketches (2009)
8. Bo, L., Sminchisescu, C.: Twin gaussian processes for structured prediction. Int. J. Comput. Vis. **87**(1–2), 28–52 (2010)
9. Bregler, C., Malik, J., Pullen, K.: Twist based acquisition and tracking of animal and human kinematics. Int. J. Comput. Vis. **56**(3), 179–194 (2004)
10. Brubaker, M.A., Fleet, D.J., Hertzmann, A.: Physics-based person tracking using the anthropomorphic walker. Int. J. Comput. Vis. **87**, 140–155 (2010)
11. Cormen, T.H., Stein, C., Leiserson, C.E., Rivest, R.L.: Introduction to Algorithms. MIT Press, Cambridge (2001)
12. Demirdjian, D., Taycher, L., Shakhnarovich, G., Graumanand, K., Darrell, T.: Avoiding the streetlight effect: tracking by exploring likelihood modes. In: IEEE Conference on Computer Vision and Pattern Recognition, pp. 357–364 (2005)
13. Deutscher, J., Reid, I.: Articulated body motion capture by stochastic search. Int. J. Comput. Vis. **61**(2), 185–205 (2005)
14. Fossati, A., Dimitrijevic, M., Lepetit, V., Fua, P.: From canonical poses to 3D motion capture using a single camera. IEEE Trans. Pattern Anal. Mach. Intell. **32**(7), 1165–1181 (2010)
15. Friborg, R., Hauberg, S., Erleben, K.: GPU accelerated likelihoods for stereo-based articulated tracking. In: European Conference on Computer Vision—Workshop on Computer Vision on GPUs (2010)
16. Gall, J., Fossati, A., van Gool, L.: Functional categorization of objects using real-time markerless motion capture. In: IEEE Conference on Computer Vision and Pattern Recognition, pp. 1969–1976 (2011)
17. Gall, J., Stoll, C., de Aguiar, E., Theobalt, C., Rosenhahn, B., Seidel, H.P.: Motion capture using joint skeleton tracking and surface estimation. In: IEEE Conference on Computer Vision and Pattern Recognition, pp. 1746–1753 (2009)
18. Ganapathi, V., Plagemann, C., Thrun, S., Koller, D.: Real time motion capture using a single time-of-flight camera. In: IEEE Conference on Computer Vision and Pattern Recognition (CVPR) (2010)
19. Girshick, R.B., Shotton, A., Kohli, P., Criminisi, A., Fitzgibbon, A.: Efficient regression of general-activity human poses from depth images. In: IEEE International Conference on Computer Vision, pp. 415–422 (2011)
20. Grest, D., Krüger, V., Koch, R.: Single view motion tracking by depth and silhouette information. In: Proceedings of the Scandinavian Conference on Image Analysis, pp. 719–729. Springer, Berlin (2007)
21. Guan, P., Weiss, A., Bălan, A.O., Black, M.J.: Estimating human shape and pose from a single image. In: IEEE International Conference on Computer Vision, pp. 1381–1388 (2009)
22. Hasler, N., Ackermann, H., Rosenhahn, B., Thormählen, T., Seidel, H.P.: Multilinear pose and body shape estimation of dressed subjects from image sets. In: IEEE Conference on Computer Vision and Pattern Recognition, pp. 1823–1830 (2010)
23. Heikkila, J., Silven, O.: A four-step camera calibration procedure with implicit image correction. In: IEEE Conference on Computer Vision and Pattern Recognition, pp. 1106–1112 (1997)

24. Knoop, S., Vacek, S., Dillmann, R.: Fusion of 2D and 3D sensor data for articulated body tracking. Robot. Auton. Syst. **57**(3), 321–329 (2009)
25. Kolb, A., Barth, E., Koch, R., Larsen, R.: Time-of-flight sensors in computer graphics. Comput. Graph. Forum **29**(1), 141–159 (2010)
26. Lewis, J.P., Cordner, M., Fong, N.: Pose space deformation: a unified approach to shape interpolation and skeleton-driven deformation. In: Proceedings of the Annual Conference on Computer Graphics and Interactive Techniques SIGGRAPH, pp. 165–172. ACM/Addison-Wesley, New York/Reading (2000)
27. Lindner, M., Schiller, I., Kolb, A., Koch, R.: Time-of-flight sensor calibration for accurate range sensing. Comput. Vis. Image Underst. **114**(12), 1318–1328 (2010). Special issue on Time-of-Flight Camera Based Computer Vision
28. López-Méndez, A., Alcoverro, M., Pardàs, M., Casas, J.R.: Real-time upper body tracking with online initialization using a range sensor. In: International Conference on Computer Vision Workshops, pp. 391–398 (2011)
29. MATLAB camera calibration toolbox. http://www.vision.caltech.edu/bouguetj/calib_doc (2012)
30. Microsoft: Kinect SDK beta. http://www.microsoft.com/en-us/kinectforwindows (2012)
31. Moeslund, T.B., Hilton, A., Krüger, V.: A survey of advances in vision-based human motion capture and analysis. Comput. Vis. Image Underst. **104**(2), 90–126 (2006)
32. Murray, R.M., Li, Z., Sastry, S.S.: A Mathematical Introduction to Robotic Manipulation. CRC Press, Boca Raton (1994)
33. Okada, R., Soatto, S.: Relevant feature selection for human pose estimation and localization in cluttered images. In: Proceedings of the European Conference on Computer Vision, pp. 434–445 (2008)
34. Okada, R., Stenger, B.: A single camera motion capture system for human–computer interaction. IEICE Trans. Inf. Syst. **E91-D**, 1855–1862 (2008)
35. Pekelny, Y., Gotsman, C.: Articulated object reconstruction and markerless motion capture from depth video. Comput. Graph. Forum **27**(2), 399–408 (2008)
36. Plagemann, C., Ganapathi, V., Koller, D., Thrun, S.: Realtime identification and localization of body parts from depth images. In: IEEE International Conference on Robotics and Automation (2010)
37. Poppe, R.: A survey on vision-based human action recognition. Image Vis. Comput. **28**(6), 976–990 (2010)
38. Primesense: Primesense NITE middleware. http://www.primesense.com (2012)
39. Romero, J., Kjellström, H., Kragic, D.: Hands in action: real-time 3D reconstruction of hands in interaction with objects. In: IEEE International Conference on Robotics and Automation, pp. 458–463 (2010)
40. Rosales, R., Sclaroff, S.: Inferring body pose without tracking body parts. In: IEEE Conference on Computer Vision and Pattern Recognition, vol. 2, pp. 721–727 (2000)
41. Rosales, R., Sclaroff, S.: Combining generative and discriminative models in a framework for articulated pose estimation. Int. J. Comput. Vis. **67**, 251–276 (2006)
42. Rosenhahn, B., Schmaltz, C., Brox, T., Weickert, J., Cremers, D., Seidel, H.P.: Markerless motion capture of man–machine interaction. In: IEEE Conference on Computer Vision and Pattern Recognition (2008)
43. Salzmann, M., Urtasun, R.: Combining discriminative and generative methods for 3D deformable surface and articulated pose reconstruction. In: IEEE Conference on Computer Vision and Pattern Recognition (2010)
44. Schwarz, L.A., Mateus, D., Castañeda, V., Navab, N.: Manifold learning for ToF-based human body tracking and activity recognition. In: British Machine Vision Conference (2010)
45. Schwarz, L., Mkhytaryan, A., Mateus, D., Navab, N.: Estimating human 3D pose from time-of-flight images based on geodesic distances and optical flow. In: IEEE Conference on Automatic Face and Gesture Recognition (2011)
46. Shakhnarovich, G., Viola, P., Darrell, T.: Fast pose estimation with parameter-sensitive hashing. In: International Conference on Computer Vision, pp. 750–757 (2003)

47. Shapiro, L.G., Stockman, G.C.: Computer Vision. Prentice Hall, New York (2002)
48. Shotton, J., Fitzgibbon, A., Cook, M., Sharp, T., Finocchio, M., Moore, R., Kipman, A., Blake, A.: Real-time human pose recognition in parts from a single depth image. In: IEEE Conference on Computer Vision and Pattern Recognition (2011)
49. Siddiqui, M., Medioni, G.: Human pose estimation from a single view point, real-time range sensor. In: Computer Vision and Pattern Recognition Workshops (2010)
50. Sigal, L., Bălan, A.O., Black, M.J.: Combined discriminative and generative articulated pose and non-rigid shape estimation. In: Advances in Neural Information Processing Systems, pp. 1337–1344 (2008)
51. Stoll, C., Hasler, N., Gall, J., Seidel, H.P., Theobalt, C.: Fast articulated motion tracking using a sums of gaussians body model. In: International Conference on Computer Vision, pp. 951–958 (2011)
52. Wang, R.Y., Popovic, J.: Real-time hand-tracking with a color glove. ACM Trans. Graph. **28**(3) (2009)
53. Wei, X., Chai, J.: Videomocap: modeling physically realistic human motion from monocular video sequences. ACM Trans. Graph. **29**(4), 42:1–42:10 (2010)
54. Weiss, A., Hirshberg, D., Black, M.J.: Home 3D body scans from noisy image and range data. In: IEEE International Conference on Computer Vision, pp. 1951–1958 (2011)
55. Ye, M., Wang, X., Yang, R., Ren, L., Pollefeys, M.: Accurate 3D pose estimation from a single depth image. In: International Conference on Computer Vision, pp. 731–738 (2011)
56. Zhu, Y., Dariush, B., Fujimura, K.: Controlled human pose estimation from depth image streams. In: Computer Vision and Pattern Recognition Workshops (2008)
57. Zhu, Y., Dariush, B., Fujimura, K.: Kinematic self retargeting: a framework for human pose estimation. Comput. Vis. Image Underst. **114**(12), 1362–1375 (2010). Special issue on Time-of-Flight Camera Based Computer Vision

Chapter 6
Home 3D Body Scans from a Single Kinect

Alexander Weiss, David Hirshberg, and Michael J. Black

Abstract The 3D shape of the human body is useful for applications in fitness, games, and apparel. Accurate body scanners, however, are expensive, limiting the availability of 3D body models. Although there has been a great deal of interest recently in the use of active depth sensing cameras, such as the Microsoft Kinect, for human pose tracking, little has been said about the related problem of human shape estimation. We present a method for human shape reconstruction from noisy monocular image and range data using a single inexpensive commodity sensor. The approach combines low-resolution image silhouettes with coarse range data to estimate a parametric model of the body. Accurate 3D shape estimates are obtained by combining multiple monocular views of a person moving in front of the sensor. To cope with varying body pose, we use a SCAPE body model which factors 3D body shape and pose variations. This enables the estimation of a single consistent shape, while allowing pose to vary. Additionally, we describe a novel method to minimize the distance between the projected 3D body contour and the image silhouette that uses analytic derivatives of the objective function. We use a simple method to estimate standard body measurements from the recovered SCAPE model and show that the accuracy of our method is competitive with commercial body scanning systems costing orders of magnitude more.

A. Weiss (✉)
Brown University, Providence, RI, USA
e-mail: aweiss@cs.brown.edu

D. Hirshberg · M.J. Black
Max Planck Inst. for Intelligent Systems, Tübingen, Germany

D. Hirshberg
e-mail: david.hirshberg@is.mpg.de

M.J. Black
e-mail: black@tue.mpg.de

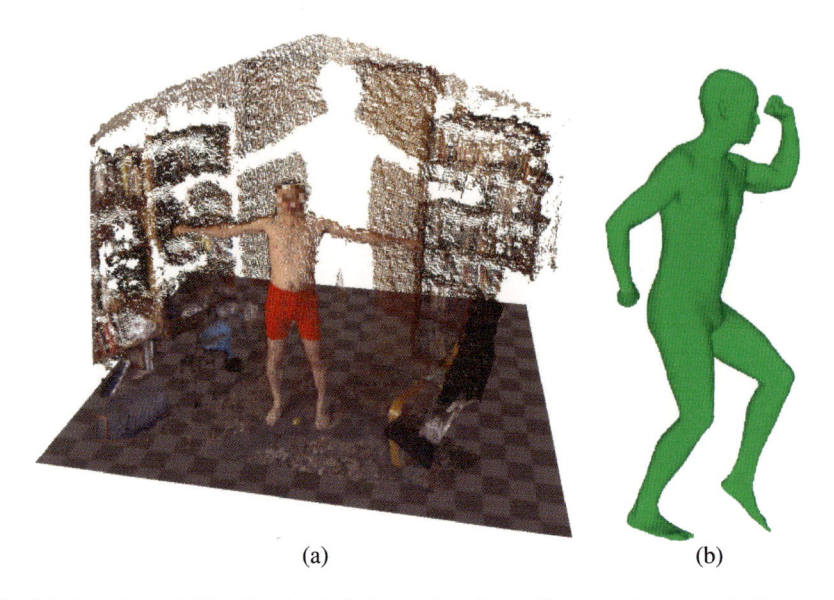

Fig. 6.1 Overview. (**a**) 3D point cloud of a human in a cluttered home environment. (**b**) Recovered shape transformed into a new pose

6.1 Introduction

For many applications an accurate 3D model of the human body is needed. The standard approach involves scanning the body using a commercial system such as a laser range scanner or special-purpose structured light system. Several such body scanners exist, costing anywhere from $35,000 to $500,000. The size and cost of such scanners limit the applications for 3D body models. Many computer vision solutions suffer the same problems and require calibrated multi-camera capture systems. Here we describe a solution that produces accurate body scans using consumer hardware that can work in a person's living room (Fig. 6.1). This opens the door to a wide range of new applications.

Recently there have been several approaches to capturing 3D body shape from a monocular image [13, 16, 17, 29], a small number of synchronized camera images [4], or from several unsynchronized cameras [14]. As requiring multiple cameras or synchronization would limit many interesting applications, we restrict our attention to the monocular case, where the common approach is to segment the person from the background and to estimate the 3D shape of the body such that the silhouette of the body matches the image silhouette. The wide variation in body shape, the articulated nature of the body, and self occlusions in a single view, however, all limit the usefulness of image silhouettes alone. To cope with these issues we combine image silhouettes with coarse monocular range data captured by a single Microsoft Kinect sensor [21].

Although the Kinect sensor itself, an IR structured light system, is not a particularly new idea, its low cost and mass distribution has the potential to bring depth

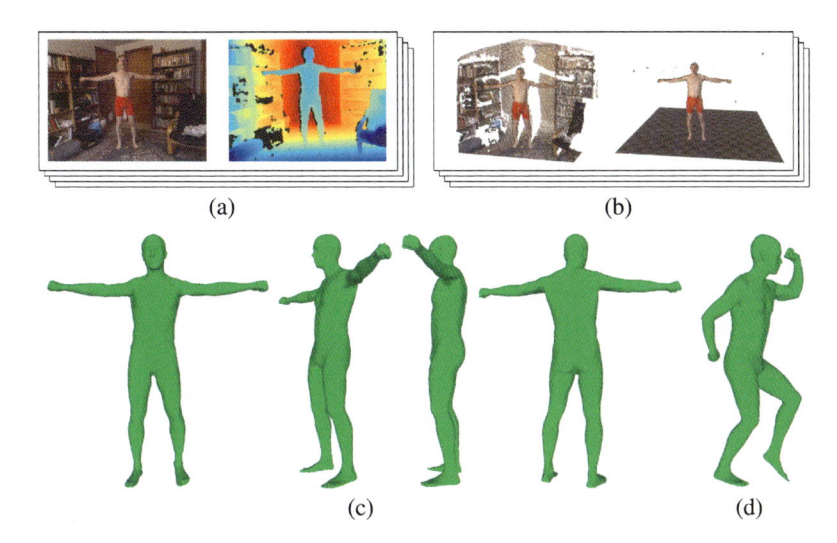

Fig. 6.2 Overview. (**a**) Four views of the body in different poses are captured from a single Kinect. (**b**) 3D point cloud and segmented 3D point cloud with ground plane for four frames (one shown). (**c**) Recovered pose and shape (4 frames). (**d**) Recovered shape reposed using the SCAPE model

sensing cameras to a level of ubiquity previously only enjoyed by visible light cameras. This makes the choice of a depth sensing camera reasonable for a much broader and more interesting range of applications then ever before.

The resolution and accuracy of the sensor are relatively poor and our key contribution is a method to accurately estimate human body pose and shape from a set of monocular low-resolution images with aligned but noisy depth information. To be scanned, a person moves in front of a single sensor to capture a sequence of monocular images and depth maps that show the body from multiple angles (Fig. 6.2). As the person moves, the body shape changes making rigid 3D alignment impossible. Such non-rigid motions make scanning the body different from scanning rigid scenes with a Kinect [22].

Rather than causing problems, changes in body pose can actually help us to isolate the person's intrinsic body shape if we model their shape in such a way that we can separate body shape from the articulated pose and posture which confounds it. Humans are often asymmetric, so a single view, which–even with depth information–leaves half the body unconstrained, is insufficient to our purposes. We are not seeking to solve a shape completion problem (as in [2]), where the unobserved side of the body is hallucinated, but to accurately recover the actual shape. Although our method will perform shape completion if it is given only a single view, we formulate it in terms of multiple frames sampled from a video sequence, showing the body from various directions. We solve for the pose in each frame and for a single common shape across all frames. To do so, we use the SCAPE model [2] which is a parametric 3D model that factors the complex non-rigid deformations induced by both pose and shape variation and is learned from a database of several thousand laser scans.

We estimate model parameters in a generative framework using an objective function that combines a silhouette overlap term, the difference between the observed range data and the depth predicted by our model, and an optional pose prior that favors similarity of poses between frames. The silhouette term uses a novel symmetric shape dissimilarity function that we locally minimize using a standard quasi-Newton method. Our silhouette formulation has significant advantages over previous methods as it allows the distance from the parametric model to the image silhouette to be explicitly differentiated, enabling accurate optimization of body shape and pose in a very high-dimensional space without resorting to ICP-based methods which are unstable for complex articulated and non-rigid objects under projection.

In summary our contributions are: (1) a system for body scanning at home; (2) the combination of multiple low-resolution, noisy, monocular views (range and/or silhouettes) to estimate a consistent 3D body shape with varying pose; (3) a new method for matching 3D models to silhouettes using an objective function that is correspondence-free, bidirectional, and can be optimized with standard methods requiring derivatives of the objective function; (4) a quantitative comparison with a commercial state-of-the-art solution for scanning and measuring the body.

6.2 Related Work

The Microsoft Kinect provides one of the first inexpensive and widely available range sensors. As discussed in the first chapter of this part of the book, existing commercial and research systems solve the problem of rough body pose estimation from this type of sensor data [10, 25] but, to date, there are no methods for accurate body shape estimation from a single Kinect.

Tong et al. [28] estimate body shape using multiple Kinect cameras. They let the body rotate on a platform and capture multiple images. To deal with body sway and small pose variations, they have a non-rigid alignment method. Because they use multiple Kinects and require calibration and a dedicated capture space, their method is more like a traditional body scanner, and is not applicable to the home scanning scenario we consider.

To estimate body shape accurately from a single Kinect, we must deal with data that are monocular, low-resolution, and noisy. Anguelov et al. [2] describe a partial solution. They show that, given a high resolution range image from a single view, the SCAPE model can be fit to the observed data. The observed data constrain the full 3D shape, enabling to hallucinate unseen parts of the body (shape completion). For our purposes, this is not sufficient since we seek an accurate model of the full body shape. We must therefore combine multiple views of the person and several low-resolution scans to obtain an accurate representation.

If the person remained rigid, or we used multiple synchronized sensors, then it would be straightforward to rigidly align multiple views to recover a composite 3D body [22]. In our case, people move relative to a single sensor and, even if they try to maintain the same pose, there will be non-rigid variations in their shape. To cope with this we need to integrate the consistent 3D body shape information across views and poses. To do so we use the SCAPE model [2] which factors body shape and pose information.

Balan and Black [5] use a similar idea to solve for body shape under clothing. They capture dressed people in multiple poses with a multi-camera system and a green-screen background. Like us, they assume that body shape is consistent across pose variations and combine information from multiple poses to estimate body shape. Our work is different in that we use monocular data. Every time instant captures the person in a different pose, so we never see the same pose from multiple views.

There have been several recent methods that estimate body shape from monocular images. For example, image contours have been used in several graphics applications [17, 29] where the metric accuracy of the body shape is not important. The recovered shapes are used for animation purposes to change the shape of people in images or videos. To achieve metrically accurate results, more information is required. Guan et al. [13] show that silhouettes alone are not sufficient for this task and introduce two innovations. First they provide a height- and weight-constrained subspace of body shape variation to constrain the problem. Second, and more importantly, they integrate a shape from shading cue into the body shape optimization (similar to [20]). The shading cue gives information about the shape inside the body contour and they show that adding this improves the recovered shape accuracy.

Shading is a relatively weak cue and if range data are available, it can provide more information about shape. In early work on body shape estimation, Plänckers and Fua [24] use depth information from a stereo camera to estimate rough body shape in a frontal view. Grest et al. [12] fit parameters of a simplified body model to silhouettes and then use these parameters to improve pose tracking from range data.

Single frame, monocular methods, whether using silhouettes, shading, depth imagery, or other cues, suffer from the problem of occlusion, where the method is forced to hallucinate unobserved surfaces. We describe a method for combining multiple frames from a single monocular sensor to obtain a pose estimate for each frame and a combined, coherent pose-independent body shape from all frames. A Kinect is used to image the body from several directions (Sect. 6.3) in potentially widely varying poses and a SCAPE model is fit to the data under the constraint that all frames, though they may have varying poses, have the same intrinsic body shape (Sect. 6.4). In a preliminary study, this estimate of body shape is then used to predict measurements with an accuracy that is competitive with a state of the art, commercial laser scan measurement system (Sect. 6.5).

6.3 Sensor and Preprocessing

The Microsoft Kinect sensor consists of an IR camera, an RGB camera, and an IR projector that casts a fixed speckle pattern. Conversion of the pattern, as seen by the IR camera, to a depth map happens on the device. It has a USB interface and images can be captured using one of several libraries. We use libfreenect, a library developed by the OpenKinect project [23], but other options include OpenNI and the Microsoft Kinect for Windows SDK, both of which provide additional features including segmentation and ground plane estimation as well as skeleton tracking. The libfreenect library provides access to both the depth map and the raw IR video, as well as to the RGB video and data from a built in accelerometer. The video streams are VGA resolution and both the RGB and IR (either raw or the depth map) can be captured together at 30 fps.

Intrinsic Calibration Intrinsic calibration of the RGB camera is carried out with a checkerboard and standard calibration techniques [6]. To calibrate the IR camera we cover the projector so that the calibration grid is not corrupted by the projected pattern; otherwise calibration is identical to that of the RGB camera. We correct for a known offset between the raw IR image and the depth map; see [19]. As the core of our method is a process of synthesizing candidate 3D bodies and testing how well they match the data from the sensor, we need this calibration to project candidate bodies into the depth image scene.

Stereo Calibration Stereo calibration between the depth and RGB cameras can be achieved with standard stereo calibration methods [6]. We use this only for visualization to map the color image onto the point cloud.

Depth Calibration The Kinect reports depth discretized into 2047 levels, with a final value reserved to mark pixels for which no depth can be calculated. These discrete levels are not uniformly distributed, but are much denser close to the device. We calibrate the depth by lining up a planar target parallel to the Kinect such that the depth values are as uniform as possible across its surface; the distance is then measured and the process repeated with depths ranging from 0.5 m to 3 m in 0.1 m increments. A curve of the form: $d(x) = \frac{1}{ax+b}$ is fit to these data, yielding the distance $d(x)$ in meters given the discrete depth level x. The resulting depth maps can be visualized either as a range image or as a point cloud, see Fig. 6.2. It is important to note that these are the distances projected onto the viewing vector of the camera, not distances from the camera center, that is, they are distances from a plane not from a point.

Ground Plane We obtain an estimate of the ground plane in the camera coordinate frame by robustly fitting a plane to the bottom of the point cloud, using the Kinect's on board accelerometer to initialize such that we locate the floor and not one of the walls.

Segmentation We segment the body from the surrounding environment using background subtraction on the depth map. Given a depth map D_{bg} taken without the subject present and a depth map D_f associated with a frame f, we take the foreground to be $D_{bg} - D_f > \epsilon$, where ϵ is a few mm. We then apply a morphological opening operation to remove small isolated false positives. Segmentations produced by the Microsoft Kinect for Windows SDK could be substituted here.

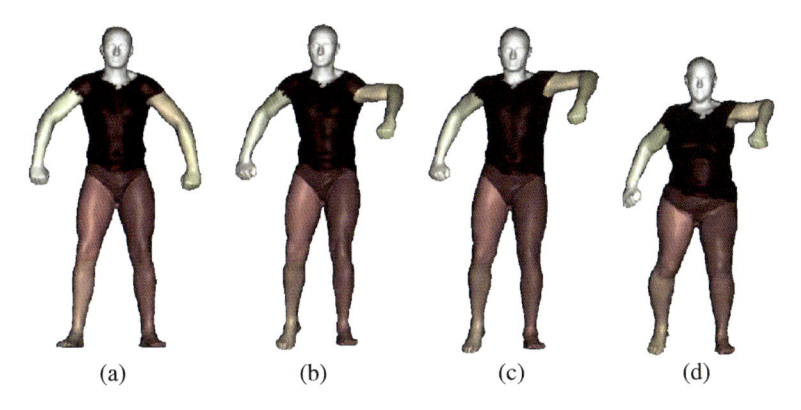

Fig. 6.3 SCAPE body model. (**a**) Template mesh. (**b**) With articulated rigid deformation applied. (**c**) With non-rigid pose deformation applied. (**d**) With body shape deformation applied. (Image credit: Alexandru Balan [3])

6.4 Body Model and Fitting

We model body shape such that we can estimate a single consistent body shape across multiple monocular frames while allowing pose to vary in each frame. Starting with a coarse initialization, we optimize an objective function that combines distance between foreground and model contours with depth error and an optional pose prior. These steps are described below.

6.4.1 SCAPE Body Model

In order to estimate a body shape that is invariant to pose, we need a model that accurately represents non-rigid shape deformations while factoring deformations caused by changes in intrinsic shape (height, weight, body type, etc.) from deformations caused by changes in pose. We use a SCAPE model, which was originally described by Anguelov et al. [2]. It is a data-driven graphics model of the human body that allows new body shapes to be synthesized with pose and intrinsic body shape independently controlled. The model is learned offline from high resolution whole body laser scans and captures the statistics of human shape variation both as an individual changes pose and intrinsically across the population.

The SCAPE model is learned from two datasets of laser scans. The first, the "pose dataset", consists of many scans of one individual in widely varying poses. The second, the "shape dataset", consists of many scans of different individuals all the same pose. In our case the pose dataset consists of approximately 70 scans and the shape dataset of approximately 1000 scans for each gender. We construct separate SCAPE models for each gender as we find a combined shape space to be distinctly multi-modal. A template mesh (Fig. 6.3(a)) is non-rigidly registered with each scan in both datasets to give a consistent topology.

Pose, in our SCAPE model, is puppeteered with a kinematic tree of 15 body parts with 3 degrees of freedom between each part; the pose parameter vector θ is the concatenation of the Rodrigues vectors for all 15 parts with a global 3D translation. Synthesis of a body in a new pose involves first rigidly rotating each part of the template (Fig. 6.3(b)) and then applying a non-rigid deformation to each triangle which both corrects collapses at the joints caused by the rigid rotation and provides muscle bulging and other pose dependent changes in body shape (Fig. 6.3(c)). The non-rigid deformation of each triangle is a linear function of the pose of nearby joints. This function is estimated using the registered pose dataset.

When subjects were scanned for the shape dataset they were directed to take a particular pose, but humans are not good at exactly replicating a pose, so there is significant pose variation in the shape dataset. Because of this, if we were simply to run Principle Component Analysis (PCA) over the registered shape dataset, we would have pose artifacts in the shape space. To mitigate this effect, the pose model is learned first and used to pose normalize the registered shape dataset, then the shape space is learned by PCA from the pose normalized, registered shape dataset. The intrinsic body shape parameter vector β is the coefficients of the 60 PCA basis vectors accounting for the most variance (Fig. 6.3(d)).

In order to allow the shape change due to pose and the shape change due to intrinsic body shape to be composed, the SCAPE model operates on triangle deformations rather than directly on the triangles [27]. This means that each triangle is effectively rotated, scaled, and sheared in place, giving inconsistent locations for vertices shared by triangles. The final consistent mesh is reconstructed from this inconsistent mesh by least squares with the global 3D translation applied as a constraint to make the problem well posed. For more details, see [2].

We use the method described in [13] to constrain body shape to a subspace that is roughly orthogonal to height variation, allowing us to freely optimize within the subspace of bodies with the subject's reported height. Our model has 48 pose parameters per frame and 60 shape parameters (i.e. 252 parameters for 4 frames).

6.4.2 Pose Initialization

As Shotton et al. [25] have demonstrated, the Kinect can be used to obtain coarse pose estimates. In contrast, we are focused on the problem of shape estimation. To this end, we assume a gross initial pose estimate; a complete, end to end system would be obtained by combining the method we describe here with an existing coarse pose tracking algorithm [10, 25]. The subject provides his or her height and the initial body shape is taken to be the average shape for the subject's height and gender [13]; gender could be automatically detected as described in [5]. We initialize the body model in the scene using the ground plane and the centroid of the point cloud. Examples of initializations for three trials can be seen in Fig. 6.5.

6.4.3 Depth Objective

For a body model represented as a triangulated 3D mesh with pose parameters θ and shape parameters β, we associate a triangle $t_x(\theta, \beta)$ with every pixel x in the overlap between the model silhouette $S(\theta, \beta)$ and observed silhouette $\tilde{S}$ by finding the front most triangle that projects into x. Let $U(\theta, \beta) = \{(x_1, t_{x_1}(\theta, \beta)), \ldots\}$ for all x in $S(\theta, \beta) \cap \tilde{S}$. For each pixel we have the observed depth $\tilde{D}_x$, and for the corresponding triangle t we find the depth, $D_t(\theta, \beta)$, along a ray through the pixel center to the plane of the triangle. Taking ρ to be a robust error function (here, Geman-McClure [11]), our depth objective is

$$E_d(\theta, \beta; \tilde{D}, U) = \frac{1}{|U|} \sum_{(x,t) \in U} \rho\big(D_t(\theta, \beta) - \tilde{D}_x\big). \tag{6.1}$$

6.4.4 Silhouette Objective

Methods for fitting 3D models to silhouettes usually approximate one of these two integrals

$$\int_{\mathbf{x} \in A} \min_{\mathbf{y} \in B} \rho(\|\mathbf{x} - \mathbf{y}\|) \tag{6.2}$$

$$\int_{\mathbf{x} \in \partial A} \min_{\mathbf{y} \in \partial B} \rho(\|\mathbf{x} - \mathbf{y}\|). \tag{6.3}$$

Here A and B are silhouettes, ∂A and ∂B are their boundaries, and ρ is a non-decreasing function (e.g. Geman-McClure [11]). Frequently, approximations to Eq. 6.2 use a discrete distance map [4, 26] and approximations to Eq. 6.3 use a discrete distance map or a correspondence-based scheme like ICP [8, 14]. The integrand of the latter is illustrated in Fig. 6.4. Integrals like these are often used to define shape distances [7], but are not widely used with parametric 3D models under projection.

Accurately fitting a body to the image evidence benefits from bi-directional shape distance functions [26] that compute the distance from the model to the image contour and vice versa. Minimizing the distance from the image to the model ensures that all image measurements are explained while minimizing the distance from the model to the image ensures that visible body parts are entirely explained by image evidence. Modeling the distance from the model to the image is straightforward using the Euclidean distance transform to approximate the distance function to the image silhouette, as this does not change during optimization. Modeling the distance from image to the model is more difficult because the distance function to the model's silhouette changes with the parameters being optimized; this makes an explicit computation of the derivatives difficult.

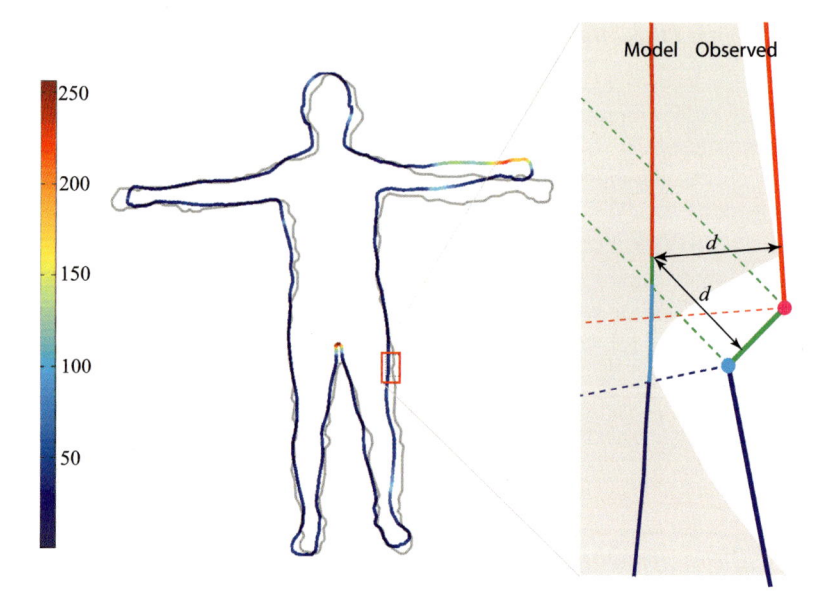

Fig. 6.4 Silhouette distance. *On the left*, the silhouette of the body model is colored by squared distance to the gray observed silhouette. *On the right*, the implicit point and line correspondence on an arc of the left leg's silhouette is shown by coloring the arc to match the colors of points and lines on the observed silhouette. The squared distance function along this arc as a function of the y-coordinate is overlaid in *gray* to illustrate the effects of changes in correspondence. *Colored dashed lines* are used to indicate the boundary of the region where a segment's point-line distance applies

Consequently, many methods that use distance maps either use uni-directional distance, from model silhouette to static, observed silhouette [18, 26] or use a derivative-free optimizer [4]. Problems with the uni-directional application of Eq. 6.2 have been discussed and addressed [26]. Similar problems arise with the use of Eq. 6.3 but are not often mentioned. The use of derivative-free methods for a high-dimensional problem like ours is impractical, so we seek a method admitting explicit computation of the derivative.

ICP methods are frequently used to minimize Eq. 6.3 for 2D to 2D and 3D to 3D shape registration problems. They can be used bidirectionally and optimization is straightforward because the average point-to-shape distance is bounded by the average distance between corresponding points, which is a smooth function of the vertices of both shapes. Under projection we lose this bound because points on the silhouette boundary no longer have a stable relationship to the 3D geometry. Without this, the use of ICP is problematic, especially with complex articulated and non-rigid objects.

If we have a set of correspondences between 3D model vertices on the silhouette boundary and points on the observed silhouette, as we minimize the average distance of the projected vertices to their corresponding 2D points, some vertices will disappear from the silhouette boundary and new vertices will appear. Since these newly visible vertices will not influence the objective function until we recompute correspondences, the optimizer may move them anywhere without penalty. When this happens, the parameters being optimized may jump away from low-error fixed points to a solution from which ICP cannot recover.

We address this problem with a well-behaved new formulation that uses implicit rather than explicit correspondences. We compute the line integral in Eq. 6.3 directly, replacing the explicit correspondences of ICP with the continuously changing ones implied by the min function. Symmetrizing this yields an objective function that is correspondence-free and bidirectional.

To compute this integral, we must know, for each point on the integration silhouette, the distance to the nearest point on the other (reference) silhouette. Each segment of the integration silhouette is broken up into pieces that are nearest to the same geometric primitive (vertex or line segment interior) in the reference silhouette. These breaks, illustrated in Fig. 6.4, occur in two circumstances: First, they can occur along lines emanating from a segment's vertices and perpendicular to the segment. These lines define the region where perpendicular distance to the segment is defined (dashed lines in Fig. 6.4). Second, these breaks can occur on linear or quadratic arcs where two points (quadratic), two segment interiors (linear), or a segment interior and a point (quadratic) are equidistant (arrows of equal distance d in Fig. 6.4).

The derivative of this integral is easily computed in terms of the derivative of the path of integration and the derivative of the integrand [9]. There is, however, a small problem. At the breaks the integrand is not differentiable with respect to the reference silhouette, as the distance functions to the two equidistant primitives vary independently. Nor is it differentiable with respect to the point of evaluation x, as variation in one direction is dictated by one primitive's distance function and variation in another will be dictated by the other's. If these breaks occur only at points, as they do for almost every pair of silhouettes, they do not matter. There are finitely many such breaks, and the value of the integrand at finitely many points, so long as it is bounded, does not effect the value of an integral. But if a segment on the integration silhouette lies along one of the arcs where two primitives are equidistant, the non-differentiability of the integrand is inherited by the integral. Despite this, in practice we optimize using a method intended for smooth functions and do not encounter problems.

De la Gorce et al. [20] use a similar integration-based approach in the context of articulated hand tracking with a generative model and formulate a differentiable objective function. Their objective focuses on a generative model of image appearance across the interior of the object. They compute a 2D integral, which allows them differentiability despite a 1D discontinuity along the occluding contour of the body. We could similarly compute a differentiable version of the area integral in Eq. 6.2, but it would require us to compute $\arg\min_{\mathbf{y} \in \tilde{S}} \|\mathbf{x} - \mathbf{y}\|$ inside a 2D region, which amounts, in our setting, to computing the Voronoi diagram for a set of line segments.

Our silhouette objective function is a symmetrized and scaled version of Eq. 6.3, averaging distance over each silhouette boundary to the other:

$$E_{\text{uni}}(A, B) = \frac{1}{|\partial A|} \int_{\mathbf{x} \in \partial A} \min_{\mathbf{y} \in \partial B} \rho(\|\mathbf{x} - \mathbf{y}\|) \tag{6.4}$$

$$E_s\big(S(\theta, \beta); \tilde{S}\big) = \frac{1}{2} E_{\text{uni}}\big(S(\theta, \beta), \tilde{S}\big) + \frac{1}{2} E_{\text{uni}}\big(\tilde{S}, S(\theta, \beta)\big) \tag{6.5}$$

where $S(\theta, \beta)$ is the silhouette of the model with pose parameters θ and shape parameters β and $\tilde{S}$ is the image silhouette.

6.4.5 Optimization

To estimate the pose parameters θ_f in each frame f (for clarity, let $\Theta = \{\theta_1, \theta_2, \ldots\}$ be the set of separate pose parameters for each frame) and the single consistent pose β for all frames, we alternately compute pixel-triangle correspondences $U(\theta_{f,i-1}, \beta_{i-1})$ for each frame f and new model parameters (Θ_i, β_i) by local minimization of

$$\Theta_i, \beta_i = \underset{\Theta, \beta}{\operatorname{argmin}} \, E(\Theta, \beta; \Theta_{i-1}, \beta_{i-1}) \tag{6.6}$$

where the combined error term E is

$$E(\Theta, \beta; \Theta_{i-1}, \beta_{i-1}) = \sum_f E_d\big(\theta_f, \beta; \tilde{D}_f, U(\theta_{f,i-1}, \beta_{i-1})\big)$$
$$+ \lambda_1 \sum_f E_s\big(S(\theta_f, \beta); \tilde{S}_f\big) + \lambda_2 E_{\text{pose}}(\Theta). \tag{6.7}$$

A simple pose prior, $E_{\text{pose}}(\Theta)$, penalizes variation in pose between frames (ignoring global rotation) and is used in cases where the subject is directed to stand in similar poses for each frame (e.g. Fig. 6.5). For local minimization, we use a symmetric rank 1 (SR1) trust region method with exact solution of the trust region subproblem.

6.5 Results

We scanned four subjects, having each stand in a T pose four times: facing the camera, in profile, facing away from the camera, and rotated 45°, halfway between frontal and profile. As demonstrated in Fig. 6.6, the choice of the four poses is relatively arbitrary; we found that more than four poses did not significantly improve the results and fewer made them worse.

Fitting results for three subjects are shown in Fig. 6.5. It is important to remember that these images are not multi-camera synchronous captures. Because these images

6 Home 3D Body Scans from a Single Kinect 111

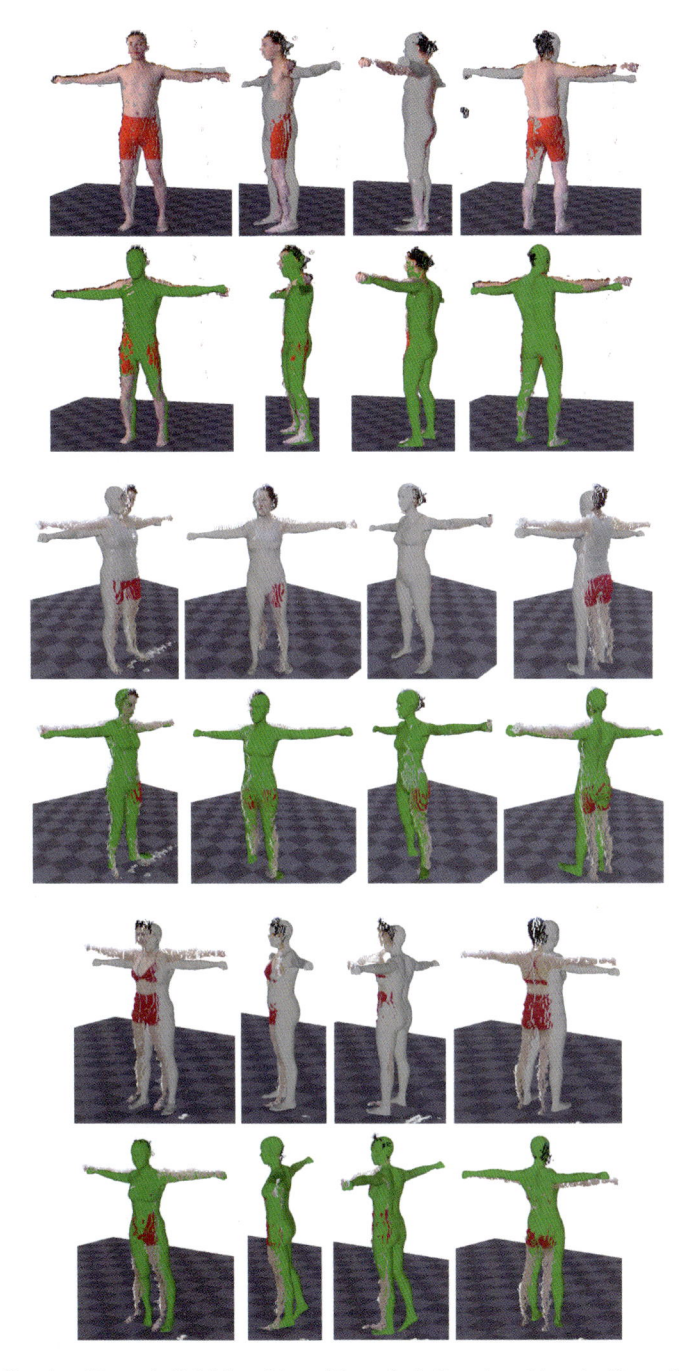

Fig. 6.5 Results. (*Rows 1–2*) Male subject. (*Rows 3–4*) Female subject 1. (*Rows 5–6*) Female subject 2. The *Grey mesh* is the initialization. The *Green mesh* shows the fitted result

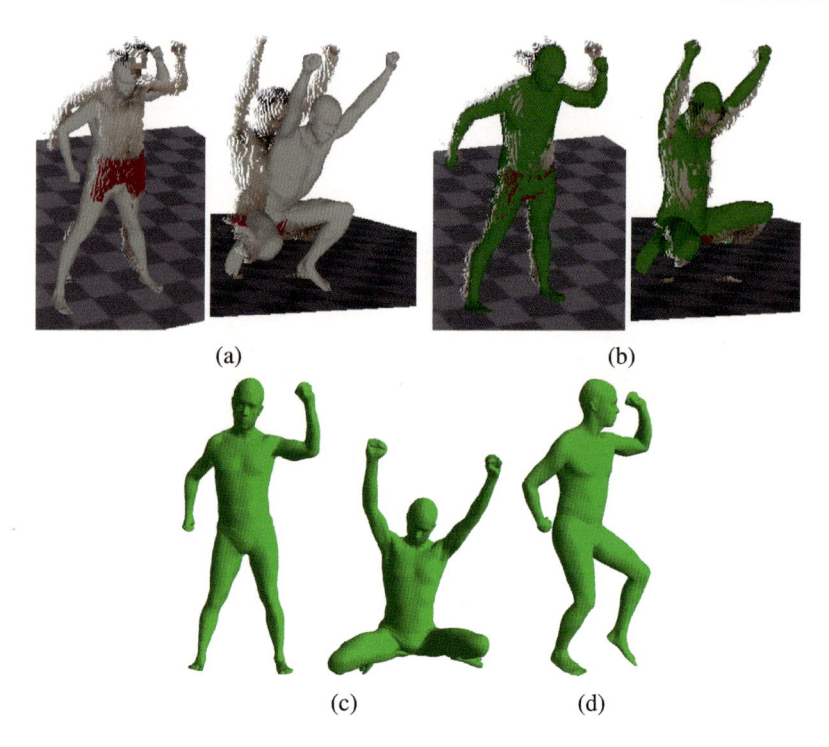

Fig. 6.6 Widely varying poses. (**a**) Initialization. (**b**, **c**) Result. (**d**) Result reposed into novel pose

are not captured simultaneously, and the subjects move from frame to frame, the pose cannot be assumed constant between frames. Consequently we let pose vary between frames and use a simple pose prior that penalizes frame-to-frame variation in the orientation of each body part independently. This helps keep the pose reasonable in cases like the third frame (profile view) for female subject 1, where the right leg is not visible from the camera and is thus otherwise unconstrained. The foot pose of female subject 1 shown here is problematic, with portions of the feet incorrectly segmented as background and a large region of floor nearby incorrectly segmented as foreground inducing incorrect ankle rotation. Despite that, the fit to the remainder of the body is quite good. With the coarse range and silhouette data used here, any individual view may not be very accurate, but the robust combination of body shape across views provides sufficient constraints to recover shape well.

Figure 6.6 shows a subject scanned in several widely varying poses and fit without the pose constancy prior to highlight the ability of the method to integrate shape across multiple disparate poses. The pose error in the second frame, where the lower legs are pulled tightly up to the upper legs, is due to a segmentation error; the lower legs were incorrectly segmented as background, so there was no image evidence to drive the lower legs to remain visible.

Optimization takes approximately 65 minutes per body. This may seem excessive but recall that the optimization involves estimating 252 parameters.

Fig. 6.7 Comparison to laser scan. (**a**) Laser scan. (**b**) SCAPE model fit to laser scan; pose and shape recovered. (**c**) Contour + depth fit to 4 views, reposed to match pose of laser scan of same subject. (**d**) Difference map showing areas of similarity (*blue*) and difference (*purple*) between (**b**) and (**c**) (scale in mm)

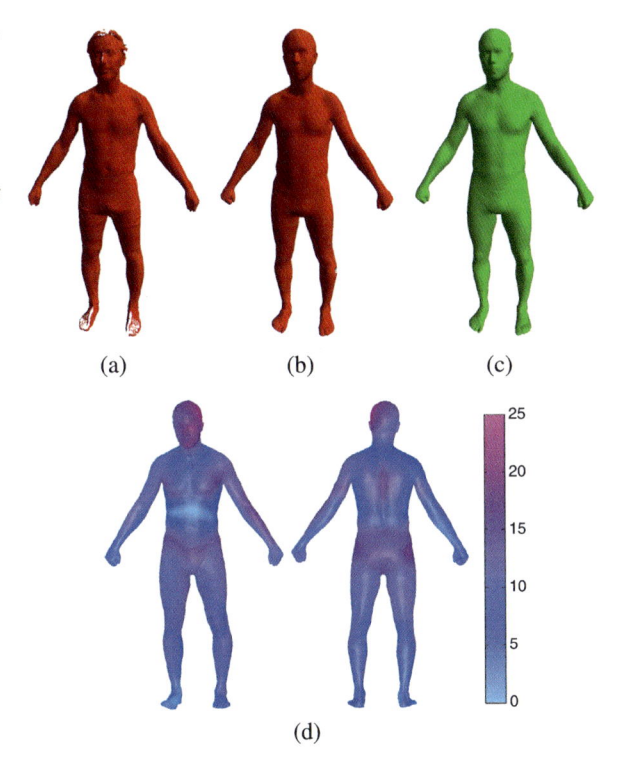

From Bodies to Measurements One of the reasons to fit a 3D body model is to extract standard measurements of the body (arm length, chest circumference, etc.) that are useful in many applications. Like Hasler et al. [15], we calculate measurements from shape parameters using a method that follows Allen et al. [1] in spirit, but is the inverse of the problem they describe. Allen et al. learn a linear function from a set of measurements to shape parameters, allowing them to synthesize new people with specified measurements. We take the same data–shape parameters and hand measurements for the several thousand subjects of the CAESAR dataset–and perform linear regression to learn a function from shape parameters to measurements (with the exception of weight, where we find it more accurate to regress from the shape parameters to the cube root of weight).

Accuracy Relative to Laser Scans We evaluate the metric accuracy of fitting body shape using just image contours and using both image contours and depth. To do so we captured reference scans of the subjects using a Vitus Smart XXL laser scanner (VITRONIC GmbH, Germany) (Fig. 6.7(a)). To test the accuracy of using the Kinect sensor versus a commercial laser scanner, we first fit the SCAPE model to the laser scans using a standard ICP method (Fig. 6.7(b)); we also fit to Kinect data as described above (Fig. 6.7(c)). This allows us to evaluate the accuracy of the fitting method and sensor data independent of the smoothing effect introduced by the SCAPE model which represents body shapes in a low-dimensional linear subspace.

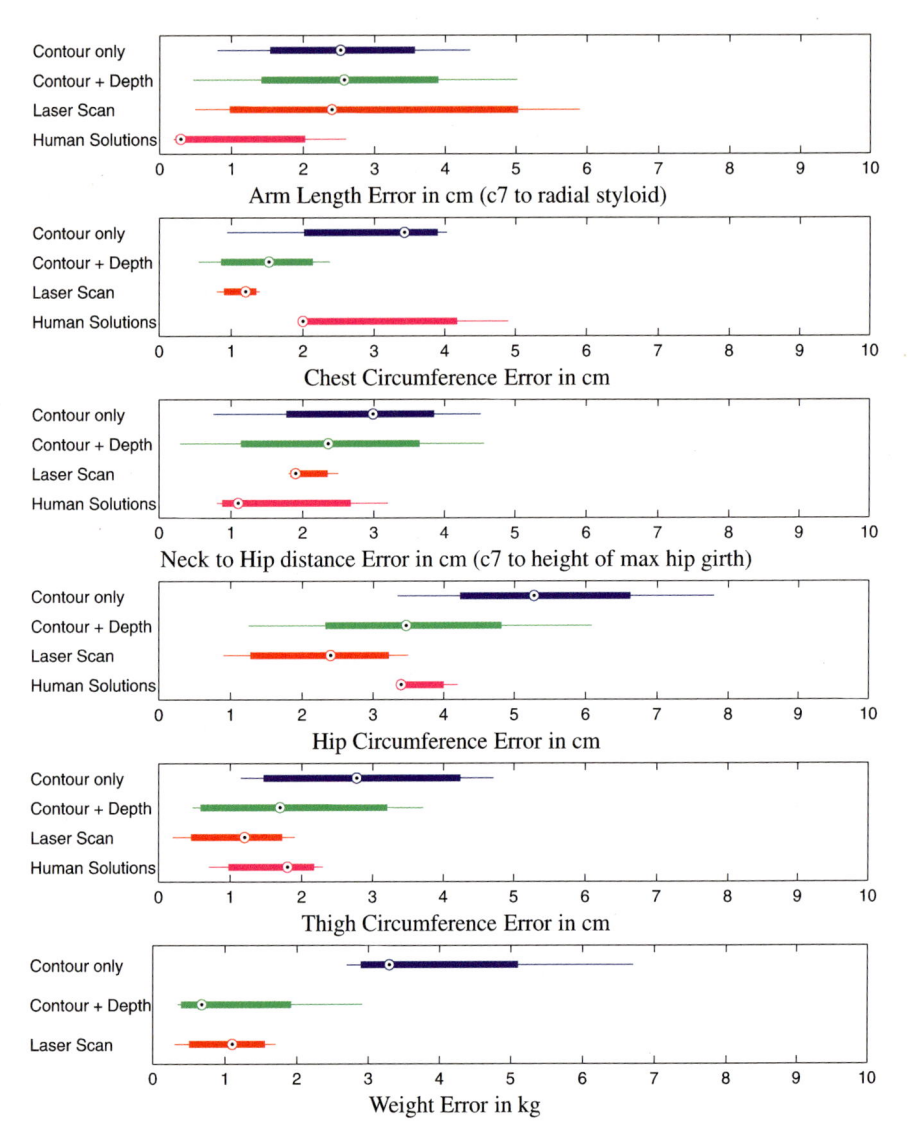

Fig. 6.8 Measurement accuracy. Error of measurements found by regression from fitted shape parameters using contour cost only (*blue*, 4 subjects), using contour and depth costs (*green*, 4 subjects), and of SCAPE fit to laser scan (*red*, 3 subjects), with respect to ground truth obtained via hand measurement. For comparison, we also show measurement error between hand measurement and measurements calculated from the laser scans by a commercial scan measurement system (Human Solutions Anthroscan) (*magenta*, 3 subjects)

The SCAPE fit to the laser scan represents a "best case scenario" since the data are high resolution and highly accurate. The difference between a model fit to laser data and Kinect data is illustrated in Fig. 6.7(d); the vertex to vertex distances are 0.53 mm (minimum), 22.23 mm (maximum), 10.17 (mean), 9.91 (median).

Fig. 6.9 With and without E_d. (**a**) Fit with contour and depth terms. (**b**) Fit with only contour term. (**c**) Same as (**b**) but seen from the camera, showing the quality of the contour match, despite the pose being wildly wrong

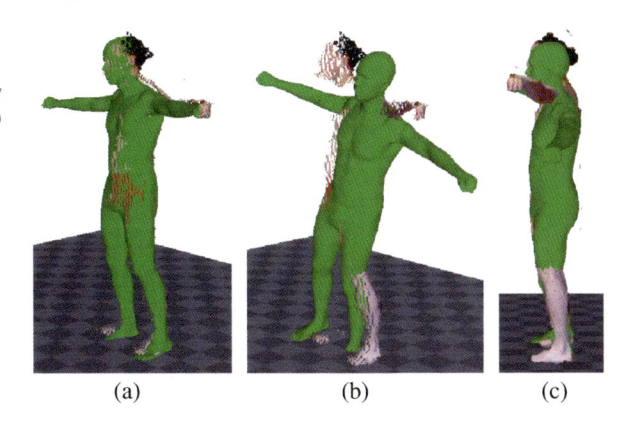

Linear Measurement Accuracy The second source of ground truth we use to evaluate accuracy is hand measurements, taken by a professional with both tailoring and anthropometric measurement experience. These are compared to measurements calculated from the optimized shape parameters using the linear predictors described above.

Figure 6.8 compares the measurement accuracy from SCAPE bodies fit to silhouettes alone, silhouettes and range, and laser data. We find that range and silhouettes together are more accurate than silhouettes alone. The reason for this is that both shape and pose are poorly constrained by a monocular silhouette (Fig. 6.9). The measurement accuracy using the Kinect-based fits is only slightly worse than with the high resolution full-body laser scans; median errors generally are within 1 cm of the laser scan measurements.

Additionally, we compare our accuracy with that of a commercially available laser scan measurement system, Human Solutions Anthroscan (Human Solutions GmbH, Germany). This system works on the raw laser scan and, consequently, factors out the effect of the SCAPE model. It is interesting to note that our inexpensive system is competitive and even outperforms the commercial system on all the circumference measurements.

6.6 Conclusions

Three-dimensional body scanning has so far had a limited range of applications due to the expense, complexity, and space requirements of existing scanning systems. All these systems are based on multiple calibrated cameras and structured light sources (including lasers). New scanners, constructed from multiple Kinects, are appearing in the marketplace for clothing applications, but like previous systems, they require a fixed installation and are not appropriate for home use.

Here we show that we can achieve accuracy similar to a state of the art laser scanner-based measurement system with a single inexpensive commodity sensor. We have demonstrated the feasibility of a body scanner that could work in a person's living room by combining information about body shape over several noisy frames. The key idea is to use the shape constancy of the body across frames to accurately estimate a single shape and varying pose. The approach combines silhouettes and depth with a novel silhouette dissimilarity term that overcomes problems of previous approaches. We show that measurements of the body can be reliably predicted using a simple linear regression approach and compare favorably to expensive commercial systems.

Future work should address the estimation of shape under clothing. This has been demonstrated in a synchronized multi-camera capture scenario with silhouettes [5] and with laser scans [15]. We believe that it should work with the Kinect sensor. We would also like to improve the optimization speed to make it interactive. An interactive system could provide the user with feedback about how to move to improve their body model.

Acknowledgements We thank Loretta Reiss for her measurement expertise and Lisa Wang for mathematical discussions. This work was supported in part by NIH EUREKA award 1R01NS066311–01 and NSF award IIS–0812364.

References

1. Allen, B., Curless, B., Popovic, Z.: The space of human body shapes: reconstruction and parameterization from range scans. ACM Trans. Graph. **22**(3), 587–594 (2003)
2. Anguelov, D., Srinivasan, P., Koller, D., Thrun, S., Rodgers, J., Davis, J.: SCAPE: shape completion and animation of people. ACM Trans. Graph. **24**(3), 408–416 (2005)
3. Balan, A.: Detailed human shape and pose from images. Ph.D. thesis, Brown University (2010)
4. Balan, A., Sigal, L., Black, M., Davis, J., Haussecker, H.: Detailed human shape and pose from images. In: IEEE Conference on Computer Vision and Pattern Recognition (2007)
5. Balan, A., Black, M.: The naked truth: estimating body shape under clothing. In: European Conference on Computer Vision (2007)
6. Bouguet, J.: Camera calibration toolbox for Matlab. http://www.vision.caltech.edu/bouguetj/calib_doc (2007)
7. Charpiat, G., Faugeras, O., Keriven, R.: Approximations of shape metrics and application to shape warping and empirical shape statistics. Found. Comput. Math. **5**(1), 1–58 (2005)
8. Delamarre, Q., Faugeras, O.: 3D articulated models and multi-view tracking with silhouettes. In: International Conference on Computer Vision (1999)
9. Flanders, H.: Differentiation under the integral sign. Am. Math. Mon. **80**(6), 615–627 (1973)
10. Ganapathi, V., Plagemann, C., Koller, D., Thrun, S.: Real time motion capture using a single time-of-flight camera. In: IEEE Conference on Computer Vision and Pattern Recognition (2010)
11. Geman, S., McClure, D.: Statistical methods for tomographic image reconstruction. Bull. Int. Stat. Inst. **LII**(4), 5–21 (1987)
12. Grest, D., Herzog, D., Koch, R.: Human model fitting from monocular posture images. In: Vision, Modeling, and Visualization (2005)
13. Guan, P., Weiss, A., Balan, A., Black, M.: Estimating human shape and pose from a single image. In: International Conference on Computer Vision (2009)
14. Hasler, N., Rosenhahn, B., Thormählen, T., Wand, M., Gall, J., Seidel, H.P.: Markerless motion capture with unsynchronized moving cameras. In: IEEE Conference on Computer Vision and Pattern Recognition (2009)

15. Hasler, N., Stoll, C., Rosenhahn, B., Thormählen, T., Seidel, H.P.: Estimating body shape of dressed humans. Comput. Graph. **33**(3), 211–216 (2009)
16. Hasler, N., Ackermann, H., Rosenhahn, B., Thormählen, T., Seidel, H.P.: Multilinear pose and body shape estimation of dressed subjects from image sets. In: IEEE Conference on Computer Vision and Pattern Recognition (2010)
17. Jain, A., Thormählen, T., Seidel, H.P., Theobalt, C.: Moviereshape: tracking and reshaping of humans in videos. ACM Trans. Graph. **29**(6), 148 (2010)
18. Knossow, D., Ronfard, R., Horaud, R.: Human motion tracking with a kinematic parameterization of extremal contours. Int. J. Comput. Vis. **79**(3), 247–269 (2008)
19. Konolige, K., Mihelich, P.: ROS.org Wiki: Kinect_calibration/technical. http://www.ros.org/wiki/kinect_calibration/technical (2011)
20. de La Gorce, M., Paragios, N., Fleet, D.: Model-based hand tracking with texture, shading and self-occlusions. In: IEEE Conference on Computer Vision and Pattern Recognition (2008)
21. Microsoft: Kinect for X-BOX 360. http://www.xbox.com/kinect (2010)
22. Newcombe, R., Izadi, S., Hilliges, O., Molyneaux, D., Kim, D., Davison, A., Kohli, P., Shotton, J., Hodges, S., Fitzgibbon, A.: KinectFusion: real-time dense surface mapping and tracking. In: International Symposium on Mixed and Augmented Reality (2011)
23. OpenKinect project. http://www.openkinect.org (2011)
24. Plänkers, R., Fua, P.: Model-based silhouette extraction for accurate people tracking. In: European Conference on Computer Vision (2002)
25. Shotton, J., Fitzgibbon, A., Cook, M., Sharp, T., Finocchio, M., Moore, R., Kipman, A., Blake, A.: Real-time human pose recognition in parts from single depth images. In: IEEE Conference on Computer Vision and Pattern Recognition (2011)
26. Sminchisescu, C., Telea, A.: Human pose estimation from silhouettes. a consistent approach using distance level sets. In: WSCG International Conference on Computer Graphics, Visualization and Computer Vision (2002)
27. Sumner, R., Popovic, J.: Deformation transfer for triangle meshes. ACM Trans. Graph. **23**(3), 399–405 (2004)
28. Tong, J., Zhou, J., Liu, L., Pan, Z., Yan, H.: Scanning 3D full human bodies using Kinects. IEEE Trans. Vis. Comput. Graph. **18**(4), 643–650 (2012)
29. Zhou, S., Fu, H., Liu, L., Cohen-Or, D., Han, X.: Parametric reshaping of human bodies in images. ACM Trans. Graph. **29**(4), 126 (2010)

Chapter 7
Real Time Hand Pose Estimation Using Depth Sensors

Cem Keskin, Furkan Kıraç, Yunus Emre Kara, and Lale Akarun

Abstract Real-time hand posture capture has been a difficult goal in computer vision. The extraction of hand skeleton parameters would be an important milestone for sign language recognition, since it would make classification of hand shapes and gestures possible. The recent introduction of the Kinect depth sensor has accelerated research in human body pose capture. This chapter describes a real-time hand pose estimation method employing an object recognition by parts approach, and the use of this method for hand shape classification. First, a realistic 3D hand model is used to represent the hand with 21 different parts. Then, a random decision forest (RDF) is trained on synthetic depth images generated by animating the hand model, which is used to perform per pixel classification and to assign each pixel to a hand part. The classification results are fed into a local mode finding algorithm to estimate the joint locations for the hand skeleton. The system can process depth images retrieved from Kinect in real time, and does not rely on temporal information. As a simple application of the system, we also describe a support vector machine (SVM)-based recognition module for the ten digits of American Sign Language (ASL) based on our method, which attains a recognition rate of 99.9 % on live depth images in real time.

7.1 Introduction

After the release of multi-touch enabled smart phones and operating systems, there has been a renewed interest in natural interfaces and particularly in hand gestures.

C. Keskin (✉) · F. Kıraç · Y.E. Kara · L. Akarun
Computer Engineering Department, Boğaziçi University, 34342, Istanbul, Turkey
e-mail: keskinc@cmpe.boun.edu.tr

F. Kıraç
e-mail: kiracmus@boun.edu.tr

Y.E. Kara
e-mail: yunus.kara@boun.edu.tr

L. Akarun
e-mail: akarun@boun.edu.tr

Hand gestures are used in these systems to interact with programs such as games, browsers, e-mail readers and a diverse set of tools. Immersive 3D displays will also depend heavily on the use of hand gestures for interaction.

Vision-based hand gesture recognition, and particularly, sign language recognition has attracted the interest of researchers for more than 20 years. Yet, a framework that robustly detects the naked hand and recognizes hand poses and gestures from color images has continued to be elusive. This can be attributed mostly to the large variance of the retrieved images, caused by changing light conditions, and to the difficulty of distinguishing the hand from other body parts.

Two developments have recently accelerated implementations of human–computer interaction using human body and hand gestures: The first is the release and widespread acceptance of the Kinect depth sensor [1]. With its ability to generate depth images in very low illumination conditions, this sensor makes the human body and hand detection and segmentation a simple task. The second development is the use of fast discriminative approaches using simple depth features coupled with GPU implementation; enabling real-time human body pose extraction [2, 3].

Recently, Kinect has been used to achieve real-time body tracking capabilities, which has triggered a new era of natural interface-based applications. In their revolutionary work, Shotton et al. fit a skeleton to the human body using their object recognition-based approach [2]. They use a large amount of labeled real and synthetic images to train a randomized decision forest (RDF) [20] for the task of body part recognition. In a later study, Girschick et al. [3] use the same methodology with a regression forest, and let each pixel vote for joint coordinates. Detailed explanation of both frameworks can be found in the first chapter of this part of the book.

The object recognition by parts approach is applicable to the hand pose estimation problem as well, but there are some notable differences between the human body and hand: (i) The projected depth image of a hand is much smaller than that of a body; (ii) a body can be assumed to be upright but a hand can take any orientation; (iii) in the case of hands, the number of possible meaningful configurations is much higher and the problem of self-occlusion is severe. On the other hand, the inter-personal variance of the shape of hands is much smaller compared to the huge differences between fully clothed human bodies.

In this work, we largely follow the approach in [2]. Adopting the idea of an intermediate representation for the object whose pose is to be estimated, we generate synthetic hand images and label their parts, such that each skeleton joint is at the center of one of the labeled parts. We form large datasets created from random and manually set skeleton parameters, and train several randomized decision trees (RDT) [20], which are then used to classify each pixel of the retrieved depth image. Finally, we apply the mean shift algorithm to estimate the joint centers as in [2]. The resulting framework can estimate hand poses in real time.

As a proof of concept, we demonstrate the system by using it to recognize ASL digits. In our approach, we first train an RDF for ASL digits using synthetic images. Then, we evaluate real depth images of ASL and fit a skeleton to each image. Finally, we classify the skeleton configuration parameters using SVM, which can then be used to infer the hand shape class for a given real hand depth image, by fitting a skeleton to it first. We demonstrate that this technique achieves a 99.9 % test accuracy on a dataset of size 15k, collected from five users. Note that there are other simpler approaches to classify ASL digits. However, using the skeletal configuration to classify hand shapes is a powerful method, since the appearance of the hand is entirely determined by the skeleton. This is reflected in the high success rate the framework achieves. More importantly, this approach does not rely on class- or application-specific heuristics and is directly applicable to all types of hand shape.

7.1.1 Related Work

With the release of Kinect, libraries for basic hand gesture recognition tasks have been developed. However, these only consider hand movement, and not hand pose. The estimation of the hand skeleton configuration has largely remained unsolved.

7.1.1.1 Hand Pose Estimation

Most approaches to hand pose estimation problem make use of regular RGB cameras. Erol et al. [4] divide the pose estimation methods into two main groups in their review: partial and full pose estimation methods. They further divide the full pose estimation methods into single frame pose estimation and model-based tracking methods. Athitsos et al. [5] estimate 3D hand pose from a cluttered image. They create a large database of synthetic hand poses using an articulated model and find the closest match from this database. Similarly, Romero et al. [6] propose a non-parametric, nearest neighbor-based search in a large database to estimate articulated hand poses. De Campos and Murray [7] use a relevance vector machine-based learning method [8] for single frame hand pose recovery. They combine multiple views to overcome the self-occlusion problem. They also report single and multiple view performances for both synthetic and real images. Rosales et al. [9] use monocular color sequences for recovering 3D hand poses. Their system maps image features to 3D hand poses using specialized mappings. Stergiopoulou and Papamarkos [10] fit a neural network into the detected hand region. They recognize the hand gesture using the grid of the produced neurons. De La Gorce et al. [11] use model-based tracking of the hand pose in monocular videos. Stenger et al. [13] apply model-based tracking using an articulated hand model and estimate the pose with an unscented Kalman filter. Bray et al. [14] propose an algorithm that wraps a particle filter around multiple stochastic meta-descent-based trackers to form a smart particle filter that can track an articulated hand pose. However, the resulting framework does not run in real time. Heap et al. [15] describe a 3D deformable point distribution model of the hand, which is used to track hands using a single RGB camera.

A number of approaches have been reported to estimate the hand pose from depth images. Mo and Neumann [16] use a laser-based camera to produce low-resolution depth images. They interpolate hand pose using basic sets of finger poses and inter-relations. Malassiotis and Strintzis [17] extract PCA features from depth images of synthetic 3D hand models for training.

In a recent study Oikonomidis et al. [12] present a solution that makes use of both depth and color images. They propose a generative single hypothesis model-based pose estimation method. They use particle swarm optimization for solving the 3D hand pose recovery problem, and report accurate and robust tracking in near real time (15 fps), with a GPU-based implementation.

7.1.1.2 Hand Shape Recognition from Depth

Uebersax et al. propose a system that segments the hand and estimates the hand orientation from captured depth data. Their letter classification method is based on average neighborhood margin maximization. Liu and Fujimura [18] recognize hand gestures using depth images acquired by a time-of-flight camera. The authors detect hands by thresholding the depth data and use Chamfer distance to measure shape similarity. Then, they analyze the trajectory of the hand and classify gestures using shape, location, trajectory, orientation and speed features. Suryanarayan et al. [19] use depth information and recognize scale and rotation invariant poses dynamically. They classify six signature hand poses using a volumetric shape descriptor which they form by augmenting 2D image data with depth information. They use SVM for classification. Uebersax et al. [21] provide a thorough review of ASL letter recognition on depth data.

In Sect. 7.2 we describe the methodology used for fitting the skeleton. Section 7.3 lists the details of conducted experiments and presents our results on ASL digit recognition. Finally, we conclude the chapter in Sect. 7.4.

7.2 Methodology

The flowchart of the system can be viewed in Fig. 7.1. The training phase is given in the upper row, and the evaluation phase in the lower row. As there is no practical way of labeling real depth images, only synthetic images are used for training. To this end, the system employs a realistic 3D hand model that can be configured to form new poses. Our framework handles automatic generation and labeling of synthetic training images by manually setting or randomizing each skeleton parameter. It can then form large datasets by interpolating poses and perturbing joints via addition of Gaussian noise to each joint angle without violating skeleton constraints. These synthetic datasets contain depth-label image pairs for each configuration. Typically, datasets consisting of 40k to 200k image pairs are generated, which are used to train the models. Each tree learns to map the pixels in a depth image to their corresponding labels in the ground truth image. Multiple decision trees are trained that form small ensembles, i.e. forests.

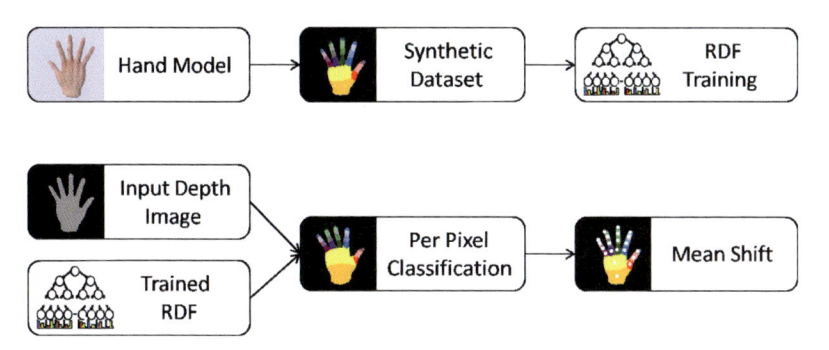

Fig. 7.1 Flowchart of the system. The *top image* depicts the training phase, and the *bottom image* depicts the evaluation phase

In the evaluation phase, an input depth image is fed into the trained RDF without the ground truth labels. The trees in the RDF classify each depth pixel into a hand part by assigning a set of posterior probabilities to it. The posterior probabilities of each tree are averaged over all the trees in the forest. Finally, the mean shift algorithm is used to estimate the 3D coordinates of the centroids of each hand part. The skeleton is formed by connecting the joint coordinates according to the model hierarchy.

The overall accuracy of the system depends on a variety of factors, such as the number of trees, the depth of individual trees, the degree of variation in the training set and other training parameters. In particular, if the training images do not reflect the variety of hand poses encountered in real life, the trees cannot generalize well to unseen poses.

By synthesizing training images, it is possible to automatically create a very large set of configurations. First, a smaller set of plausible and common hand poses is manually created, from which new poses are generated by extrapolating and randomizing these configurations.

7.2.1 Data

To generate the synthetic images, we use a 3D skinned mesh model with a hierarchical skeleton, consisting of 19 bones, 15 joints and 21 different parts as viewed in Fig. 7.2. Hand parts are defined such that all significant skeleton joints are located near the centroids of corresponding parts. Hence, the thumb contains three parts and all the other fingers contain four parts that signify each bone tip. The palm is divided into two different parts, so that the deformations are better captured.

The model is animated and rendered with the texture depicting the hand parts, without shading. The final color image is the label image, and the content of the Z-buffer, which contains the depth map of the rendered pixels, is the depth image. The magnitudes of the depth pixels are mapped to the interval [0, 255] to minimize

Fig. 7.2 The 3D hand model with a hierarchical skeleton and 21 labeled parts that is used to generate a synthetic training set. (**a**) The skeleton is depicted with *yellow parts* indicating the joint locations. Image (**b**) shows the parts, each of which correspond to a joint or bone tip in the skeleton

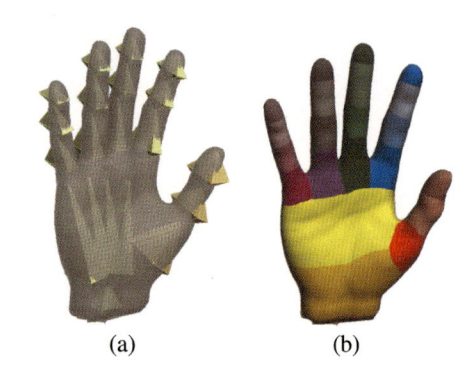

memory cost. To retain compatibility with the incoming Kinect data, the input depth images are also normalized to the same interval.

The training sets are designed with target applications in mind, so that the trained trees can generalize well to previously unseen hand poses that can be encountered during common tasks, such as hand poses used for games, natural interfaces and sign languages, all of which are manually modeled using a tool. The animator tool can interpolate between these poses using the hierarchical skeleton model, and add slight variations to each frame by perturbing joint locations, while changing the camera pose. Skeletal constraints are applied to each interpolated pose, ensuring that the resulting configurations are feasible. A data glove, which measures the joint angles of the hand in real time, can also be used to manipulate the digital model and create realistic hand poses. It can also be used to estimate and better model the inter-personal variations in hand shape, such as size, finger lengths and thickness. However, the models trained on a synthetic dataset formed by manipulating a single hand shape has been found to be sufficient for all types of hand, as inter-personal variance is low for the hands, and the trained models can easily be adapted to different hand sizes by scaling feature parameters if necessary.

7.2.2 Decision Trees

Decision trees consist of split nodes, which are the internal nodes used to test the input; and leaf nodes, which are the terminal nodes used to infer a set of posterior probabilities for the input, based on statistics collected from training data. Each split node sends the incoming input to one of its children, according to the test result. The test associated with a split node is usually of the form

$$f_n(F_n) < T_n \tag{7.1}$$

where $f_n(F_n)$ is a function of a subset of features and T_n is a threshold, at split node n. The input is injected at the root node, which is forwarded by the split nodes according to the test results; and the posterior probabilities associated with the leaf node that is reached are used to infer the class label. Hence, the training of a deci-

Fig. 7.3 A decision tree. The input pixels are tested at each node and guided *down the tree*, finally reaching a leaf node that is associated with a set of posterior probabilities, which is estimated from the label histogram of data collected during the training

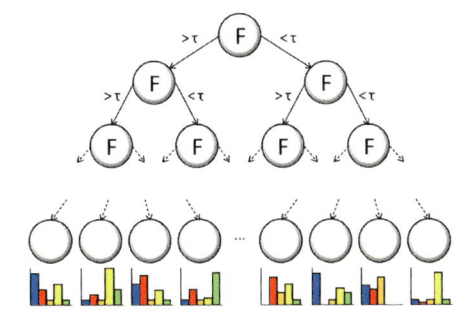

sion tree involves determining the tests and collecting statistics from a training set. A decision tree is depicted in Fig. 7.3.

In the case of an RDT, the features do not need to be determined beforehand. Instead, the feature parameters are randomly sampled several times, and the test that provides the best split, i.e. the maximum amount of information gain, is chosen. This approach is particularly useful if the feature space is very large.

7.2.3 Randomized Decision Forest for Hand Pose Estimation

An RDF is an ensemble of RDTs trained on the same or slightly different datasets. The input to an RDF is a depth image I, and a pixel location x. The output is a set of posterior probabilities for each hand part label c_i.

We use the same features as in [2]. Given a depth image $I(x)$, where x denotes location, we define a feature $F_{u,v}(I, x)$ as follows:

$$F_{u,v}(I, x) = I\left(x + \frac{u}{I(x)}\right) - I\left(x + \frac{v}{I(x)}\right). \quad (7.2)$$

The offsets u and v are relative to the pixel in question, and normalized according to the depth at x. This ensures that the features are 3D translation invariant. Note that they are neither rotation nor scale invariant, and the training images should be generated accordingly. The depth of background pixels and the exterior of the image are taken to be a large constant.

Each split node is associated with the offsets u and v and a depth threshold τ. The data is split into two sets as follows:

$$C_L(u, v, \tau) = \{(I, x) | F_{u,v}(I, x) < \tau\} \quad (7.3)$$
$$C_R(u, v, \tau) = \{(I, x) | F_{u,v}(I, x) \geq \tau\}. \quad (7.4)$$

Here, C_L and C_R are the mutually exclusive sets of pixels assigned to the left and right children of the split node, respectively.

In the training phase, each split node randomly selects a set of features, partitions the data accordingly and chooses the feature that splits the data best. Each split is scored by the total decrease in the entropy of the label distribution of the data:

$$S(u, v, \tau) = H(C) - \sum_{s \in \{L,R\}} \frac{|C_s(u, v, \tau)|}{|C|} H(C_s(u, v, \tau)) \qquad (7.5)$$

where $H(K)$ is the Shannon entropy estimated using the normalized histogram of the labels in the sample set K. The process ends when the leaf nodes are reached. Each leaf node is then associated with the normalized histogram of the labels estimated from the pixels reaching it.

Starting at the root node of each RDF, each pixel (I, x) is assigned either to the left or the right child until a leaf node is reached. There, each pixel is assigned a set of posterior probabilities $P(c_i|I, x)$ for each hand part class c_i. For the final decision, the posterior probabilities estimated by all the trees in the ensemble are averaged:

$$P(c_i|I, x) = \frac{1}{N} \sum_{n=1}^{N} P_n(c_i|I, x) \qquad (7.6)$$

where N is the number of trees in the ensemble, and $P_n(c_i|I, x)$ is the posterior probability of the pixel estimated by the tree with index n. Another option is to multiply the posteriors. However, the trees are correlated, and multiplication is more prone to the effects of noise.

The RDF assigns each leaf node a set of posterior probabilities by counting the number of training pixels from every label that reach that node. This approach poses a balance problem if the number of training pixels significantly differ for labels. Indeed, the number of training pixels for the palm is several orders of magnitude larger than that of the finger tips. Hence, even a small portion of pixels from the palm area dominates the posterior likelihoods of the leaf nodes it reaches. One solution is to increase tree depth until all the leaves are pure. However, this causes overtraining or over-confident posteriors, and reduces performance on test set. To prevent this, (i) we stratify the sampling process and ensure that an almost equal number of pixels from each label are used for training; (ii) we stop the splitting process if fewer than a certain number of pixels are assigned to a node. This prevents overfitting and allows better generalization.

Since only synthetic images are used for training, the RDFs must also generalize to real data as retrieved by the depth sensor. To ensure this, and to prevent the RDF from memorizing artifacts or patterns associated with synthetic images, we perturb both the skeletal configurations and the generated depth maps. In particular, Gaussian noise is applied to each angle in the skeleton as well as to the depth information. The Gaussian noise is applied to each depth pixel separately. The effect of the resulting depth noise is depicted in Fig. 7.4. The image on the left is a synthetic depth image. Here, the contrast is maximized to make the artifacts visible. Note that the actual noise model of Kinect is very complex due to underlying algorithms. Here, Gaussian noise is not applied to imitate the Kinect sensor, but rather to prevent the RDF from memorizing the very precise depth information provided by a single

Fig. 7.4 The effect of added depth noise. The *image on the left* is the original synthetic depth image. The *image on the right* is the same image with added Gaussian noise ($\sigma = 3$)

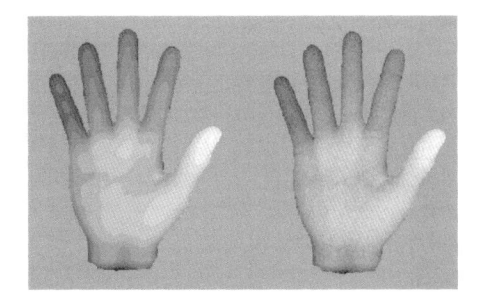

digital hand model, and to better generalize to the slightly different hand shapes of actual people.

7.2.4 Joint Position Estimation

After each pixel is assigned posterior probabilities, the result is used to estimate the joint positions. To locate the actual joint coordinates, a number of approaches can be employed, such as calculating the centroid of all the pixels belonging to a hand part. However, finding the centroid is not robust against outliers, which is especially a greater problem for smaller hand parts.

To reduce the effect of outliers, the mean shift local mode finding algorithm [22] is preferred over finding the global centroid of the points belonging to the same class. The mean shift algorithm estimates the probability density of each class label with weighted Gaussian kernels placed on each sample. Each weight is set to be the pixel's posterior probability $P(c_i|I, x)$ corresponding to the class label c_i, times the square of the depth of the pixel, which is an estimate of the area the pixel covers, indicating its importance. The joint locations estimated using this method are on the surface of the hand and need to be pushed back to find an exact match for the actual skeleton.

Starting from a point estimate, or *seed*, the mean shift algorithm uses a gradient ascent approach to locate the nearest mode of the distribution. As the maxima are local, several different starting points are used and the one converging to the maximum score is selected. Finally, a decision regarding the visibility of the joint is made by thresholding the highest score reached during the mean shift phase. The joint positions estimated in this manner are then connected according to their configuration in the hand skeleton, forming the final pose estimate.

At this point, it is possible to make use of temporal or spatial information to infer a better skeleton estimate. For instance, a particle filter can be used to eliminate sudden jumps in joint locations, and skeletal constraints can be used to disregard some of the local maxima reached by the mean shift phase. An important constraint is that the joints on a finger lie on a 3D plane, which can also be used to detect occluded joints.

7.3 Experiments

Here, we report quantitative results for the hand pose estimation and hand shape classification methods. First, we introduce the synthetic and real datasets used in experiments.

7.3.1 Datasets

7.3.1.1 Synthetic Dataset

Performance of RDFs on previously unseen poses depends heavily on the training set provided. Ideally, we want the trained RDF to generalize to all possible hand poses. However, the number of images that need to be synthesized for this ambitious task is immense. A static hand pose is a single configuration of the 22-dof skeleton. The number of possible configurations, even with a modest step size for each angle, is huge. Moreover, simply rotating a single static pose in 3D to generate all possible views with a step size of 15 degrees, produces 15k images per pose. This suggests that the target application should determine the extent of the dataset. Here, we choose the 24 static ASL letters, the 10 ASL digits, and six hand poses that are widely known and used, such as the sign for OK. For the 40 poses selected and manually synthesized with the hand model, we rotate the camera in 3D, perturb the angles, and interpolate between the poses to generate 200k synthetic images. The offline learning method of Sect. 7.2 can be used to train an RDF on this dataset. However, to incorporate a larger dataset, incremental learning methods should be preferred [23].

7.3.1.2 Real Dataset

For the hand shape classification task, both synthetic and real images can be used. However, only the accuracy on a real set is of importance. Therefore, a dataset consisting of real depth images retrieved from a Kinect depth camera is collected. Data collection is simple; one needs to perform the sign for several seconds in front of the sensor, while slightly moving and rotating the hand. We collected a dataset for the ten ASL digits from five different people. Each shot takes ten seconds, amounting to a total of 300 frames for each digit per person. Hence, the dataset consists of 15k images.

7.3.2 Effect of Model Parameters

The RDF parameters that have an effect on the classification accuracy are as follows: (i) The number of trees; (ii) the tree depth; (iii) the limits of u, v and τ; (iv) the number of feature samples tried at each node; (v) mean shift weight threshold; (vi) the number of mean shift seeds.

7 Real Time Hand Pose Estimation Using Depth Sensors

Fig. 7.5 The effect of the forest size on the test accuracy

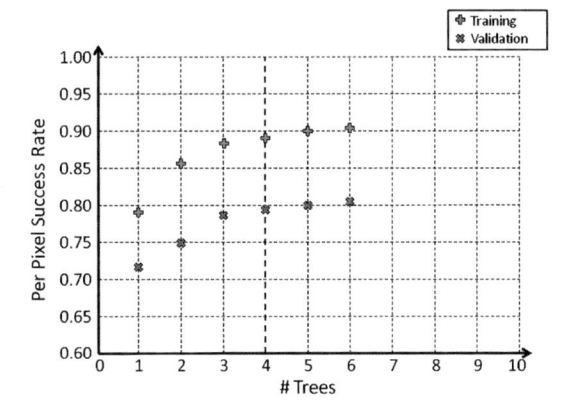

7.3.2.1 The Effect of the Forest Size

Training a large RDT by maximizing information gain is likely to produce overconfident posteriors. Since posterior probabilities are averaged over all trees, increasing the forest size produces smoother posteriors, alleviates overtraining, and allows better generalization, while monotonously increasing test accuracy. This is illustrated in Fig. 7.5. The trade-off is the linear increase in memory and the time it takes to test. We typically use one to four trees, as real-time performance is of importance in most application areas.

7.3.2.2 The Effect of the Tree Depth

The depth of a tree determines the number of tests to apply to the input. If the depth is too large, noisy training data will be isolated by the tests, causing overtraining. Likewise, a shallow tree will produce low-confidence, high entropy posteriors. Therefore, it is important to optimize the tree depth.

The effect of the tree depth is illustrated in Fig. 7.6. Overtraining starts at around depth 22, and the gain from increasing depth over 20 is minimal. As the need for memory increases exponentially, we prefer setting the depth to 20.

In our implementation, a tree of depth D evaluates pixels using exactly D binary comparisons. The number of internal nodes is $2^D - 1$, and the number of leaves is 2^D.

7.3.2.3 The Effect of the Feature Space

The feature space is determined by the maximum range of the offset parameters u, v and τ. We use a single limit for both x and y coordinates of the u and the v parameters, and a separate limit for the τ parameter. This defines the spatial context that can be used for tests in the form of a cube around the pixel. Intuitively,

Fig. 7.6 The effect of the tree depth on the test accuracy

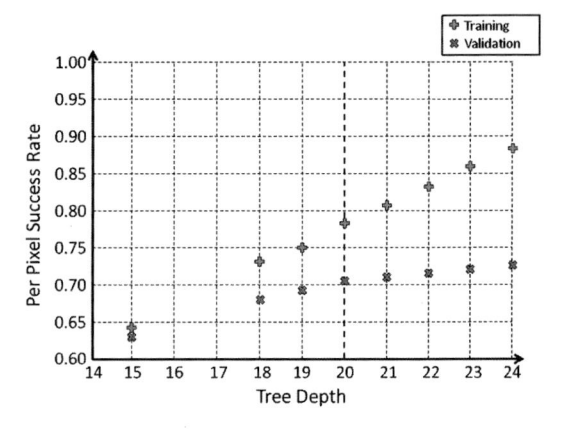

Fig. 7.7 The effect of the limits of the offset parameters u and v on the test accuracy

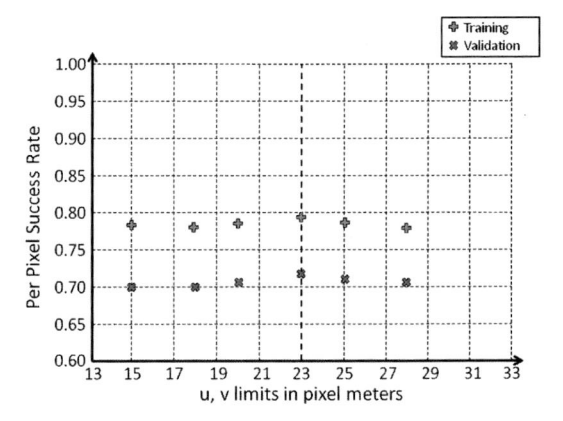

taking a larger context into account should increase the test accuracy. However, a fixed number of parameter values are sampled at each node. Hence, incorporating a larger context may reduce the probability of selecting good features that maximize information gain for a split. Moreover, the training dataset must be large enough to prevent the RDT from overtraining, if it uses a large spatial context. This effect is visible for different values of u and v limits in Fig. 7.7. The optimum value for the limit of u and v is estimated to be 23 pixel meters, i.e. 23 pixels if the hand is 1 m away, 46 pixels if the hand is 50 cm away, or 11.5 pixels if the hand is 2 m away from the camera. In our tests, we estimated the optimum value of τ to be 60 mm.

7.3.2.4 The Effect of the Sample Size

The sample size is the number of parameter values sampled from the feature space for each internal node. Increasing the sample size increases the test accuracy, as it is more likely to sample features that increase the information gain with a larger sample size. The trade-off is the increase in training time. Since forest size must

Fig. 7.8 The effect of the sample size on the test accuracy

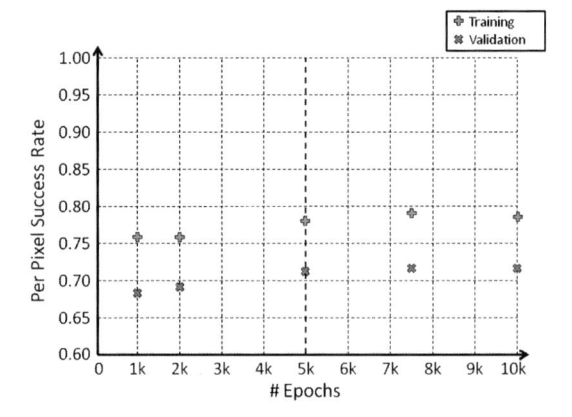

be small due to memory constraints, the RDTs must produce confident posteriors. However, as we are sampling from a fixed feature space, the effect of the sample size levels off after some value. This is illustrated in Fig. 7.8. For the fixed limit of 23 pixel meters for u and v, the gain from increasing the number of trials is negligible after sample size reaches 5000.

7.3.2.5 The Effect of the Mean Shift Parameters

Since hands are highly articulate and flexible objects, self-occlusion of entire hand parts is natural and happens frequently. In the ideal case, there should be no pixel assigned to the hidden hand part. However, it is common that some pixels are misclassified. In such cases, the mean shift algorithm determines the joint location for the hidden hand part based on the misclassified pixels only. Therefore, such spurious joint estimates need to be eliminated.

A decision regarding the visibility of the joint is made by thresholding the highest score reached during the mean shift phase. The effect of the thresholding process is shown in Fig. 7.9. Here, the images on the first column are the original pixel classification results, with colors assigned according to the highest posterior. The images in the second column are the same images, with the corresponding joint locations as estimated by the mean shift algorithm. The images on the third column are produced by eliminating joints that have low confidence values. Here, the confidence is defined as the value of the peak reached during the mean shift phase, which is evaluated using a combination of the pixel posteriors, joint bandwidth, which is a measure of the spread of the joint, and the importance of the pixel, which is the square of its depth, i.e. a measure of its area. The range of values depends on the implementation, and we empirically estimated it to be around 0.4. In the upper row of Fig. 7.9, the threshold is set to 0.5, which eliminates legitimate joints. In the middle row, the threshold is set to 0.4, and only spurious joints are eliminated. In the lower row, the threshold is set to 0.2, leaving one spurious joint intact.

Mean shift is a local mode finding method that only finds the closest maximum. To increase the likelihood of converging to the global maximum, we start multiple

Fig. 7.9 In the *upper row*, the confidence score threshold is set too high (0.5), eliminating true joints. In the *middle row*, the threshold is set correctly (0.4) and only the spurious joints are eliminated. In the *lower row*, the threshold is set too low (0.2), leaving one spurious joint intact

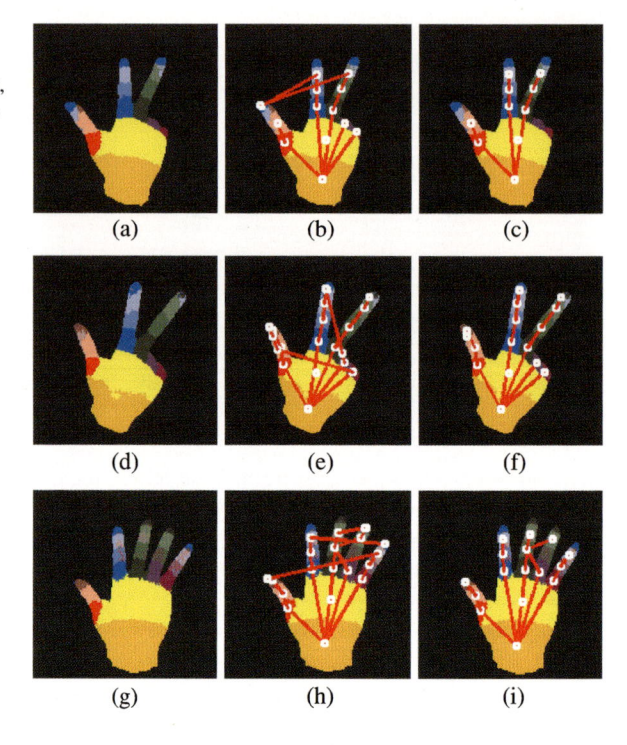

(a) (b) (c)
(d) (e) (f)
(g) (h) (i)

times from different seed points. The maximum with the highest score is selected, once all iterations converge. Seeds are randomly selected from the list of pixels with posterior probabilities higher than a certain value. We empirically determined this likelihood to be 0.35. The effect of the number of seeds is illustrated in Fig. 7.10. Here, the rows depict two examples, and the columns correspond to seed numbers 1, 2, 3 and 4, respectively. The higher this number, the more likely it is to converge to the correct joint locations. The trade-off is the increase in joint estimation time. In practice, we start from up to 20 different seeds.

7.3.3 Hand Pose Estimation Results

A synthetic dataset of size 200k formed with 40 hand poses is used to conduct hand pose estimation experiments. First, 5×2 cross-validation strategy is used to determine the best parameters. In this method, the dataset is randomly divided into two sets. In the first run, the model is trained on the first set and tested on the second set. In the second run, the model is trained on the second set and tested on the first set. This procedure is repeated on five randomly created pairs, and the average accuracy is regarded as a robust estimation of the success rate. The optimal forests are achieved with the parameters reported in Sect. 7.2: (i) Forest size $= 4$; (ii) Tree depth $= 20$; (iii) Offset limit $= 23$ pixel-meters; (iv) Sample size $= 5000$;

7 Real Time Hand Pose Estimation Using Depth Sensors

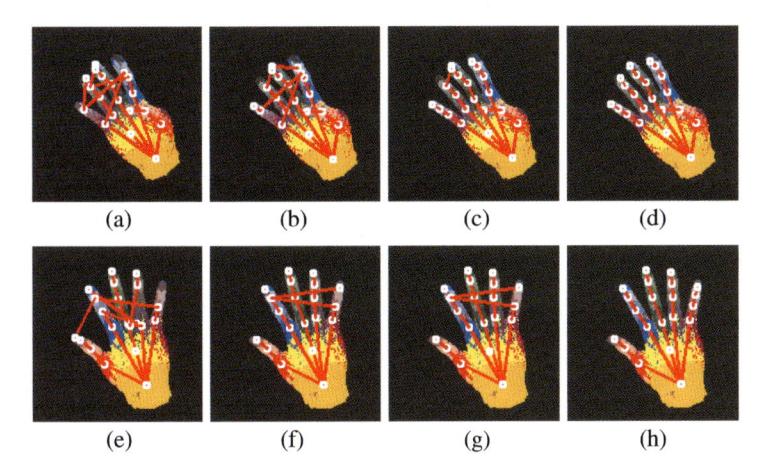

Fig. 7.10 The effect of the number of starting points for the mean shift algorithm. The *columns* correspond to number of seeds 1, 2, 3 and 4, respectively

(v) Mean shift seed posterior threshold $= 0.35$; (vi) Number of seeds $= 20$. The test accuracy of the resulting RDF is also determined with 5×2 cross-validation. The per-pixel classification accuracy (using hard labels) on this dataset is 67.5 %.

Another important measure of error is the average distance between the estimated joint coordinates and the ground truth. However, spurious joints, especially misplaced finger tips, have a large effect on this type of error. Therefore, we estimate the number of spurious or missing joints as an indicator of the error instead. Hence, we count the number of correct joints in the test dataset, and divide it over the number of visible joints. The visibility of the joints is determined automatically, and correctness of a joint estimation is determined by thresholding the projected distance between the estimated and actual joint coordinates. For the synthetic dataset of size 200k, with 40 poses, 82.1 % of the visible joints are estimated correctly. For a smaller dataset of size 20k, formed by ASL digits only, the method is able to find 97.3 % of the joints correctly. Most of the error in the latter case is attributable to misplaced finger tips.

7.3.4 Proof of Concept: American Sign Language Digit Recognizer

To test the system on a real world application, we developed a framework for classifying ASL digits in real time. The method described in Sect. 7.2 gives estimates of the hand skeleton as output. The pose classifier uses these estimates to recognize the digits by mapping the estimated joint coordinates to known hand poses.

First, the RDF is trained on a synthetic ASL digit dataset of size 20k, so that it learns to extract the skeleton from poses that closely resemble ASL digits. Then, this RDF is used to evaluate the real depth images acquired from the Kinect, while a

Table 7.1 Classification rates and evaluation times of each classifier on the ASL digit dataset consisting of 20k synthetic images

Method name	Accuracy	Classification duration (ms)
ANN	99.89	0.0045
SVM	99.96	0.3

user is performing ASL digits. A training set is formed using the extracted skeleton parameters by properly labeling each hand skeleton according to its corresponding hand shape. Such a training set can be used to train classifiers in a supervised manner. These shape classifiers can then be used to map the extracted hand skeletons into ASL digits in real time.

7.3.4.1 Hand Shape Classifiers

As the intended usage of the system is real-time recognition of ASL digits, speed is as important as the recognition rate. We choose artificial neural networks (ANN), since they are fast, and SVMs, since they are accurate. We use 5×2 cross-validation strategy for both model selection and to test accuracy. Model selection for the RDF is done only on the synthetic dataset.

7.3.4.2 Model Selection on the Synthetic Dataset

Both the RDFs and the skeleton classifiers need to be optimized. To select an RDF model, a synthetic dataset needs to be used, since there is no ground truth labels that are associated with real data. We optimized ANN and SVM separately for both synthetic and real datasets. The synthetic dataset consists of 20k samples, formed by 2k synthetic images for each of the ASL digits. The RDF parameters are as reported in Sect. 7.3.3. For the ANN, the optimum number of hidden nodes is estimated to be 20. For SVMs, the optimal parameters are found to be 2^6 for the cost parameter and 2^{-4} for the Gaussian spread (γ).

The test accuracies and evaluation times are listed in Table 7.1. The first column gives the average accuracies achieved by the cross-validation tests. The second column gives the evaluation times. Evidently, ANN is significantly faster than SVM. However, SVM performs slightly better on the test data. The intermediate phases and the final skeletons for several examples are given in Fig. 7.11.

7.3.4.3 ASL Digit Classification Results on Real Data

We conducted 5×2 cross-validation and grid search to estimate the optimal parameters of ANN and SVM again for the real dataset. Table 7.2 shows the parameters tested.

7 Real Time Hand Pose Estimation Using Depth Sensors

Fig. 7.11 Examples of extracted skeletons on synthetic ASL images. *Upper row* lists the depth images. *Middle row* shows the per pixel classification results. *Third row* displays the estimated joint locations on top of the labeled images. The finalized skeleton is shown in the *bottom row*

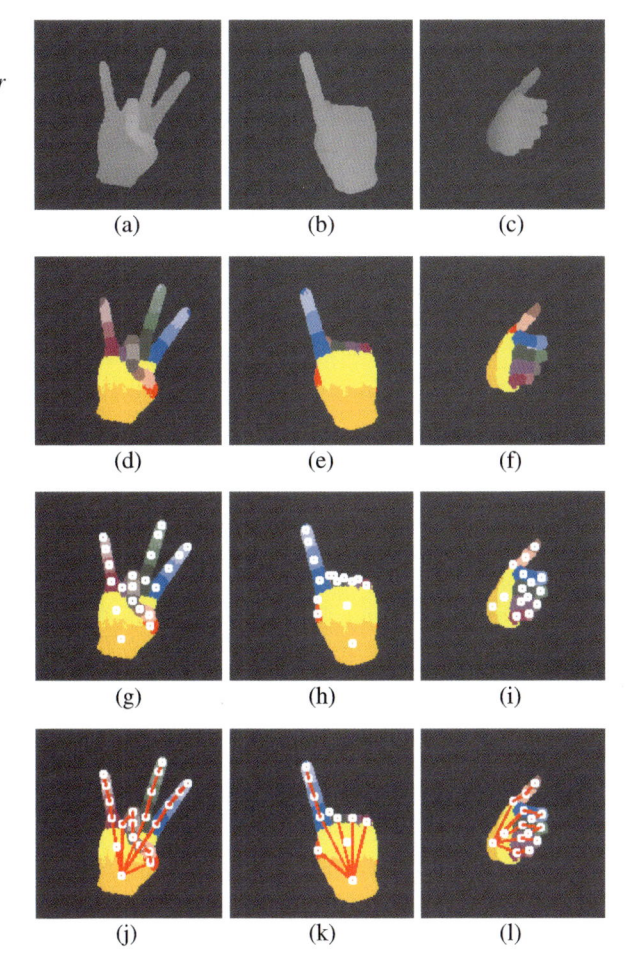

Table 7.3 lists the optimal parameters and recognition rates on training and validation sets for ANNs and SVMs for real data. SVMs outperform ANNs and reach nearly perfect accuracy on the validation set, indicating that the descriptive power of the estimated skeleton is sufficient for the task of hand shape classification on real depth images.

7.4 Conclusion

In this study, we described a depth image-based real-time skeleton fitting algorithm for the hand, using RDFs to classify depth image pixels into hand parts. To produce the huge amount of samples that are needed to train the decision trees, we developed a tool to generate realistic synthetic hand images. Our experiments showed that the system can generalize well when trained on synthetic data, backing up the

Table 7.2 Tested parameter values (H: hidden nodes, C: SVM cost, γ: Gaussian spread)

Method name	Parameter values
ANN	$H = \{5, 10, 15, 20, 25, 30, 35, 40, 45, 50, 55\}$
SVM	$C = \{2^{-1}, 2^0, 2^1, 2^2, 2^3, 2^4, 2^5, 2^6, 2^7\}$
SVM	$\gamma = \{2^{-5}, 2^{-4}, 2^{-3}, 2^{-2}, 2^{-1}, 2^0, 2^1\}$

Table 7.3 Optimal parameters, average training and validation accuracies

Method name	Optimal parameters	Training accuracy	Validation accuracy
ANN	Hidden nodes = 40	99.27	98.81
SVM	Cost = 2^5, $\Gamma = 2^{-2}$	100	99.90

claims of Shotton et al. in [2]. In particular, just by feeding manually designed hand poses corresponding to ASL digits to the RDFs, the system learned how to correctly classify the hand parts for real depth images of hand poses that are close enough. This in turn enabled us to collect real data labeled by the RDFs that can be used for further pose classification tasks. We demonstrated the efficiency of this approach by reaching a recognition rate of 99.9 % using SVMs on real depth images retrieved with Kinect. The features used by SVMs are the mean shift-based joint estimates calculated in real time from the per pixel classification results.

We focused on optimizing the speed and accuracy of the system, in particular by performing grid search over all model parameters. The resulting framework is capable of retrieving images from Kinect, applying per pixel classification using RDFs, estimating the joint locations from several hypotheses in the mean shift phase, and finally using these locations for pose classification in real time. The system is optimized for multicore systems and is capable of running on high end notebook PCs without experiencing frame drops. Further enhancement is possible through the utilization of the GPU, as described in [24], and this framework can be used along with more CPU intensive applications such as games and modeling tools. This method is one of the first to retrieve the full hand skeleton in real time using a standard PC and a depth sensor, and has the extra benefit of not being affected by illumination.

The main focus of this study is skeleton fitting to the hands from a single frame. Consequently, temporal information is ignored, which can certainly be used to enhance the quality of the fitted skeleton, via methods such as Kalman [25] or particle filtering [26].

References

1. Microsoft Corp. Redmond, WA. Kinect for Xbox 360
2. Shotton, J., Fitzgibbon, A., Cook, M., Sharp, T., Finocchio, M., Moore, R., Kipman, A., Blake, A.: Real-time human pose recognition in parts from single depth images. In: IEEE Conference on Computer Vision and Pattern Recognition (2011)

3. Girshick, R., Shotton, J., Kohli, P., Criminisi, A., Fitzgibbon, A.: Efficient regression of general-activity human poses from depth images. In: International Conference on Computer Vision (2011)
4. Erol, A., Bebis, G., Nicolescu, M., Boyle, R.D., Twombly, X.: Vision-based hand pose estimation: a review. Comput. Vis. Image Underst. **108**, 52–73 (2007)
5. Athitsos, V., Sclaroff, S.: Estimating 3D hand pose from a cluttered image. In: IEEE Conference on Computer Vision and Pattern Recognition (2003)
6. Romero, J., Kjellstrom, H., Kragic, D.: Monocular real-time 3D articulated hand pose estimation. In: Humanoids, pp. 87–92 (2009)
7. De Campos, T.E., Murray, D.W.: Regression-based hand pose estimation from multiple cameras. In: IEEE Conference on Computer Vision and Pattern Recognition (2006)
8. Tipping, M.E., Smola, A.: Sparse Bayesian learning and the relevance vector machine. J. Mach. Learn. Res. **1**, 211–244 (2001)
9. Rosales, R., Athitsos, V., Sigal, L., Sclaroff, S.: 3D hand pose reconstruction using specialized mappings. In: International Conference on Computer Vision (2001)
10. Stergiopoulou, E., Papamarkos, N.: Hand gesture recognition using a neural network shape fitting technique. Eng. Appl. Artif. Intell. **22**, 1141–1158 (2009)
11. De La Gorce, M., Fleet, D.J., Paragios, N.: Model-based 3D hand pose estimation from monocular video. IEEE Trans. Pattern Anal. and Mach. Intell., Feb. 1–14 (2011)
12. Oikonomidis, I., Kyriazis, N., Argyros, A.: Efficient model-based 3D tracking of hand articulations using Kinect. In: British Machine Vision Conference (2011)
13. Stenger, B., Mendonça, P.R.S., Cipolla, R.: Model-based 3D tracking of an articulated hand. In: IEEE Conference on Computer Vision and Pattern Recognition (2001)
14. Bray, M., Koller-Meier, E., Van Gool, L.J.: Smart particle filtering for high-dimensional tracking. Comput. Vis. Image Underst. **106**, 116–129 (2007)
15. Heap, T., Hogg, D.: Towards 3D hand tracking using a deformable model. In: International Conference on Automatic Face and Gesture Recognition, pp. 140–145 (1996)
16. Mo, Z., Neumann, U.: Real-time hand pose recognition using low-resolution depth images. In: IEEE Conference on Computer Vision and Pattern Recognition (2006)
17. Malassiotis, S., Strintzis, M.: Real-time hand posture recognition using range data. Image Vis. Comput. **26**, 1027–1037 (2008)
18. Liu, X., Fujimura, K.: Hand gesture recognition using depth data. In: Automatic Face and Gesture Recognition (2004)
19. Suryanarayan, P., Subramanian, A., Mandalapu, D.: Dynamic hand pose recognition using depth data. In: International Conference on Pattern Recognition (2010)
20. Breiman, L.: Random forests. Mach. Learn. **45**, 5–32 (2001)
21. Uebersax, D., Gall, J., Van den Bergh, M., Van Gool, L.: Real-time sign language letter and word recognition from depth data. In: International Conference on Computer Vision—Workshop on Human Computer Interaction: Real-Time Vision Aspects of Natural User Interfaces (2011)
22. Comaniciu, D., Meer, P.: Mean shift: a robust approach toward feature space analysis. Pattern Anal. Mach. Intell. **24**, 603–619 (2002)
23. Basak, J.: Online adaptive decision trees: pattern classification and function approximation. Neural Comput. **18**, 2062–2101 (2006)
24. Sharp, T.: Implementing decision trees and forests on a GPU. In: European Conference on Computer Vision (2008)
25. Welch, G., Bishop, G.: An Introduction to the Kalman Filter (1995)
26. Isard, M., Blake, A.: CONDENSATION—conditional density propagation for visual tracking. Int. J. Comput. Vis. **29**, 5–28 (1998)

Part III
RGB-D Datasets

In recent years, there has been significant progress on methods for visual recognition and categorization. Besides novel methods for image representations, a lot of research effort has been put in advanced machine learning methods. Critical to this success has been the creation of large datasets. Examples are the Pascal VOC Challenge, LabelMe, and ImageNet, just to mention a few ones. Furthermore, with the help of Amazon Mechanical Turk or other crowd-sourcing platforms the labeling process has been sped up tremendously and many new applications have become feasible.

However, the design and acquisition of a dataset is not always trivial. A good dataset should contain a fair representation of all the sub-categories. As datasets contain labeled instances (e.g., a particular image contains a face) they are important for at least two reasons: First of all, the data can be used to build the models. As mentioned above, and demonstrated in the previous parts of the book, machine learning methods usually have the need for a lot of training data. Secondly, the dataset together with a proper evaluation metric can be used to evaluate the available methods and make fair comparisons among them.

In this part three newly built datasets for consumer depth cameras are introduced. Synchronized images or videos of both color (RGB) and depth are acquired. In the first chapter by Janoch et al. (A Category-Level 3D Dataset: Putting the Kinect to Work) the main target applications are object class detection and recognition. The second chapter by Lai et al. (RGB-D Object Recognition: Features, Algorithms, and a Large Scale Benchmark) arranges objects in a hierarchical manner and also aims for detection and recognition and even pose recognition of a particular object instance. Finally, the chapter by Ni et al. (RGB-HuDaAct: A Color-Depth Video Database For Human Daily Activity Recognition) focuses on human activity recognition in videos. In addition to setting up the database, all three chapters discuss proper RGB-D features and modeling techniques.

Chapter 8
A Category-Level 3D Object Dataset: Putting the Kinect to Work

Allison Janoch, Sergey Karayev, Yangqing Jia, Jonathan T. Barron, Mario Fritz, Kate Saenko, and Trevor Darrell

Abstract The recent proliferation of the Microsoft Kinect, a cheap but quality depth sensor, has brought the need for a challenging category-level 3D object detection dataset to the forefront. Such a dataset can be used for object recognition in a spirit usually reserved for the large collections of intensity images typically collected from the Internet. Here, we will review current 3D datasets and find them lacking in variation of scene, category, instance, and viewpoint. The Berkeley 3D Object Dataset (B3DO), which contains color and depth image pairs gathered in read domestic and office environments will be presented. Baseline object recognition performance in a PASCAL VOC-style detection task is established, and two ways that inferred world size of the object van be used to improve detection are suggested. In an effort to make more significant performance progress, the problem of extracting useful features from range images is addressed. There has been much success in using the histogram of oriented gradients (HOG) as a global descriptor for object detection in intensity images. There are also many proposed descriptors designed specifically for depth data (spin images, shape context, etc.), but these are often focused on the local, not global descriptor paradigm. We explore the failures of gradient-based de-

---

A. Janoch (✉) · S. Karayev · Y. Jia · J.T. Barron · K. Saenko · T. Darrell
University of California at Berkeley, Berkeley, CA, USA
e-mail: allie@eecs.berkeley.edu

S. Karayev
e-mail: sergeyk@eecs.berkeley.edu

Y. Jia
e-mail: jiayq@eecs.berkeley.edu

J.T. Barron
e-mail: barron@eecs.berkeley.edu

K. Saenko
e-mail: saenko@eecs.berkeley.edu

T. Darrell
e-mail: trevor@eecs.berkeley.edu

M. Fritz
Max Plank Institute for Informatics, Campus E1.4, 66123 Saarbrücken, Germany
e-mail: mfritz@mpi-inf.mpg.de

scriptors when applied to depth, and propose that the proper global descriptor in the realm of 3D should be based on curvature, not gradients.

8.1 Introduction

The task of object recognition has made significant advances in the past decade and crucial to this success has been the creation of large datasets as well as simple but effective features. Unfortunately, these successes have been limited to the use of intensity images and have chosen to ignore the very important cue of depth. Depth has long been thought to be an essential part of successful object recognition, but the reliance on large datasets has minimized the importance of depth. Collection of large datasets of intensity images is no longer difficult with the wide spread availability of images on the web and the relative ease of annotating datasets using Amazon Mechanical Turk. Recently, there has been a resurgence of interest in available 3D sensing techniques due to advances in active depth sensing, including techniques based on LIDAR, time-of-flight (Canesta), and projected texture stereo (PR2). The Primesense sensor used on the Microsoft Kinect [4] gaming interface offers a particularly attractive set of capabilities, and is quite likely the most common depth sensor available worldwide due to its rapid market acceptance (8 million Kinects were sold in just the first two months).

There is a large body of literature on instance recognition using 3D scans from the computer vision and robotics communities. However, there are surprisingly few existing datasets for category-level 3D recognition, or for recognition in cluttered indoor scenes, despite the obvious importance of this application to both communities. As reviewed below, published 3D datasets have been limited to instance tasks, or to a very small numbers of categories. Described here is the Berkeley 3D Object dataset (B3DO) [21], a dataset for category level recognition, collected using the Kinect sensor in domestic and office environments. Figure 8.1 shows images representative of B3DO. The dataset has an order of magnitude more variation than previously published datasets.

Since B3DO was collected using Kinect hardware, which uses active stereo sensing, the quality of the depth scans is much higher than in datasets based on passive stereo or sparsely sampled LIDAR. The full dataset can be downloaded at http://www.kinectdata.com.

As with existing 2D challenge datasets such as the Pascal VOC [12], B3DO has considerable variation in pose and object size, with objects covering a range of sizes from nearly 5 % to almost 75 % of image width. An important observation the dataset enables is that the actual world size distribution of objects has less variance than the image-projected, apparent size distribution. The statistics of these and other quantities for categories in the dataset are reported in Sect. 8.3.4.

A key question is what value do depth data offer for category level recognition? Conventional wisdom is that ideal 3D observations provide strong shape cues for recognition, but in practice even the cleanest 3D scans may reveal less about an

Fig. 8.1 Typical scenes found in the B3DO. The intensity image is shown *on the left*, the depth image *on the right*

object than available 2D intensity data. Numerous schemes for defining 3D features analogous to popular 2D features for category-level recognition have been proposed and can perform in uncluttered domains. Section 8.4 evaluates the application of histogram of gradients (HOG) descriptors on 3D data and evaluates the benefit of such a scheme on our dataset. Observations about world size distribution can also be used to place a size prior on detections, which can improve detection performance as evaluated by average precision, as well as provide a potential benefit for detection efficiency.

For more significant performance improvements, features besides HOG must be explored. Much of the recent success of object recognition based solely on intensity images begins with the use of features derived from histograms of gradients. Detectors such as the deformable parts model proposed by Felzenszwalb et al. [14] begin with feature inspired by the HOG features described by Dalal and Triggs [10]. Such features have been demonstrated to have some success when used on range images [23] as shown in Sect. 8.4, but the feature was not originally designed to be used as a depth descriptor. In fact, a gradient-based descriptor tends to identify discontinuities in depth, which in many cases is very similar to the representation that is learned by computing HOG features on intensity images. There will be some differences in the features computed using gradients on intensity and range images and both will be useful at times. For example, in Fig. 8.2 the back of the office chair would be easier to identify using HOG on the depth image.

Fig. 8.2 The *office chair on top* illustrates an example where the depth discontinuities identified by HOG on a depth image would offer additional information not as easily identified from the intensity image. The *bowl on the bottom* shows an example where gradients on the depth image would not be expected to yield much that could not be understood from the intensity image

Merely identifying discontinuities in depth does not capture much of the signal provided by depth. For example, an important characteristic of a bowl, like the one in Fig. 8.2, is that it is concave on the inside, something that will not be captured by HOG on range images. There have been a number of features proposed for depth as described in Sect. 8.2.2, including both local features such as spin images [22], 3D shape context [16], the VFH model [25] and the features used for pose estimation in the Microsoft Kinect [26].

We propose that the proper feature to use in coordination with HOG should be similar, but instead of being based on first-order statistics and gradients, should be based on second-order statistics or curvature. Curvature is an appealing concept because the same surface in a range image will have the same Gaussian and mean curvature from any viewpoint under orthographic projection. This is because both Gaussian and mean curvature encode the first and second principal curvature in a way that is invariant to rotation, translations and changes in parameterization [6]. The curvature-based feature, which we call a histogram of curvature or HOC, would be able to capture the fact that a bowl is concave on the inside, while maintaining the spatial binning that is appealing in HOG.

8.2 Related Work

There have been numerous previous efforts in collecting datasets with aligned 2D and 3D observations for object recognition and localization. Below is a review of the most pertinent ones, and a brief highlight of how B3DO is different. Also included in this section is an overview of previous work highlighting the integration of 2D appearance and depth modalities.

8.2.1 3D Datasets for Detection

We present an overview of previously published datasets that combine 2D and 3D observation and contrast our dataset from those previous efforts:

RGBD-Dataset of [23] This dataset from Intel Research and University of Washington features 300 objects in 51 categories. The category count refers to nodes in a hierarchy, with, for example, *coffee mug* having *mug* as parent. Each category is represented by four to six instances, which are densely photographed on a turntable. For testing object eight short video clips of distinct scenes are available, which lend themselves to evaluation of four categories (bowl, cap, coffee mug, and soda can) and 20 instances. There does not appear to be significant viewpoint variation in the detection test set. This dataset will be presented in detail in the following chapter.

UBC Visual Robot Survey [3, 20] This dataset from University of British Columbia provides training data four categories (mug, bottle, bowl, and shoe) and 30 cluttered scenes for testing. Each scene is photographed in a controlled setting from multiple viewpoints.

3D Table Top Object Dataset [28] This dataset from University of Michigan three categories (mouse, mug and stapler) and provides 200 test images with cluttered backgrounds. There is no significant viewpoint variation in the test set.

Solutions in Perception Challenge [2] This dataset from Willow Garage forms the challenge which took place in conjunction with International Conference on Robotics and Automation 2011, and is instance-only. It consists of 35 distinct objects such as branded boxes and household cleaner bottles that are presented in isolation for training and in 27 scenes for test.

Max Plank Institute Kinect Dataset [8] This dataset was designed for category level recognition and contains 82 objects for training and 72 objects for testing across 14 different categories. Objects were photographed densely in isolation for both training and testing. The same object (but at a different viewing angle) was included in both the training and test sets.

Fig. 8.3 A random sample of instances of the "chair" class in B3DO. There is significant variety amongst the examples in the model of chair, the viewpoint, the level of occlusion and illumination

Indoor Scene Segmentation Dataset [27] This dataset from NYU includes videos of 64 different scenes seven different types of room. Approximately 2300 of the 100,000 frames are segmented into regions.

Other Datasets Beyond these, other datasets have been made available which do include simultaneous capture of image and depth but serve more specialized purposes like autonomous driving [1], pedestrian detection [11] and driver assistance [29]. Their specialized nature means that they cannot be leveraged for the multi-object category localization task that is our goal.

In contrast to all of these datasets, B3DO contains both a large number of categories and many different instances per category. Both training and testing data are photographed "in the wild" instead of in a controlled turntable setting, and images contain significant variation in lighting and viewpoint throughout the dataset. For an illustration, consider Fig. 8.3, which presents examples of the "chair" category in B3DO. These qualities make B3DO more representative of the kind of data that can actually be seen in people's homes; data that a domestic service robot would be required to deal with and use for online training.

8.2.2 3D and 2D/3D Recognition

There have been a number of 3D features proposed for object recognition as well as a number of systems that combine intensity images with depth for object recognition. Although this is by no means an inclusive list, some local 3D features that have been proposed include spin images [22], 3D shape context [16], and the VFH model [25]. Both spin images and 3D shape context define a support region around interest points and then compute a histogram centered at that point. The support region is oriented with the surface normal in both cases, but for spin images the support region is a cylinder and for 3D shape context it is a sphere. For spin images the cylinder is broken up into bins radially and with the cylinders height. In contrast, 3D shape context breaks up the sphere into bins in the azimuth, elevation and radial dimensions, thus unlike spin images, 3D shape context is not rotationally invariant. Recently, Shotton et al. [26] proposed a pose detector based on a random forest of decision trees. The features used in the trees examine a specific point and compare its depth to two other random points to traverse the tree.

A number of 2D/3D hybrid approaches have been recently proposed, and B3DO should be a relevant testbed for these methods. A multi-modal object detector in which 2D and 3D are traded off in a logistic classifier is proposed by Gould et al. [17]. The method leverages additional handcrafted features derived from the 3D observation such as "height above ground" and "surface normal", which provide contextual information. Sun et al. [28] show how to benefit from 3D training data in a voting-based method. Fritz et al. [15] extend branch and bound's efficient detection to 3D and add size and support surface constraints derived from the 3D observation.

Most prominently, a set of methods have been proposed for fusing 2D and 3D information for the task of pedestrian detection. The popular HOG detector [10] to disparity-based features is extended by Hattori et al. [19]. A late integration approach is proposed by Rohrbach et al. [24] for combining detectors on the appearance as well as the depth image for pedestrian detection. Instead of directly learning on the depth map, Walk et al. [29] use a depth statistic that learns to enforce height constraints of pedestrians. Ess et al. [11] explore pedestrian detection by using stereo and temporal information in a hough voting framework also using scene constraints. Recently, Lai et al. [23] evaluated object detection on a challenging dataset collected with the Kinect, as shown in the following chapter. They combined three features: HOG on intensity images, HOG on depth images and a histogram calculated based on the estimated scale of an object. They found the combination of the three features yields significantly improved results over a detector based solely on intensity images.

8.3 The Berkeley 3D Object Dataset

The Berkeley 3D Object Dataset is a large-scale dataset of images taken in domestic and office settings with the commonly available Kinect sensor. The sensor provides a color and depth image pair, and is processed for alignment and inpainting (see Sect. 8.3.3). The data were collected by many members of the research community, as well as an Amazon Mechanical Turk (AMT) worker, providing an impressive variety in scene and object appearance. As such, the dataset is intended for evaluating approaches to category-level object recognition and localization.

The dataset was collected with ten different Kinects that were taken to the homes and offices of 19 different volunteers who collected 849 images from 75 different scenes or rooms. Volunteers were given a list of objects that would be labeled and were told to take images that did not looked staged containing one or more of these objects. Simple instructions should enable the dataset to grow more easily in the future.

Over 50 different object classes are represented in the dataset by crowd-sourced labels. The annotation was done by AMT workers in the form of bounding boxes on the color image, which are automatically transferred to the depth image.

8.3.1 Data Annotation

Crowd sourcing on AMT was used to label the data collected. AMT is a well-known service for "Human Intelligence Tasks" (HITs), which are typically small tasks that are too difficult for current machine intelligence. Our labeling HIT gives workers a list of eight objects to draw bounding boxes around in a color image. Each image is labeled by five workers for each set of labels in order to provide sufficient evidence to determine the validity of a bounding box. A proposed annotation or bounding box is only deemed valid if at least one similarly overlapping bounding box is drawn by another worker. The criteria for similarity of bounding boxes is based on the PASCAL VOC [12] overlap criterion (described in more detail in Sect. 8.4.1), with the acceptance threshold set to 0.3. If only two bounding boxes are found to be similar, the larger one is chosen. If more than two are deemed similar, the bounding box which overlaps the most with the other bounding boxes is kept and rest are discarded.

8.3.2 The Kinect Sensor

The Microsoft Xbox Kinect [4] was originally designed as a video game peripheral for controller-free gaming through human pose estimation and gesture recognition. The sensor consists of a horizontal bar with cameras, a structured-light projector, an accelerometer and an array of microphones mounted on a motorized pivoting foot. Across the horizontal bar are three sensors: two infrared laser depth sensors with a depth range of approximately 0.6 to 6 meters, and one RGB camera (640 × 480 pixels) [4]. Depth reconstruction uses proprietary technology from Primesense, consisting of continuous infrared structured-light projection onto the scene. Since its release in November 2010, much open source software has been released allowing the use of the Kinect as a depth sensor [9].

The Kinect color and infrared cameras are a few centimeters apart horizontally, and have different intrinsic and extrinsic camera parameters, necessitating their calibration for proper registration of the depth and color images. Calibration parameters differ significantly from unit to unit, which poses a problem to totally indiscriminate data collection. Fortunately, the calibration procedure is made easy and automatic due to efforts of the open source community [7, 9].

8.3.3 Smoothing Depth Images

The structured-light method used for recovering ground-truth depth-maps necessarily creates areas of the image that lack an estimate of depth. In particular, glass surfaces and infrared-absorbing surfaces can be missing in depth data. In addition, "shadows" may occur along the edge of some objects. Tasks such as getting the average depth of a bounding box, or applying a global descriptor to a part of the depth image therefore benefit from some method for "inpainting" these missing data.

This work assumes that proper inpainting of the depth image requires some assumption of the behavior of natural shapes and that objects have second-order smoothness (that curvature is minimized)—a classic prior on natural shapes [18, 31]. In short, the inpainting algorithm minimizes

$$\|h * Z\|_F^2 + \|h^\mathrm{T} * Z\|_F^2 \tag{8.1}$$

with the constraints $Z_{x,y} = \hat{Z}_{x,y}$ for all $(x, y) \in \hat{Z}$, the measured depth, and where $h = [-1, +2, -1]$, is an oriented 1D discrete Laplacian filter, $*$ is a convolution

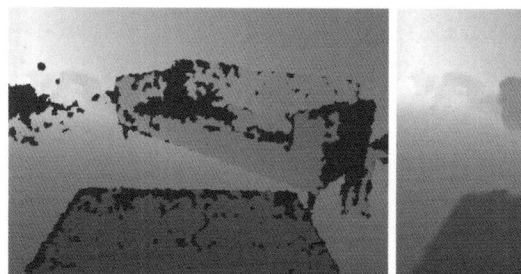

Fig. 8.4 Illustration of our depth smoothing method. The original depth image is shown *on the left* where *black pixels* demonstrate missing depth data. The smoothed image is shown *on the right*

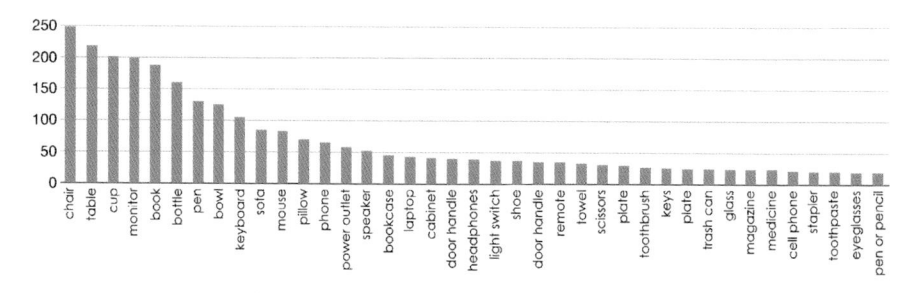

Fig. 8.5 Object frequency for the 39 classes with 20 or more examples. A heavy tail can be observed, which is common in other vision datasets

operation, and $\|\cdot\|_F^2$ is the squared Frobenius norm. The solution to this optimization problem is a depth-map Z in which all observed pixels in $\hat{Z}$ are preserved, and all missing pixels have been filled in with values that minimize curvature in a least-squares sense. This problem is occasionally ill-conditioned near the boundaries of the image, so a small additional regularization term is introduced for first-order smoothness. For speed considerations, the hard constraints in the problem above are relaxed to heavily penalized soft constraints to solve the induced least-square problem. Figure 8.4 illustrates this algorithm operating on a typical input image from B3DO with missing depth to produce the smoothed output.

8.3.4 Data Statistics

The distribution of objects in household and office scenes as represented in B3DO is shown in Fig. 8.5. The typical long tail of unconstrained datasets is present, and suggests directions for targeted data collection. There are 12 classes with more than 70 examples, 27 classes with more than 30 examples, and over 39 classes with 20 or more examples.

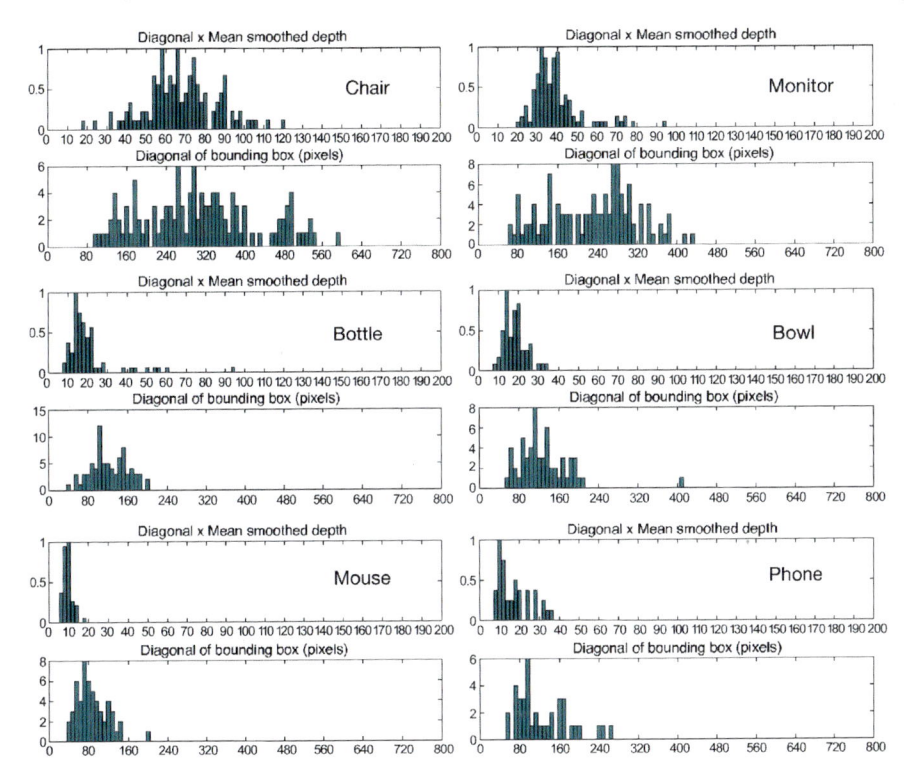

8 A Category-Level 3D Object Dataset: Putting the Kinect to Work

Fig. 8.6 Statistics of object size. For each object class, the *top histogram* is inferred world object size, obtained as the product of the bounding box diagonal and the average depth of points in the bounding box. The *bottom histogram* is the distribution of the length of the diagonal of the bounding box. (Note the difference in scale on the x-axis for these histograms)

Unlike other 3D datasets for object recognition, B3DO features large variability in the appearance of object class instances. This can be seen in Fig. 8.3, presenting random examples of the chair class in the dataset; the variation in viewpoint, distance to object, frequent presence of partial occlusion, and diversity of appearance in this sample poses a challenging detection problem.

The apparent size of the objects in the image, as measured by the bounding box containing them, can vary significantly across the dataset. The real-world size of the objects in the same class varies far less, as can be seen in Fig. 8.6. As a proxy for the real-world object size, the product of the diagonal of the bounding box l and the distance to the object from the camera D is used, which is roughly proportional to the world object size by similar triangles (of course, viewpoint variation slightly scatters this distribution–but less so than for the bounding box size).

We found that mean smoothed depth is roughly equivalent to the median depth of the depth image ignoring missing data, and so this is used to measure distance. The Gaussian was found to be a close fit to these size distributions, allowing estimation of the size likelihood of a bounding box as $\mathcal{N}(x|\mu, \sigma)$, where μ and σ are estimated on the training data. This result will be used further in Sect. 8.4.3.

8.4 Detection Baselines

The cluttered scenes of B3DO provide for a challenging object detection task, where the task is to localize all objects of interest in an image. Here, the task is constrained to finding eight different object classes: chairs, monitors, cups, bottles, bowls, keyboards, computer mice, and phones. These object classes were among the most well-represented in our dataset.[1]

8.4.1 Sliding Window Detector

The baseline system is based on a standard detection approach of sliding window classifiers operating on a gradient representation of the image [10, 14, 30]. Such detectors are currently the state of the art on cluttered scene datasets of varied viewpoints and instance types, such as the PASCAL-VOC challenge [12]. The detector considers windows of a fixed aspect ratio across locations and scales of an image pyramid and evaluates them with a score function, outputting detections that score above some threshold.

Specifically, the implementation of the Deformable Part Model detector [14] is followed. This uses the LatentSVM formulation

$$f_\beta(x) = \max_z \beta \cdot \Phi(x, z) \tag{8.2}$$

for scoring candidate windows, where β is a vector of model parameters and z are latent values (allowing for part deformations). Optimizing the LatentSVM objective function is a semi-convex problem, and so the detector can be trained even though the latent information is absent for negative examples.

Since finding good negative examples to train on is of paramount importance in a large dataset, the system performs rounds of data mining for small samples of hard negatives, providing a provably exact solution to training on the entire dataset.

To featurize the image, HOG with both contrast-sensitive and contrast-insensitive orientation bins, four different normalization factors, and 8-pixel wide cells is used. The descriptor is analytically projected to just 31 dimensions, motivated by the analysis in Felzenszwalb et al. [14].

Two feature channels for the detector are explored. One consists of featurizing the color image, as is standard. For the other, we apply HOG to the depth image (Depth HOG), where the intensity value of a pixel corresponds to the depth to that point in space, measured in meters. This application of a gradient feature to depth

---

[1]We chose not to include a couple of other well-represented classes in this test set because of extreme variation in interpretation of instances of object by the annotators, such as the classes of "table" and "book."

images has little theoretical justification, since first-order statistics do not matter as much for depth data (this is why we use second-order smoothing in Sect. 8.3.3). Yet this is an expected first baseline that also forms the detection approach on some other 3D object detection tasks, such as in [23]. Section 8.5 will explore features based on second-order statistics.

Detections are pruned by non-maximum suppression, which greedily takes the highest-scoring bounding boxes and rejects boxes that sufficiently overlap with an already selected detection. This procedure results in a reduction of detections on the order of ten, and is important for the evaluation metric, which penalizes repeat detections.

8.4.2 Evaluation

Evaluation of detection is done in the widely adopted style of the PASCAL detection challenge, where a detection is considered correct if

$$\frac{area(B \cap G)}{area(B \cup G)} > 0.5, \qquad (8.3)$$

where B is the bounding box of the detection and G is the ground-truth bounding box of the same class. Only one detection can be considered correct for a given ground-truth box, with the rest considered false positives. Detection performance is represented by precision-recall (PR) curves, and summarized by the area under the curve, the average precision (AP). Evaluation is done on six different splits of the dataset, averaging the AP numbers across splits.

The goal of this work is category, not instance-level recognition. As such, it is important to keep instances of a category confined to either training or test set. This makes the recognition task much harder than if training on the same instances of a category as exists in the test set was allowed (but not necessarily the same views of them). To enforce this constraint, images from the same scene or room are never in both the training and test sets. This is a harder constraint than needed, and is not necessarily perfect (for example many different offices might contain the same model laptop). As there is no scalable way to provide per-instance labeling of a large, crowd-sourced dataset of cluttered scenes, this method is settled upon, and the problem is kept open for future research.

Figure 8.7 shows the detector performance eight different classes. Note, depth HOG is never better than HOG on the 2D image. This can be attributed to the inappropriateness of a gradient feature on depth data, as mentioned earlier, and to the fact that due to the limitations of the infrared structured-light depth reconstruction, particular objects (such as monitors) tend to have significant missing depth data. Figure 8.8 provides an illustration of cases in which objects are missing depth data, along with objects from the same class which are missing much fewer depth data.

Fig. 8.7 Performance of the baseline detector on our dataset, as measured by the average precision. The *darker gray bars* represent the detector which extracted features from the color image, and the *light gray bars* represent the detector which extracted features from the depth map. Average results over six different splits of the data are shown with *error bars*. Depth HOG fails completely on some categories, for reasons explained in the text

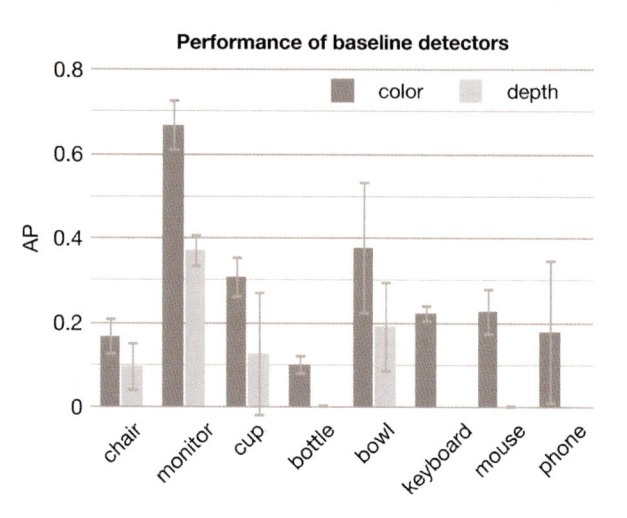

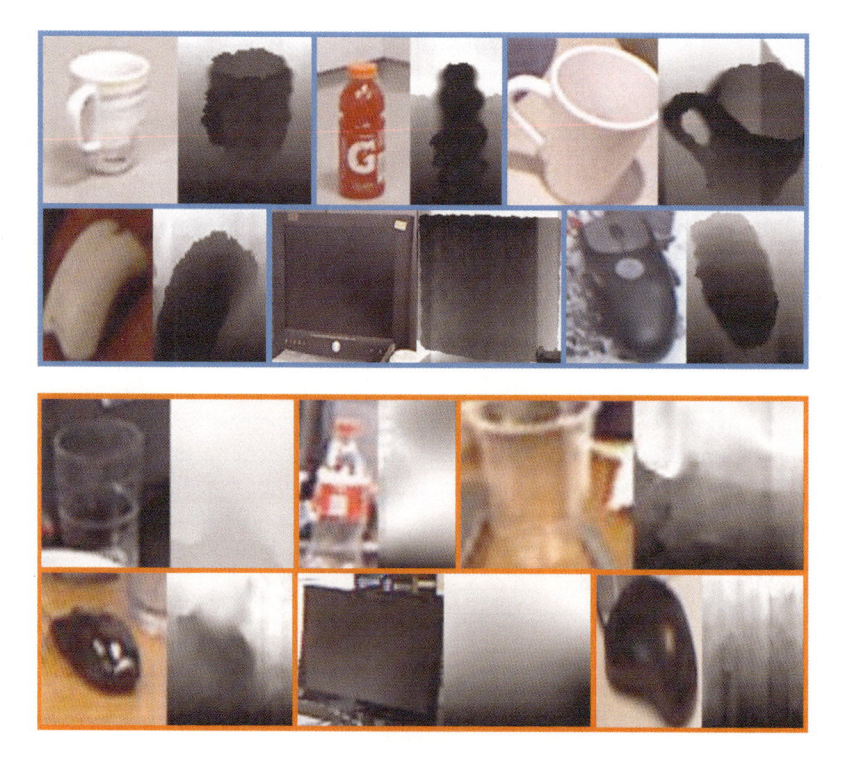

Fig. 8.8 The *top two rows of images* show examples of good depth data for various objects. The *bottom two rows* show examples of missing depth data for objects of the same classes as shown in the *top two rows*. All examples illustrate depth after smoothing as described in Sect. 8.3.3

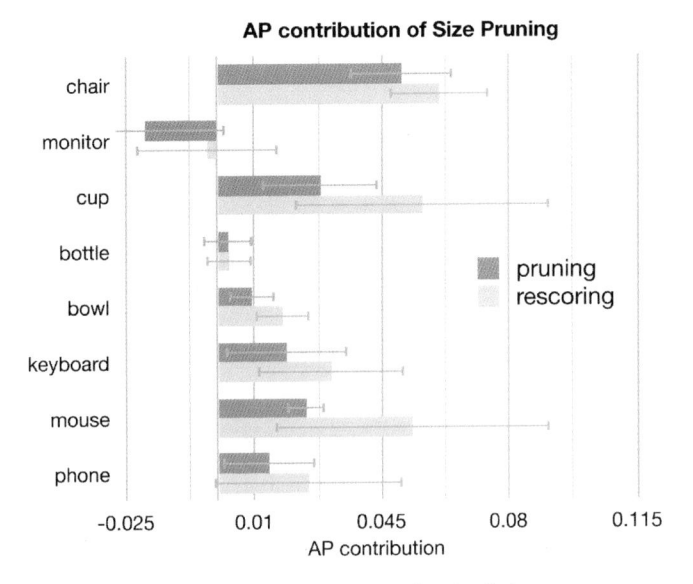

Fig. 8.9 The gain (or loss) in average precision from using depth data to prune or rescore detections. Average precision was averaged across six different splits of the data, and *error bars* are shown. In all cases the rescoring strategy is superior to the pruning strategy. In all but the case of the monitor, both pruning and rescoring improved performance over the baseline

8.4.3 Pruning and Rescoring by Size

In Sect. 8.3.4, the distributions of object size demonstrated that true object size, even as approximated by the product of object projection in the image and median depth of its bounding box, varies less than bounding box size. In the following, two ways of using approximated object size as an additional source of discriminative signal to the detector are investigated.

The first way of using size information consists of pruning candidate detections that are sufficiently unlikely given the size distribution of that object class. The object size distribution is modeled with a Gaussian, which is a close fit to the underlying distribution; the Gaussian parameters are estimated on the training data only. Boxes that are more than $\sigma = 3$ standard deviations away from the mean of the distribution are pruned.

Figure 8.9 shows that the pruning results provide a slight increase in detection performance, while Fig. 8.10 shows that 12 % to 68 % of the suggested bounding boxes are pruned (on average across the classes, 32 % of candidate detections are rejected). This observation can be leveraged as part of an "objectness" filter or as a thresholding step in a cascaded implementation of this detector for a gain in detection speed [5, 13]. The classes chair and mouse are the two classes most helped by size pruning, while monitors and bottle are the least helped (likely because many bottles and monitors have significant missing depth data). Using bounding box size of the detection (as measured by its diagonal) instead of inferred world size results in no improvement to AP performance on average.

Fig. 8.10 Average percentage of past-threshold detections pruned by considering the size of the object. The *light gray* rectangle reaching to 32 % is the average across classes. In both cases, *error bars* show standard deviation across six different splits of the data

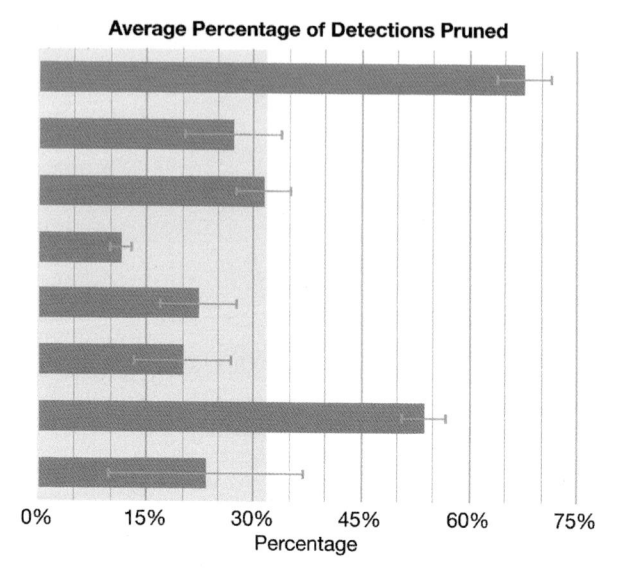

The second way we use size information consists of learning a rescoring function for detections, given their SVM score and size likelihood. A simple combination of the two values is learned:

$$s(x) = \exp(\alpha \log(w(x)) + (1-\alpha) \log(\mathcal{N}(x|\mu,\sigma))), \quad (8.4)$$

where $w(x) = 1/(1 + \exp(-2f_\beta(x)))$ is the normalized SVM score, $\mathcal{N}(x|\mu,\sigma)$ is the likelihood of the inferred world size of the detection under the size distribution of the object class, and α is a parameter learned on the training set. This corresponds to unnormalized Naïve Bayes combination of the SVM model likelihood and object size likelihood. Since what matters for the precision-recall evaluation is the ordering of confidences and whether they are normalized is irrelevant, $s(x)$ can be evaluated directly.

As Fig. 8.9 demonstrates, the rescoring method works better than pruning. This method is able to slightly increase recall as well as precision by assigning a higher score to likely detections in addition to lowering the score (which is, in effect, pruning) of unlikely detections.

8.5 A Histogram of Curvature (HOC)

The previous section demonstrated how HOG could be used to featurize range images. As mentioned earlier, this is not the ideal use of HOG since it is designed to be used on intensity images. We seek to define a feature representation analogous to HOG that is more appropriate for range images. Curvature is an appealing feature to work with when range data are available because it is potentially less sensitive to changes in viewpoint than gradient-based descriptors (such as HOG). As mentioned in the introduction, a surface in a range image will have the same Gaussian and mean curvature from any viewpoint under orthographic projection.

8.5.1 Curvature

Curvature is a measurement of the rate of change of the orientation of the tangent vector to a curve. The principal curvatures for a point P is the maximum (K_1) and minimum (K_2) curvature for all curves passing through P. To further reduce curvature to a single measurement one can either calculate the Gaussian curvature,

$$K_{\text{gauss}} = K_1 K_2 \tag{8.5}$$

or mean curvature,

$$K_{\text{mean}} = (K_1 + K_2)/2. \tag{8.6}$$

The sign of the Gaussian and mean curvature are enough to characterize the surface at a point P into one of eight fundamental surface types: peak, pit, ridge, valley, saddle ridge, saddle valley, flat or minimal [6].

8.5.2 HOC

The first step to compute a histogram of curvature is to compute curvature at every pixel. A simple computation of curvature using second derivatives is very sensitive to noise and the Kinect sensor is by no means a noiseless sensor. As a first attempt to remove noise, range images are smoothed using a simple convolution with an averaging filter. In order to further overcome the obstacle of noise, Besl describes how Gaussian and mean curvature can be computed robustly for points on a surface [6]. We follow this method to compute Gaussian and mean curvature with the only modification being that the following 3×3 filter windows are used instead of 7×7 windows.

$$F_u = 1/8 \begin{pmatrix} 1 & 0 & -1 \\ 2 & 0 & -2 \\ 1 & 0 & -1 \end{pmatrix}$$

$$F_v = 1/8 \begin{pmatrix} 1 & 2 & 1 \\ 0 & 0 & 0 \\ -1 & -2 & -1 \end{pmatrix}$$

$$F_{uu} = 1/4 \begin{pmatrix} 1 & -2 & 1 \\ 2 & -4 & 2 \\ 1 & -2 & 1 \end{pmatrix}$$

$$F_{vv} = 1/4 \begin{pmatrix} 1 & 2 & 1 \\ -2 & -4 & -2 \\ 1 & 2 & 1 \end{pmatrix}$$

$$F_{uv} = 1/4 \begin{pmatrix} 1 & 0 & -1 \\ 0 & 0 & 0 \\ -1 & 0 & 1 \end{pmatrix}.$$

Just as in [6], these filters are then convolved (denoted by $*$) with the depth Z to produce intermediate values that can be used to compute mean and gaussian curvatures in Eqs. 8.8 and 8.9:

$$\begin{aligned} g_u(i,j) &= F_u * Z(i,j) & g_v(i,j) &= F_v * Z(i,j) \\ g_{uu}(i,j) &= F_{uu} * Z(i,j) & g_{vv}(i,j) &= F_{vv} * Z(i,j) \\ g_{uv}(i,j) &= F_{uv} * Z(i,j) & & \end{aligned} \tag{8.7}$$

$$K_{\text{mean}}(i,j)$$
$$= \frac{(1+g_v^2(i,j))g_{uu}(i,j) + (1+g_u^2(i,j))g_{vv}(i,j) - 2g_u(i,j)g_v(i,j)g_{uv}(i,j)}{2(\sqrt{1+g_u^2(i,j)+g_v^2(i,j)})^3} \tag{8.8}$$

$$K_{\text{gauss}}(i,j) = \frac{g_{uu}(i,j)g_{vv}(i,j) - g_{uv}^2(i,j)}{(1+g_u^2(i,j)+g_v^2(i,j))^2}. \tag{8.9}$$

After computing both Gaussian and mean curvature at every point in the range image, the goal is to compute some sort of histogram over a window of the image based on curvature. Below are the results for with four different types of feature with varying number of bins.

The feature vector for each window is computed for a pyramid of different resolution windows similarly to [14]. Windows are divided into spatial bins or cells, more specifically the number of cells in the horizontal direction is equal to w/k, where w is the width of the window and k is some constant, in this case $k = 8$. The number of cells in the vertical direction is equal to h/k, where h is the height of the window. A histogram is then computed for each cell and the resulting histograms for each cell and each level of the pyramid are concatenated to create a feature vector for the entire window.

The first HOC methods are inspired by the fact that mean curvature might be a sufficient feature because if the boundary of a curve is specified, mean curvature uniquely determines the shape of the surface [6]. Since noise is such a concern when computing curvature the first two HOC features are not actually histograms, but simply averages over a spatial area. For each spatial cell (i, j), the average mean curvature is denoted $a_{\text{curv}}(i, j)$.

A single number is assigned for that cell based on the average:

$$\text{HOC}_1(i, j) = \begin{cases} -1 & \text{if } a_{\text{curv}}(i, j) < -t \\ 0 & \text{if } -t < a_{\text{curv}}(i, j) < t \\ 1 & \text{if } a_{\text{curv}}(i, j) > t. \end{cases} \quad (8.10)$$

Experiments were also conducted using two thresholds instead of just one. Using one threshold approximately assigns negative, zero and positive curvature to different values (or in the case of the histograms below, different bins). Using two thresholds assigns strongly negative, weakly negative, zero, weakly positive and strongly positive curvature to different values. This is an intuitively desirable effect because we might bin depth discontinuities (strong curvature) into different bins than small changes in curvature that can be seen within the edges of an object. This intuition leads to the hypothesis that without two thresholds the features would be dominated by the strong curvature at depth discontinuities, thus making HOC similar to HOG on a range image. Obviously, this should be avoided so the second HOC feature is assigned using two thresholds:

$$\text{HOC}_2(i, j) = \begin{cases} -2 & \text{if } a_{\text{curv}}(i, j) < -t_2 \\ -1 & \text{if } -t_2 < a_{\text{curv}}(i, j) < -t_1 \\ 0 & \text{if } -t_1 < a_{\text{curv}}(i, j) < t_1 \\ 1 & \text{if } t_1 < a_{\text{curv}}(i, j) < t_2 \\ 2 & \text{if } a_{\text{curv}}(i, j) > t_2. \end{cases} \quad (8.11)$$

Since the features described in Eqs. 8.10 and 8.11 are not actually histograms, the following similar features are actually histograms of the average curvature in a spatial bin:

$$\text{HOC}_3(i, j, 1) = \begin{cases} 1 & \text{if } a_{\text{curv}}(i, j) < -t \\ 0 & \text{otherwise} \end{cases}$$

$$\text{HOC}_3(i, j, 2) = \begin{cases} 1 & \text{if } -t < a_{\text{curv}}(i, j) < t \\ 0 & \text{otherwise} \end{cases} \quad (8.12)$$

$$\text{HOC}_3(i, j, 3) = \begin{cases} 1 & \text{if } a_{\text{curv}}(i, j) > t \\ 0 & \text{otherwise.} \end{cases}$$

As before a fourth feature that uses two thresholds instead of one can be defined:

$$\text{HOC}_4(i, j, 1) = \begin{cases} 1 & \text{if } a_{\text{curv}}(i, j) < -t_2 \\ 0 & \text{otherwise} \end{cases}$$

$$\text{HOC}_4(i, j, 2) = \begin{cases} 1 & \text{if } -t_2 < a_{\text{curv}}(i, j) < -t_1 \\ 0 & \text{otherwise} \end{cases}$$

$$\text{HOC}_4(i, j, 3) = \begin{cases} 1 & \text{if } -t_1 < a_{\text{curv}}(i, j) < t_1 \\ 0 & \text{otherwise} \end{cases} \quad (8.13)$$

$$\text{HOC}_4(i, j, 4) = \begin{cases} 1 & \text{if } t_1 < a_{\text{curv}}(i, j) < t_2 \\ 0 & \text{otherwise} \end{cases}$$

$$\text{HOC}_4(i, j, 5) = \begin{cases} 1 & \text{if } a_{\text{curv}}(i, j) > t_2 \\ 0 & \text{otherwise.} \end{cases}$$

Of course, averaging might not be the right solution, a lot of signal might be lost in attempts to denoise. As mentioned before, Gaussian curvature may or may not be useful, so the following HOC features continue to use just mean curvature (K_{mean}). (Gaussian curvature will be used later.) In the following feature descriptor, instead of averaging, a true histogram is computed by counting the number of pixels in each cell that fall into each of the three bins of the histogram:

$$\text{HOC}_5(i, j, 1) = \sum_{\text{pixel}(x,y) \in \text{cell}(i,j)} \left(K_{\text{mean}}(x, y) < -t \right)$$

$$\text{HOC}_5(i, j, 2) = \sum_{\text{pixel}(x,y) \in \text{cell}(i,j)} \left(-t < K_{\text{mean}}(x, y) < t \right) \quad (8.14)$$

$$\text{HOC}_5(i, j, 3) = \sum_{\text{pixel}(x,y) \in \text{cell}(i,j)} \left(K_{\text{mean}}(x, y) > t \right).$$

As before, a 5-bin version of the feature vector can also be formulated:

$$\text{HOC}_6(i, j, 1) = \sum_{\text{pixel}(x,y) \in \text{cell}(i,j)} \left(K_{\text{mean}}(x, y) < -t_2 \right)$$

$$\text{HOC}_6(i, j, 2) = \sum_{\text{pixel}(x,y) \in \text{cell}(i,j)} \left(-t_2 < K_{\text{mean}}(x, y) < -t_1 \right)$$

$$\text{HOC}_6(i, j, 3) = \sum_{\text{pixel}(x,y) \in \text{cell}(i,j)} \left(-t_1 < K_{\text{mean}}(x, y) < t_1 \right) \quad (8.15)$$

$$\text{HOC}_6(i, j, 4) = \sum_{\text{pixel}(x,y) \in \text{cell}(i,j)} \left(t_1 < K_{\text{mean}}(x, y) < t_2 \right)$$

$$\text{HOC}_6(i, j, 5) = \sum_{\text{pixel}(x,y) \in \text{cell}(i,j)} \left(K_{\text{mean}}(x, y) > t_2 \right).$$

After experimenting with different thresholds, we found empirically that $t = t_1 = 0.005$ and $t_2 = 0.05$ worked best.

Finally, it is necessary to evaluate feature descriptors that use Gaussian curvature as well as mean curvature. To do this additional bins must be added to either HOC_5 or HOC_6. A six bin histogram of mean and gaussian curvature (K_{gauss}) is computed as follows:

$$\text{HOC}_7(i, j, k) = \text{HOC}_5(i, j, k) \quad \text{for } k = 1, 2, 3$$

$$\text{HOC}_7(i, j, 4) = \sum_{\text{pixel}(x,y) \in \text{cell}(i,j)} \left(K_{\text{gauss}}(x, y) < -t_g \right)$$

$$\text{HOC}_7(i, j, 5) = \sum_{\text{pixel}(x,y) \in \text{cell}(i,j)} \left(-t_g < K_{\text{gauss}}(x, y) < t_g \right) \quad (8.16)$$

$$\text{HOC}_7(i, j, 6) = \sum_{\text{pixel}(x,y) \in \text{cell}(i,j)} \left(K_{\text{gauss}}(x, y) > t_g \right).$$

A similar feature descriptor (HOC$_8$) can be computed for an eight-bin histogram using two thresholds for mean curvature:

$$\text{HOC}_8(i, j, k) = \text{HOC}_6(i, j, k) \quad \text{for } k = 1, 2, 3, 4, 5 \quad (8.17)$$

$$\text{HOC}_8(i, j, k) = \text{HOC}_7(i, j, k - 2) \quad \text{for } k = 6, 7, 8. \quad (8.18)$$

We found empirically that $t_g = 0.00005$ worked well.

8.5.3 *Experimental Setup and Baselines*

All the experiments in this section are based on a sliding window linear SVM classifier trained in two phases, one using random negative examples and one using "hard" negatives generated using the code from Felzenszwalb et al. [14]. Two mirrored models are trained for each class and windows are constrained to a fixed aspect ratio but varying position and scale. All features are evaluated as a pyramid of scales. In contrast to the experiments in Sect. 8.4, the models computed in this section were not based on the deformable parts model. As in Sect. 8.4, nonmaximal suppression is used at test time and the same evaluation paradigm (Eq. 8.3) is used.

Two baselines were performed, both based on the use of a HOG feature descriptor that uses both contrast-sensitive and contrast-insensitive bins, and four different normalization schemes [14]. The first baseline simply ignores depth and just computes HOG features for the color image. The second baseline concatenates HOG features for both color and depth images.

Experimental results were computed for 16 different feature vectors. The first eight consist of a HOG feature descriptor for intensity image concatenated with one of the eight different HOC features. The second eight features consist of the concatenation of HOG on the intensity image, HOG on the range image and one of the eight HOC features.

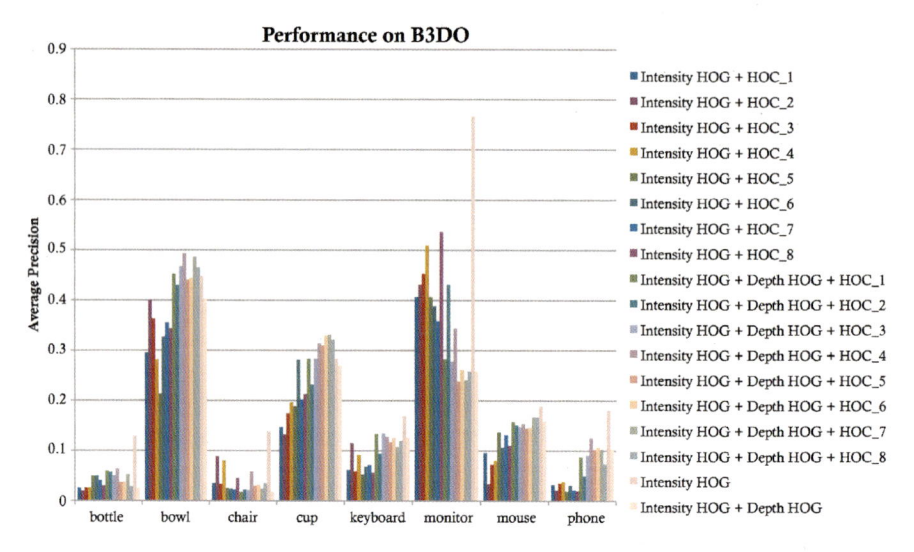

Fig. 8.11 Average precision for all 16 different feature vectors as well as the two baselines. Performance is averaged by six different splits of the data

8.5.4 Results

Figure 8.11 shows average precision, eight different classes of objects and all 16 feature vectors in addition to the two baselines (Intensity HOG and Intensity HOG + Depth HOG). For most categories, using HOG on intensity images and depth images in conjunction with HOC performed better than leaving out HOG on the depth images. The biggest exception to this is for computer monitors. Most of the monitors in B3DO are turned off and are thus completely black. The structured-light sensor used by the Kinect does not always work well for black objects, and monitors are an example of a surface that often has significant missing data. Thus, increased performance by adding a depth channel should not be expected.

In order to visualize results more clearly, Fig. 8.12 shows results for only the features that combine HOG on intensity and depth images with HOC, as well as the baselines. The most noticeable result is that the best performance for bottle, chair, keyboard, monitor, computer mouse and phone occurs when depth is ignored. There are positive results for the categories of cup and bowl. For bowls, both HOC_4 and HOC_7 outperform the baseline that ignores depth by approximately 5 % and the baseline that uses HOG on depth and no curvature by approximately 10 %. Similar results can be observed for cups, but for cups the best performing features are HOC_6 and HOC_7. This result is somewhat intuitive, the shape of cups and bowls is very simple, and likely easier to learn than the shape of more complicated objects like chairs and telephones.

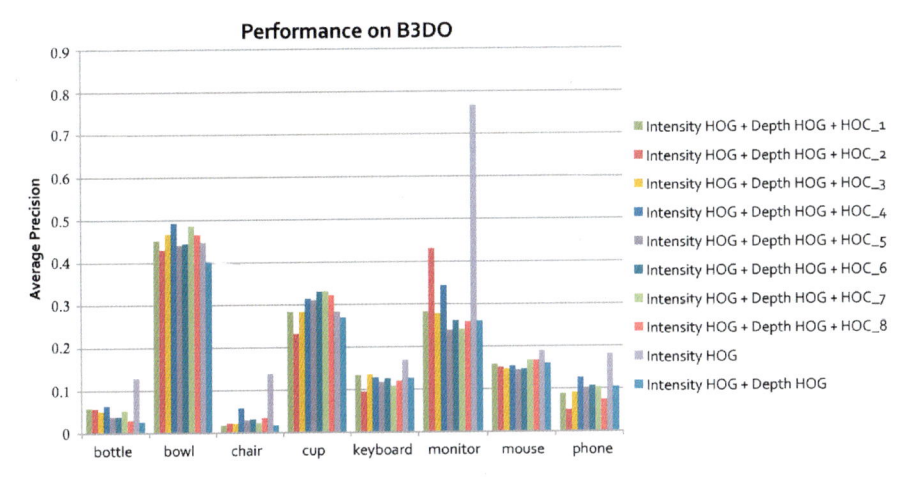

Fig. 8.12 Similar to Fig. 8.11, the chart shows performance just for the features that combine HOG on the intensity image and depth image with a HOC feature

8.6 Discussion

The Berkeley 3D Object Dataset provides a challenging dataset on which to test the ability of object detectors to take advantage of 3D signal. This dataset provides a unique opportunity for researchers to test their methods in the face of large variation in pose and viewpoint. In addition, the lack of dense training data (for example on a turntable) and the simple collection process enables this dataset to continue to grow with contributions from the world outside the research community.

Section 8.4 demonstrated that techniques based on estimating the size of objects can be used to slightly improve performance. Simple solutions such as computing a histogram of gradient for range images can extract some of the information present in the range image but not all. In order to extract all the available information from depth signal, features that can learn the shape of the objects that one wishes to recognize must be used. To this end, this work proposes the histogram of curvature, or HOC. Performance could be improved in a number of ways. It is possible that linear classifiers are not powerful enough. HOG has been hand tuned with various normalization factors in order to work well with linear classifiers, but as HOC is missing this, it may require nonlinear kernels. In addition, by simply concatenating feature vectors, the fact that the three feature vectors were obtained by different processes is lost. A multiple kernel learning framework may be better able to handle the fact that there are in fact three feature vectors without simply concatenating them.

References

1. Ford campus vision and Lidar dataset. http://robots.engin.umich.edu/Downloads

2. Solution in perception challenge. http://opencv.willow-garage.com/wiki/SolutionsInPerceptionChallenge
3. UBC Robot Vision Survey. http://www.cs.ubc.ca/labs/lci/vrs/index.html
4. Introducing Kinect for Xbox 360. http://www.xbox.com/en-US/Kinect/ (2011)
5. Alexe, B., Deselaers, T., Ferrari, V.: What is an object? In: IEEE Conference on Computer Vision and Pattern Recognition (2010)
6. Besl, P.J., Jain, R.C.: Segmentation through variable-order surface fitting. IEEE Trans. Pattern Anal. Mach. Intell. **10** (1988). doi:10.1109/34.3881
7. Bradski, G.: The OpenCV library. Dr. Dobb's Journal of Software Tools (2000)
8. Browatzki, B., Fischer, J., Birgit, G., Bulthoff, H., Wallraven, C.: Going into depth: evaluating 2d and 3d cues for object classification on a new, large-scale object dataset. In: International Conference on Computer Vision—Workshop on Consumer Depth Cameras for Computer Vision (2011)
9. Burrus, N.: Kinect RGB demo V0.4.0. http://nicolas.burrus.name/index.php/Research/KinectRgbDemoV4?from=Research.KinectRgbDemoV2 (2011)
10. Dalal, N., Triggs, B.: Histograms of oriented gradients for human detection. In: IEEE Conference on Computer Vision and Pattern Recognition (2005)
11. Ess, A., Schindler, K., Leibe, B., Gool, L.V.: Object detection and tracking for autonomous navigation in dynamic environments. Int. J. Robot. Res. (2010). doi:10.1177/0278364910365417
12. Everingham, M., Van Gool, L., Williams, C.K.I., Winn, J., Zisserman, A.: The PASCAL Visual Object Classes Challenge 2010 (VOC2010) Results. http://www.pascal-network.org/challenges/VOC/voc2010/workshop/index.html
13. Felzenszwalb, P.F., Girshick, R.B., McAllester, D.: Cascade object detection with deformable part models. In: IEEE Conference on Computer Vision and Pattern Recognition (2010)
14. Felzenszwalb, P.F., Girshick, R.B., McAllester, D., Ramanan, D.: Object detection with discriminatively trained part based models. IEEE Trans. Pattern Anal. Mach. Intell. (2009). doi:10.1109/TPAMI.2009.167
15. Fritz, M., Saenko, K., Darrell, T.: Size matters: metric visual search constraints from monocular metadata. In: Advances in Neural Information Processing Systems (2010)
16. Frome, A., Huber, D., Kolluri, R., Bulow, T., Malik, J.: Recognizing objects in range data using regional point descriptors. In: European Conference on Computer Vision (2004)
17. Gould, S., Baumstarck, P., Quigley, M., Ng, A.Y., Koller, D.: Integrating visual and range data for robotic object detection. In: European Conference on Computer Vision—Workshop on Multi-camera and Multi-modal Sensor Fusion Algorithms and Applications (2008)
18. Grimson, W.: From Images to Surfaces: A Computational Study of the Human Early Visual System. MIT Press, Cambridge (1981)
19. Hattori, H., Seki, A., Nishiyama, M., Watanabe, T.: Stereo-based pedestrian detection using multiple patterns. In: British Machine Vision Conference (2009)
20. Helmer, S., Meger, D., Muja, M., Little, J.J., Lowe, D.G.: Multiple viewpoint recognition and localization. In: Asian Conference on Computer Vision (2010)
21. Janoch, A., Karayev, S., Jia, Y., Barron, J.T., Fritz, M., Saenko, K., Darrell, T.: A category-level 3-D object dataset: putting the Kinect to work. In: International Conference on Computer Vision—Workshop on Consumer Depth Cameras for Computer Vision (2011)
22. Johnson, A., Hebert, M.: Using spin images for efficient object recognition in cluttered 3d scenes. IEEE Trans. Pattern Anal. Mach. Intell. **21**(5), 433–449 (1999)
23. Lai, K., Bo, L., Ren, X., Fox, D.: A large-scale hierarchical multi-view RGB-D object dataset. In: International Conference on Robotics and Automation (2011)
24. Rohrbach, M., Enzweiler, M., Gavrila, D.M.: High-level fusion of depth and intensity for pedestrian classification. In: Annual Symposium of German Association for Pattern Recognition (2009)
25. Rusu, R.B., Bradski, G., Thibaux, R., Hsu, J.: Fast 3d recognition and pose using the viewpoint feature histogram. In: International Conference on Intelligent Robots and Systems (2010)

26. Shotton, J., Fitzgibbon, A., Cook, M., Sharp, T., Finocchio, M., Moore, R., Kipman, A., Blake, A.: Real-time human pose recognition in parts from single depth images. In: IEEE Conference on Computer Vision and Pattern Recognition (2011)
27. Silberman, N., Fergus, R.: Indoor scene segmentation using a structured light sensor. In: International Conference on Computer Vision—Workshop on 3D Representation and Recognition (2011)
28. Sun, M., Bradski, G., Xu, B.X., Savarese, S.: Depth-encoded hough voting for joint object detection and shape recovery. In: European Conference on Computer Vision (2010)
29. Walk, S., Schindler, K., Schiele, B.: Disparity statistics for pedestrian detection: combining appearance, motion and stereo. In: European Conference on Computer Vision (2010)
30. Wang, X., Han, T.X., Yan, S.: An HOG-LBP human detector with partial occlusion handling. In: International Conference on Computer Vision (2009)
31. Woodford, O., Torr, P., Reid, I., Fitzgibbon, A.: Global stereo reconstruction under second-order smoothness priors. IEEE Trans. Pattern Anal. Mach. Intell. (2009). doi:10.1109/ICCV.2009.5459207

Chapter 9
RGB-D Object Recognition: Features, Algorithms, and a Large Scale Benchmark

Kevin Lai, Liefeng Bo, Xiaofeng Ren, and Dieter Fox

Abstract Over the last decade, the availability of public image repositories and recognition benchmarks has enabled rapid progress in visual object category and instance detection. Today we are witnessing the birth of a new generation of sensing technologies capable of providing high quality synchronized videos of both color and depth, the RGB-D (Kinect-style) camera. With its advanced sensing capabilities and the potential for mass adoption, this technology represents an opportunity to dramatically increase robotic object recognition, manipulation, navigation, and interaction capabilities. We introduce a large-scale, hierarchical multi-view object dataset collected using an RGB-D camera. The dataset consists of two parts: The RGB-D Object Dataset containing views of 300 objects organized into 51 categories, and the RGB-D Scenes Dataset containing 8 video sequences of office and kitchen environments. The dataset has been made publicly available to the research community so as to enable rapid progress based on this promising technology. We describe the dataset collection procedure and present techniques for RGB-D object recognition and detection of objects in scenes recorded using RGB-D videos, demonstrating that combining color and depth information substantially improves quality of results.

K. Lai (✉) · L. Bo · D. Fox
Department of Computer Science & Engineering, University of Washington, Seattle, WA 98195, USA
e-mail: kevinlai@cs.washington.edu

L. Bo
e-mail: lfb@cs.washington.edu

D. Fox
e-mail: fox@cs.washington.edu

X. Ren
Intel Science and Technology on Pervasive Computing, Seattle, WA 98195, USA
e-mail: xiaofeng.ren@intel.com

A. Fossati et al. (eds.), *Consumer Depth Cameras for Computer Vision*, Advances in Computer Vision and Pattern Recognition, DOI 10.1007/978-1-4471-4640-7_9, © Springer-Verlag London 2013

9.1 Introduction

The availability of public image repositories on the Web, such as Google Images, and visual recognition benchmarks like Caltech 101 [11], LabelMe [36], and ImageNet [9] has enabled rapid progress in visual object recognition in the past decade. Today we are witnessing the birth of a new generation of sensing technologies capable of providing high quality synchronized videos of both color and depth, the RGB-D (Kinect-style) camera [22, 35]. This technology represents an opportunity to dramatically increase the capabilities of robotics object recognition, manipulation, navigation, and interaction. We describe the RGB-D Object Dataset, a large-scale, multi-view object data set collected using an RGB-D camera that was first introduced in [23]. The dataset and its accompanying software has been made publicly available to the research community to enable rapid progress based on this promising technology. The dataset and accompanying software tools are available at http://www.cs.washington.edu/rgbd-dataset.

Unlike many existing recognition benchmarks that are constructed using Internet photos, where it is impossible to keep track of whether objects in different images are physically the same object, our dataset consists of multiple views of a set of objects. This is similar to the 3D Object Category Dataset presented by Savarese et al. [37], which eight object categories, 10 objects in each category, and 24 distinct views of each object. The RGB-D Object Dataset presented here is at a much larger scale, with RGB and depth video sequences of 300 common everyday objects from multiple view angles totaling 250,000 RGB-D images. The objects are organized into a hierarchical category structure using WordNet hyponym/hypernym relations. The dataset also includes the RGB-D Scenes Dataset, which eight RGB-D video sequences of office and kitchen environments.

In addition to introducing a large RGB-D object and scene dataset, we also present techniques for object recognition in RGB-D data and detection of objects in scenes recorded using RGB-D videos. We demonstrate that combining color and depth information can substantially improve results on three object recognition tasks: (1) *Category-level* recognition involves classifying previously unseen objects as belonging in the same category as objects that have previously been seen (e.g., coffee mug). (2) *Instance-level* recognition is identifying whether an object is physically the same object that has previously been seen. We use the word *instance* to refer to an object with a particular appearance. (3) *Pose-level* recognition is estimating the orientation of the object relative to the camera. The ability to solve all three recognition tasks is important for applications such as service robotics. For example, identifying an object as a generic "coffee mug" or as "Amelia's coffee mug" can have different implications depending on the context of the task. Determining the accurate pose of an object is necessary for manipulation.

9.2 RGB-D Object Dataset Collection

The RGB-D Object Dataset contains visual and depth images of 300 physically distinct objects taken from multiple views. The chosen objects are commonly found in home and office environments, where personal robots are expected to operate. Objects are organized into a hierarchy taken from WordNet hypernym/hyponym relations and are a subset of the categories in ImageNet [9]. Figure 9.1 shows several subtrees in the object category hierarchy. *Fruit* and *Vegetable* are both top-level subtrees in the hierarchy. *Device* and *Container* are both subtrees under the *Instrumentation* category that covers a very broad range of man-made objects. Each of the 300 objects in the dataset belongs to one of the 51 leaf nodes in this hierarchy, with between 3 to 14 instances in each category. The leaf nodes are shaded blue in Fig. 9.1 and the number of object instances in each category is given in parentheses. Figure 9.2 shows some example objects from the dataset. Each shown object comes from one of the 51 object categories. Although the background is visible in these images, the dataset also provides segmentation masks (see Fig. 9.4). The segmentation procedure using combined visual and depth cues is described in Sect. 9.3.

The dataset is collected using a RGB-D camera manufactured by PrimeSense [35], whose optical hardware is identical to the Microsoft Kinect [22]. The RGB-D camera simultaneously records both color and depth images at 640×480 resolution. In other words, each 'pixel' in an RGB-D frame contains four channels: red, green, blue and depth. The 3D location of each pixel in physical space can be computed using known sensor parameters. The RGB-D camera creates depth images by continuously projecting an invisible infrared structured light pattern and performing stereo triangulation. Compared to passive multi-camera stereo technology, this active projection approach results in much more reliable depth readings, particularly in textureless regions. Figure 9.3 (top) shows a single RGB-D frame which consists of both an RGB image and a depth image. Driver software provided with the RGB-D camera ensures that the RGB and depth images are aligned and time-synchronous.

Using this camera setup, we record video sequences of each object as it is spun around on a turntable at constant speed. The camera is placed around one meter from the turntable. We found this to be the minimum distance required for the RGB-D camera to return reliable depth readings. Data was recorded with the camera mounted at three different heights relative to the turntable, at approximately $30°$, $45°$ and $60°$ above the horizon. One revolution of each object was recorded at each height. Each video sequence is recorded at 20 Hz and contains around 250 frames, giving a total of 250,000 RGB + Depth frames in the RGB-D Object Dataset. The video sequences are all annotated with ground truth object pose angles between $[0, 360°]$ by tracking the red markers on the turntable. A reference pose is chosen for each category so that pose angles are consistent across video sequences of objects in a category. For example, all videos of coffee mugs are labeled such that the image where the handle is on the right is $0°$.

9.3 Segmentation

Without any post-processing, a substantial portion of the RGB-D video frames is occupied by the background. We use visual cues, depth cues, and rough knowledge

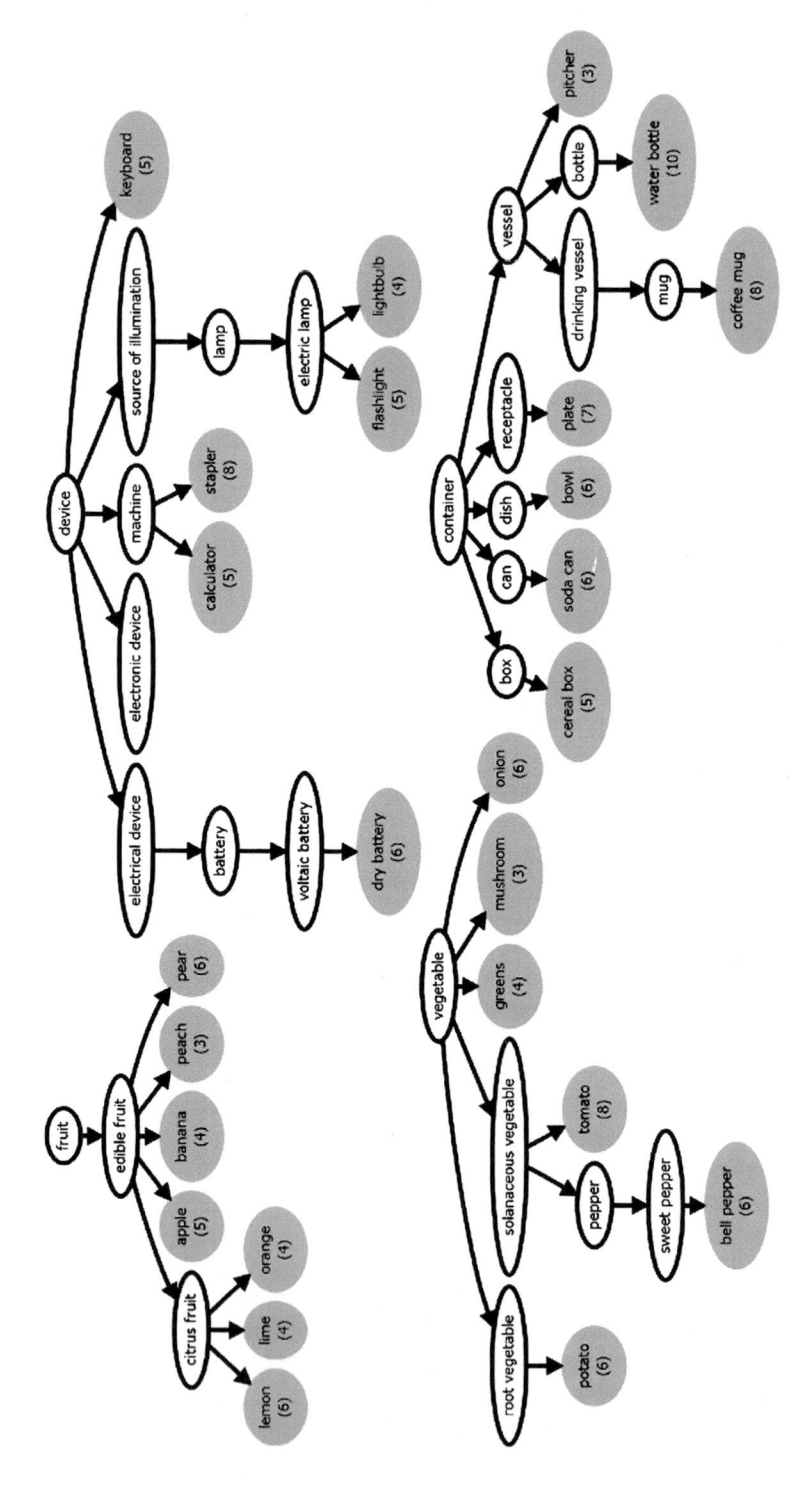

Fig. 9.1 The fruit, device, vegetable, and container subtrees of the RGB-D Object Dataset object hierarchy. The number of instances in each leaf category (*shaded in blue*) is given in parentheses

9 RGB-D Object Recognition: Features, Algorithms, and a Large Scale Benchmark

Fig. 9.2 Objects from the RGB-D Object Dataset. Each object shown here is in a different category

Fig. 9.3 Each RGB-D frame consists of an RGB image (*left*) and a depth image (*right*)

of the configuration between the turntable and camera to produce fully segmented objects from the video sequences.

The first step in segmentation is to remove most of the background by taking only the points within a 3D bounding box where we expect to find the turntable and object, based on the known distance between the turntable and the camera. This prunes most pixels that are far in the background, leaving only the turntable and the object. Using the fact that the object lies above the turntable surface, we can perform RANSAC plane fitting [13] to find the table plane and take points that lie above it to be the object. This procedure gives very good segmentation for many objects in the dataset, but is still problematic for small, dark, transparent, and reflective objects. Due to noise in the depth image, parts of small and thin objects like rubber erasers and markers may get merged into the table during RANSAC plane fitting. Dark, transparent, and reflective objects cause the depth estimation to fail, resulting in pixels that contain only RGB but no depth data. These pixels would be left out of the segmentation if we only used depth cues. Thus, we also apply vision-based background subtraction to generate another segmentation. The top row of Fig. 9.4 shows several examples of segmentation based on depth. Several objects are correctly segmented, but missing depth readings cause substantial portions of the water bottle, jar and the marker cap to be excluded.

To perform vision-based background subtraction, we applied the adaptive gaussian mixture model of KaewTraKulPong and Bowden [21], using the implementa-

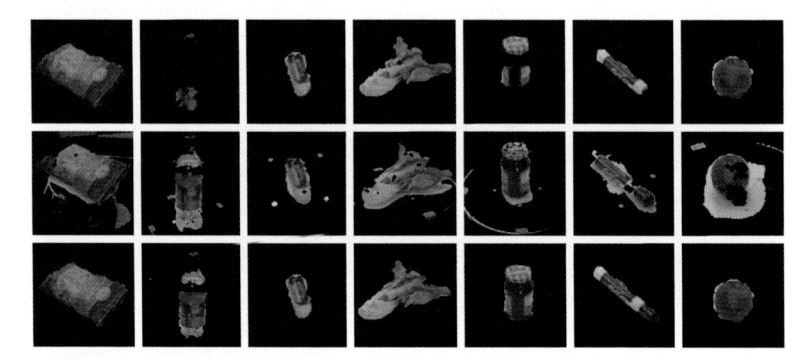

Fig. 9.4 Segmentation examples, *from left to right*: bag of chips, water bottle, eraser, leaf vegetable, jar, marker and peach. Segmentation using depth only (*top row*), visual segmentation via background subtraction (*middle row*), and combined depth and visual segmentation (*bottom row*)

tion provided by the OpenCV library. Each pixel in the scene is modeled with a mixture of K gaussians that is updated as the video sequence is played frame-by-frame. The model is adaptive and only depends on a window W of the most recent frames. A pixel in the current frame is classified as foreground if its value is beyond σ standard deviations from all gaussians in the mixture. For our object segmentation we used $K = 2$, $W = 200$, and $\sigma = 2.5$. The middle row of Fig. 9.4 shows several examples of visual background subtraction. The method is very good at segmenting out the edges of objects and can segment out parts of objects where depth failed to do so. However, it tends to miss the centers of objects that are uniform in color, such as the peach in Fig. 9.4, and pick up the moving shadows and markers on the turntable.

Since depth-based and vision-based segmentation each excel at segmenting objects under different conditions, we combine the two to generate our final object segmentation. We take the segmentation from depth as the starting point. We then add pixels from the visual segmentation that are not in the background nor on the turntable by checking their depth values. Finally an image erosion filter is run on this segmentation mask to remove isolated pixels. The bottom row of Fig. 9.4 shows the resulting segmentation using combined depth and visual segmentation. The combined procedure provides high quality segmentations for all the objects.

9.4 Video Scene Annotation

In addition to the views of objects recorded using the turntable (the RGB-D Object Dataset), we also eight video sequences of natural scenes, which we call the RGB-D Scenes Dataset. The scenes cover common indoor environments, including office workspaces, meeting rooms, and kitchen areas. The video sequences were recorded by holding the RGB-D camera at approximately human eye-level while walking around in each scene. Each video sequence contains several objects from

Table 9.1 Number of frames and objects in the eight annotated videos of natural scenes in the RGB-D Scenes Dataset

Video sequence	# of frames	# of objects
Desk_1	1748	3
Desk_2	1949	3
Desk_3	2328	4
Kitchen_small_1	2359	8
Meeting_small_1	3530	13
Table_1	2662	8
Table_small_1	2037	4
Table_small_2	1776	3

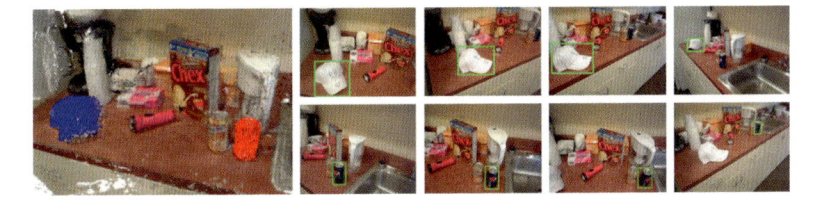

Fig. 9.5 (*Left*) 3D scene reconstruction of a kitchen scene with a *cap highlighted in blue* and a soda can *in red* using the labeling tool. (*Right*) Ground truth bounding boxes of the cap (*top*) and soda can (*bottom*) obtained by labeling the reconstruction

the RGB-D Object Dataset. The objects are visible from different viewpoints and distances and may be partially or completely occluded in some frames. Table 9.1 summarizes the number of frames and number of objects in each video sequence. In Sect. 9.6 we demonstrate that the RGB-D Object Dataset can be used as training data for performing object detection in these natural scenes. Here we will first describe how we annotated these natural scenes with the ground truth bounding boxes of objects in the RGB-D Object Dataset. Traditionally, the computer vision community has annotated video sequences one frame at a time. A human must tediously segment out objects in each image using annotation software like the LabelMe annotation tool [36] and more recently, *vatic* [39]. Temporal interpolation across video frames can somewhat alleviate this, but is only effective across a small sequence of frames if the camera trajectory is complex. Crowd-sourcing (e.g. Amazon Mechanical Turk) can also shorten annotation time, but does so merely by distributing the work across a larger number of people. We propose an alternative approach. Instead of labeling each video frame, we first stitch together the video sequence to create a 3D reconstruction of the entire scene, while keeping track of the camera pose of each video frame. We label the objects in this 3D reconstruction by hand. Figure 9.5 (left) shows the reconstruction of a kitchen scene with a cap labeled in blue and a soda can labeled in red. Finally, the labeled 3D points are projected back into the known camera poses in each video frame and this segmentation can be used to compute an object bounding box. Figure 9.5 (right) shows some bounding boxes obtained by projecting the labeled 3D points into several video frames.

Our labeling tool uses the technique proposed by Henry et al. [19] to reconstruct 3D scenes from the RGB-D video frames. The RGB-D mapping technique consists of two key components: (1) spatial alignment of consecutive video frames, and (2) globally consistent alignment of the complete video sequence. Successive frames are aligned by jointly optimizing over both appearance and shape matching. Appearance-based alignment is done with RANSAC over SIFT features annotated with 3D position (3D SIFT). Shape-based alignment is performed through Iterative Closest Point (ICP) using a point-to-plane error metric [7]. The initial alignment from 3D SIFT matching is used to initialize ICP-based alignment. Henry et al. [19] show that this allows the system to handle situations in which only vision or shape alone would fail to generate good alignments. Loop closures are performed by matching video frames against a subset of previously collected frames using 3D SIFT. Globally consistent alignments are generated with TORO, a pose-graph optimization tool developed for robotics SLAM [17].

The overall scene is built using small colored surface patches called *surfels* [34] as opposed to keeping all the raw 3D points. This representation enables efficient reasoning about occlusions and color for each part of the environment, and provides good visualizations of the resulting model. The labeling tool displays the scene in this surfel representation. When the user selects a set of surfels to be labeled as an object, they are projected back into each video frame using transformations computed during the scene reconstruction process. Surfels allow efficient occlusion reasoning to determine whether the labeled object is visible in the frame and if so, a bounding box is generated.

9.5 RGB-D Object Recognition

In object recognition the task is to assign a label (or class) to each query image. The possible labels that can be assigned are known ahead of time. State-of-the-art approaches to tackling this problem are usually supervised learning systems. A set of images are annotated with their ground truth labels and given to a classifier, which learns a model for distinguishing between the different classes. We evaluate object recognition performance on two tasks: category recognition and instance recognition. In category recognition, the system is trained on a set of objects. At test time, the system is presented with an RGB and depth image pair containing an object that was not present in training and the task is to assign a category label to the image (e.g. coffee mug or soda can). In instance recognition, the system is trained on a subset of views of each object. The task here is to distinguish between object instances (e.g. Pepsi can, Mountain Dew can, or Aquafina water bottle). At test time, the system is presented with an RGB and depth image pair that contains a previously unseen view of one of the objects and must assign an instance label to the image.

Two important problems to address for object recognition using RGB-D cameras are designing the appropriate feature representation for RGB-D data, and devising the appropriate classification method. In Sect. 9.5.1 we describe the experimental setup for using the RGB-D Object Dataset to evaluate recognition techniques. We then describe our work on distance learning in Sect. 9.5.2, demonstrating that it outperforms existing state-of-the-art classifiers. In Sect. 9.5.3, we present Kernel Descriptors, a novel family of features for RGB-D Object Recognition, and show that it outperforms existing state-of-the-art features for image and 3D point cloud recognition. Finally, in Sect. 9.5.4 we present a technique for efficiently performing RGB-D object recognition and pose estimation jointly.

9.5.1 Experimental Setup

The experiments performed in this section use the turntable data containing cropped and segmented views of objects in the RGB-D Object Dataset. The video sequences in the RGB-D Scenes Dataset are not used. We subsampled the turntable data by taking every fifth video frame, giving around 45000 RGB-D images. For category recognition, we randomly leave one object out from each category for testing and train the classifiers on all views of the remaining objects. For instance recognition, we consider two scenarios:

- Alternating contiguous frames: Divide each video three contiguous sequences of equal length. There are three heights (videos) for each object, so this gives nine video sequences for each instance. We randomly select seven of these for training and test on the remaining two.
- Leave-sequence-out: Train on the video sequences of each object where the camera is mounted 30° and 60° above the horizon and evaluate on the 45° video sequence.

We do not make use of the WordNet organization of the dataset in our experiments. We average accuracies across 10 trials for category recognition and instance recognition with alternating contiguous frames. There is no randomness in the data split for leave-sequence-out instance recognition so we report numbers for a single trial.

9.5.2 Distance Learning for RGB-D Object Recognition

In its simplest form, nearest neighbor classifiers place a set of examples with known labels in a euclidean feature space and a test example is classified based on the labels of the k nearest known examples (the k-nearest neighbor classifier). The idea behind distance learning is that nearest neighbor classification can be improved by learning a distance function because euclidean feature distances may not be the best measure of similarity, particularly when different types of feature are combined [40, 41]. Instead of learning a single global distance metric, recently researchers have looked into local distance learning, which learns different distance functions for different regions of the feature space [38]. Local distance learning has been extensively studied and demonstrated for object recognition, both for color images [15, 16, 31] and 3D shapes [27]. A key property of these approaches is that they are non-parametric, meaning that they can learn decision boundaries whose shape and complexity is determined by the data.

9.5.2.1 Instance Distance Learning

We proposed instance distance learning in [25]. Many existing distance learning approaches for image classification are designed for recognition of image collections on the web, such as Flickr and Google Images. In these applications it is impossible to tell whether two images in the collection are of the exact same object. In contrast, there are applications, particularly in robotics, where the data come from a known set of objects and consist of a collection of views taken from different camera positions, as is the case in the RGB-D Object Dataset. Our proposed approach exploits this structure by learning a distance function for each object instance. An object instance is an object with a particular appearance, and we assume that we have a collection of views of each object. We learn view-to-instance distances that measure the similarity between a query view of an object and each of the 300 object instances in the RGB-D Object Dataset.

Given a set of M features, let $\mathbf{d}(x, y)$ be the M-dimensional vector of L_2 distances between two views x and y computed for each feature separately. We define the distance between a view x and an instance Y as the weighted average of feature distances from x to all the views y that constitute instance Y:

$$f(x, Y) = \frac{1}{|Y|} \sum_{y \in Y} \mathbf{w}_y^\top \mathbf{d}(x, y) + b \qquad (9.1)$$

where $\mathbf{w}_y$, the vector of weights for y, and b, the bias term, are learned parameters. Classification of a test view is performed by computing the above distance to every object instance in the training set and taking the label of the nearest neighbor.

Parameter learning is formulated as a convex optimization problem with a margin-based loss function. Group-Lasso regularization [33] is used to encourage sparsity across views by encouraging $\mathbf{w}_y$ to not be the zero vector for only a small subset of $y \in Y$. In other words, the approach can, via supervised learning, choose to retain a small subset of views that provide good coverage of the visual variation of each object. On the RGB-D Object Dataset, instance distance learning can learn distance functions that depend only on 30 % of the views in the training data without compromising classification accuracy, outperforming uniform random downsampling at equal levels of data sparsification [25].

9.5.2.2 RGB-D Feature Set

To evaluate Instance Distance Learning we used existing state-of-the-art features developed separately for RGB images and 3D point clouds.

Shape features are extracted from 3D point clouds of each view. The 3D point cloud is obtained from the depth image using known camera intrinsic parameters. We first compute spin images [20] for a randomly subsampled set of 3D points. We generate a feature vector for the view using this collection of local descriptors using efficient match kernels (EMK) [4]. To incorporate spatial information, we divide each view using a $3 \times 3 \times 3$ axis-aligned bounding cube. We compute a 1000-dimensional EMK features in each of the 27 cells separately. We perform principal component analysis (PCA) on the EMK features in each cell and take the first 100 components. We also include as shape features the width, depth and height of the bounding cube. For SVM and random forest classifiers, we concatenate these features to yield a 2703-dimensional shape descriptor. For distance learning approaches, we compute euclidean feature distances for each of the 27 spin image cells, as well as each dimension of the bounding box separately, meaning we learn weighted distances over 30 shape features.

Visual features are extracted from the RGB image to capture the appearance of a view. We extract SIFT descriptors [30] densely on an 8×8 grid. To generate image-level features we use EMK on a two-level spatial pyramid: First we compute a 1000-dimensional EMK feature from the entire image. Then we divide the image into 2×2 blocks and extract EMK features in each block. We perform PCA on each block and take the first 300 components, giving a 1500-dimensional EMK SIFT descriptor. We also extract texton histogram [28] features. We used 100 textons learned from images on LabelMe and computed histograms five image regions, as was done in [31]. We also include a color histogram (11 bins three color channels) and the mean and standard deviation color. For SVM and random forest classifiers, we concatenate all the features to yield a 2039-dimensional visual descriptor. For distance learning approaches, we compute euclidean feature distances for each of five spatial pyramid blocks of SIFT features, five image regions of texton histograms, the color histogram, the mean color, and the color standard deviation separately. Hence, we learn weighted distances over 13 visual features.

9.5.2.3 Evaluation

We compared instance distance learning with the exemplar-based distance learning approach of [31]. This approach learns a distance function independently for each view of an object, i.e. an exemplar. Classification of a test view is performed by computing distances to every view in the training set and taking the label of the nearest neighbor. We also compared with three standard classifiers including linear and gaussian kernel support vector machine (LinSVM and kSVM) [6, 10], and random forests(RF) [5, 14]. We compared the performance of the proposed instance distance learning approach and alternative classification methods on two recognition tasks: Table 9.2 shows the classification accuracy on category recognition, and Table 9.3 for shows the accuracy on instance recognition with alternating contiguous frames (refer to Sect. 9.5.1 for a description of the different experimental setups). We report classification accuracies when using only shape features, only visual features,

Table 9.2 Category recognition on leave-out objects. Performance of various classification methods on the RGB-D Object Dataset using shape features, visual features, and with all features

Method	Category recognition		
	Shape	Vision	All
LinSVM	53.1 ± 1.7	74.3 ± 3.3	81.9 ± 2.8
kSVM	64.7 ± 2.2	74.5 ± 3.1	83.8 ± 3.5
RF	66.8 ± 2.5	74.7 ± 3.6	79.6 ± 4.0
EBLocal [31]	58.9 ± 2.1	70.1 ± 3.4	78.4 ± 2.8
IDL [25]	70.2 ± 2.0	78.6 ± 3.1	85.4 ± 3.2

Table 9.3 Instance recognition on alternating contiguous frames. Performance of various classifiers on the RGB-D Object Dataset using shape features, visual features, and with all features

Method	Instance recognition (alternating contiguous frames)		
	Shape	Vision	All
LinSVM	32.4 ± 0.5	90.9 ± 0.5	90.2 ± 0.6
kSVM	51.2 ± 0.8	91.0 ± 0.5	90.6 ± 0.6
RF	52.7 ± 1.0	90.1 ± 0.8	90.5 ± 0.4
EBLocal [31]	41.2 ± 0.6	81.2 ± 0.6	84.5 ± 0.5
IDL [25]	54.8 ± 0.6	89.8 ± 0.2	91.3 ± 0.3

Table 9.4 Instance recognition on left-out sequence. Performance of various classifiers on the RGB-D Object Dataset using shape features, visual features, and with all features

Method	Instance recognition (leave-sequence-out)		
	Shape	Vision	All
LinSVM	32.3	59.3	73.9
kSVM	46.2	60.7	74.8
RF	45.5	59.9	73.1

and using both shape and visual features. From the results, we see that the proposed instance distance learning outperforms per-exemplar distance learning and the three standard classifiers on both category and instance recognition.

Aside from comparing the instance distance learning with existing classification methods, we also investigated the usefulness of shape and visual features for category and instance recognition. For this we also report in Table 9.4 the performance of the three standard classifiers on instance recognition on left-out video sequences. We find that regardless of the classification technique used, the chosen visual features are more useful than shape features for both category and instance recognition (see Tables 9.2, 9.3, and 9.4). However, shape features are relatively more useful in category recognition, while visual features are relatively more effective in instance recognition. This is because a particular object instance has a fairly constant visual appearance across views, while objects in the same category can have different texture and color. On the other hand, shape tends to be stable across a category in many cases. The most interesting and significant conclusion is that combining both shape and visual features gives higher overall performance regardless of classification technique. The features complement each other, which demonstrates the value of a large-scale dataset that can provide both shape and visual information. For alternating contiguous frames instance recognition, using visual features alone already gives very high accuracy, so including shape features does not increase performance. The leave-sequence-out evaluation is much more challenging, and here combining shape and visual features significantly improves accuracy.

9.5.3 Kernel Descriptors for RGB-D Object Recognition

The core of building a robust object recognition system is to extract underlying representations (features) from high-dimensional sensor data such as images, depths and 3D point clouds. Given the wide availability of RGB-D cameras, it is an open question what is the best way to extract features over RGB-D images. The standard approach to object recognition is to compute pixel attributes in small windows around (a subset of) pixels. For example, in SIFT [29], gradient orientation and magnitude attributes are computed from 5×5 image windows. Another example is Spin Images [20] over local 3D point clouds. A key question for object recognition is then how to measure the similarity of local patches based on the attributes of pixels within them, because this similarity measure is used in classifiers such as linear support vector machines (SVM). Techniques based on histogram features, such as SIFT and Spin Images, discretize individual pixel attribute values into bins and then compute a histogram over the discrete attribute values within a patch. The similarity between two patches can then be computed based on their histograms. Unfortunately, the binning restricts the similarity measure and introduces quantization errors, which limit the accuracy of recognition.

9.5.3.1 Kernel Descriptors

Kernel descriptors, which we proposed in [1–3], aim to discover underlying representations of RGB-D sensor data using machine learning methodology. We highlight the kernel view of SIFT and Spin Images, and show that histogram features are a special, rather restricted case of efficient match kernels. This novel insight allows us to design a family of kernel descriptors. Kernel descriptors avoid the need for pixel attribute discretization and are able to turn any pixel attribute into compact patch-level features. Here, the similarity between two patches is based on a kernel function, called the match kernel, that averages over continuous similarities between all pairs of pixel attributes in the two patches. Match kernels are extremely flexible and it is easy to incorporate domain knowledge, since the similarity measure between pixel attributes can be any positive definite kernel, such as the popular Gaussian kernel function. While match kernels provide a natural similarity measure for image patches, evaluating these kernels can be computationally expensive, in particular for large image patches. To compute kernel descriptors, one has to move to the feature space forming the kernel function. Unfortunately, the dimensionality of these feature vectors is high, or even infinite, if for instance a Gaussian kernel is used. Thus, for computational efficiency and for representational convenience, we reduce the dimensionality by projecting the high/infinite dimensional feature vector to a set of finite basis vectors using kernel principal component analysis. This procedure can approximate the original match kernels very well, as shown in [1–3].

As an example, we briefly describe the gradient kernel descriptors over depth patches. We treat depth images as grayscale images and compute gradients at pixels. The gradient kernel descriptors F_{grad} is constructed from the pixel gradient similarity function k_o

$$F_{\text{grad}}^t(Z) = \sum_{i=1}^{d_o} \sum_{j=1}^{d_s} \alpha_{ij}^t \left\{ \sum_{z \in Z} \tilde{m}_z k_o(\tilde{\theta}_z, p_i) k_s(z, q_j) \right\} \quad (9.2)$$

where Z is a depth patch, and $z \in Z$ are the 2D relative position of a pixel in a depth patch (normalized to $[0, 1]$). $\tilde{\theta}_z$ and $\tilde{m}_z$ are the normalized orientation and magnitude of the depth gradient at a pixel z. The orientation kernel $k_o(\tilde{\theta}_z, \tilde{\theta}_x) = \exp(-\gamma_o \|\tilde{\theta}_z - \tilde{\theta}_x\|^2)$ computes the similarity of gradient orientations. The position Gaussian kernel $k_s(z, x) = \exp(-\gamma_s \|z - x\|^2)$ measures how close two pixels are spatially. $\{p_i\}_{i=1}^{d_o}$ and $\{q_j\}_{j=1}^{d_s}$ are uniformly sampled from their support region, d_o and d_s are the numbers of sampled basis vectors for the orientation and position kernels. α_{ij}^t are projection coefficients computed using kernel principal component analysis. Other kernel descriptors are constructed in a similar fashion from pixel-level similarity functions (see [2] and [3] for details).

To summarize, extracting kernel descriptors involves the following steps: (1) define pixel attributes; (2) design match kernels to measure the similarities of image patches based on these pixel attributes; (3) determine approximate, low dimensional match kernels. While the third step is done automatically by learning low dimensional representations and the defined kernels, while the first two steps allow the user to tune the approach for specific scenarios and application. Thus, kernel descriptors provides a unified and principled framework for extracting rich features from sensor data. We have developed eight types of kernel descriptor [1–3] for RGB-D images; a relatively complete feature set to capture rich cues for robust object recognition. Kernel descriptors outperform state-of-the-art recognition algorithms on many benchmarks, including USPS, extended Yaleface, Scene-15, Caltech-101, CIFAR-10, CIFAR-10-ImageNet, and the RGB-D Object Dataset. More importantly, the features have exhibited very robust performance in several real-world recognition systems, including the autonomous chess playing manipulator robot [32] and the object-aware situated interactive system (OASIS) [24]. The source code for RGB-D kernel descriptors is available at http://www.cs.washington.edu/rgbd-dataset/software.html.

9.5.3.2 Evaluation

We evaluated the proposed kernel descriptors on the RGB-D Object Dataset for both category and instance recognition (leave-sequence-out). For each RGB-D image, we compute seven kernel descriptors on dense regular grids: gradient kernel descriptors (GradKDES) over image and depth patches, local binary pattern kernel descriptors (LBPKDES) over image and depth patches, normalized RGB kernel descriptors (NRGBKDES) over image patches, spin kernel descriptors (SpinKDES) and size kernel descriptors (SizeKDES) over 3D point clouds. NRGBKDES is a variant of RGB kernel descriptors [2] that normalizes RGB values by subtracting the mean and dividing by the standard deviation in order to be robust to lighting condition changes. We extract gradient, local binary patten, and normalized RGB kernel descriptors on 16×16 depth or image patches with spacing of eight pixels. For size kernel descriptors, we consider the whole point cloud and subsample the number of 3D points to be no more than 200 for each interest point. For spin kernel descriptors, we set the radius of the local region around interest points to be 4 cm and again subsample the number of neighboring points to be no larger than 200. We consider 1×1, 2×2 and 4×4 pyramid sub-regions and form object-level features using EMK [4] with 1000 basis vectors learned by K-means on about 500,000 kernel descriptors sampled from training data. The dimensionality per kernel descriptor is $(1+4+16) \times 1000 = 21000$. The total feature extraction time per kernel descriptor is around 0.2 seconds using unoptimized MATLAB code. We train linear SVMs for recognition, which our experiments suggest are sufficient for good accuracy when using kernel descriptors.

We report the results of RGB-D kernel descriptors in Table 9.5. Results from using the existing shape and visual feature set (FeaSet, see Sect. 9.5.2) is also repeated here for comparison. First of all, we observe that combining all kernel descriptors performs much better than the best single kernel descriptors for both category and instance recognition. There are two reasons at least. Firstly, RGB-D kernel descriptors capture different recognition cues of objects including shape, color and size, which are strong in their own right and complement each other. The weights learned by the linear SVM using label information can automatically balance the contribution of each kernel descriptors for a specific task. The results in Table 9.5 show that RGB-D kernel descriptors significantly outperform the set of existing shape and visual features used in Sect. 9.5.2.

For category recognition, we observe in Table 9.5 that the best single kernel descriptor is gradient over RGB images, achieving 77.7 % accuracy. Combining depth and image kernel descriptors achieves 86.3 %, much higher than that obtained by gradient kernel descriptors only. We observe that the performance of depth kernel descriptors is comparable with image kernel descriptors, indicating that depth information is as important as visual information for category recognition. For instance

Table 9.5 Category recognition (leave-objects-out) and instance recognition (leave-sequence-out). Performance of each kernel descriptor and their combination is reported. Results using the feature set in Sect. 9.5.2 is repeated here for comparison. The classifier is linear SVM in all cases

Features	Category	Instance
FeaSet (RGB)	74.3 ± 3.3	59.3
FeaSet (Cloud)	53.1 ± 1.7	32.3
FeaSet Combination	81.9 ± 2.8	73.9
GradKDES (RGB)	77.7 ± 2.7	82.2
LBPKDES (RGB)	77.5 ± 2.5	80.9
NRGBKDES (RGB)	64.7 ± 3.3	83.4
GradKDES (Depth)	72.8 ± 2.4	40.1
LBPKDES (Depth)	72.1 ± 2.1	33.5
SpinKDES (Cloud)	60.2 ± 2.5	33.1
SizeKDES (Cloud)	56.3 ± 3.5	25.2
Combination of all KDES	86.5 ± 1.0	91.2

recognition, we observe in Table 9.5 that the best single feature is the normalized RGB kernel descriptor (83.4 %). Combining depth and image kernel descriptors achieves 91.2 %, substantially better than that obtained by normalized RGB kernel descriptors. We also notice that depth features are much worse than image features in the context of instance recognition. This is not very surprising since the different instances in the same category could share very similar shape.

9.5.4 Joint Object Category, Instance, and Pose Recognition

Object perception has multiple levels of semantics. When an autonomous robot encounters an object, we may want it to answer any or all of the following questions: *Is this a coffee mug or a plate?* (**category** recognition); *Is this Alice's coffee mug or Bob's coffee mug?* (**instance** recognition); *Am I looking at the mug with the handle facing left or right?* (**pose** recognition or approximate pose estimation). Although it is clear that category, instance, and pose recognition are closely connected and multiple facets of a single object perception problem, they have traditionally been studied in different contexts and solved using different techniques.

9.5.4.1 Object-Pose Tree

We investigated a technique, called the Object-Pose Tree, for simultaneously addressing three object recognition tasks: category recognition, instance recognition, and pose estimation [24]. These three object recognition tasks form a tree as naturally defined by the semantic structures: a category covers multiple object instances,

Fig. 9.6 Recognition of a box of Bran Flakes cereal using the Object-Pose Tree. The system labels the test image by starting with the category level *at the top* and traversing down the tree to the instance, view, and finally pose level *at the bottom*. The system finds the most similar (but not identical) pose in the training set

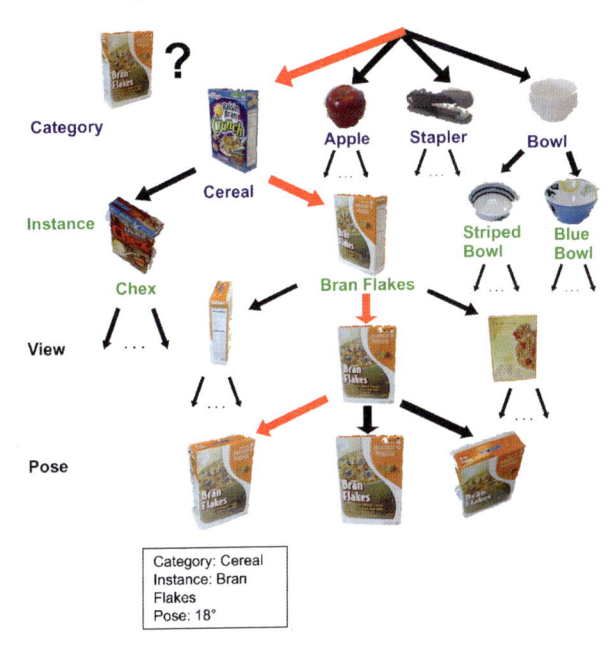

an instance covers multiple (discrete) "views", and each view is a collection of (continuous) object poses (see Fig. 9.6). Each node in the tree is a linear decision function. Given a test image containing a cropped and segmented view of an object, the system first evaluates the score that each node at the first (category) layer assigns to the image using the corresponding linear functions. The test image proceeds down the node with the highest score, and scores are computed for nodes in the second (instance) layer under that subtree. This process is repeated until the image reaches a leaf node, which represents one example in the training set (a view of an object in a particular pose). The system then assigns the category, instance, and pose based on the path traced by the test image.

Parameter learning of the entire Object-Pose Tree is formulated as structured SVM learning, where the path traced by the test image is the structured output of the system. A single convex objective function is defined that takes into account a margin-based loss on all three recognition tasks. This objective function is optimized using stochastic gradient descent. The learning procedure is detailed in [24].

9.5.4.2 Evaluation

We evaluated the Object-Pose Tree on the RGB-D Object Dataset, which annotates the pose of every view of every object as the angle about the vertical axis. Each object category has a canonical pose that is labeled as $0°$, and every image in the dataset is labeled with a pose in $[0, 360°]$. As features, we use gradient and shape (local binary pattern) kernel descriptors [2] extracted over both RGB and depth images. We use the leave-sequence-out procedure for train/test data split: the tree is

Table 9.6 Category, instance, and pose recognition results using the SVM Tree and the Object-Pose Tree

Approach	Category accuracy	Instance accuracy	Pose error
SVM Tree	92.0	77.4	44.6°
Object-Pose Tree	94.3	78.4	30.2°

Fig. 9.7 Recognition results from the Object-Pose Tree for two objects: *Red Mug* (top left), and *Ultrabrite Toothpaste* (top right). (*Bottom*) From left to right, *the top five objects* with the highest classifier response at the instance level and at the pose level for *Red Mug* and *Ultrabrite toothpaste*

trained on views of all 300 objects at 30° and 60° with the horizon (not to be confused with the pose angle about the vertical axis that the system is to estimate), and evaluated on views taken at 45° with the horizon.

Table 9.6 shows results from using the Object-Pose Tree and from using a tree of SVM classifiers. The SVM Tree has the same structure as the Object-Pose Tree, but the parameters are learned differently. For the SVM Tree, we first train a multi-class linear SVM for the category layer. Then we train SVMs for distinguishing instances within each category separately. We repeat this procedure down to the view and pose layers. We report category and instance recognition accuracies, as well as the median pose error for cases where the object instance is correctly identified. The results show that the Object-Pose Tree outperforms the SVM Tree, demonstrating that learning the parameters of the entire tree jointly through a single objective function is better than learning for each task independently. Figure 9.7 shows recognition results on two images using the Object-Pose Tree, a red mug and an Ultrabrite toothpaste. For each image, the top five matching instances and poses are shown.

9.6 Object Detection in Scenes Using RGB-D Cameras

In Sect. 9.5 we demonstrated how to perform RGB-D object recognition, where images are already cropped and segmented so that they contain only one object. In some applications such segmentations may not be easy to obtain. In this section, we demonstrate how to use the RGB-D Object Dataset to perform object detection in real-world scenes that can contain multiple objects. Given an image, the object detection task is to identify and localize all objects of interest. Like in object recognition, the objects belong to a fixed set of class labels. The object detection task can also be performed at both the category and the instance level. Existing work generally localizes objects to one of two levels of granularity: (1) localize the object to a rectangular subregion of the image (bounding box), and (2) assign an object label to every pixel or 3D point, leading to a pixel/point-level segmentation of the scene.

We present approaches for detecting objects at both levels of granularity. Experiments are performed where object detectors are trained using views of objects in the RGB-D Object Dataset, and evaluated on scenes in the RGB-D Scenes Dataset. During training, videos in the RGB-D Scenes Dataset that contain the objects are not used. A set of videos of taken in similar office and kitchen environments but without the presence of objects in the RGB-D Object Dataset are used for sampling negative training examples. These videos are available as "background" scenes in the RGB-D Scenes Dataset.

9.6.1 RGB-D Object Detection

Our RGB-D object detection system uses sliding window detectors [8, 12, 18], where the system evaluates a score function for all positions and scales in an image, and thresholds the scores to obtain object bounding boxes. Each detector window is of a fixed size and we search across 20 scales on an image pyramid. For efficiency, we here consider a linear score function (so convolution can be applied for fast evaluation on the image pyramid). We perform non-maximum suppression to remove multiple overlapping detections.

Let H be the feature pyramid and p the position of a subwindow. p is a three-dimensional vector: the first two dimensions is the top-left position of the subwindow and the third one is the scale of the image. Our score function is

$$s_w(p) = w^\top \phi(H, p) + b \qquad (9.3)$$

where w is the filter (weights), b the bias term, and $\phi(H, p)$ the feature vector at position p. We train the filter w using a linear support vector machine (SVM):

$$L(w) = \frac{w^\top w}{2} + C \sum_{i=1}^{N} \max\left(0, 1 - y_i\left(w^\top x_i + b\right)\right) \qquad (9.4)$$

where N is the training set size, $y_i \in \{-1, 1\}$ the labels, x_i the feature vector over a cropped image, and C the trade-off parameter.

The performance of the classifier heavily depends on the data used to train it. For object detection, there are many potential negative examples. A single image can be

Fig. 9.8 Original depth image (*left*) and filtered depth image using a recursive median filter (*right*). The *black pixels in the left image* are missing depth values

used to generate 10^5 negative examples for a sliding window classifier. Therefore, we follow a bootstrapping hard negative mining procedure. The positive examples are object windows we are interested in. The initial negative examples are randomly chosen from background images and object images from other categories/instances. The trained classifier is used to search images and select the false positives with the highest scores (hard negatives). These hard negatives are then added to the negative set and the classifier is retrained. This procedure is five times to obtain the final classifier.

As features we use a variant of histogram of oriented gradients (HOG) proposed in [12]. The gradient orientations in each cell (8 × 8 pixel grid) are encoded using two different quantization levels into 18 (0°–360°) and nine orientation bins (0°–180°), respectively. This yields a 4 × (18 + 9) = 108-dimensional feature vector. A 31-D analytic projection of the full 108-D feature vectors is used [12].

Aside from HOG over RGB image, we also compute HOG over depth image where each pixel value is the object-to-camera distance. Before extracting HOG features, we need to fill up missing values in the depth image. Since missing values tend to be grouped together, we use a recursive median filter. Instead of considering all neighboring pixel values, we take the median of the non-missing values in a 5 × 5 grid centered on the current pixel. We apply this median filter recursively until all missing values are filled. An example original depth image and the filtered depth image are shown in Fig. 9.8.

Finally, we also compute a feature capturing the scale (true size) of the object. Observe that the distance d of an object from the camera is inversely proportional to its scale, o. For an image at a particular scale s, we have $c = \frac{o}{s}d$, where c is constant. For sliding window detection the detector window is fixed, meaning that o is fixed. Hence, $\frac{d}{s}$, which we call the normalized depth, is constant. Since the depth is noisy, we use a histogram of normalized depths over 8 × 8 grid to capture scale information. For each pixel in a given image, d is fixed, so the normalized depth histogram can choose the correct image scale from the image pyramid. We used a histogram of 20 bins with each bin having a range of 0.15 m. Helmer et al. [18] also used depth information, but they used it as a prior in their probabilistic model while we construct a scale histogram feature from normalized depth values.

We evaluated RGB-D object detection on eight natural scene video sequences described in Sect. 9.4. Since consecutive frames are very similar, we subsample the video data and run our detection algorithm on every 5th frame. We constructed four category detectors (bowl, cap, coffee mug, and soda can) and 20 instance detectors from the same categories. We follow the PASCAL Visual Object Challenge (VOC)

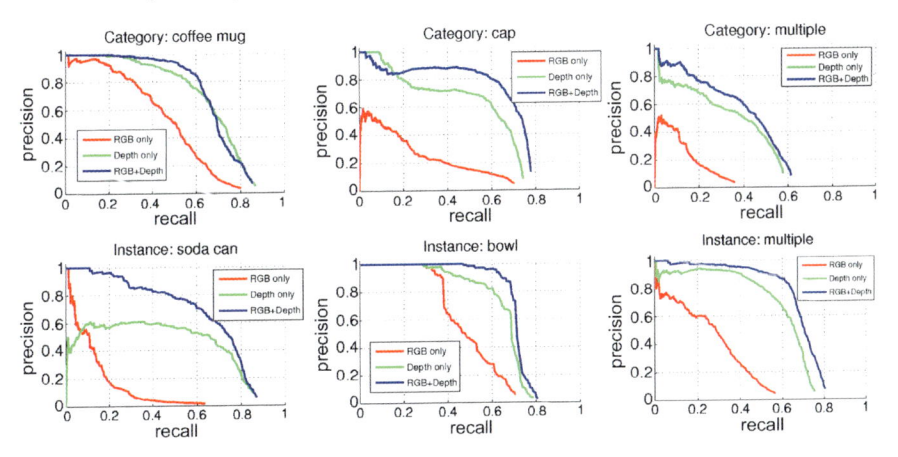

Fig. 9.9 Precision-recall curves comparing performance with image features only (*red*), depth features only (*green*), and both (*blue*). The *top row* shows category-level results. *From left to right, the first two plots* show precision-recall curves for two binary category detectors, while the *last plot* shows precision-recall curves for the multi-category detector. The *bottom row* shows instance-level results. *From left to right, the first two plots* show precision-recall curves for two binary instance detectors, while the *last plot* shows precision-recall curves for the multi-instance detector

evaluation metric. A candidate detection is considered correct if the size of the intersection of the predicted bounding box and the ground truth bounding box is more than half the size of their union. Only one of multiple successful detections for the same ground truth is considered correct, the rest are considered as false positives. We report precision-recall curves and average precision, which is computed from the precision-recall curve and is an approximation of the area under this curve. For multiple category/instance detections, we pool all candidate detection across categories/instances and images to generate a single precision-recall curve.

In Fig. 9.9 we show precision-recall curves comparing detection performance with a classifier trained using image features only (red), depth features only (green), and both (blue). We found that depth features (HOG over depth image and normalized depth histograms) are much better than HOG over RGB image. The main reason for this is that in depth images strong gradients are mostly from true object boundaries (see Fig. 9.8), which leads to much less false positives compared to HOG over RGB image, where color change can also lead to strong gradients. The best performance is attained by combining image and depth features. The combination gives higher precision across all recall levels than image only and depth only, if not comparable. In particular, combining image and depth features gives much higher precision when high recall is desired.

Figure 9.10 shows multi-object detection results in three scenes. The leftmost scene contains three objects observed from a viewpoint significantly different from what was seen in the training data. The multi-category detector is able to correctly detect all three objects, including a bowl that is partially occluded by a cereal box. The middle scene shows category detections in a very cluttered scene with many distracting objects. The system is able to correctly detect all objects except the par-

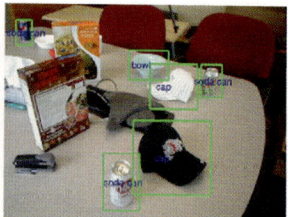

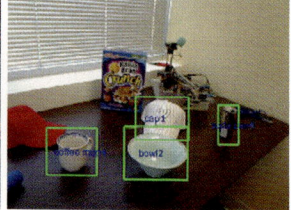

Fig. 9.10 Three detection results in multi-object scenes. *From left to right, the first two images* show multi-category detection results, while the *last image* shows multi-instance detection results

tially occluded white bowl that is far away from the camera. Notice that the detector is able to identify multiple instances of the same category (caps and soda cans). The rightmost scene shows instance detections in a cluttered scene. Here the system was able to correctly detect both the bowl and the cap, even though the cap is partially occluded by the bowl. Our current single-threaded implementation takes approximately 4 seconds to run the four object detectors to label each scene. Both feature extraction over a regular grid and evaluating a sliding window detector are easily parallelizable. We are confident that a GPU-based implementation of the described approach can perform multi-object detection in real-time.

9.6.2 Scene Labeling

For robotics applications such as object grasping, localizing objects with a bounding box is not enough. Instead, a pixel-level classification is needed, which provides both recognition and segmentation of objects in the scene. In [26], we presented a technique for pixel-level object labeling in 3D scenes reconstructed from RGB-D videos. To do this, we used sliding window detectors to assign a class probability to every pixel. Evidence is aggregated over multiple video frames by transforming the pixels into points in a 3D scene. The transformation is computed based on camera poses estimated using the RGB-D Mapping algorithm [19]. The scene is voxelized and a Markov Random Field (MRF) over the voxels that combines cues from view-based detection and 3D geometry is used to obtain the final object labeling.

We evaluated our object labeling approach on labeling five object categories in the RGB-D Scenes Dataset, bowls, caps, cereal boxes, coffee mugs, and soda cans. We achieve an overall F-score of 89.8 % when evaluated on all eight scenes in the dataset, where equal weight is assigned to each of the five object categories and to the background class. Table 9.7 shows the per-category and overall precisions and recalls of the proposed approach (Det3DMRF), as well as picking the label of each point uniformly at random (Random). The precisions for Random is 16.7 % for each of the six classes as expected, while the recalls show that the vast majority (87.5 %) of points in our scenes is background. The proposed approach performs consistently well for six classes, achieving close to overall 90 % precision and recall.

9 RGB-D Object Recognition: Features, Algorithms, and a Large Scale Benchmark

Table 9.7 Per-category and overall (macro-averaged across categories) precisions and recalls for the proposed detection-based 3D scene labeling approach and for random labeling. Our approach works very well for all object categories in the RGB-D Scene Dataset

Technique	Precision/recall						
	Bowl	Cap	Cereal box	Coffee mug	Soda can	Background	Overall
Random	16.7/2.9	16.7/2.2	16.7/6.5	16.7/1.0	16.7/0.9	16.7/87.5	16.7/16.7
Det3DMRF	91.5/85.1	90.5/91.4	93.6/94.9	90.0/75.1	81.5/87.4	99.0/99.1	91.0/88.8

Fig. 9.11 3D scene labeling results for three complex scenes in the RGB-D Scenes Dataset. 3D reconstruction (*top*), our detection-based scene labeling (*bottom*). Objects colored by their category: bowl is *red*, cap is *green*, cereal box is *blue*, coffee mug is *yellow*, and soda can is *cyan*

In Fig. 9.11 we we show three complex scenes that were labeled by our 3D scene labeling technique (Det3DMRF). The top row shows the reconstructed 3D scene and the bottom row shows results obtained by Det3DMRF. Objects are colored by their category label, where bowl is red, cap is green, cereal box is blue, coffee mug is yellow, and soda can is cyan. More detailed comparisons with alternative approaches are presented in [26].

If the desired output is bounding boxes in the original RGB-D video frames, it is possible to use the labeled 3D scene to validate object detections. We do this by running object detectors with a low threshold and pruning out bounding box candidates whose labels do not agree with the majority label of points in a central sub-rectangle of the bounding box. Figure 9.12 shows precision-recall curves obtained from both the individual frame-by-frame object detections (red) and detections validated by 3D scene labeling (blue). Each point along the curve is generated by ranking detections from all five category detectors together and thresholding on the detection score. It is clear that 3D scene labeling can significantly reduce false positives by aggregating evidence across the entire video sequence. While the precision of frame-by-frame

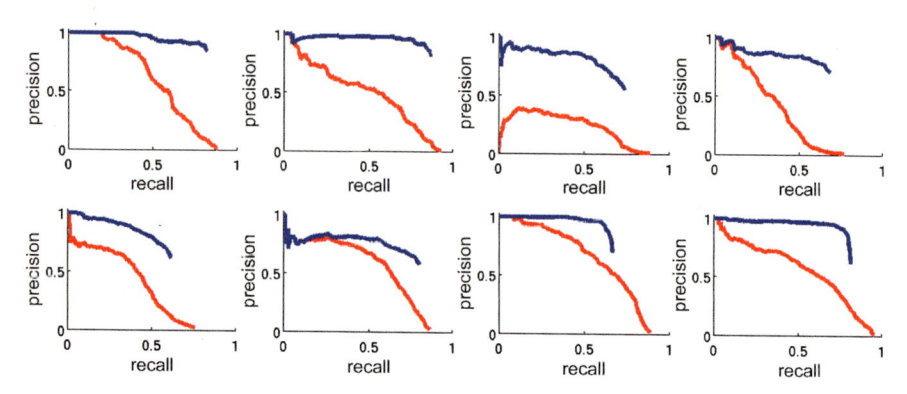

Fig. 9.12 Precision–recall curves comparing the performance of labeling images with bounding boxes of detected objects. Each plot shows results on one of the eight video sequences in the RGB-D Scenes Dataset, aggregated over all five category detectors. Frame-by-frame object detection is drawn in *red*, while 3D scene labeling (our approach) is drawn in *blue*

detection rapidly decreases beyond 60 % recall for all eight scenes, using 3D scene labeling it is possible to obtain 80 % recall and 80 % precision in a majority of them.

9.7 Discussion

We presented a large-scale, hierarchical multi-view object dataset collected using an RGB-D camera. We demonstrated methods for doing segmentation by combining depth and visual background subtraction and video ground truth annotation via 3D reconstruction. We also presented and evaluated state-of-the-art features and classification techniques for doing object recognition, object detection, and 3D scene labeling in RGB-D data. The RGB-D Object Dataset, the RGB-D Scenes Dataset, and accompanying software tools are publicly available at http://www.cs.washington.edu/rgbd-dataset.

Acknowledgements This work was funded in part by the Intel Science and Technology Center for Pervasive Computing and by ONR MURI grant N00014-07-1-0749.

References

1. Bo, L., Lai, K., Ren, X., Fox, D.: Object recognition with hierarchical kernel descriptors. In: IEEE Conference on Computer Vision and Pattern Recognition (2011)
2. Bo, L., Ren, X., Fox, D.: Kernel descriptors for visual recognition. In: Advances in Neural Information Processing Systems (2010)
3. Bo, L., Ren, X., Fox, D.: Depth kernel descriptors for object recognition. In: Intelligent Robots and Systems (2011)
4. Bo, L., Sminchisescu, C.: Efficient match kernel between sets of features for visual recognition. In: Advances in Neural Information Processing Systems (2009)

5. Breiman, L.: Random forests. Mach. Learn. **45**(1), 5–32 (2001)
6. Chang, C.-C., Lin, C.-J.: LIBSVM: a library for support vector machines (2001)
7. Chen, Y., Gérard, M.: Object modelling by registration of multiple range images. Image Vis. Comput. **10**(3), 145–155 (1992)
8. Dalal, N., Triggs, B.: Histograms of oriented gradients for human detection. In: IEEE Conference on Computer Vision and Pattern Recognition (2005)
9. Deng, J., Dong, W., Socher, R., Li, L., Li, K., Fei-fei, L.: ImageNet: a large-scale hierarchical image database. In: IEEE Conference on Computer Vision and Pattern Recognition (2009)
10. Fan, R., Chang, K., Hsieh, C., Wang, X., Lin, C.: Liblinear: a library for large linear classification. J. Mach. Learn. Res. **9**, 1871–1874 (2008)
11. Fei-Fei, L., Fergus, R., Perona, P.: One-shot learning of object categories. IEEE Trans. Pattern Anal. Mach. Intell. **28**(4), 594–611 (2006)
12. Felzenszwalb, P., McAllester, D., Ramanan, D.: A discriminatively trained, multiscale, deformable part model. In: IEEE Conference on Computer Vision and Pattern Recognition (2008)
13. Fischler, M., Bolles, R.: Random sample consensus: a paradigm for model fitting with applications to image analysis and automated cartography. Commun. ACM **24**(6), 381–395 (1981)
14. Freund, Y., Schapire, R.E.: Experiments with a new boosting algorithm. In: International Conference on Machine Learning, pp. 148–156 (1996)
15. Frome, A., Singer, Y., Malik, J.: Image retrieval and classification using local distance functions. In: Advances in Neural Information Processing Systems (2006)
16. Frome, A., Singer, Y., Sha, F., Malik, J.: Learning globally-consistent local distance functions for shape-based image retrieval and classification. In: International Conference on Computer Vision (2007)
17. Grisetti, G., Grzonka, S., Stachniss, C., Pfaff, P., Burgard, W.: Estimation of accurate maximum likelihood maps in 3d. In: Intelligent Robots and Systems (2007)
18. Helmer, S., Lowe, D.G.: Using stereo for object recognition. In: International Conference on Robotics and Automation, pp. 3121–3127 (2010)
19. Henry, P., Krainin, M., Herbst, E., Ren, X., Fox, D.: RGB-D mapping: using depth cameras for dense 3d modeling of indoor environments. Int. J. Robot. Res. (2012). doi:10.1177/0278364911434148
20. Johnson, A., Hebert, M.: Using spin images for efficient object recognition in cluttered 3D scenes. IEEE Trans. Pattern Anal. Mach. Intell. 21(5) (1999). doi:10.1109/34.765655
21. KaewTraKulPong, P., Bowden, R.: An improved adaptive background mixture model for realtime tracking with shadow detection. In: European Workshop on Advanced Video Based Surveillance Systems (2001)
22. Microsoft Kinect. http://www.xbox.com/en-us/kinect
23. Lai, K., Bo, L., Ren, X., Fox, D.: A large-scale hierarchical multi-view RGB-D object dataset. In: International Conference on Robotics and Automation (2011)
24. Lai, K., Bo, L., Ren, X., Fox, D.: A scalable tree-based approach for joint object and pose recognition. In: Conference on Artificial Intelligence (2011)
25. Lai, K., Bo, L., Ren, X., Fox, D.: Sparse distance learning for object recognition combining RGB and depth information. In: International Conference on Robotics and Automation (2011)
26. Lai, K., Bo, L., Ren, X., Fox, D.: Detection-based object labeling in 3d scenes. In: International Conference on Robotics and Automation (2012)
27. Lai, K., Fox, D.: Object Recognition in 3D point clouds using web data and domain adaptation. Int. J. Robot. Res. (2010). doi:10.1177/0278364910369190
28. Leung, T., Malik, J.: Representing and recognizing the visual appearance of materials using three-dimensional textons. Int. J. Comput. Vis. **43**(1), 29–44 (2001)
29. Lowe, D.: Distinctive image features from scale-invariant keypoints. Int. J. Comput. Vis. **60**, 91–110 (2004)
30. Lowe, D.G.: Object recognition from local scale-invariant features. In: International Conference on Computer Vision (1999)

31. Malisiewicz, T., Efros, A.: Recognition by association via learning per-examplar distances. In: IEEE Conference on Computer Vision and Pattern Recognition (2008)
32. Matuszek, C., Mayton, B., Aimi, R., Deisenroth, M., Bo, L., Chu, R., Kung, M., LeGrand, L., Smith, J., Fox, D.: Gambit: an autonomous chess-playing robotic system. In: International Conference on Robotics and Automation (2011)
33. Meier, L., Van De Geer, S., Bühlmann, P.: The group lasso for logistic regression. J. R. Stat. Soc., Ser. B **70**, 53–71 (2008)
34. Pfister, H., Zwicker, M., van Baar, J., Gross, M.: Surfels: surface elements as rendering primitives. ACM Trans. Graph. (2000). doi:10.1145/344779.344936
35. PrimeSense. http://www.primesense.com/
36. Russell, B., Torralba, K., Murphy, A., Freeman, W.: Labelme: a database and web-based tool for image annotation. Int. J. Comput. Vis. 77(1–3) (2008). doi:10.1007/s11263-007-0090-8
37. Savarese, S., Fei-Fei, L.: 3d generic object categorization, localization and pose estimation. In: International Conference on Computer Vision (2007)
38. Schultz, M., Joachims, T.: Learning a distance metric from relative comparisons. Adv. Neural Inf. Process. Syst. (2003)
39. Vondrick, C., Ramanan, D., Patterson, D.: Efficiently scaling up video annotation with crowd-sourced marketplaces. In: European Conference on Computer Vision (2010)
40. Weinberger, K.Q., Saul, L.K.: Distance metric learning for large margin nearest neighbor classification. J. Mach. Learn. Res. **10**, 207–244 (2009)
41. Xing, E., Ng, A., Jordan, M., Russell, S.: Distance metric learning with application to clustering with side-information. Adv. Neural Inform. Process. Syst. (2002)

Chapter 10
RGBD-HuDaAct: A Color-Depth Video Database for Human Daily Activity Recognition

Bingbing Ni, Gang Wang, and Pierre Moulin

Abstract In this chapter, we present a home-monitoring oriented human activity recognition benchmark database, based on the combination of a color video camera and a depth sensor. Our contributions are two-fold: (1) We have created a human activity video database named RGBD-HuDaAct, which contains synchronized color-depth video streams, for the task of human daily activity recognition. This database aims at encouraging research in human activity recognition based on multi-modal video data (color plus depth). (2) We have designed two multi-modality fusion schemes which naturally combine color and depth information from two state-of-the-art feature representation methods for action recognition, namely, spatio-temporal interest points (STIPs) and motion history images (MHIs). These depth-extended feature representation methods are evaluated comprehensively, and superior recognition performance related to their uni-modal (color only) counterparts is demonstrated.

10.1 Introduction

Automatic recognition and analysis of human daily activities (e.g., *go to bed*, *mop the floor*, *eat meal*, etc.) is helpful in a variety of applications, e.g., to facilitate effective delivery of health and medical services to isolated, elderly people. In general, video-based human activity recognition has been an active research topic in computer vision over the last decade. However, the inherent limitations of standard sensing devices restrict previous methods [2, 4, 10, 23] to recognition and analysis of lateral motions. However, human bodies and motions are 3-dimensional, and

---

B. Ni (✉) · G. Wang
Advanced Digital Sciences Center, Singapore, Singapore
e-mail: bingbing.ni@adsc.com.sg

G. Wang
e-mail: gang.wang@adsc.com.sg

P. Moulin
University of Illinois at Urbana Champaign, Urbana, IL 61801, USA
e-mail: moulin@ifp.uiuc.edu

so the information loss in the depth channel could cause significant degradation in recognition performance. The recent emergence of Microsoft Kinect depth sensors has made it feasible and economically sound to capture in real-time not only the color images, but also depth maps with appropriate spatial resolution (640 × 480 in pixel) and amplitude accuracy (≤ 1 cm accuracy). Both 3-dimensional scene structure information and the 3-dimensional motion information can be extracted. Therefore the motion ambiguity of the color camera resulting from the projection of the 3-dimensional motion onto the 2-dimensional image plane can be circumvented.

To date, very few databases provide joint color and depth data for human activity recognition. To encourage such research, we have constructed a video database named **RGBD-HuDaAct** for human activities captured with a RGB-D (i.e., *color plus depth*) sensor. This database is available upon request to the first author. Though the database is developed under the application scenario of daily activity recognition, it could be used as a common test bed for general activity recognition.

Although it is widely believed that combining color and depth provides complementary information, to our knowledge, no studies have yet shown how much gain (in terms of recognition accuracy) could be obtained by exploring the additional depth modality. To demonstrate the capability of the depth information, we develop two color-depth fusion schemes for feature representation from the most representative feature representation methods in human action recognition. Specifically, we first extend the spatio-temporal interest points methods (STIPs) into a depth-layered multi-channel representation; then, we augment the motion history images (MHIs) with two depth-change induced motion history channels. Extensive experimental results demonstrate the superior performance gained by fusing color and depth information for human activity recognition.

The rest of this chapter is organized as follows: Sect. 10.2 gives a brief review of feature representation methods in activity recognition literature. A detailed introduction to the color-depth human daily activity video database is given in Sect. 10.3. The proposed color-depth fusion schemes for activity feature representation are described in Sect. 10.4. Comprehensive experimental evaluations are given in Sect. 10.5 and Sect. 10.6 draws the conclusion and presents possible directions for future work.

10.2 Related Works

Many feature representation methods have been developed for recognizing activities (actions) from video sequences based on color cameras. Sequences of human silhouettes are utilized to model both spatial and temporal characteristics of human actions. In [4], silhouettes are temporally accumulated to form motion energy images (MEIs) and motion history images (MHIs). Seven Hu moments [14] are extracted from both MEIs and MHIs to serve as action descriptors. Davis and Tyagi [8] use Gaussian mixture models (GMM) to capture the distribution of the moments of silhouette sequences. Several other approaches utilize motion flow patterns to represent human actions. Typically, optical flows [11] are calculated for the entire image by matching consecutive video frames. Then the motion patterns [10] or the estimated motion parameters [2] are used for action representation. However, ambiguity arises when the real-world 3-dimensional motion is projected onto the 2-dimensional image plane.

Recently, a series of spatio-temporal interest points (STIPs)-based methods have been proposed, which achieve state-of-the-art performances in activity recognition. These methods include Harris3D [18], HOG3D [15] and Cuboid [9]. Although slightly different from each other, these methods share the common feature extraction and representation framework, which involves detecting local extrema of the image gradients and describing the point using histogram of oriented gradients (HOG) [7] and histogram of optic flows (HOF).

The first work using RGB-D sensor for activity recognition is [20]. In [20], a bag of $3D$ points (BOPs) are efficiently sampled from the depth map and Gaussian mixture models are used to model the human postures. This method yields superior results over the conventional method which uses $2D$ silhouettes. However, it has several limitations: (1) Instead of direct utilization of the 3-dimensional motion information, it uses 2-dimensional projections of key poses, which could essentially lead to sub-optimal feature representations; (2) only depth information is used for recognition while color information is completely ignored; however, color and depth information are rather complementary than exclusive.

More recently, Sung et al. [26] directly use skeleton motion data extracted from Kinect SDK for activity representation; however, this method cannot be applied when skeleton data cannot be reliably obtained.

10.3 RGBD-HuDaAct: Color-Depth Human Daily Activity Database

10.3.1 Related Video Databases

A summarization of the existing video activity benchmark databases is given in Table 10.1. **KTH** [25] a**nd Weizmann** [3] **Databases**: These databases aim at simple action recognition, including: *walking, jogging, running, hand-waving*, etc. However, the simplicity of the action categories as well as the clean backgrounds make the recognition tasks easy. As the reported accuracies on both databases approach 94.53 % [16] and 100 % [3, 12], respectively, they are no longer considered as good benchmarks. Instead, the RGBD-HuDaAct aims at realistic human daily activities, which are challenging for recognition tasks. **Movie Action Database** [22]: This database is widely used for activity recognition in movies. Given the large variations of the visual contents and the camera movements, this database is challenging. Note that although some of its activity categories overlap with the RGBD-HuDaAct database, the two databases focus on different applications, i.e., the former deals with movie actions under uncontrolled environment with moving cameras, while the latter is for daily activity monitoring under fixed environment and camera settings. **Sports Event Databases** [21, 24]: The UCF sports event database [24] and

Table 10.1 Comparisons of the RGBD-HuDaAct database over other benchmark activity databases

Database	Modality	Resolution	Sample #	Category descriptions
KTH [25]	RGB	160 × 120	2391	6 classes: walking, jogging, running, etc.
Weizmann [3]	RGB	180 × 144	90	10 classes: run, walk, skip, jumping-jack, side, etc.
Hollywood2 [22]	RGB	600 × 450	3669	12 classes: answering the phone, driving car, eating, etc.
UCF Sports [24]	RGB	720 × 480	184	10 classes: swinging, golf swinging, walking, etc.
UCF YouTube [21]	RGB	320 × 240	3040	11 classes: basketball shooting, biking, diving, etc.
MSR Action3D [20]	Depth	320 × 240	4020	20 classes: high arm wave, hand catch, forward punch, etc.
Indoor Activity [26]	RGB-Depth	640 × 480	NA	12 classes: cooking, writing, working on computer, etc.
RGBD-HuDaAct	RGB-Depth	640 × 480	1189	12 classes (plus background activity): drink water, eat meal, phone call, etc.

the UCF YouTube sports database [21] consist of a set of actions collected for various sports events which are typically obtained from websites including BBC Motion gallery, GettyImages, and YouTube.com. These two databases are very challenging due to large variations in camera motion, object appearance and pose, object scale, viewpoint, cluttered background, and illumination condition, etc. While these two databases consider only outdoor sports, the daily activities in the RGBD-HuDaAct database are all indoor. **MSR Action3D Database** [20]: The only existing depth sensor-based action database is collected by Li et al. [20], which aims at recognizing actions (gestures) in game interaction. However, this database only contains depth maps without corresponding color images. In contrast, the RGBD-HuDaAct database contains synchronized and registered color-depth videos. Used for gesture recognition, this database contains only atomic actions such as hand wave, punch, etc. In contrast, our database aims at higher level human behavior such as mopping the floor, eating meal, etc. **Indoor Kinect Activity Database** [26]: Very recently, Sung et al. [26] use Kinect sensor to construct and indoor (e.g., office, kitchen, bedroom, bathroom, and living room) activity dataset for the task of activity detection, which includes four subjects and 12 activity categories. In addition to RGB-D images, the database also provides skeleton motion data. Most of their categories do not overlap with ours. To have more inter-personal variations, the number of subjects participating our data collection (i.e., 30) is much larger than theirs.

Differently from these databases, our motivation is driven by the application of assisted living in health-care. Monitoring the daily activities of senior citizens has recently become an urgent demand due to the aging population problem. There only exists a very recent video database for senior home monitoring [6], however, it does

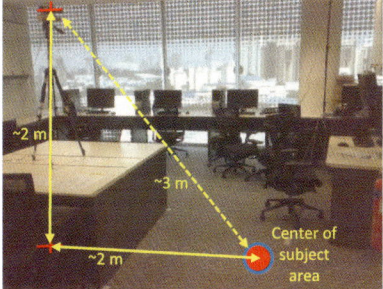

Fig. 10.1 The Kinect camera setup. (*Left*) The video capture environment. (*Right*) The geometric configuration of the Kinect camera

not utilize the depth modality. In contrast, the RGBD-HuDaAct database contains synchronized color and depth videos, which are more suitable for 24 hours monitoring, since the depth sensor also works without visible lighting.

10.3.2 Database Construction

We utilize the recently released Microsoft Kinect sensor to construct the RGBD-HuDaAct video database, collected in a lab environment, which is illustrated in Fig. 10.1. There are minor variations in the camera position and orientation due to repeated mountings of the camera. From Fig. 10.1, it can be noted that the horizontal and vertical distances from the camera to the center of the scene under capture are about 2 and 2 meters, respectively and the average depth of the human subject in the scene is about 3 meters (i.e., which is the optimal operation range of the depth camera). This geometric setting is appropriate for home or hospital ward monitoring. The resolutions of both color image and depth map are 640×480 in pixel. The color image is of 24-bit RGB values; and each depth pixel is a 16-bit integer. Both sequences are synchronized and the frame rates are 30 frames per second (fps). The color and depth frames are stereo-calibrated using the standard stereo-calibration method with a chessboard pattern object available in OpenCV (four corners of the chessboard object are used as corresponding points for depth calibration, as in [1]). We repeat the camera calibration procedure at the beginning of each video capture session and the camera is fixed throughout the session. The database can be downloaded at: http://adsc.illinois.edu/research/ADSC-RGBD-dataset-download-instructions.pdf.

10.3.3 Database Statistics

We are interested in 12 categories of human daily activities motivated by the definitions provided by health-care professionals [17] for *Activity of Daily Living (ADL)*, which includes: *make a phone call, mop the floor, enter the room, exit the room, go to bed, get up, eat meal, drink water, sit down, stand up, take off the jacket and put on the jacket*. These defined activities are directly corresponding to the ADL category: *using the telephone, maintaining the home, eating, transferring, dressing*, respectively (note that other ADL categories such as *toileting, bathing, managing finances, shopping* are not suitable for visual recognition). We also have a category named as *background activity* that contains different types of random activity. We invited 30 student volunteers to perform these daily activities, which are organized into 14 video capture sessions. The subjects were asked to perform each activity 2–4 times. Finally, we captured about 5,000,000 frames (approximately 46 hours long) for a total of 1189 labeled video samples. Each video sample spans about 30–150 seconds. Note that the size of our database is still growing to include more activity classes and video samples.

Two example frames from each activity category are illustrated in Fig. 10.2, in terms of both color (left) and depth (right) frames. We can make two observations from Fig. 10.2: (1) There exist distinctive depth layers for the moving human body parts in different activities, which implies that incorporating the depth layer information could bring additional discriminating capability for activity feature representation; (2) there exist rich intra-class variations for each activity category.

For example, for the activities *make a phone call* and *drink water*, the subject could be either standing still or sitting on the chair and either hand could be used for phone answering and water drinking. As another example, for the activities *put on the jacket* and *take off the jacket*, different persons have their own styles of performing these actions and they might be facing or not facing the camera. These variations make our database more realistic and challenging.

Note that although the background of the current database is of limited variations and only a single subject is present (i.e., compared to the movie action or YouTube databases), we must emphasize that for the application of indoor home monitoring, using a fixed camera and the current background environment are very typical. One limitation of the current sensor is that the operation range is fixed at about 3 meters and the camera view angle is also fixed. However, in real applications, the actions can occur at any distance with different view angles. Therefore, we are currently collecting more data with various distance ranges and view angles. Also the effective range of the Kinect is limited within 6 meters, and we are currently investigating a multiple-Kinect setup to cover the whole space.

10.4 Color-Depth Fusion for Activity Recognition

In this section, we introduce two feature representation methods for fusing color and depth information for activity recognition, which are straightforwardly developed from two state-of-the-art action representation methods, i.e., spatial-temporal interest points (STIPs) and motion history images (MHIs). On the one hand, we derive a **Depth-Layered Multi-Channel STIPs** (DLMC-STIPs) framework which

Fig. 10.2 Example color and depth frames from each activity category. Note for the depth map, *brighter pixels* mean larger depth values. *Some black regions* correspond to depth measurement errors due to surface reflections, i.e., the PC screen

divides the spatio-temporal interest points into several depth-layered channels, and then STIPs within different channels are pooled independently, resulting in a multiple depth-channel histogram representation. On the other hand, we propose a **3-Dimensional Motion History Images** (3D-MHIs) approach which equips the conventional motion history images (MHIs) with two additional channels encoding the motion recency history in the depth-changing directions. In the experiments, these two color-depth-based feature representation methods are comprehensively evaluated over their color-only counterparts. It is demonstrated that by modeling the 3-dimensional spatial structure of the detected spatio-temporal feature points as well as the 3-dimensional motion history of the human subjects, the discriminating capabilities of the features are boosted.

10.4.1 Depth-Layered Multi-channel STIPs (DLMC-STIPs)

Spatio-temporal interest points (STIPs) are widely used for action recognition. The most representative versions of STIPs employ the Harris3D detector, which was proposed by Laptev and Lindeberg in [18]. The Harris3D detector is a space-time extension of the 2-dimensional Harris detector [13]. At each space-time video point, a spatio-temporal second-moment matrix is computed as $\mu(.; \sigma, \tau) = g(.; s\sigma, s\tau) * (\Delta V(.; \sigma, \tau))(\Delta V(.; \sigma, \tau))^T$ (i.e., V is the video volume), in terms of different spatial and temporal scale values $s\sigma, s\tau$. Namely, space-time gradients ΔV are computed and smoothed by a separate Gaussian smoothing function $g(.; s\sigma, s\tau)$. The detected locations of space-time interest points are given by local extrema of $H = \det(\mu) - \kappa \operatorname{trace}^3(\mu)$, in terms of both spatial and scale space. To characterize local shapes and motions, histograms of oriented gradients (HOG) and histograms of optic flows (HOF) are calculated within the space-time neighborhoods of the detected interest points, see [18]. The HOG and HOF feature descriptors are first quantized into visual words and then each video sequence is represented as a bag of such visual words [27] (i.e., as a histogram vector over the visual word vocabulary).

However, the human subject is in essence a 3-dimensional structure and the detected spatio-temporal feature points are associated with local motions taking place at different 3-dimensional locations; however, the previous pooling methods of STIPs can only utilize this spatial information up to 2-dimensional, i.e., feature poolings are performed within each x–y–t sub-volume, and the spatial information along the depth direction is totally lost. The availability of depth map enables us to recover this lost information. The most straightforward way to utilize the spatial information along the depth direction is to perform the feature pooling by dividing the entire scene into different depth layers, and form a multi-channel STIPs histogram. This basic idea is similar with the space partition in [18], where STIPs are spatially pooled within each x–y–t sub-volume, i.e., the entire 3-dimensional space-time video volume is divided into several x–y–t sub-volumes. Our proposed framework is named as **Depth-Layered Multi-Channel STIPs (DLMC-STIPs)**, which is formulated as follows.

Each video sample V could be represented as a set of (N) STIP feature descriptors (i.e., HOG and HOF), which is denoted $V = \{\mathbf{x}_1, \mathbf{x}_2, \ldots, \mathbf{x}_N\}$. Each STIP feature descriptor is denoted $\mathbf{x}_i = (x, y, z, t, \sigma, \mathbf{x}_{\text{HOG}}^T, \mathbf{x}_{\text{HOF}}^T)^T$. Here, x, y, z, t, σ represent the $3D$ coordinate (x, y, z), temporal index and the scale of the detected feature point, respectively. $\mathbf{x}_{\text{HOG}}$ and $\mathbf{x}_{\text{HOF}}$ are the $72D$ HOG and $90D$ HOF feature vectors, respectively. We first perform unsupervised clustering on the set of HOG and HOF feature descriptors to construct a visual word vocabulary (codebook). We denote the visual codebook encoded vector (by nearest visual word assignment according to the Euclidean distance) of the feature descriptor $\mathbf{x}_i$ as $\mathbf{v}_i$, i.e., $\mathbf{v}_i$ is a K-dimensional (K is the codebook size) assignment vector with one of the element as 1 and the others as 0s. Then the histogram representation $\mathbf{h}$ for the video sample V is given by

$$\mathbf{h} = \frac{1}{N} \sum_{i=1}^{N} \mathbf{v}_i. \tag{10.1}$$

This aggregation process is usually referred as *feature pooling*, i.e., aggregating the set of local features into a global representation vector.

We can also incorporate the spatial information in the feature pooling process. In [18], the entire 3-dimensional space-time volumes are divided into several x–y–t sub-volumes and pooling is performed within each sub-volume. Then the pooled histogram vectors from all the sub-volumes are concatenated to form a multi-channel representation. When the depth value of each detected STIP point is available, we can also form depth-layered multi-channel representations. Namely, we introduce a set of (M) depth layers $L_1^z = [z_1^l, z_1^u], L_2^z = [z_2^l, z_2^u], \ldots, L_M^z = [z_M^l, z_M^u]$, with lower and upper boundaries denoted as z_m^l and z_m^u for the mth depth layer. Then, we form multi-channel histograms $\mathbf{h}_1, \mathbf{h}_2, \ldots, \mathbf{h}_M$, as

$$\mathbf{h}_m = \frac{1}{N} \sum_{z(\mathbf{x}_i) \in L_m^z} \mathbf{v}_i, \quad \forall m = 1, 2, \ldots, M. \tag{10.2}$$

These multiple channel histograms could be concatenated into an $M \times K$-dimensional feature vector $\mathbf{h} = (\mathbf{h}_1^T, \mathbf{h}_2^T, \ldots, \mathbf{h}_M^T)^T$, as the input to the classification framework, e.g., support vector machines. The distance metric for calculating the kernel matrix could be χ^2 distance. Moreover, we can also use the spatial pyramid matching kernel (SPM) proposed in [19] to better explore the spatial information given in the depth axis. An illustration of the DLMC-STIPs generation process is given in Fig. 10.3. Note the following. (1) The DLMC-STIPs method is not fully 4D representation, since the interest point detection and local volume representation are both performed in the x–y–t space. However, improvement has been observed when the local features are not distinctive with this naive extension (see Sect. 10.5). We believe this trial idea (together with the database) will inspire the research community to develop more sophisticated approaches which represent activities in a fully 4D manner. (2) The DLMC-STIPs framework does not explicitly model the motion along the depth axis, and a 3D-MHIs approach which explicitly models the 3-dimensional motion is introduced in the next subsection.

10.4.2 3-Dimensional Motion History Images (3D-MHIs)

Another widely used feature representation method for action classification is motion history images (MHIs) developed by Bobick and Davis [4], which is capable of encoding the dynamics of a sequence of moving human silhouettes. In an MHI, each pixel intensity is a function of the motion recency at that location, where brighter value corresponds to more recent motion. This single image contains the discriminative information for determining how a person has moved (spatially and temporally) during the action. Denoting $I(\mathbf{x}, \mathbf{y}, t)$ as an image sequence, each pixel intensity value in an MHI is a function H^I of the temporal history of motion at that point, namely:

$$H_\tau^I(x, y, t) = \begin{cases} \tau, & \text{if } |I(x, y, t) - I(x, y, t-1)| > \delta I_{th} \\ \max(0, H_\tau^I(x, y, t-1) - 1), & \text{else.} \end{cases} \tag{10.3}$$

Here τ is the longest time window we want the system to consider and δI_{th} is the threshold value for generating the mask for the region of motion. The result is a scalar-valued image where brighter pixels indicate more recent motion. Statistical descriptions of the motion history images are then computed based on seven Hu

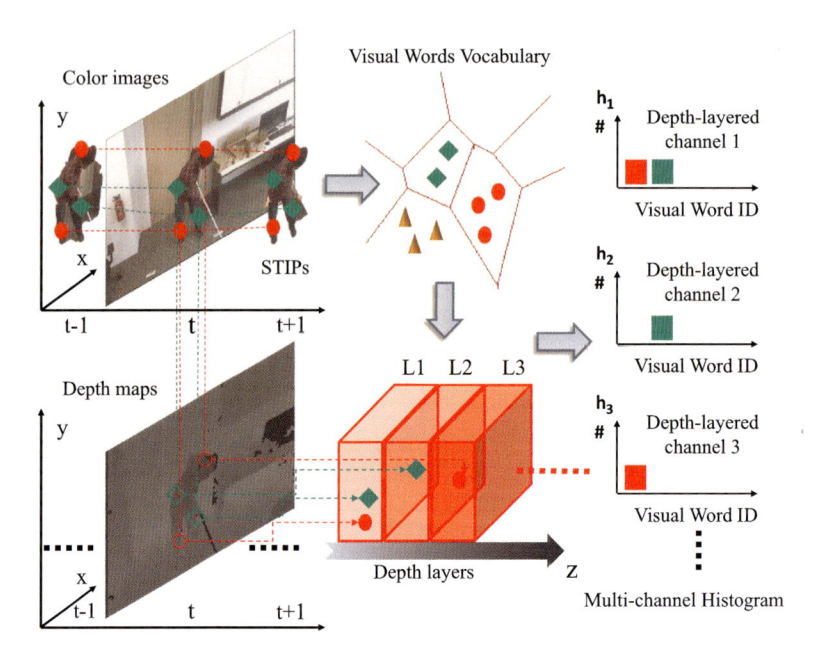

Fig. 10.3 A diagram of the generation process of DLMC-STIPs representation

moment-based features [14], which are known to yield reasonable shape discrimination in a translation- and scale-invariant manner.

However, using only RGB camera, MHIs can only encode the history of motion induced by the lateral component of the scene motion parallel to the image plane. With the additional depth sensor, we can now develop an extended framework which is capable of encoding the motion history along the depth-changing directions. In particular, we propose two depth-change induced motion history images named as DMHIs. DMHIs contain forward-DMHIs (fDMHIs) which encode the forward motion history (increase of depth) and backward-DMHIs (bDMHIs) which encode the backward motion history (decrease of depth). To generate fDMHIs, the following process is adopted:

$$H_\tau^{fD}(x,y,t) = \begin{cases} \tau, & \text{if } (D(x,y,t) - D(x,y,t-1)) > \delta D_{th} \\ \max(0, H_\tau^{fD}(x,y,t-1) - 1), & \text{else.} \end{cases} \quad (10.4)$$

Here, H_τ^{fD} denotes the forward motion history image and $D(x,y,t)$ denotes the depth sequence. δD_{th} is the threshold value for generating the mask for the region of forward motion. The backward-DMHI (i.e., H_τ^{bD}) is generated in a similar way with the thresholding function replaced by $(D(x,y,t) - D(x,y,t-1)) < -\delta D_{th}$. The conventional MHIs are combined with fDMHIs and bDMHIs to represent 3-dimensional motion history and we denote the combined feature representation as **3D-MHIs**. To represent each action video, similar to MHIs, Hu moments are calculated for all three channels (i.e., MHIs, fDMHIs and bDMHIs) and are concate-

| MHI | fDMHI | bDMHI |

Fig. 10.4 Illustration of the MHI, fDMHI and bDMHI in a *sit down* sequence

nated to form a representation vector. An example 3D-MHI is illustrated in Fig. 10.4 in the context of a *sit down* sequence. From Fig. 10.4, we notice obvious motion patterns in fDMHI in contrast to bDMHI, which indicates the subject is moving away from the camera. This example implies that by using fDMHIs and bDMHIs, we can distinguish different actions which present similar motion patterns in the x–y directions but with distinctive motion patterns in the depth-changing directions.

10.5 Experimental Evaluations

10.5.1 Evaluation Schemes

In this work, we use 59 % (i.e., by random sampling a fixed number of samples from each category) of the video samples in the RGBD-HuDaAct database for experiment. The subset we use in the experiments include 18 subjects with nine capture sessions, yielding a total of 702 video samples belonging to 13 activity classes, including the *background activity* videos which are added to the existing 12 activity classes to test how algorithms can recognize the specified activities from some random daily activities such as walk around, stand still, pick-up some object, etc.

To test the generalization capability of the methods for novel input, we use the leave-one-subject-out (LOSO) scheme for algorithmic evaluations. In each run, we choose the samples from one subject as the testing samples, and the remaining samples from the database serve as the training samples. The overall recognition performance is calculated by gathering the results from all training-testing runs.

The evaluation results are reported in terms of classification accuracy as well as class confusion matrix. We regard our human daily activity recognition problem as a multi-class classification problem and each video sample has one and only one activity label (i.e., out of 13 classes). For the LOSO scheme, the classification accuracy is given by the ratio of the correctly classified testing samples over the total number of testing samples, by gathering the classification results from all testing runs. In our experiments, the class confusion matrix C is a 13×13 matrix where each element C_{ij} denotes how many testing samples of the ith class are classified into the jth class. Larger values for the diagonal elements and smaller values for the off-diagonal elements indicate better discriminating capability.

Table 10.2 Comparisons of the classification accuracies (%) for STIPs and DLMC-STIPs under different experimental settings

Setting	$K=128$	$K=256$	$K=512$
STIPs (χ^2)	68.95	76.78	79.77
DLMC-STIPs (χ^2, $M=2$)	72.43	77.10	79.91
DLMC-STIPs (χ^2, $M=4$)	74.22	77.91	79.23
DLMC-STIPs (χ^2, $M=8$)	76.64	79.49	79.49
DLMC-STIPs (SPM)	**77.64**	**81.05**	**81.48**

Prior to feature extraction, we down-sample the original color and depth video sequences in both spatial and temporal dimensions by a factor of 2, yielding 320 × 240 pixels and 15 fps video samples (i.e., this setting is similar with [20]). We use support vector machines (SVM) [5] (*one-against-one* scheme for multi-class classification) for all classification tasks with different kernels. The penalty parameter $\mathcal{C}$ of SVM is optimized by cross-validation. The bandwidth parameters for χ^2 and RBF kernels are set as the average of the squared distances (χ^2 and Euclidean, respectively) of the training sample pairs.

10.5.2 DLMC-STIPs vs. STIPs

We compare the classification performances between the proposed DLMC-STIPs and the conventional STIPs. We perform K-means clustering to the set of HOG + HOF descriptors, which yields codebooks with size K. We vary the value of K as 128, 256 and 512 for more comprehensive evaluations. For the conventional STIPs, a K-dimensional histogram vector is calculated for representing each video sequence. Note that in order to better reveal the discriminating capability gained by depth-layered multi-channel representation, we fix the setting of other configurations as simple as possible, i.e., we do not partition the STIPs into different x–y–t sub-volume as in [18]. Obviously, space partition in terms of x–y–t for both methods could bring more discriminative information on an equal basis. For DLMC-STIPs, we divide the depth axis into $M=2, 4, 8$ equally spaced layers according to the depth value distributions of the SITPs. As both DLMC-STIPs and STIPs are histogram-based representations, we use χ^2 distance for calculating the kernel matrix. We also explore the spatial pyramid matching kernel (SPM) [19] for DLMC-STIPs representations with $l=3$ depth spatial levels. Various classification accuracies under different parameter combinations are given in Table 10.2. We also illustrate the class confusion matrices for both methods in Fig. 10.5, at the setting of $K=256$.

It can be observed from Table 10.2 that by using depth-layered multi-channel histogram representation, the classification accuracies can be improved consistently; also, by using the spatial pyramid matching kernel (SPM), the classification performances can be further boosted.

	PJ	EX	SD	DW	EN	EM	TJ	MF	MP	SU	GB	GU	BG
PJ	.83	.00	.00	.02	.00	.00	.11	.02	.00	.00	.00	.00	.02
EX	.00	.80	.00	.00	.17	.00	.00	.00	.02	.00	.00	.00	.02
SD	.02	.02	.65	.09	.00	.00	.00	.00	.04	.15	.00	.00	.04
DW	.00	.00	.03	.82	.00	.03	.01	.00	.11	.00	.00	.00	.00
EN	.00	.11	.04	.00	.85	.00	.00	.00	.00	.00	.00	.00	.00
EM	.00	.00	.00	.06	.00	.93	.02	.00	.00	.00	.00	.00	.00
TJ	.26	.00	.04	.00	.00	.00	.63	.00	.04	.00	.00	.00	.04
MF	.02	.00	.00	.00	.00	.00	.00	.98	.00	.00	.00	.00	.00
MP	.00	.00	.00	.11	.00	.06	.07	.00	.74	.03	.00	.00	.00
SU	.02	.00	.23	.17	.02	.00	.02	.00	.08	.47	.00	.00	.00
GB	.00	.00	.00	.00	.00	.00	.00	.00	.00	.00	.82	.16	.02
GU	.00	.00	.00	.00	.00	.00	.00	.00	.00	.00	.13	.87	.00
BG	.11	.03	.03	.03	.00	.00	.05	.05	.08	.00	.05	.03	.54

	PJ	EX	SD	DW	EN	EM	TJ	MF	MP	SU	GB	GU	BG
PJ	.83	.00	.00	.04	.00	.00	.11	.02	.00	.00	.00	.00	.00
EX	.00	.93	.00	.00	.07	.00	.00	.00	.00	.00	.00	.00	.00
SD	.02	.00	.65	.07	.02	.00	.02	.00	.06	.15	.00	.00	.02
DW	.01	.00	.03	.79	.00	.03	.01	.00	.10	.03	.00	.00	.00
EN	.00	.06	.02	.00	.93	.00	.00	.00	.00	.00	.00	.00	.00
EM	.00	.00	.00	.04	.00	.94	.00	.00	.02	.00	.00	.00	.00
TJ	.19	.00	.00	.02	.00	.00	.76	.00	.04	.00	.00	.00	.00
MF	.02	.00	.00	.00	.00	.00	.00	.98	.00	.00	.00	.00	.00
MP	.01	.00	.00	.11	.00	.03	.07	.01	.75	.00	.00	.00	.01
SU	.00	.00	.21	.15	.00	.00	.00	.00	.06	.58	.00	.00	.00
GB	.00	.00	.00	.00	.00	.00	.00	.00	.00	.00	.89	.11	.00
GU	.00	.00	.00	.00	.00	.00	.00	.00	.00	.00	.09	.91	.00
BG	.05	.05	.03	.03	.00	.00	.03	.11	.11	.00	.00	.03	.57

Fig. 10.5 Class confusion matrices for STIPs (*left*) and DLMC-STIPs (*right*, SPM kernel) under the setting of $K = 256$. For better view, we use two characters to represent each activity category, i.e., PJ: *put on the jacket*, TJ: *take off the jacket*, EN: *enter the room*, EX: *exit the room*, SD: *sit down*, SU: *stand up*, DW: *drink water*, EM: *eat meal*, MF: *mop the floor*, MP: *make a phone call*, GB: *go to bed*, GU: *get up* and BG: *background activity*

Table 10.3 Comparisons of the classification accuracies (%) for MHIs and 3D-MHIs under different experimental settings

Kernel	MHIs	fDMHIs + bDMHIs	3D-MHIs
Linear	34.19	68.66	**70.51**
RBF	37.18	66.81	**69.66**

10.5.3 3D-MHIs vs. MHIs

We also compare the classification performances between the proposed 3D-MHIs and the conventional MHIs. For both methods, the τ value is chosen by cross-validations. We further normalize the 3D-MHIs and MHIs by multiplying a scale factor $\frac{1}{\tau}$ to achieve scale invariance. Note that the original implementation of MHIs as in [4] uses a multiple view configuration. In this work, however, we use a single view instead. For SVM classification, we explore both the linear kernel and the RBF kernel, and the classification results are given in Table 10.3. We again show the class confusion matrices for both methods in Fig. 10.6, for the case of linear SVM.

From Table 10.3 and Fig. 10.6, it is noted obviously that by adding the two depth-changing induced motion history images, the discriminating capability of the feature representation is significantly boosted (by nearly 30 %). Furthermore, from Fig. 10.6, we see that the activity *enter the room* is quite easy to confuse with the activities *exit the room* and *mop the floor* due to their similar lateral motion patterns; however, by using 3D-MHIs, these ambiguities are significantly eliminated, since both *enter the room* and *exit the room* include abundant and distinctive depth-changing information.

We also compare the best results obtained from our RGB-D-based methods, i.e., 3D-MHIs and DLMC-STIPs (SPM) with the state-of-the-art action recognition

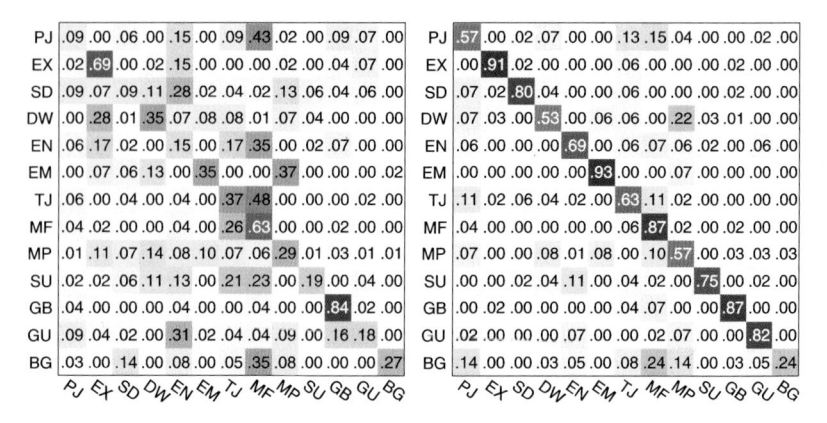

	PJ	EX	SD	DW	EN	EM	TJ	MF	MP	SU	GB	GU	BG
PJ	.09	.00	.06	.00	.15	.00	.09	**.43**	.02	.00	.09	.07	.00
EX	.02	**.69**	.00	.02	.15	.00	.00	.00	.02	.00	.04	.07	.00
SD	.09	.07	.09	.11	.28	.02	.04	.02	.13	.06	.04	.06	.00
DW	.00	.28	.01	**.35**	.07	.08	.08	.01	.07	.04	.00	.00	.00
EN	.06	.17	.02	.00	.15	.00	.17	**.35**	.00	.02	.07	.00	.00
EM	.00	.07	.06	.13	.00	**.35**	.00	.00	**.37**	.00	.00	.00	.02
TJ	.06	.00	.04	.00	.04	.00	**.37**	**.48**	.00	.00	.00	.02	.00
MF	.04	.02	.00	.00	.04	.00	.26	**.63**	.00	.00	.02	.00	.00
MP	.01	.11	.07	.14	.08	.10	.07	.06	**.29**	.01	.03	.01	.01
SU	.02	.02	.06	.11	.13	.00	.21	**.23**	.00	**.19**	.00	.04	.00
GB	.04	.00	.00	.00	.04	.00	.00	.04	.00	.00	**.84**	.02	.00
GU	.09	.04	.02	.00	**.31**	.02	.04	.04	.09	.00	.16	.18	.00
BG	.03	.00	.14	.00	.08	.00	.05	**.35**	.08	.00	.00	.00	**.27**

	PJ	EX	SD	DW	EN	EM	TJ	MF	MP	SU	GB	GU	BG
PJ	**.57**	.00	.02	.07	.00	.00	.13	.15	.04	.00	.00	.02	.00
EX	.00	**.91**	.02	.00	.00	.00	.06	.00	.00	.00	.02	.00	.00
SD	.07	.02	**.80**	.04	.00	.00	.06	.00	.00	.00	.02	.00	.00
DW	.07	.03	.00	**.53**	.00	.06	.06	.00	.22	.03	.01	.00	.00
EN	.06	.00	.00	.00	**.69**	.00	.06	.07	.06	.02	.00	.06	.00
EM	.00	.00	.00	.00	.00	**.93**	.00	.00	.07	.00	.00	.00	.00
TJ	.11	.02	.06	.04	.02	.00	**.63**	.11	.02	.00	.00	.00	.00
MF	.04	.00	.00	.00	.00	.00	.06	**.87**	.02	.00	.02	.00	.00
MP	.07	.00	.00	.08	.01	.08	.00	.10	**.57**	.00	.03	.03	.03
SU	.00	.00	.02	.04	.11	.00	.04	.02	.00	**.75**	.00	.02	.00
GB	.00	.02	.00	.00	.00	.00	.04	.07	.00	.00	**.87**	.00	.00
GU	.02	.00	.00	.00	.07	.00	.00	.02	.07	.00	.00	**.82**	.00
BG	.14	.00	.00	.03	.05	.00	.08	.24	.14	.00	.00	.03	.05	.24

Fig. 10.6 Class confusion matrices for MHIs (*left*) and 3D-MHIs (*right*), at the setting of linear SVM

Fig. 10.7 Comparison of recognition accuracies using DT, B3D, 3D-MHIs and DLMC-STIPs (SPM)

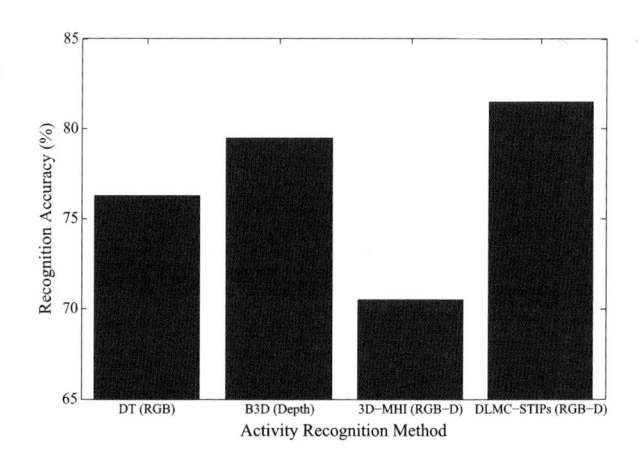

methods using RGB images, e.g., dense trajectories (DT) [28] and depth images, e.g., bag of 3D points (B3D) [20]. The related parameters for these comparing methods (e.g., trajectory length, number of visual words of trajectory descriptors, number of mixtures and number of states for bag of 3D points method, the 3D points sampling rate) are tuned optimally on a validation subset. The comparison is illustrated in Fig. 10.7. We can see that fusion RGB and depth information (DLMC-STIPs (SPM)) outperforms single modality-based methods.

10.6 Conclusions

In this work, we introduced a publicly available color-depth video database for human daily activity recognition. We also presented two fusion schemes combining color and depth modalities for action representation, which have shown superior recognition performances over their color-only counterparts. We hope this database could serve as a benchmark test bed of color-depth-based algorithms for home monitoring oriented activity recognition. In the future, we will extend the current database with actions captured from different distance ranges and view angles.

Acknowledgements This study is supported by the research grant for the Human Sixth Sense Programme at the Advanced Digital Sciences Center from Singapore's Agency for Science, Technology and Research (A*STAR).

References

1. http://nicolas.burrus.name/index.php/research/kinectcalibration
2. Black, M.J., Yacoob, Y., Jepson, A.D., Fleet, D.J.: Learning parameterized models of image motion. In: IEEE Conference on Computer Vision and Pattern Recognition, pp. 561–567 (1997)
3. Blank, M., Gorelick, L., Shechtman, E., Irani, M., Basri, R.: Actions as space-time shapes. In: International Conference on Computer Vision, pp. 1395–1402 (2005)
4. Bobick, A., Davis, J.: The representation and recognition of action using temporal templates. IEEE Trans. Pattern Anal. Mach. Intell. **23**(3), 257–267 (2001)
5. Chang, C.C., Lin, C.J.: LIBSVM: a library for support vector machines. ACM Trans. Intell. Syst. Technol. **2**, 27:1–27:27 (2011)
6. Cheng, H., Liu, Z., Zhao, Y., Ye, G.: Real world activity summary for senior home monitoring. In: IEEE International Conference on Multimedia and Expo (2011)
7. Dalal, N., Triggs, B.: Histograms of oriented gradients for human detection. In: IEEE Conference on Computer Vision and Pattern Recognition (2005)
8. Davis, J.W., Tyagi, A.: Minimal-latency human action recognition using reliable-inference. Image Vis. Comput. **24**(5), 455–472 (2006)
9. Dollar, P., Rabaud, V., Cottrell, G., Belongie, S.: Behavior recognition via sparse spatiotemporal features. In: IEEE International Workshop on Visual Surveillance and Performance Evaluation of Tracking and Surveillance (2005)
10. Efros, A.A., Berg, A.C., Mori, G., Malik, J.: Recognizing action at a distance. In: International Conference on Computer Vision (2003)
11. Fleet, J.L.B.D.J., Beauchemin, S.S.: Performance of optical flow techniques. Int. J. Comput. Vis. **12**(1), 43–77 (1994)
12. Gorelick, L., Blank, M., Shechtman, E., Irani, M., Basri, R.: Actions as space-time shapes. IEEE Trans. Pattern Anal. Mach. Intell. **29**(12), 2247–2253 (2007)
13. Harris, C., Stephens, M.: A combined corner and edge detector. In: Alvey Vision Conference, pp. 147–151 (1998)
14. Hu, M.: Visual pattern recognition by moment invariants. IRE Trans. Inf. Theory **8**(2), 179–187 (1962)
15. Klaser, A., Marszalek, M., Schmid, C.: A spatio-temporal descriptor based on 3d gradients. In: British Machine Vision Conference (2008)
16. Kovashka, A., Grauman, K.: Learning a hierarchy of discriminative space-time neighborhood features for human action recognition. In: IEEE Conference on Computer Vision and Pattern Recognition
17. Krapp, K.: Activities of Daily Living Evaluation. Encyclopedia of Nursing and Allied Health (2002)
18. Laptev, I., Lindeberg, T.: Space-time interest points. In: IEEE International Conference on Computer Vision (2003)

19. Lazebnik, S., Schmid, C., Ponce, J.: Beyond bags of features: spatial pyramid matching for recognizing natural scene categories. In: IEEE Conference on Computer Vision and Pattern Recognition (2006)
20. Li, W., Zhang, Z., Liu, Z.: Action recognition based on a bag of 3d points. In: IEEE Conference on Computer Vision and Pattern Recognition—Workshop on Human Communicative Behavior Analysis (2010)
21. Liu, J., Luo, J., Shah, M.: Recognizing realistic actions from videos "in the wild". In: IEEE Conference on Computer Vision and Pattern Recognition (2009)
22. Marszałek, M., Laptev, I., Schmid, C.: Actions in context. In: IEEE Conference on Computer Vision and Pattern Recognition (2009)
23. Ni, B., Yan, S., Kassim, A.: Recognizing human group activities with localized causalities. In: IEEE Conference on Computer Vision and Pattern Recognition (2009)
24. Rodriguez, M., Ahmed, J., Shah, M.: Action MACH: a spatio-temporal maximum average correlation height filter for action recognition. In: IEEE Conference on Computer Vision and Pattern Recognition (2008)
25. Schuldt, C., Laptev, I., Caputo, B.: Recognizing human actions: a local SVM approach. In: IEEE International Conference on Pattern Recognition (2004)
26. Sung, J., Ponce, C., Selman, B., Saxena, A.: Human activity detection from RGBD images. In: AAAI Workshop on Pattern, Activity and Intent Recognition (2011)
27. Ullah, M.M., Parizi, S.N., Laptev, I.: Improving bag-of-features action recognition with non-local cues. In: British Machine Vision Conference (2010)
28. Wang, H., Kläser, A., Schmid, C., Cheng-Lin, L.: Action recognition by dense trajectories. In: IEEE Conference on Computer Vision and Pattern Recognition, pp. 3169–3176 (2011)

Index

0–9
3D Datasets, 145
3D Features, 52, 143, 176

A
Activity recognition, 198
American sign language, 133
Annotation, 74, 148, 172, 173, 188

B
Background subtraction, 80, 104
Body pose estimation, 64, 72, 101
Body shape estimation, 101, 105

C
Classification, 65, 135
Conditional regression forest, 67
Connected component, 82
Correspondences, 68, 81, 108
CUDA, 53
Curvature, 157

D
Database retrieval, 87
Decision forest, 65, 124
Decision tree, 65, 124
Dijkstra's algorithm, 82
Displacement, 52
Distance learning, 175
Distance measure, 88, 108
Distance metric, 88
Distortion, 9

F
Feature extraction, 53
Features, 65, 81

G
Geodesic distance, 83
Geodesic extrema, 80

H
Hand pose estimation, 121
Hough forest, 67
Human–computer interaction, 120

I
ICP, 29, 36, 50, 58, 68, 75, 108, 174
    photogeometry, 33
Implicit Shape Model, 66

K
Kd-tree, 79
Kernel descriptors, 179
Kinect, 3, 32, 49, 66, 72, 76, 77, 89, 100, 120, 128, 142, 149, 197
    calibration, 14, 104, 149, 197
    depth resolution, 6
    evaluation, 19
    geometrical model, 8
    intrinsic parameters, 14
    measuring device, 4
    residual errors, 15
Kinematic chain, 77, 106, 123

L
Linear blend skinning, 68, 77
Local optimization, 81, 110

M
Mean-shift, 79, 127
Motion capture, 65, 78
Motion history images, 201

N
Naïve Bayes, 156
Non-maximum suppression, 153

O
Object detection, 185
Object recognition, 147, 174
Object–pose tree, 182

P
PMD Camcube, 89
Pose initialization, 106
Precision analysis, 55

Q
Quantization step, 56, 77

R
Random Ball Cover, 34
  approximation, 43
  construction, 37
  on GPU, 37
Random forest
  Classification, 65
  Regression, 66

RANSAC, 171
Registration, 49
Regression, 64

S
SCAPE, 101, 105
Segmentation, 169
Skeleton model, 68, 77, 106, 123
Sliding window, 152
Smoothing, 149
Sparse structures, 51
Spatio-temporal interest points, 199
Surface mesh, 68, 77, 105, 123
Surfels, 174
SwissRanger, 4, 21, 24, 89
Synthetic training data, 65, 123

T
Time-of-flight, 21, 29, 76, 122
Tracking, 88

V
Vitruvian manifold, 68
Voting, 66

Printed by Printforce, the Netherlands

I Have Hundreds of Stories, Some of them True

Russell Garcia

Cover photo of poster painted by Reynold Brown of the 1960 MGM film "The Time Machine", with original music score written by Russell Garcia. This film has become a 'cult classic' and there are even Time Machine clubs around the world. Without a doubt, this is Russell's best known film score which is still selling today on CD.

Back cover photo: personal photo of RG when working on film The Time Machine.

I Have Hundreds of Stories, Some of them True
©2013 Russell Garcia. All Rights Reserved.
No part of this book may be reproduced in any form or by any means, electronic, mechanical, digital, photocopying or recording, except for the inclusion in a review, without permission in writing from the publisher.

Published in the USA by:
BearManor Media
P O Box 71426
Albany, Georgia 31708
www.bearmanormedia.com

ISBN: 978-1-59393-729-4
Printed in the United States of America
Book design by Robbie Adkins

I Have Hundreds of Stories, Some of them True

CONFESSION:
My wife, Gina, really wrote this book. I just take credit for it.
- rg.

Russell Garcia on his 95th Birthday – April 12, 2011

I Have Hundreds of Stories, Some of them True

ACKNOWLEDGEMENTS

I am eternally grateful to Bo Goldsen of Criterion Music Publishers for his help in so many ways and especially for finding a publisher for my darling Russell's autobiography.

A 'zillion' thanks go across the thousands of miles to Marc Myers in New York, who with all his deadlines, put them aside to write a wonderful Introduction for this book. As he said, "I pushed my work to the side and wrote from the heart."

I have to say I was not very "computer literate" when I first started working on this project. I want to give special thanks to Deb Green for helping me to learn so much about the computer. This project could never have happened without her help.

- Gina Garcia

FOREWORD

"Are you crazy," I shouted, laughing out loud, when my husband Russell suggested we sell up everything in Hollywood and buy a sailboat and sail around the world. "I can't even swim." Hysterical with laughter, I kept looking at him expecting him to say, that he was really just joking. But instead he said, "So, why can't you learn to swim?"

We'd been married 14 years by then and I guess I should have known that Russell wasn't joking. Sure, I knew he really was an adventurous guy, but come on, sail around the world?

"It's not just the swimming," I said trying to be reasonable, "We don't know how to sail or navigate. It's madness, we'd be crazy to attempt it." In his mild calm way he said, "We can learn all that and just think what an adventure it will be." And learn all that we did. I really knew he was serious when he bought me a 30 foot trimaran for my birthday. Not that I feel one can ever really be prepared because there were plenty of scary times with screaming winds and 40 foot waves, that I wondered what on earth we were doing. All the things we did to get ready for such an adventure weren't really enough. You don't know how you'll react until the moment comes even though you think you are well prepared. Our dear friend, Don Gumpertz who was a yachtie himself, gave us a medical kit to take on the boat. I even learned how to inject an orange with a shot of morphine for emergency accidents when we were out at sea.

Family and friends all thought we were mad. We had such a fantastic life. Russell was at the peak of his career composing and arranging in Hollywood and Europe. Our two children were adults and doing well. We had a gorgeous house in the Hollywood Hills, we each drove a Porsche, mine was red and his was black, and most important of all, we were active in the Baha'i Faith.

We bought a 41 foot trimaran that was built in Florida and named her Dawn-Breaker. Originally, we thought we'd go around the world in three years, but the Suez Canal closed while we were under way, so we decided there was no rush after all and spent almost six years on the boat.

In Florida, we had to use the inland waterways with some 60 bascule bridges. As a yacht approached the bridge, it had to give three blasts on its horn for the bridge to open. When we approached the first bridge, Russ pressed the horn and got no sound whatsoever, so he shouted,

"Quick, grab my cornet." Having played trumpet professionally, he decided he wanted to carry his instrument aboard. Weren't we lucky he did because who would have guessed that the horn on a new boat wouldn't work? He gave three blasts on his horn and the bridge opened and we motored through. So it went for all 60 bridges until we got into open sea.

From Florida, we sailed to the Bahamas and then on to Jamaica, giving both Haiti and Cuba a wide berth because they would confiscate a U.S. yacht if you got into their waters. We sailed on from Jamaica to Panama through the Canal and into the Pacific. Our first stop was the Galapagos Islands famous for those giant iguanas that really look like dragons. I wouldn't pose for a photo near one. I knew they were not meat eaters, but then who knew when it last had a feed.

Our longest crossing was to the Marquesas Islands in French Polynesia. It took us 25 days to cover 3,000 miles. Next, we sailed to the Tuamotu Islands where they had a pool with several six foot sharks. The children would jump in the pool and ride on their backs. We were invited to jump in, and thanking them politely we decided we weren't quite ready for that adventure. We went on to Tahiti, Moorea, Bora Bora, Raiatea, and Huahine, which smells like vanilla because of the many vanilla plantations they have there.

We continued on to the Cook Islands, Samoa, Tonga, Fiji and the Ellice and Gilbert Islands. Now called Tuvalu and Kiribati, It was when we returned to Fiji from the Gilberts, that we met New Zealand musicians who were entertaining on a big Russian Liner. We had not planned to sail to New Zealand so when the offer to fly us down to do concerts, radio, TV, and master classes at universities, we accepted.

When our tour was finished, a friend in Auckland insisted we had to see the Bay of Islands. He even let us borrow his car. When we arrived there and got our first view of all these islands scattered around the sparkling blue ocean, Russell said, "Let's get a real estate agent and look for a piece of property." I will let you read Russell's account regarding the miracle of how it all came about because it was a miracle. And it changed our whole life around.

I have to say that our crossing from Fiji to New Zealand a couple of years later, when we finally got our residency visas, was the only time I thought we might not make it. We hit a horrendous storm, with winds screaming across the turnbuckles, we tore sails, and were blown many miles off course. But we made it! I'm sure our guardian angels were looking after us.

Back in the 50s, when Russ wanted to take me skiing in Europe, and my response was, "But I can't ski," his comment was, "So why can't you learn to ski?" And before long, he had me skiing down glaciers in the beautiful Swiss Alps and the Dolomite mountains of northern Italy.

And would you believe it, he even had me hiking to the top of the highest mountain in the U.S. Back in 1953, Mount Whitney at 14,494 feet high (4,418 meters) was the highest mountain. When Alaska joined the U.S., that all changed. The highest mountain in the U.S. is Mount McKinley at 20,320 feet high (6,194 meters). It is located in south central Alaska in the Alaska Range and is known locally as Denali (the Great One).

Russ had promised our son David that when he was 12 years old they'd hike to the top of the highest mountain in the U.S. I foolishly thought it was a father and son adventure, but Russ' comment was, that's right, you've guessed it, "So why can't you hike with us?" So I did.

It took us four days to get to the summit and only one day to come down.

We each carried a heavy backpack. And we did a dumb thing by camping above timber- line. Once the sun went down, it was so cold it even hailed big chunks of ice in the middle of summer. The air was so rare at that height, that during the relatively warm day we made very slow progress. We didn't feel like eating much either, so most of the food we carried up also came down with us.

I guess it's not too bad, considering I was a concrete jungle kid raised in Brooklyn, New York and actually had never been on a hike until the age of 17 when Russ introduced me to hiking.

I first met Russ in 1949 when he was playing trumpet at the Figueroa Ball Room. My date, who had taken me dancing, knew Russ. We were chatting during intermission, and then when my date went to the bathroom, Russ moved in fast and asked me to have dinner with him the next night. I was so startled that I actually agreed. Later, I had second thoughts. I really didn't know this guy and seriously considered not showing up.

At that time, I was studying philosophy at night at Los Angeles University and the way Russ had invited me to have dinner actually seemed harmless since he had to go on to work at the ball room and I had to go on to school. Besides, he was very charming with a wonderful twinkle in his blue eyes and his sense of humor really intrigued me. East Coast humor is sharp and sarcastic but West Coast humor was full of puns and shaggy dog stories (which I really love).

Interestingly enough, after we got to know each other better, he confessed, "I've never ever moved so fast like that before with someone I just met," and I confessed, "I almost didn't show up cause I liked to know someone first before agreeing to a date." Coincidence? Or was it written in the stars?

The more I got to know him, I saw less and less of other guys. My Italian parents started to worry. What they didn't know yet was that Russ was 16 years older than me, had been married twice before and had complete custody of his two children, David age eight and Judy age seven.

When Russ asked how old I was, I knew if he realized I was only 17 years old, I'd never see him again. And my mama taught us never to lie. So when he asked my age, I just casually said, "I'll be 20 on Dec 4th." I didn't say what year. Well, when Dec 4th came round, he showed up with 20 long stemmed red roses and a beautiful wristwatch. That's when my folks really started to worry. Not because of the flowers, but because of the jewelry. In Italian custom, jewelry signifies serious intentions. Of course, I knew then, I had to tell him I was 18 not 20 years old. I knew full well he might want out but as it turned out, he didn't.

The first night I brought Russell home to meet the family and to have dinner, I pleaded with the folks to be on best behavior mode, "But, of course," Papa answered immediately. "We know how to welcome guests."

When Mama brought the pasta to the table, Papa shouted, "Dig in boys!"

The decibels were always loud at our house. I got in there quickly to fix Russell a plate. Then Mama said something to Papa and he said, "What'd ya say?" She shouted back, "Aah, wash out ya eahrs." To which Papa promptly shouted in return, "Shad ap, I'll blind ya." And he held up his hand pointing with two fingers at her. Best behavior! Ha! More like mealtime at the zoo.

To be honest though, we kids were used to it and realized that was how Mama and Papa showed their love for each other but to someone new to the family, who was especially on the quiet side, like Russell, it must have been shocking. Did I make a fuss after he left? You bet I did, but I knew the folks were hoping to get rid of him. And I thought they just might succeed, too. Especially when one time, Papa, who knew that Russ didn't like hot peppers, made a salad and said the peppers were not very hot. Russ not only lost his voice, tears came streaming down his face, and I swear smoke came out of his ears. And everybody laughed. But, surprise, surprise! My darling hung in there.

On my 21st birthday, Russ asked me to marry him. It was 1952, and though I really did want to marry him, I knew it would really be settling down to a husband with two children, because just four days after he proposed, we found our daughter Judy, who had been taken illegally by her mother from the boarding school where she and David were living. By this time, my folks had learned to love Russ and the kids and so I was thrilled when they gave us their blessings to marry.

Still I surprised myself when I said to him, "I really feel that I should travel a bit and see the world, before we marry." "Well, can't we get married and travel together?" he replied in his typical practical way. So I said, "OK." And did he keep his promise? He certainly did. I think it got to be a bit of a game. He'd come home from the studio and say, "Oh by the way, honey, we're flying to London, Paris, Munich, Rome, Beijing or wherever, tomorrow night." Did it worry me? Not a bit. I was always ready. I knew from our very first trip overseas, we carried the music in our suitcases and sent our clothes as unaccompanied baggage.

When Russ wrote this book, we had been married 57 years. We actually almost made our 59th. He passed on to the spiritual world just over a month before our anniversary. We were always romanticists at heart and believe it or not, we actually got married 58 times, that is, apart from our actual wedding day or should I say "night" since it was Christmas Eve at midnight. We didn't know about the Baha'i Faith then, so had a non-denominational pastor perform our ceremony which consisted of two passages, one on the subject of Love and one on Marriage from a book called The Prophet written by Khalil Gibran.

Getting married every year seemed to evolve in a very natural way. Every Christmas Eve, at the folks' house, we always had a big special seafood extravaganza with course after course of food. When it was our first anniversary, just before midnight, Russ and I decided to go to The Little Brown Church in the Valley to remarry by reading to each other those passages on Love and Marriage as a way to looking forward to another year of being together. Then when we went back to the folks place, all the kids and grown-ups, too, had a great time opening presents.

As it happened, we became Baha'is in 1955, and because we loved the beautiful Marriage Tablet in the Baha'i Writings, which gives the greatest advice to two lovers starting out on a physical and spiritual journey together, we added that Tablet to our little remarrying ceremony on our third anniversary. When we were in Munich for our eleventh anniversary, we just decided to carry on our little tradition wherever we were in the world.

Life was never dull with my darling. He had a wicked sense of humor and was a master at keeping a straight face. He loved to tease in a fun way of course, and could take as good as he gave. I used to accuse him of staying up nights thinking of all the silly things he used to start the day with because he had me laughing before we were even out of bed in the morning.

One evening, when we were having friends over for dinner, I felt sure I would be able to cope with building the fire I'd need to BBQ the chicken. Russell was recording until 6 p.m. so I wasn't going to be able to shout, "Hey honey, I need your help." As the time was flying by and the fire kept going out, I realized I wasn't going to get the coals ready in time to BBQ.

In a state of panic, I finally called the studio. "This is Russell's wife and I have to talk to him, please, it's an emergency." I did have the presence of mind to make sure they weren't making a take. "What's wrong, sweetheart?" came Russell's very concerned voice. Almost in tears, I said, "How do I keep the fire lit, I'll never get the chicken cooked in time for dinner." Well, very patiently, he told me how to build the fire and to keep it going. I had a hard time living that down, cause all the musicians at the recording session heard about my EMERGENCY. I did mention I was a concrete jungle kid and never a girl scout, didn't I?

At a recording session, after an especially beautiful rendition of a ballad, when Russ came into the booth to listen to the playback I asked, "What tune is that? It's absolutely beautiful!" "That's called 'Round Midnight'" he said. "Who wrote it?" I asked. "Thelonius Monk," he answered. "Thelonius Monk, that's a name?" I scoffed. And, in his sweet quiet way, he said, "Oh honey, I'd like you to meet Thelonius Monk," and he motioned to some guy I'd never seen before who was also in the booth. He wasn't Thelonius Monk of course, and everyone who knew, burst out laughing. Horror and relief mingled together when I realized he was putting me on.

Walking out of the premiere showing of *The Ugly American*, for which Russell had written all of the exotic, indigenous music, I said to Russell, "That Marlon Brando is such a great actor, I wish he wouldn't mumble so. The man walking in front of us turned around and just silently glared at me. To my horror, it was Marlon Brando! My darling Russell, in his sweet quiet way said to me, "Sometimes, my honey, you're like a gum ball machine, every thought you have in your head rolls out of your mouth."

Skiing in Europe was always fun. We were in St Moritz because Russell was writing the music for a film featuring Olympic Skiers. Every day, I would go off skiing with friends and Russell would join the filming crew up above St. Moritz. I heard the dreaded cry "Avalanche!" spreading through the crowd of skiers. The word was that there was an avalanche where they were filming. But there was no word regarding whether there were any survivors.

Whenever we were together and by some miracle, our lives were spared, we always felt it surely must not be our time to go. But this time, we were not together, and all I heard were the wild rumors flying around that the whole filming group had been wiped out. I immediately went off by myself to pray. For five hours, we waited to hear what had really happened. And once again, we were blessed by our guardian angels.

We spent so much time together working on songs, shows and musical dramas, that when I wanted to give Russell a surprise 90th Birthday Party, in 2006, I had to work very surreptitiously. Had it not been for our dear friends Karl and Sharon Kneisel it could never have happened. They were kind enough to allow me to use their e-mail address and telephone. All our wonderful friends had already agreed to bring chocolate cake, Russell's favorite.

The very talented singing star Tim Beveridge, not only performed, singing "All the Things You Are," which was always one of Russ's favorite songs for beautiful melody plus lyric, but Tim also acted as MC for the other talented singers like Mike Riwai and the lovely Barbie Davidson and pianist Bronwyn Case Gilbert. Yvonne Sharp, the Mayor at that time, presented Russell with a Distinguished Citizen Of The Far North Award. Shortly after that, the Kerikeri Rotary Club presented him with the Paul Harris Fellow.

I couldn't believe we actually pulled it off. There were a couple of times when I thought the cat was out of the bag, but friends on the phone were quick to notice that I was not answering their questions, but making up something completely unrelated cause Russ had walked into the room. I got such a kick out of being able to surprise him, because he was really shocked.

Technically, getting him to the beautiful Centre at Kerikeri, was quite simple. We had recently had a meeting with the Centre Committee about doing some concerts and perhaps a concert version of the opera Porgy and Bess. On our birthdays, we always went out for dinner at the Copthorne Hotel in Paihia, so it was very easy for me to say, "Darling, after dinner, would you mind if we had a quick meeting with the Centre Committee? It has to do with possibly doing Porgy and Bess and I know you'd enjoy such a project." "No problem," he answered.

The amazing thing is when we had gone out to dinner and had to drive past the Music Centre, it was packed with cars because of a big rug sale that was on. So, on our return from dinner, I was quick to comment, "Oh that big rug sale, must still be on, look at all the cars still here." Just as he was going to open the door for me to go into the lounge first, I said, "Oh, I have to use the bathroom, honey, you go on ahead." Well, soon as he opened the door, 160 people began singing "Happy Birthday." He was speechless. And I have to say I was delighted and surprised because my darling was never at a loss for words.

What fun, to hear Russell say later, "At first, I thought it very unusual that Gina had suddenly started going to morning or afternoon tea with lady friends. She had never done that in all our years of marriage. But, if it made her happy, that was wonderful." Though he always would add, "I would never believe she could be so devious as to pull it off." But the truth was, I never really was going to morning and afternoon tea parties, but would go to Karl and Sharon's place to check e-mail and take care of the zillion details to keep it a surprise for him. Sharon would even give me cake or cookies to bring him from our so-called "tea party."

Since his birthday was in the middle of the week, a lot of our friends from Auckland were not able to join us in Kerikeri. Our dear friends, Hussain and Christine Reyhani, insisted that we had to have a party at their beautiful home in Auckland on the weekend and that it had to be a surprise as well. So they invited us down to have dinner at a very nice restaurant and told Russ that they wanted us to meet some of their friends who were directors at the Auckland Museum.

Well, he certainly never imagined I would organize two surprise birthday parties in one week for him, but, you know, I did fool him big time again, with a lot of help from many dear friends, of course.

A few years later, I was again able to surprise him, for a little while, at least, again, with the help of Karl and Sharon. I got a surprise phone call from Karl one day. "Are you able to talk freely, or is Russ there with you?" he said. "Russ is in the studio writing music," I said, "What's all this mystery?" "Well, your Russell has been nominated as a recipient for the Queens Service Medal for his Contribution to Music for 2009," he said. "Wow, what an honor!" I squealed with joy.

I was able to keep it a surprise until one day, in the mail, came a letter addressed to him saying he had been nominated and that the Attorney General's Office wanted to know if he would consider accepting the award before they could proceed any further. I was completely blown away when I opened a letter addressed to me, saying that I had been nominated also for my Services to Music and would I consider accepting the Queens Service Medal. I had no idea that my name had also been put forth. Karl and Sharon never let on that I had also been nominated. Would you believe, to this day in 2013, I still have no idea who felt we each were deserving of such an honor.

After as many years together as we had, we actually knew each other for sixty-two years, it got so I'd say something he was thinking about or he'd say something I was thinking about. It was like two souls really becoming one. I still look back and feel: "What a charmed life we shared."

- Gina Garcia, January 2013

*Gravestone for Russell Garcia created by sculptor Chris Booth
Kerikeri Cemetery, Bay of Islands, New Zealand*

INTRODUCTION

Russell Garcia saw West Coast jazz coming. In the late 1940s, he sensed that the future rested in high-octane brass, conversational trombones, surfing reeds and a hard-charging rhythm section-all working together with a dramatic, cinematic script. Only Russ didn't call them scripts. To him, they were scores—blueprints that musical architects like Russ crafted and then handed out to musicians in the form of parts. When the parts were played together, the audio results could be as contemporary as a glass house or as cool as a new car with fins. Listening to the big band music recorded in the '50s at the studios of far Hollywood, you heard space, speed, sunsets, and surf.

Russ anticipated all of it. Growing up in Oakland, California in the 1930s, Russ found himself glued to the family radio. Sounds from the New York Philharmonic as well as the Swing Era-Ellington, Lunceford, Shaw, Hines, Goodman, James, Dorsey and so many others-poured out, helping him imagine an orchestral Eden. Bands were outfitted in the finest clothes, women were graceful and elegant, and money was plentiful. The price of admission? The ability to play an instrument-or write for those who could.

Russ's obsession with radio and records in the '30s only grew, so his brother bought him a broken-down cornet for $5-held together by Band-Aids. Russ taught himself to play the instrument-with help from Bix Beiderbecke and Louis Armstrong 78s. As Russ developed, his parents bought him a trumpet. So Russ took lessons, and in grade school he started a small jazz group. But what would they play? No worries, Russ said he'd whip up a few arrangements—figuring out on his own how to transpose music for the different instruments. By his own admission, his first arrangement of "Me and My Shadow" was a disaster. So he bought a stock arrangement of the song to see how he had goofed. Then he fixed the problems.

Later, in high school, Russ's ability for arranging really blossomed because he had two wonderful teachers who taught him all of the basics-harmony, counterpoint, conducting and orchestration. Russ soaked up the smarts and played trumpet in two school bands plus his own. He also developed quite an ear. Just by listening to Armstrong's "I Can't Give You Anything But Love, Baby," he was able to write down Pop's solo-note for note.

After high school, nothing could hold Russ back from the big band Shangri-La heard on his family radio. He enrolled at San Francisco University to study music, but soon faced a problem. He was already arranging and playing trumpet on a professional level and felt he was already ahead of his professors. Confident in his ability, he quit University and took his trumpet on the road with the bands of Al Donahue and Horace Heidt, leaving Heidt to arrange for Bob Crosby. In 1947, he began arranging for Harry James.

To supplement his income, the newly married Russ and his wife Gina decided that teaching would be a way for Russ to generate extra income. Thanks to the passage of the G.I. Bill in 1944, musicians returning from World War II were able to attend college or study privately for free. The G.I. Bill was a boon for music schools and teachers who now could receive federal funds when taking on veterans. The ranks of music departments at established West Coast universities topped out fast in the late '40s. To meet the surging number of veteran musicians seeking higher education, new schools were formed. But instead of providing formal training-like most universities-many of the new schools began to offer courses in commercial arranging for the recording and movie studios.

One of these new schools was the Westlake School of Music in Los Angeles. Russ was offered a job there and took it. But what was he going to teach? As Russ told me, "I wrote a four page outline. Then I added musical examples to illustrate each of the points. My course guide eventually became the basis for my book, *The Professional Arranger-Composer*. Why has the book been so successful? I don't know. I guess I've always been a synthesizer, finding ways to make things simpler. I just took what I knew about arranging and composing, broke it down into parts and added musical illustrations. I guess the techniques were explained in a way that many musicians could grasp quickly." His *Arranger-Composer Book II* followed a few years later.

Among Russ's many students was the young tenor saxophonist Bill Holman, who told me that Russ's course guide changed his way of thinking about arranging. In fact, Los Angeles in the early '50s was filled with new thinkers-making it an expanding hotbed of experimentation and exploration. With the proliferation of long-playing records and magnetic tape recorders, newly formed record companies needed as much new music as they could get their hands on.

This lab environment gave Russ room to grow. As he told me, "I had studied every style of music I could. I took lessons in the Schillinger System, which was a mathematical theory for composing. Then I studied composer Arnold Schoenberg's tone-row method. I think I was one of the first arrangers to use tone rows on my 1955 Wigville album."

But how could Russ possibly have figured all of this sophisticated stuff out on his own? Let me tell you a little secret. After Russ left San Francisco University and played trumpet with big bands, he went to Hollywood and studied with the finest teachers he could find. These teachers included Ernst Toch, Edmund Ross, and Mario Castelnuovo-Tedesco. He also studied conducting with Sir Albert Coates. Russ told me, "Every Wednesday, I got to conduct a movement from a tone poem or a symphony. For two years, I got to do this in West Hollywood. It was a great experience."

Soon other opportunities emerged in L.A.-a town that invented lucky breaks. Russ said, "Someone told Norman Granz, the owner and producer of Clef and Norgran Records, about me. He decided to use me to score part of an album with Buddy DeFranco's Orchestra in 1953. Then he brought me in at the end of 1954, to arrange strings for an entire Buddy DeFranco and Oscar Peterson album called *The George Gershwin Songbook*. I loved working with both Oscar and Buddy."

From there, Russ became a go-to arranger just as the recording studios were running at full tilt. Brilliant albums followed, including *Four Horns and a Lush Life* (1955), *Oscar Peterson's In a Romantic Mood* (1955), *Listen to the Music of Russell Garcia* (1956), *Buddy DeFranco's Broadway Showcase* (1956), *Charlie Barnet's Lonely Street* (1956), and *Russ Garcia and His Orchestra* (1956).

With the introduction of the 12-inch LP in the mid-1950s, vocalists who were once novelty acts on recordings became album stars-especially as covers began to feature their color photos in moody, romantic settings. Russ arranged albums for many of them, including Anita O'Day, Frances Faye, Helen Grayco, Bobby Troup, Herb Jeffries, Julie London, Tony Travis, the Axidentals, Margaret Whiting, Sylvia Mora, Blossom Dearie, and Mel Torme. He also scored Porgy and Bess for Ella Fitzgerald and Louis Armstrong. Many film scores followed. Russ said, "I was always amazed that the MGM films I did for producer George Pal in the early '60s, are still popular and being shown around the world." Russ and Gina relocated to New Zealand in the early '70s where the outflow of prolific music continued.

But to fully understand how Russ managed to balance a driven and relaxed personality, you must know a little something about the trombone—his favorite instrument. The instrument's tones have soul, notes slide, and it's probably the most conversational of all the band instruments, since so much of the music it produces comes from the players' voice. Here's what Russ told me, "I love the instrument because it can be strong and gutsy and swinging, or it can be soft and beautiful." That's all you need to know about Russ.

- Marc Myers (March 2013)

Marc Myers writes frequently on music for the Wall Street Journal and posts daily at JazzWax.com. He is author of Why Jazz Happened (University of California Press)

PROLOGUE

This book is a collection of, I hope, interesting stories about many of the great Film, TV and Recording Stars I've had the good fortune to work with in the last seventy years plus some incidents out of my own life that seem to amuse friends and enemies.

I'm the luckiest person that ever lived on this ridiculous planet. I've never worked a day in my life.

I write music and they give me money for it.

Anyway, I hope you will enjoy hearing about another side of the antics of some of these stars that differs from what their publicists make up to get their clients' names into those horrible gossip magazines.

This book is a bit of an ego trip, but a lot of these stories are just too good to not share. Please don't count the number of "I"s.

And, I realize it's a no-no for most publishers, but, when I put in my little confidential asides for the reader, I print them in italics.

- rg. 2009

TABLE OF CONTENTS

Acknowledgements v

Foreword vii

Introduction xvii

Prologue xxi

Odd Jobs 1

Film Stars 5

Singers 19

Jazz Instrumental Stars 27

Symphony Orchestras 35

Speaking Of Symphonies 37

Film Scores 41

In The Beginning 47

Some Early Memories 49

World War Two 57

To The U.S. After The War 63

Into The Recording Biz 73

The Fabulous 50s And 60s 81

Europe Again 85

Back To The U.S. Again 93

Sailing Away 97

Last Chapter In A Charmed Life 111

A Partial List of R.G. CD's/Albums 113

About the Author 115

Photography Credits 117

I Have Hundreds of Stories, Some of them True

Odd Jobs

    Yes, I've had some weird musical jobs. The topper I think, was being hired as a Technical Adviser on a film being made in Las Vegas. The musical director of Hal Roach Studios was Leon Klatzkin. I had known him since we were kids studying trumpet and recently he had hired me to work on two TV series with him. I guess he felt he owed me a few favors, so he had the studio send my lovely wife, Gina and I, two air tickets and all expenses paid in a top Las Vegas hotel, plus paying me several hundred dollars a day (*would you believe it?*), to watch Jayne Mansfield take her clothes off.

    She was one smart and very nice chick who knew how to play the "dumb blonde" role to the hilt. They were making a film called *Nights In Las Vegas* and Jayne was to do a strip tease dance in it. She was one of the 'well endowed' (*in the Dolly Parton mode*) sex bomb actresses of the day. We had pre-recorded a version of "Night Train" and my job was to see that she bumped on the right beats.

Night Train

Doo dl ly	Doo dl ly	Doo dl ly	Doo dl ly
Doo dl ly	Doo dl ly	Doo dl ly	Doo dl ly
Doo daht	BUMP	BUMP	BUMP

The whole Vegas show room was full of extras, people who are hired to be there. Jayne's husband, Mickey Hargitay, who was Mr. Universe, a bulging muscle man, was sitting at a front table watching his wife do a strip tease dance.

Both of them were so in love with their bodies, their whole bedroom ceiling was a big mirror. (*No, Gina, I never saw it. I just heard about it.*)

Jayne enjoyed doing this "strip act" so much that, I swear, she kept making mistakes on purpose. It took all afternoon to make the one scene.

Sophia Loren, Jayne Mansfield

Jobs like this don't come along very often. One of the witty musicians said, "If Jayne fainted, it would take four men to carry her out—two abreast." The sax player next to him said, "Don't be a boob. That's udderly ridicu- louse."

I did an arranging job on Sophia Loren's film, *The Brass Target*, but unfortunately never got to meet her. It was a very violent scene in a penthouse. They thought it wouldn't be quite so brutal if, instead of underscoring the fight, they had the hi-fi playing 50s music. I never did know whether they used what I wrote in the Glen Miller style or what I wrote in the style of Les Brown's Band.

The gorgeous Zsa Zsa Gabor, a very likeable smart woman, also knew how to play the 'dumb blonde' part to perfection. Her mother, was just as, if not more, beautiful than her two daughters, Zsa Zsa and Eva. Mom taught them every trick in the book to catch a rich husband. (*They each married several of the richest men in the world.*) When Zsa Zsa would get out of her automobile, her dress would slide up to her hips and show off those gorgeous legs. She did all these things unconsciously without even thinking, I'm sure.

When I was hired to do Zsa Zsa's musical arrangements for her Vegas Show, she said, in her gawjus Hungarian accent, "Russ, I know I don't sing so vell, but I have a gown cut down to here." And she pointed below her

Zsa Zsa Gabor

belly button. And I assured her, "Don't worry, Zsa Zsa, you'll WOW them." (*Today, where anything goes, it wouldn't raise an eyebrow, but back then, it was a bit shocking.*) A few years later Zsa Zsa was on the Laugh In TV show. At that time, the Funk and Wagnall Dictionary was popular. Steve Martin used a big word and said, "Look that up in your Funk and Wagnalls" and Zsa Zsa's innocent sounding voice came in, "What's a wagnalls??"

I used to be an arranger on the Andy Williams TV show. His pianist, who later became a top arranger in Hollywood, (*He must have read my text books*) would get the keys and routines for the singers and I would then write arrangements. I walked into rehearsal one afternoon and this sloppily dressed woman with stringy uncombed hair, was sitting in the first row with one ankle on her other knee, and I thought "What's a cleaning woman doing in here acting like she owns the place?" When I looked closer—Shock! It was Bette Davis, whose arrangements I had done for the show. I guess she was still in her "Baby Jane" mode. With all these ladies who aren't singers, the arranger must write the melody very strong in the orchestra or the singer can't stay on the melody. With one chick singer I recorded, I had four trombones in octaves playing her entrance note and she still came in way off. One of the musicians explained, "She doubles on singing."

Another interesting experience was Gail Storm. (*A fictitious name if I ever heard one*). She had two very popular TV series, *My Little Margie* and *Oh, Susanna* for which I wrote a lot of the music. She actually sang quite well and had a couple of hit records.

I was hired to do the arranging-conducting for a record date with her. She had an operation on her vertebrae just a week before the session and they gave her male hormones, which caused her voice to drop a perfect fifth. Naturally, the arrangements now were all in too high a key for her. The wonderful Hollywood musicians could have, of course, transposed their parts down, but it put them all in the wrong range for their instruments. We had to send everyone home so I could rewrite all the music and we had to come in the next week to record.

Film Stars

Fred Astaire was one of the greatest film actor-dancing stars. When I was a kid, my mother used to take me to the Saturday movie matinee to see Astaire and Ginger Rogers, and later with his other dance partners, Eleanor Powell and Cyd Charisse. I never dreamt that one day I would work with them all and have them for friends. My mother would have been so proud.

I did lots of music for Eleanor Powell and also the beautiful young Jane Powell. No relation between the two except beauty and great singing voices.

When Eleanor Powell made her big "comeback," I did all her arrangements. Her opening show in Vegas was fabulous, and a lot of us were backstage congratulating her. Several people were praising my music very highly, but the fellow that did the set designs kept interrupting and saying things like, "Did you hear the people all gasp when the curtains opened and they saw the sets?" Nick Castle, Hollywood's most well-known choreographer at the time, said, "Yes, did you notice? As the audience was walking out, they were all whistling the sets."

A few months later, I was in Dallas doing a one-week clinic on Composing and Arranging at the University. A friend of mine, Earl Humphreys, who was singing at an exclusive club, invited me to come in for dinner. I started dinner alone and as friends of his came in, he introduced us and had them make the table bigger. Soon, there must have been twenty of us. When I excused myself to go to the loo (*toilet*), this drop dead gorgeous blonde followed me, gave me her phone number which she had written in a match book cover with an eyebrow pencil and said, "Please phone me when you get back to Hollywood." (*She must have heard I worked for Universal Studios and thought I could make her a movie star*). Of course, I threw it away. (*I'm under contract to my own gorgeous girl*). Later in the evening, someone said to me, "You know who that blonde girl is? She's Mickey Cohen's girlfriend." Mickey Cohen was one of the most well-known gangsters in California. (*You don't mess with a chick that belongs to those fellows*).

Not long after that, he was shot and killed thru his Beverly Hills window. (*Don't look at me like that. I didn't do it.*)

As we continued dinner in the Dallas Club, I happened to mention that Eleanor Powell was opening her show at a Hotel in San Antonio that night. Two men in unison said, "I have an aero plane, let's fly down." One was the mayor of Tyler, Texas. (*Only in Texas could this happen*). So we flew down and caught her second show. They of course, ordered expensive wines and desserts. And when the time to pay the check came, (*would you believe it?*), Eleanor Powell had paid the whole thing.

Two months before, when I was at Eleanor's Vegas opening night, a new show opened the same night at the Stardust Hotel. They had used about 12 minutes out of Gershwin's "Rhapsody in Blue" for the grand opening with full cast on stage. Ira Gershwin, George's brother, who had control of the Gershwin Estate, happened to be in the audience and he ran to the hotel manager and told him, "We want George's Rhapsody to be a concert piece. We don't want it to be background for fifty almost nude chorus girls parading on stage. If you don't have it out of your show in two weeks, I'm going to sue you for four million dollars." The manager went to Eddie O'Neal, the orchestra conductor and said, "What can we do?" He said, "Call Russ." They were trying to call my phone service in Hollywood, and someone told them, "Russ is across the street for Eleanor Powell's opening." So, they came and got me, and I had a week and a half to write a piece with the same tempos and phrase lengths, but it could not sound anything like Rhapsody in Blue. (*They could never have built new choreography to teach such a big cast in such a short time*). We called it the "Rhapsody In Green."

Ira Gershwin never liked anything done differently than his brother had originally written it, though; I'm sure George would have loved hearing his music in different settings, like jazz or modernized arrangements.

Ira, I feel, spoiled the MGM film of Porgy and Bess by insisting that they do no location shots and film on a set like the Broadway Show. And he insisted that the original keys in which George wrote all the songs not be changed. Therefore, none of the great-featured singing stars could sing their songs except Sammy Davis.

Studio singers had to record the songs and let all these famous singers lip-sync. Marnie Nixon and Loulie-Jean Norman did most of this kind of work for films.

Also, it's hard to imagine, but Ira didn't like the CD of Porgy and Bess with Ella Fitzgerald and Louis Armstrong that I did in 1960. It's still a very big seller today.

Louis Armstrong, Ella Fitzgerald, Russ Garcia

When Louis walked into the studio he always had a few friends carrying his trumpet case and a case full of medications, lip salves, gargles, mouthwash, and his Swiss Kris, a mild laxative he enjoyed sharing with everyone. I told him, "Pops, you should stop by Thrifty Drug Store and see if they need anything."

When we were thru recording for the day, he would go out and eat dinner and then go down to Central Ave. and jam half the night. He'd come in the next morning to the session and when he'd try to play his horn, the air would all come out of the sides of his mouth with no sound. He'd face the wall and keep trying and all of a sudden, BANG, the sound came thru, his lips would be vibrating and all was well. He didn't know the song, "Bess Oh Where's My Bess"; so we recorded the orchestra track and later I sang the part and sent it to him in Las Vegas. He phoned one night and said, "Hey Russ, I'm listenin' to ya' every night before I go to sleep." Of course, then he flew down and recorded it.

The cult classic *Porgy and Bess* I did with all the jazz stars of Bethlehem Records that featured Mel Torme and Francis Faye, and Johnny Hartman, Sally Blair, George Kirby, Betty Roche, Frank Rosolino, Loulie-Jean Norman, Bob Dorough, Joe Derise, Australian Jazz Quartet and the Stan Levey Group, also upset Ira. We used Jazzbo Collins, a colorful disk jockey to do narration, describing the story as if he was seeing it happen in front of him, which led us from one scene or song to the next. I took musical fragments from Gershwin's score and developed them, in a very modern jazz idiom, as background and transitions between songs. Of course, this horrified Ira. George would have loved it, I'm sure. So, you might gather that Ira and I crossed swords over many issues.

Before the recording of this album, I had a piano player come in and I sang the parts, in my froggy voice, for the lead singers on all the music they couldn't be expected to know. Francis Faye would sometimes play some of these for friends and let them try to guess who was singing. Then they'd all have a good laugh.

Bethlehem Records owned a two-minute tape of "Summer Time" played by the Ellington Band, which they put at the beginning of this *Porgy and Bess* production so they could use the Ellington name. A later release by Hallmark of all the songs without the narration, gave complete credit to Ellington for the arranging, even though I wrote every note in this whole monster six-sided album, except for the two minute Ellington recording, which he probably didn't arrange. Most people give Ellington credit for a lot of songs and arrangements made by Ellington's very close, and very talented friend, the little giant, Billy Strayhorn.

When Bethlehem flew me to New York to discuss this project, they talked about swinging *Carmen*. Since *Carmen* had been done this way, I suggested *Porgy and Bess*. When they said they would use Frances Faye and Mel Torme, I asked, "Which one is Porgy?" (*Frances was big and muscular and loud, while the great jazz singer Torme was a bit vertically challenged and velvety voiced*).

Cyd Charrise was considered by many to be the most beautiful actress in Hollywood, (*Her legs reached all the way to the ground*). She was married to Tony Martin who used to play tenor sax. We were in the same band when we were kids in Oakland. His name was Hal Morris then and he got fired because he didn't play the sax very well, though he had great success later in Hollywood as a singing-acting star. I found Cyd, who was a great dancer and fine actress, quite shy.

It's amazing how many gorgeous girls don't seem to have great self-esteem. When they are acting, they are playing a part and lose their shyness.

Judy Garland's pianist-conductor, Mort Lindsey, a talented musician, used to work out the routines and keys for Judy's stage show act and give them to me to write orchestra arrangements. One night, Judy went to hear Vic Damone and after his show, went back stage to compliment him. Judy said, "What beautiful arrangements, Vic. Who wrote them?" He said, "Russ Garcia." And she said, "I must get him to do some arrangements for me." (*She didn't know that most of the music arrangements she was singing I had written*).

Mickey Rooney was also a good friend who would come pounding on my door in the morning and shout, "Hey, Russ, wake up. I've written another song I need you to write down." I

Cyd Charrise

hated to ride in his convertible. He'd roar down those Hollywood hills curvy canyons talking with both hands. But he was a happy fun person to be with, and a wonderful actor. For some reason all good comedians are excellent actors.

Gina and I met Liz Taylor, when she was quite young, at La Scala, the "in" restaurant in Beverly Hills at the time. We were having dinner with Louella Parsons and her friend Jimmy MacHugh, famous songwriter, and Pete Rugalo, well-known film and big band music writer. Louella was the top media columnist writing gossip about the Hollywood stars. Of course, all the ambitious young actors were coming to our table to "butter up" Louella hoping to get their name in her column. The gorgeous young Liz Taylor sat with us for a bit. She wore a leather cowgirl outfit that was stunning. Later, Louella said to us, "All these actors make a fuss over me, but I'll bet not one of them will come to my funeral." I was quick to promise that we would but, unfortunately, we couldn't keep that promise because we were in Europe when it happened.

Around this time, Sinatra was romancing a beautiful young girl, Peggy Connelly, and had me do an album with her. It's recently been re-released as a CD.

Sinatra was assured of becoming known. He had the mafia behind him. When he would arrive in L.A. on the train, they hired several girls to scream and swoon. It convinced young girls all over the country to do the same. Later, I heard (*which means I don't know if it's true or not*), that when a producer refused to star Frank in a film, the producer came home after a few days away, and found the bloody head of the horse he loved on his pillow. Needless to say, the studio insisted that Frank get the part. Of course, Sinatra deserved his fame. He sang with a good beat, sang the meaning of the lyric with feeling, had a good sound, and was a good performer. But I wonder how many great talents fall by the wayside because they never had that lucky break or had the promotion that is so necessary these days.

I also knew Ann Miller as a 16 year old, a beautiful child who became a star soon after. She did an act, mostly tap dancing, in the Deauville Club in San Francisco, where I was working in the band when I was just out of high school. The gangster owners protected her like hawks from any smart alecks that tried to make a play for her.

Mitzi Gaynor was a wonderful friendly young kid. When she played in a stage show I was working on in L.A. called *Louisiana Purchase*, the choreographer Gene Loring had me write a special modern ballet sequence. When Irving Berlin, who wrote the show, came to California for the opening, he said, "How dare you have someone I never heard of write some music for a show of mine?" But when he heard the music, he was happy with it. Berlin couldn't read or write music, but was a great songwriter. You can always get a composer, like ol' uncle Russell to put your songs on paper. He worked out his songs on the piano only in the key of Gb. They say his piano had a big lever that could put the whole keyboard up a half step.

An amusing thing happened after one matinee performance. Next to the artist's entrance there was a juice bar and I stopped for a cup of coffee. Seeing a little shaker of nutmeg, I sprinkled a bit on my coffee. One of the musicians sat down next to me and said, "What's that on your coffee?" I told him and he started to put a bit on his coffee. (*In my silly mode*) I said, "You better not do that. You'll go home and be chasing your wife all over the house and you may not get back for the evening performance." When I arrived for the show that evening, I walked in the juice bar and most of the musicians, including all the girl fiddle players, had nutmeg floating on their coffee. (*Shows how a superstition can get started*).

Later, after Mitzi was famous for her role in South Pacific, I was asked by Norman Granz of Verve records to do an album with her. She had a vocal coach from the film studio come to the sessions. He had her concentrating on so many things, she could never sing freely, (*with her natural lovely voice*), the meaning of the lyric. If only he had been barred from the session, we could have had much better results.

Remember Alan Jones? He had a big hit, in a major film *The Donkey's Serenade*. He called me to do a CD with him. (*He wanted to make a big comeback*). I went to his house several times to plan songs and style. He was always trying to get me to join him in a nip from bottles of booze he had hidden from his wife all over the house. (*It was like a scene from* Lost Weekend). After all the time spent planning and sketching, I got a telephone call from him telling me how lucky he was. He had found an arranger who was really up there in Beverly Hills society. So, what could I do but wish Alan luck and success with the project. I never did hear if this album ever came out.

I did do several arrangements for Jack Jones, Alan's talented son, one of the best singers around.

I got a call from Charlie Chaplin's conductor at that time, Keith Williams. They wanted me to work with Chaplin and Ray Rasch, Chaplin's pianist, on the film *Limelight*. Chaplin was a genius. He wrote the script, produced, directed and acted in the film and knew every camera angle he wanted. He even picked out the main music themes with one finger on the piano. (*One became a hit song*). And, he could do all the steps the ballet did in the film and helped with the choreography. Of course, he couldn't write for the 65-piece orchestra, so needed an arranger. The film turned out beautifully, BUT, then some congressman, who wanted publicity, accused Chaplin of being a communist, and said Chaplin had earned all his money in the U.S. and had never bothered to become a citizen. Chaplin had gone to one communist meeting many years back to see what it was all about. He was not a communist. He wasn't much interested in politics. So, when he and his beautiful very, very, young wife, Oona, (*the daughter of Eugene O'Neill, the famous playwright*), took a short trip to England, they wouldn't grant them visas to come back to the U.S. The American Legion threatened to picket the film if it came to the theatres, so it didn't get shown in America for a long time. (*The witch hunts.*) So Chaplin and Oona went to live in the beautiful mountains above Lucerne, Switzerland.

Twenty years later, Hollywood wanted to honor Chaplin and decided to award him an Oscar for the music of *Limelight*. He was getting a bit older and said, "Someone by the name of Russell worked on this with us and should share this award." (*This is the story I got from his conductor Keith*). They went to the house of Charlie's pianist, Ray Rasch. Ray had died and his wife thought it could have been Larry Russell, a close friend of Ray's, and an excellent arranger in Hollywood. They went to Larry's house. He had died and his wife said, "Yes, I think he probably did it," so they gave the Award to Chaplin and Larry Russell, whose son accepted it for him. The next day my phone was busy ringing with calls from people including Keith Williams, the conductor, and Ray Rasch's son. They thought I should have shared this award. Actually, I think Ray did most of this work with Chaplin, so maybe he, not me or Larry, should have shared the Oscar. And, even though lots of people want to make a fuss over this, I don't want to cause a big kafuffle over something that happened 50 years ago. It's ancient history. I'm sure Larry's kids and grandkids are proud of the Oscar, and my Baha'i Faith says I should be the source of grief to no one. (*Besides, I think awards are for kids to post on the refrigerator.*)

I Have Hundreds of Stories, Some of them True

I do have a nice photo of Chaplin and me taken at the film scoring session.

Russell Garcia, Charlie Chaplin

There are so many award shows now; an award should be awarded to the best award show. The latest award sent to me was from MAC (Manhattan Actors and Cabaret entertainers,) for Best New Song of the Year 2009. It was "I Remember" recorded recently with Shaynee Rainbolt, a wonderful N.Y. jazz singer who also helped co-write the lyric.

Remember Will Rogers, the cowpoke with the great homespun, dry wit? He would spin a lariat and quietly drop fabulous little remarks like, "Some people learn by reading or listening, but others have to learn by peeing on the electric fence." Roger's most famous saying was, "I never met a man I didn't like." At one of the film studios, Marvin Hamlish must have had a disagreement with one of the orchestra musicians. One morning, we came into the sound recording stage and here was a little sign on the wall saying, "Will Rogers never met Marvin Hamlish."

Charles Laughton and his wife Elsa Lanchester lived in a spooky looking old wooden house in the hills above Hollywood Boulevard West. When Verve Records asked me to do a CD of Cockney Songs with Elsa, she wanted to do this in their home, not in a studio. So we brought Ampex recorders to their house, and recorded every day for a week or so. Charles Laughton's collection hobby was ancient Columbian Pottery and modern French paintings that looked like someone dipped a broom in creosote and made a few slashes and a blob on a giant canvas. I would have valued them at about $10, but I'm sure they were worth a fortune. (*What ever happened to beauty and good taste?*)

The art director at Verve came with us the first day and fawned over Charles so much it sickened him and he told me, "Please don't let him come here anymore." (*I think that stars would rather be treated like people.*)

We would start recording at 10:30 in the morning with Elsa and piano, planning to add bass and drums and strings, or whatever we needed, later. Usually, after 11:00 a.m., Charles would come down stairs and dive in their pool. If only I could have taken a photo of him dripping wet, stringy hair, his big belly hanging out above his wet boxer shorts, his before lunch glass of gin in his hand, it would have been worth a fortune, but of course, one wouldn't dare.

Later after Charles had passed away, I would often run into Elsa at Universal Studios where she was featured in one of those ghoulish family series. I think it was *The Addams Family*. She would say, "Hey, Russ, why don't you ever come by the house to see me?" But I wasn't sure what was on her mind, so I never did.

Around this time, NBC decided they would do a radio show with Laurel and Hardy. The script was written and I wrote all the music. The orchestra and all of us came in for the recording and these two fantastic showmen showed up so drunk they couldn't read the script without a load of mistakes. So everyone was sent home and told to come back next week same time. The same thing happened again and NBC said, "Forget it." So sad. These great men who had given so many happy laughs to the world now caused a few tears.

Spike Jones and wife Helen Grayco, a singer that I did a very nice album with called *Round Midnight*, had in their Beverly Hills home as much humor as he put into his comic, hilarious music hits. They had wonderful copies of famous paintings, but when you looked closely, you'd see Whistler's Mother had a racing form on her lap, and Blue Boy had Spike's face and was cross-eyed. And, they had a funny little poodle named Irving. They lived in Beverly Hills and Spike said when he went out on the front porch and called out, "Irving," heads would pop out all along the street.

Clint Eastwood, a real music lover, especially of jazz, did his first TV series at Universal. It was "Laredo" and your old uncle Russell composed and conducted the music. I loved it, when in the beautiful artistic town of Carmel, where Eastwood had a home, city regulations wouldn't let him build a retaining wall, so he ran for mayor, got elected, changed the regulation, built his wall and refused to run for mayor at the next election.

(I'll bet there's been a time you've wished you could buy a hotel so you could fire some rude employee. Howard Hughes actually did something like this in Las Vegas.)

Other TV series I provided music for, at this time, were *Perry Mason, Twilight Zone, Mr. District Attorney, The Virginian, The Fugitive, Captain Newman M.D., Wild Wild West, Petticoat Junction*, etc. Universal and Columbia now often drop music I wrote way back then, into current TV series, which of course makes me very happy when the royalty statements come in.

Gina and I sponsored a beautiful young Japanese girl named Yoriko who came and lived with us in our Mulholland house for a time. She was totally in love with Geoff Clarkson, Bob Hope's pianist-conductor. She was available any time Geoff wanted, and Gina said, "If you really want to marry this guy, here's how we do it." She had friends make dates to take Yoriko

Rainbow House in Hollywood Hills, California

Whare Koa in Bay of Islands, New Zealand

to the movies. After Geoff called a second time to find out she had a date, he said, "Where are you meeting these fellows?" Her answer, "Thru Gina." Geoff said, "Gina wouldn't do that to me." Result: He proposed marriage and they were happily married in our Mulholland mountainside house two weeks later. *(A man doesn't stand a chance against two women working together.)*

This house, designed by John Lautner, (one of Frank Lloyd Wright's best students), built in 1960-62, is still being featured in Sunday newspapers and architectural magazines today. We called it "The Rainbow House" because the roof is a hundred and fifty foot arc, and we put various colored windows here and there. But the two young fellows that own it now insist on calling it "The Garcia House." They went to Lautner's office, got the plans and brought the house back to the original way we had it. A couple of owners in the interim had made small changes. The house was featured all the way through *Mel Gibson's film Lethal Weapon 2. (Would you believe they paid the then owner more to do the filming than we sold the house for?)* It was so different in design it took two years to get permits through City Hall bureaucracy and took two years to build. The banks all refused, because it was so unorthodox, to loan us the money to build it. Luckily, I got a couple of films to compose music for and we were able to pay as we built.

Our builder was formerly in charge of building sets for MGM films, so wasn't afraid of so many innovative ideas. Eventually, we went from the most modern house in Hollywood to one of the oldest in New Zealand, and loved them both.

Singers

Anita O'Day was a wonderful kook, and a joy to arrange for. She was one of the very few singers that never phrased way behind the beat. She *made* the band swing. She could be out all night dissipating and come into a recording next morning looking as healthy as a high school cheerleader. She walked into one session and Bud Shank, the great jazz alto sax player, was warming up on his flute. Anita said, "Who's that?" When I told her she said, "I don't like his embouchure." I think she was showing off a new word she had learned. Anita had a wonderful sense of rhythm, sang with feeling, could skat with the best, and had a distinctive sound. What more could you want? She chose the name O'Day because it's Pig Latin for 'dough'.

Ella Fitzgerald was another great with those same good qualities. Would you believe that Ella, the world's "champeen" singer, would be in a panic before each performance? But the minute she got that microphone in her hand and got into the song, she'd forget herself and sang like an angel.

Strangely enough, I've been able to help lots of singers and actors to completely get rid of stage fright by telling them to say aloud to themselves, "I love my audience, but I don't give one damn what they think about me."

Sarah Vaughn had perfect pitch, so I started the arrangement of "My Ship" with no one playing in back of her, then after seven or eight bars,

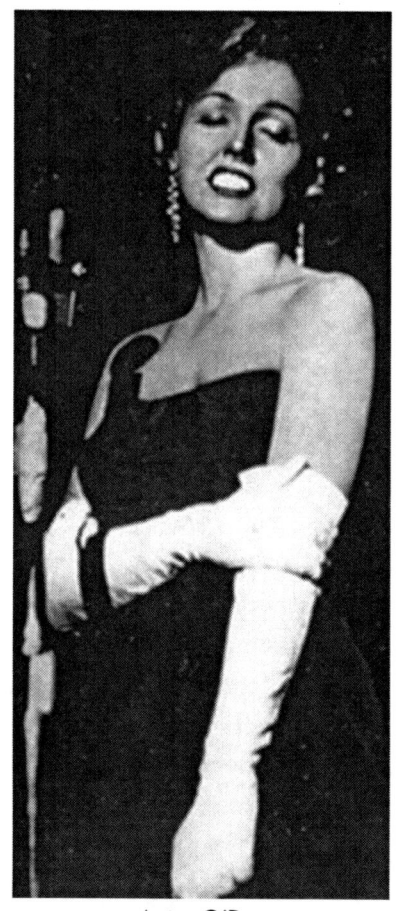

Anita O'Day

added a pizzicato bass and then celeste, and gradually the whole big orchestra was playing. As we started rehearsing this, Billy May walked into the booth and seeing the whole big orchestra not playing, he switched on the intercom and said, "Hey, Russ. Is this what you get twenty dollars a page for?"

I did twenty or twenty-five arrangements for Sarah and when Columbia released them they just credited the Hal Mooney Orchestra. Hal was the A and R man for Columbia at the time.

When I'd work with Mel Torme, he had already planned exactly what he was going to do and even suggested chord progressions and where he wanted to modulate up a half step. Sammy Davis was the opposite. I'd go to his house and we'd find the best keys for the songs he wanted to sing and he'd say, "Surprise me, Russ." He would come to the recording session having no idea what the orchestra was going to do, but he was such a natural musician he'd create great things to fit in perfectly with my arrangement. I heard that he used "Slow Boat To China" and "In The Still Of The Night" that I recorded with him, in his nightclub act for a long time. When I took Gina to see him perform in Vegas, he walked on stage and she said, "He's ugly." Then he started to sing, and she said. "He's beautiful."

On hearing a Blossom Dearie recording, with her jazz piano and high little voice, I pictured her as a big, fat, black mama. What a surprise, meeting her to discuss a record date, (*we did several CDs together*), to find she was a wee small blond. She was a master at finding great old songs that were little known.

Margaret Whiting was a real pro and a joy to work with. The CD we did of Jerome Kern's fabulous songs is one of her best and one I'm quite proud of. Kern songs and Harold Arlen songs are such fun to arrange with their perfect melodies and wonderful sophisticated harmonic progressions, and they most always collaborated with my favorite lyricist, Oscar Hammerstein.

Shaynee Rainbolt, a wonderful and popular New York jazz singer, heard a song I had recorded with Julie London called "Go Slow." She saw that I had written it and searched the internet to find me. But when she saw my birth date 1916, she thought, "This guy must be dead." But a musician friend told her, "No, he's still alive and working." She found an e-mail address and asked me to send a copy of the song.

Margaret Whiting

Shaynee Rainbolt Sings Russell Garcia - "CHARMED LIFE"

Years before, a fellow had walked into my little office in the Otto K. Oleson building on Vine St. where a lot of arrangers lived in little cube offices that were formerly dressing rooms for the first Film Studio in Hollywood. Nelson Riddle, who later became famous as Sinatra's arranger, was one of us and was struggling to get a little work then. But, anyway, this fellow that looked like a university professor came in and said, "I've written a lyric and I hope you'll write me a tune for it." I said, "Leave it here, and I'll see if it inspires anything." It was a surprisingly sexy lyric and I was preparing a CD with Julie London at the time, so I quickly scribbled a melody for it. Julie liked it and recorded it. Nothing much happened with it. Twenty years or more later, I'd almost forgotten it, and a surprise royalty check for several thousand came in. The publisher had placed it in two movies and on the airlines. A lot of girl singers all over the world, heard the song, and wanted to sing it. We can't find the lyric writer, Ned Kronk, who would be overjoyed to know he had a song, probably the only one he ever wrote, that was getting popular, plus a good lump of money coming to him. The tune went over so well in Shaynee's act, she asked me for other tunes. When I sent a lot of them, she decided she must do a CD of all R.G. songs. Of course, I was overjoyed.

Tierney Sutton

I had done a CD years ago featuring four trombones that Bethlehem Records called "4 Horns and a Lush Life." Later they reissued it as, "I'll Never Forget What's Her Name," (*the name of one of the originals I wrote for it*). It featured Frank Rosolino, Maynard Fergusson (*on valve trombone instead of his trumpet*), Herbie Harper and Tommy Pederson and Marty Paich on piano. It got a lot of play. Frances Faye, Mel Torme, Anita O'Day and now, Shaynee Rainbolt asked for this sound in back of them on their CDs. We recently performed the music from Shaynee's CD *Charmed Life* in N.Y., S.F. and L.A. to standing ovations. Trombones can play exciting swing, or play soft like a French Horn behind a ballad, and are in a range to contrast a girl singer.

Tierney Sutton is another rising star that can sing jazz or classical like an angel. She and her group of three great musicians, Christian Jacob, piano, Trey Henry, bass, Ray Brinker, drums, work out very imaginative arrangements. Tierney's husband Alan Kaplan, one of the best Trombonists in America, called the musicians for me, and is featured on Shaynee Rainbolt's CD, *Charmed Life*.

Frances Faye used me for arranger-conductor every chance she could. She was at our house one evening when the *Frances Faye Sings Folk Songs* album was just released. A young person said, "Russ, who's this fellow with you in the photo?"

Frances thought this was hilarious. She had a drop dead gorgeous Swedish girlfriend living with her who wowed the musicians whenever she walked in, but the girl only had eyes for Frances.

Award winner Terese Genecco, a wonderful N.Y. jazz musician, can do a perfect "Frances Faye."

Remember Doris Day, the gorgeous young singer with the Les Brown Band? At that time, I think there wasn't a red blooded male in the whole wide world who wasn't in love with her exquisite beauty. Later in films, she was always cast as the pure untouchable girl next-door type. And Groucho made his classic remark, "I knew Doris Day before she was a virgin."

Isn't it odd that some of the things you toss off in a hurry often make the most noise? I was in the tiny village of Ngawha Springs in New Zealand, population 40 or 50, and an English friend making a cup of tea in the kitchen whistled a little tune. I said, "Where on earth did you learn that melody?" I had tossed that off for a publisher in Germany years ago. He wanted a light little happy tune with pizzicato strings and harp and bells. Our friend said, "That's the theme song for one of the most popular TV game shows in England, *Call My Bluff*.

I would have never received a penny from that publisher if I hadn't found this out and called him on it.

(*A lot of people say the term, "Honest Publisher" is an oxymoron*). But, for the record, I have to say that Criterion Music Publishers and Londontown have always been very fair with me.

I can't figure out the sudden demand for music I wrote in the 60s. But I won't argue about it. On royalty statements, film themes from *Time Machine* and *Atlantis, The Lost Continent* keep showing up on *Saturday Night Live* TV. How they can use these I can't imagine.

The famous dancer, Renee De Marco built a great act with four fellows that danced, sang, and did comedy. She took all of us, her special material writers, her choreographer, her arranger (*me*), and the four dancers to Las Vegas for a week to prepare for her opening show. All nine of us in her troupe, except me, of course, were as gay as a golly woggle. One of them came and sat next to me while I was having a cup of coffee in the bar, and it was obvious (*to me*) he had been sent to sound out my preferences. So when a chorus girl walked by, I said, loud and clear, "Wow, what a gawjus chick," to set that record straight.

Russ Garcia and Frances Faye

Jazz Instrumental Stars

It was such a privilege to be good friends with Oscar Peterson, Stan Getz, Buddy Childers, Gil Evans, Roy Eldridge, Johnny Hodges, Bud Shank, Don Fagerquist, Stan Kenton, George Shearing, Dizzy Gillespie, Lester Young, Harry James, Sam Donahue, Charlie Barnett, Cappy Lewis, Bobby Shew, the Nash brothers... (*This list could go on and on. In a few days I know I'll think of a few dozen talented friends I left out.*)

At the Finland Pori Jazz festival for several years, I did a nine-day master class in Arranging and Composition. One year Maynard Ferguson and his band of great young nice clean looking kids were playing. Maynard was playing a solo and glanced down at the side of the stage and back at the audience and suddenly did a double take. He stopped playing and turned to me and said, "Russ, what the hell are you doing way over here?" Then went on with his solo. The young musicians in Maynard's band were all flipping over a gorgeous young girl working the desk at our hotel, but she had no time for any of them. On the day we were leaving, I overslept and rushed down to the desk and said, "Get me a cab, quick. I have to be at the airport in 15 minutes." She said, "It takes 20 minutes to get a cab here, but I'm just getting off work, I'll drive you to the airport." All Maynard's band was sitting on the long bench in front of the wooden shack that was the Pori airport, and here comes bleary eyed old uncle Russell driving up with this beautiful kid, and they're all looking at me like, "You dirty old man."

Another wonderful Trumpet player was Buddy Childers. He played lead trumpet with the Kenton Band when he was only 16 years old. (*That's a rough chair to sit in*). On recording dates, I had always used Buddy as a strong lead player. Then one day at a Baha'i Jazz Fireside in Hollywood he was playing flugel horn with just bass, Jim Hughart, and guitar, Jaimie Findley. He played such melodic emotional jazz, I said, "Buddy, I never knew you played so beautifully. Some day we should do a CD with strings." The next day he phoned and said, "When can we do it?" He paid for the orchestra and studios and I did the arranging-conducting. On piano, we used the wonderful Brian O'Rourke who always surprises me with something refreshingly inventive in every solo. On bass was John Leitham (*There's a pretty wild story here, too*) and Greg Field, drums. This was one of Sinatra's favorite rhythm sections. For Latin percussion, we used Cun Yungo who worked on Miles Davis' CDs. We recorded a lot of beautiful ballads from the 40s, and 50s. To keep it moving and exciting we used a light Latin rhythm on every other piece. I'm quite proud of this CD. We never tire of listening to it.

A few months later I was in Phoenix working with the Symphony musicians during a World Thinkers Conference and Doc Severenson conducted a Concert with the Symphony a few days after. He offered us tickets to his

CD Cover - Buddy Childers with the Russ Garcia Strings - "COME HOME AGAIN"

concert and at an after-concert jam session, the young girl bass player played a great solo in the key of Db, a rough key for bass players.

When I complimented her on it she said, "Russ, I know you. I played bass on the Buddy Childers's CD." (*This was John Leitham, who was now Jennifer Leitham with red hair, a dress and ear rings. She had an operation and was now Jennifer. Shock!*)

Buddy was to marry the gorgeous and talented Diane Varga three weeks before our CD session. She went in for a face-lift, which she didn't really need as far as I could see, and never came out of the anaesthetic.

As shocked as Buddy was, he insisted on going ahead with our CD and dedicated it to Diane. (*He played his heart out*). The CD is all beautiful standards except for one song Buddy wrote called "My Diane" and one written by my Gina and I, "Come Home Again" which is the name of the CD. Buddy has joined Diane now.

Diane Varga

Diane Varga, Buddy Childers with Gina and Russ Garcia

(*Don't ever get old. When I looked in the* Hollywood Union Magazine *for December, ten of my old friends had gone on. I half expected to see my own name in there, but I guess they don't want me up there. They must be saying, "Keep him down there on earth, we don't want him up here." Or, should I have said, "Down here").*

When Stan Kenton formed his big Neophonic Orchestra he asked me to write something really far out. He said, "Russ, experiment. Go all the way." So I wrote a five movement piece called "Adventure In Emotions" using every device I could think of. In the first movement, I had the orchestra playing a flurry of sound on a dissonant cluster (scale) and had Bud Shank, on alto, express Pathos on the leftover notes not in the scale the band was playing. When he had gone on for a while, then the conductor gives a downbeat for the next section. Of course, I also used my system of symmetric tone rows, and polytonality and every other far out device I had learned or could create. All in all, a quite dissonant suite. At its premier in L.A., of course, Stan was conducting, and Gina and I were sitting in the balcony. When they started my piece, the woman next to me put her hands over her ears and said, "My God, do they call this music?" At the finish, there were enough people in the audience who enjoyed this kind of thing, so there was monstrous applause. Stan called, "Russ, where are you? Take a bow." So I did, and smiled at the lady next to me. (*Of course, we must respect everyone's right to their own opinion and taste*).

A few years later when Ken Poston had me do this piece at the Big Band Jazz Festival he puts on yearly at the Sheraton Hotel near the L.A. Airport, I wrote a shockingly consonant 6th movement for this Suite, all major triads, but with no constant key feeling. I hope the same lady was there.

At this Festival, before each movement, I told the audience what to listen for, and explained what devices we were using, and how the band was doing more creating than I, and they loved it. Capitol Records recorded it with all the great Kenton musicians, Shelley Manne, Buddy Childers, Maynard Fergusson, Frank Rosolino, Milt Bernhardt, Harry Betts, etc.

Years later, when we were in our boat in Suva, Fiji, I got a phone call asking for permission to use some of this rather dissonant music for a video of the Muhammad Ali - Joe Frasier fight.

At one Monterey Jazz Festival, Gil Fuller, who used to write for Dizzy Gillespie's Band, asked me to do this same far out piece. At rehearsal, the day before the concert, about a quarter of the band didn't show up and several that were there had hangovers or had been indulging in something stronger than booze. I almost called the whole thing off, but I thought, "What the Hell. Maybe they'll come thru on the job." It didn't come off too well. (*This is called 'A learning experience'*). I was ready to swear off doing Jazz Festivals, but Pori, Finland, and L.A., and Munich and others were always a joy.

Gina and I became very close friends with George Shearing and his wife Ellie, who was an excellent opera and session singer. Even though I never worked with George, the four of us always had dinner together when we happened to be in the same city. And we kept in touch through telephone and email. He overcame his handicap of blindness since birth to become one of the best pianists in the jazz field, and even performed with symphonies performing the Mozart Piano Concerto, (*If he learned it by listening or by Braille I never found out*). The Queen knighted him so he is now Sir George.

Back stage at a European Jazz Festival, Dizzy Gillespie walked over and put his arm around Shearing and said, "George, probably no one ever told you, but you're black." Everyone, including Shearing, roared with laughter.

George had such a wonderful sense of humor. Sometimes, he would phone me in New Zealand, all the way from N.Y. to tell me a joke. The last time he did this he told me about the musician excusing himself for being late for a Chicago recording session saying, "Traffic was so terrific, I got stuck on the bridge from Indiana." The conductor said, "Don't give me that. There is no bridge in Indiana." (Explanation: The song, 'Back Home Again In Indiana' is an A B A C form and has no contrasting middle section they call 'the bridge' in the usual A A B A form.)

If you ever phoned George and his lovely wife Ellie long distance, you'd have to listen to a mini-opera with them singing and playing, while your phone bill is piling up, before they pick up the phone. Now, it is so sad this great artist had a stroke and is in a wheel chair and can't play anymore.

I thank the Creator that we have CDs to keep the music and the memory of timeless musicians alive.

After Dizzy passed away, we gave him tribute concerts, playing all the wonderful Diz and Bird (Charlie Parker) compositions.

Two hours of Be Bop is a little heavy for some audiences, so I asked a lot of Diz's close friends, Oscar Peterson, George Shearing, Ella Fitzgerald, Mike Longo, Ray Brown, etc., to make me 2 to 5 minute videos. Plus we got the

Dizzy Gillespie

video of Diz on the Muppet show (*which is hilarious*), and a concert with Diz clowning with Jon Faddis (*A Diz clone*). We played these videos between band numbers in the concert, and I told stories about Diz. I was able to tell them about a lot of our beliefs by saying, "Diz was my Baha'i brother and he believed there was just one race, the human race and all of the religions are worshipping the same unknowable force that created this universe, and the earth is really just one country."

We did this Diz Tribute for a sold out concert in Auckland and the three other big cities in NZ, and then in Prague, in the Czech Republic, at the Rudolfinum, across the river from the castle. I think it's the most beautiful Concert Hall in Europe. The gas lamps are still hanging from the ceiling (*but of course, electrified now*). We also featured singer Judy Rafat on this concert.

The managers of the Rudolfinum, still in communist thinking mode, said, "This is the first jazz concert we've ever had here. Our quota is an audience of 200, but for jazz we doubt you'll get *that* many." We attracted over 1500, standing room only.

I made Gina promise not to buy any of the famous Prague crystal. It's heavy, and we carry so much heavy music, my arms get longer every year. But, at the end of the concert up came the usual flowers and a black box, of course, with a beautiful heavy crystal vase in it. Also, a young girl came up and put a long bead necklace around my neck and kissing me on the cheek said, "When you started that music I got so excited, I wanted to rush right up on the stage and kiss you," and I replied, "What was your name? I'd like you to meet my wife." (*Gina was standing near us on the stage*).

At the end of World War II, (*which I won single handed in Europe*), the Red Cross set up places where we could get donuts and coffee and they had a few recordings. I found a Dizzy Gillespie - Charlie Parker recording and was I wowed. This had all happened while I was away. A new exciting style of music called Be Bop. After the war, when we returned to Camp Kilmer, New Jersey, they said, "No one is to leave camp." As soon as it was dark, another friend and I crawled under the fence and hitch hiked into N.Y. and went down to 52nd Street and the Club where Diz and Bird were playing. I sat there with my mouth (*and ears*) open till closing time, never dreaming that Diz and I would be good friends one day.

Gina and Russ Garcia in front of the Rudolfinum - Prague, Czech Republic

I met that genius Charlie Parker a few times but drugs wiped him out in his early 30s, so I can't say I really knew him that well. So sad that that amazing talent destroyed himself at such an early age.

In Prague, I was also asked to give master classes at the Conservatorium of Music, and several concerts with big orchestra, plus write music for a short film for Prague TV. At the finish of one concert, they had a VIP reception. I was telling a very nice fellow about my beliefs, which I believe can bring about the happy peaceful world we all long for. He gave me his card and said, "Look me up if you ever get to Bratislava." His card said, Vice President of Czechoslovakia. What a surprise. When the countries separated a few years later, he became Prime Minister of Slovakia.

Inspired by Havel, (a writer-poet that had spent time in jail for writings that were considered anti-communist), 300,000 citizens collected in

Wenceslaus Square and told the communists they were thru. (*A velvet revolution*). No one was killed or injured. And then, when Slovakia wanted to become independent from the Czechs, again there was no argument. It came about peacefully. In the centre of Prague, the communists had put up a tank on a pedestal with a plaque saying, "This monument is dedicated to the day that Russia liberated the Czechs from their oppressive government." (*Ha!*)

After Czechoslovakia became independent, some students at night painted the tank pink and were put in jail and it was painted brown again. All the newly elected government officials on a night soon after, put on old clothes and painted the tank pink again. They couldn't put the government leaders in jail, so now it's there as a tourist attraction, and called "The Pink Tank."

At the end of the concert VIP reception, we started to leave and someone said, "Let's catch the last show of the Fountains." This is a thrilling display of streaming water and multi-colored lights programmed to catch the accents and crescendos of recorded symphony music. We all went and it was glorious. As I got up to go, all of a sudden, I heard music of mine coming out of the speakers. The technicians had stayed up late the night before and computer-programmed the show to fit a symphonic piece of mine they had found on a CD.

I nearly fell into the fountains. Everyone, including Gina, knew it was going to happen except me. What a beautiful surprise.

Symphony Orchestras

A Symphony performance is one of the highest forms of co-operation of our human race. Each member does his individual part with precision and emotion and the resultant whole is far, far greater than the sum of the parts. But now, Symphonies are worried that they are an 'endangered species'. When the Mozart lovers die off, they'll have no audience. Most young kids now, have never had the thrill of hearing a live Symphony. Lots of them have never heard a Big Band. All they know is the 'screamin-meemies'. A good share of the recordings now are made of a two bar, or four bar loop and the singer has a lyric and finds something that will work, often out of meter, against the two or three chords that are endlessly repeating. Or, the raps are mostly speaking in rhythm with a rhythmic figure under it. A hundred years ago they called this "Spreche Stimme."

So, the worried Symphonies are bringing in young singers, and they need arrangements, so that's where old uncle Russell comes in. I've studied all my life to write Symphony music, but grew up in California in the midst of jazz, so feel at home in both fields. Recently, they brought over Marlena Shaw from Las Vegas to NZ and had me do 13 arrangements. And then I did a lot of arrangements for a wonderful Maori singer, Whirimako Black. She is used to going into a studio with a small group with no music or just a lead sheet and recording. She innocently asked, "Why does the Symphony need you? What do you do?" My explanation was, "There are 65 musicians in the orchestra and every one of them needs music in front of them to play. That's why I'm called in.

So many times now on re-releases of CDs from the past they give me no credit at all. Some of the young "A and R" people don't know the importance of the arrangement and the conductor. It's disappointing on some CDs that I was really proud to have done, like a new re-release of Porgy and Bess with Ella and Louis, and Anita O'Day's Verve classics, and Blossom Dearie's Verve things, etc., etc., to get no credit at all.

When, because of my family name, I was getting calls to do Latin music, I went down to Sunset Blvd. in Los Angeles to the salsa clubs, with music pad in hand, and made notes of what the bass and piano and drums were all doing and so became proficient enough in Latin rhythms. This paid off when I was called by RCA Victor to do whole albums they put out under Louis Arcaraz' name, plus the album called Carioca, and two CDs with the trumpet virtuoso Rafael Mendez, and then Laurindo Almeido, the fabulous guitarist as well as Big Film Latin Productions.

I studied lots of instruments privately for three months or so; violin, cello, flute, french horn, piano, etc. etc., not to perform on them, but so I could write for them without writing impossible fingerings or awkward passages to play. This may be why I am still working at my age.

Russ Conducting in Auckland during his 95th Birthday Concert

Speaking of Symphonies

I like the story of Toscanini bawling out the clarinet player. I think it might have been Glen Johnston. Glen talked back to him, and the temperamental Toscanini shouted, "Get out." Glen picked up his clarinet and as he was walking out, said, "Go 'bleep' yourself." (*I've edited this*) and Toscanini said, "It's a too late to apologize. Get out."

A lot of conductors think it's necessary to be the tyrant, the drill sergeant, but I love the musicians' attitude in Hollywood. You all work together to make beautiful music and everyone enjoys doing it. There's none of the attitude, "employee versus employer. The one in charge is the enemy." I've had big orchestras say, "We can do a better take, Russ. Can't we go ten minutes overtime, at no charge, and do it again?"

I was so lucky. Sir Albert Coates had a conducting class and his six students each got to conduct a movement from a Symphony or a Tone Poem with the West Hollywood Symphony each Wednesday for a couple of years. I never wanted to be a full time symphony conductor, but it was wonderful to be able to conduct my own music for TV series or films, or recordings or concerts. Alfred Wallenstein told me he spent more time drinking tea with sweet little old ladies that helped keep the Symphony afloat, than he spent on music. But I was fortunate enough to conduct Symphony orchestras in Vienna, Hamburg, Hannover, Prague, Hollywood Bowl, Munich, Orange County Calif., all the major cities in NZ, plus Changchun, China.

And, It was such an honor to get to know some of the famous Symphonic composers. Three other Composers, Lyn Murray, the Morton brothers and I, had the great joy of a three-hour lunch with one of my favorite composers, Dimitri Shoshtakovitch. They let him out of Russia for a two-week music festival at UCLA. We took him to the Bel Aire Hotel, one of the most posh restaurants anywhere. He was so happy when I told him

I had learned so much from him, when I was very young, by making myself a two line piano sketch from the scores of his 5th and his 1st Symphonies so I could study and analyze them. He knew our table couldn't be bugged at this restaurant and said, "We get along so wonderfully on a personal level, it's a shame our governments act like children." He lived in fear for his life in Russia. An accusation of writing music in our Western world style could mean the end. There is an excellent book called *Testimony* about his life.

Igor Stravinsky brought his "Circus Polka," a modern humorous piece, to our West Hollywood Symphony rehearsal to hear it for the first time. A few months later, I was with him in the booth when they were recording a Stockhausen piece. Stockhausen had only allowed a couple of bars for the upright tuba player to put in a mute, an impossibility, so Arthur Morton stood on a chair in back of the tuba holding the mute and put it in and out at the proper moments. Stravinsky put a two-dollar bill and a one-dollar bill on the counter for Morton with a note saying, "Two dollars for putting mute in. One dollar for taking mute out." (*Yes, we had two-dollar bills in those days.*)

I met Schoenberg at his home in Westwood. He taught for a short while at UCLA. I had studied his tone row method with Ernst Krenek. I didn't tell him that I enjoyed his student Alban Berg's music much more than his. Still, I was able to use a lot from studying Schoenberg's Tone Row method and tempering it with mercy. In Krenek's classes, the professional composers wrote interesting music while most of the students wrote very dull things.

It's very difficult for composers to get new Symphonic Compositions played because Orchestras are inundated with scores, mostly from University student composers. Though, a few years back, the Munich Rundfunk Symphony recorded ten pieces of mine for a CD called "Kaleidoscope," and the NZSO (New Zealand Symphony Orchestra) recorded for radio a lot of my music, and recently recorded my "Dungeon Chal" at a concert which was recorded for a CD, and I've had occasional concert performances or recordings with Hamburg, Vienna, and other Orchestras or Chamber Groups.

Russell Garcia Conducting the New Zealand National Symphony Orchestra

Film Scores

I did a CD of beautiful Johnny Green songs, called "Johnny Evergreens." Johnny was musical director of MGM Studios. We all went back to N.Y. for the big send off. Johnny had a load of big names come to a monster dinner. Richard Rodgers was there. He told me, "Always insist on first billing, Russ." Walter Winchell, Betty Furness, and lots of others were there also. One well known woman said, "Russ, you've hardly said anything. Tell us a little about yourself." As I started to open my mouth, she turned to the woman on the other side of her and said, "Did you see that stunning dress that Agatha wore to the theatre last night?" (*Glumph*)

Dave Kapp, who owned Kapp Records, was there. He said to me, "Russ, I'd like you to record me an album. Go into a studio in L.A. and do whatever you want." I had an idea for an Outer Space Album (there wasn't anything like that out at the time) so I went into the studio and recorded the first four pieces and sent the tapes back to him. He phoned and said, "Gee, Russ, I thought you would do something like Leroy Anderson." Anderson had some clever hit instrumental singles out at the time. My reply was, "If that's what you wanted, all you had to do was ask. Send me back the tapes. I'll send you a check for what you have spent for the musicians and the studio." Which he did. I took it to Liberty Records who bought it immediately, and it became a good seller. But I never said, "Nyaah, Nyaah, Ha, ha." It was called, *Fantastica* recently released again on CD by Basta Records in the Netherlands, and is suddenly getting quite popular again.

When George Pal heard this *Fantastica* Science Fiction type music he hired me to write the music for his next films, *The Time Machine* and *Atlantis, The Lost Continent*. He talked to me about a third one, based on Phillip Wylie's *The Disappearance* but Pal passed away before he got to do this last one.

George Pal was a genius at getting wild effects at a time when we had no computers to make it easy. In one scene, it was a laborious job shooting a few frames of film, changing the make up on an actor or dummy, and taking a few frames more, till he had a person decaying to a skeleton and eventually into dust.

Also, in those days, we composers had no computers to get weird sounds. So I had to make up my own effects. Before recording the big MGM 65 piece orchestra, I brought two percussion men into the studio and had one hit the big MGM gong and the other take a microphone from the centre slowly to the rim. This sound I ran backwards so it started with very high frequencies and crescendoed into the low loud smash, then ran it forwards to a high fade; we recorded: Blowing thru a straw into gelatin water; hitting a musical saw with a soft mallet and wavering the saw (*an unearthly sound*); All sorts of wood block hits; Vibrating a table knife from the tip on a table edge and pulling it in towards the hilt. I ran a lot of these effects backwards, and at different speeds, thru feedback echo. This way, I made weird loops to dub into the music track later. *The Time Machine* we made in 1960 has become a cult classic with a website and Time Machine Clubs. I still get very complementary email fan letters every week.

This film was the first Hollywood feature film for two unknowns, Rod Taylor and Yvette Mimieux, who both went on up from this to stardom. Arnold Leibovit of Talking Rings Records put out a CD of *Time Machine* that was later released by Crescendo Records. And just two years ago, FSM (Film Score Monthly) went to MGM, got the original 24 track tapes we scored for *The Time Machine* and *Atlantis The Lost Continent* and digitally re-mastered them and have released two wonderful CDs (*AND happily, I get credit as composer*).

For Atlantis, I think George Pal thought he would try two more unknown actors, but he wasn't quite so lucky this time. When the head of MGM Studios saw the film he said, "Cut thirty minutes out of this film." (*Can you imagine what this does to the already recorded music that is timed to the original?*) I had to work for a week with the music editor, Bud Cates, and edit the music to fit with the new film timings. What a job! Bud seemed amazed that I "kept my cool." He said, "Most composers would have a kicking screaming tantrum." He decided it must be my Baha'i Faith and asked Gina and I to come to his house and tell he and his wife Merle of our beliefs. Before long they joined us in trying to build a beautiful world for all people.

It just happened a very dear friend of mine, the genius Joseph Smith, painted the poster that publicized the Atlantis film. He also did them for several other film studios and many George Pal films. When I first started working at Universal Studios, the music department was one of three old wooden houses, which I imagine were old sets. (Now they are replaced by gigantic modern buildings). Alfred Hitchcock's office was in one spooky looking old house next door, and across the street was the art department. They paid these fantastic artists Joseph Smith and Reynold Brown only 350 dollars for paintings, which I consider masterpieces. These amazing modern masters could do these intricate paintings in a few days. Sad that both the paintings for the posters for my two Pal films were lost when George Pal's beautiful home in Bel Aire burned to the ground.

My first two film composing jobs were for Lippert Films. Two garment manufacturers from N.Y. came to Hollywood and hired Dick Hazard and I to write the music. They shot each film in one week and demanded we score them in three hours. Almost impossible. One was "Radar Secret Service" it was so bad it was comedic. The other was "Operation Hay Lift." Its whole plot was dropping hay to starving cattle. A complete bore.

But then, when Hank Mancini (None of his friends could call him Henry), was doing the score for *The Glen Miller Story*, they found Miller's wife had the whole library except for five pieces they wanted to use. They asked Hank, (I just *can't* call him, Henry), "Who can take this music off of the recordings note for note?" He said, "Call Russ." Apparently I did it OK, and then worked with this talented man on Orson Welles' *Touch of Evil*. Then the studio had me work on *Come September* (Gina Lolobrigida and Rock Hudson). So, my foot was in the door at Universal Studios. They gave me an office there and I did composing, arranging, conducting jobs, any one or all three, for many, many years.

The wonderful musician Benny Carter and I wrote the score together for *Fame Is The Name Of The Game* pilot film for a TV series. I was conducting, because Benny didn't like to, and during one 10-minute break a friend said, "I'd like you to meet a friend from Australia." I told this gentleman that one day I would sail thru those Sydney Heads. He gave me his card and said, "Look me up if you do." Years later when we flew to Sydney for a week, I called him and went to see him. It turns out he was the head-man of the whole Australian Broadcasting Commission. When I asked if he remembered me, he hauled out two magazine articles he had sold, telling how relaxed it was, and how much fun we had recording a film score in Hollywood. He talked me into staying five months, instead of one week, and working for ABC. Our sailboat was safe up in the islands and it was hurricane season (*which prohibits long sailing trips*) so, "Why not?"

Often a film producer or director would be spending an evening in a N.Y. restaurant and the pianist may have written a nice tune. Not knowing the difference between a songwriter and a composer, they would say to him, "How would you like to score our next film?" Of course, he's going to say yes. Soon, Joe Gershensen, head of the film music department at Universal, would be phoning me saying, "Russ, they've done it again." (*I've done so much ghost writing you should be able to see thru me*). Still, they did pay very well for this.

Sometimes wonderful talents would get the job to compose the music for a film, but lacked film experience. It is much different than writing an orchestra piece. It's necessary, when writing music for films, to fit the timings and moods of a scene. So they hired me to help and do the arranging. All the studios seemed to value me enough to pay me double scale for arranging.

They had me do two films with the talented Mort Lindsey and two with Cy Coleman who wrote the music for many very successful Broadway Shows. Cy asked me to come to New York and arrange for and conduct Shows but I was too happy and successful in Hollywood to think about leaving.

Universal also hired me to work, arranging for the great creative talent, Quincy Jones, on his first two films. (*He was the only one who ever gave me ASCAP credit for the few sequences I had written for which he hadn't given me a theme or a sketch.*)

On one film, they had hired Bobby Darrin as composer. He was a wonderful singer, but had absolutely no composing experience. He gave me an 8 bar melody and a two bar very ordinary blues riff from which he supposed I would write the whole score. At the recording he said to me, "I don't recognize that cue as being from the material I gave you." So, to appease him, I answered, "Sometimes, Bobby, we turn a theme upside down or backwards for variety." After the film came out, I just happened to turn on TV one evening and there was Darrin doing an interview. He played his little theme on the piano and said, "And sometimes I turned it upside down or backwards for variety." (*I think he actually thought he had written the score*).

The star in the film was Sandra Dee, a popular teen who had done well in TV and recording. They asked me to record some songs with her. At the session I had a big orchestra with some of the best musicians in the world. Sandra walks in two minutes late and seeing a piano, she sits down and starts playing the 'boompa-chicka, bompa-chicka' intro to "Heart and Soul" that every kid in the world played then. She was showing off, trying to impress all these great musicians who are sitting there grimacing and waiting at over a hundred dollars an hour.

Often, my Gina and I would go out to dinner with people in the film industry who were loaded with money. Some of the wives would have designer dresses that must have cost well over 2000 dollars. They often admired a dress Gina was wearing. She would never tell them she had paid 30 dollars for it.

In the Beggining

I was born in Oakland, California (*because I wanted to be near my mother. I was so shocked; I didn't say a word for a whole year*).

You must have noticed, I was born with an incurable malady. You might call it, "Hooked on Silliness."

Thank heaven my Gina is a great "Foible Coper" cuz I do have foibles. 'Anything for a laugh' gets me into big trouble sometimes.

Probably, I would have been born in San Francisco but the giant 1906 earthquake and fire drove my parents out. They lost everything and had escaped, walking around giant cracks in the earth to catch the last ferryboat to Oakland.

My kindly, loving old grandfather later told me that his father was born in the Azores Islands, (*the last peaks of Atlantis that didn't sink in the ocean*), and brought the family to the Boston - Nantucket area when grand-dad was a baby. Hence, my Latin name. He married a very strong little Irish Catholic lady who never called me Russell. I was "Little Mark" because they had me christened 'Mark' as a baby. I'm sure she was horrified when her son, my father, married a Protestant of English, Irish, Scots, German, French (and who knows what else) descent. My mom's sister had their family tree traced back to that old roué Ben Franklin who had a reputation for having a brilliant mind. (*I wonder what brilliant mind would fly a kite while holding its metal string in a lightning storm?*)

I have always loved the Italians. (Gina is Italian from both parents. Emotion *can* kick in before logic), but they don't backpack resentments. It's all out in the open *right now*. We have nothing but laughs when we travel in Italy. Nothing is simple. Everything's an Opera. In Naples, we asked two fellows, "Which way to the Concert Hall? They each pointed in opposite directions and a big argument started. A crowd gathered and applauded any especially vitriolic remark. I said to Gina, "A.I.A.C." That's our code for "All Italians are crazy" and we walked off and asked someone else.

But, back to my childhood. I must have been four or five when an aunt and uncle visited on Xmas day. They must have thought, "We don't have anything to bring to the little kid"; so they neatly wrapped up a washcloth. I opened it and ran around waving it, shouting, "It's a joke. It's a joke." If I embarrassed them, it serves them right. They tell me that as a tiny fellow, I once knocked on the back door. My mother, who was all love, (*She'd have tears in her eyes if any of her five boys had to go away for two weeks*), said, "Who's there?" I answered, "General." She asked, "General who?" My answer was, "General Nuisance." and my parents told everyone their son was already a stand-up comedian.

Some Early Memories

My first memory. I must have been a tiny tot, imitating the grown-ups. I waddled down to the river and dove in. Someone pulled me out, but I'll never be a great swimmer, because of a little panic in the water. Was sailing across the ocean an over-compensation?

I'd never forgotten holidays in Mill Valley with an aunt and uncle (*who weren't related, just family friends*). Their kids were very musical. One became first French horn player with the San Francisco Symphony for years. We would hike to the top of Mt Tamalpius and then talk the driver of the steam engine into giving us a ride down to Mill Valley on 'The Crookedest Railroad in the World'. Now autos can drive all these switchbacks to the top. My family was kind of dignified and I was startled and delighted when my 'uncle' squeezed a watermelon seed between his fingers and shot it at one of the boys, which started a five-minute seed war at the dinner table.

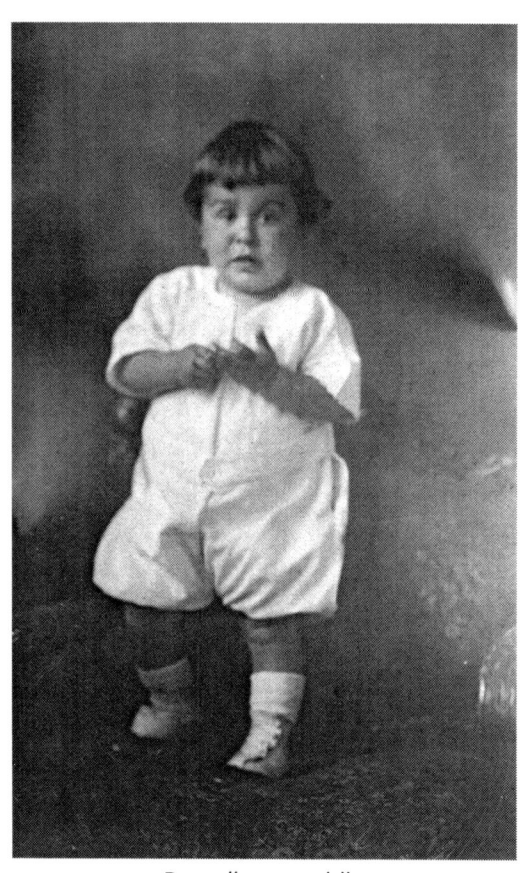

Russell as a toddler

Other memorable holidays were taking the train and ferry to San Francisco, then a ferry to Sausalito, no bridges then, and on the narrow-gauge steam train to Russian River.

A certain amount of music ability showed up in primary school. Our teacher noticed I could read a bit of music, enough to hold a harmony part in her little choir. She trained a small group and took us to the University of California in Berkley to show us off.

As a five and six year old, I devoured books about Daniel Boone and Kit Carson, and read all my older brother's books on Pop Psychology.

As a seven year old, every Sunday morning, I would wait by the radio, no TV then, for the N.Y. Philharmonic to come on. My older brother saw my love of music and brought me home a cornet held together with band-aids and tape. He had paid 5 dollars for it. I was soon playing it, so they got me a better trumpet. We formed a little jazz band at school. I was the youngest kid in my grade. They had skipped me forward a year and a half. (*The schools must have been too crowded.*) Until the middle of High School, I was always the littlest kid in the class. The girls especially towered way above me.

In Junior High, I had a great desire to write for our little jazz band so I bought a piano copy of "Me And My Shadow," a popular tune at the time. I knew my trumpet was in Bb and my part was written a whole step above concert key, so I figured out the Eb sax must be transposed up a sixth, and wrote my first arrangement. It sounded HORRIBLE. I had tried to put everything in the printed piano part in the instruments. So I analyzed stock arrangements and started listening to records and radio music analytically. After many tries, I was able to write a fairly decent sounding arrangement. Finally, when I got to High School, in my early teens, I had two wonderful teachers, Herman Trutner and a Mrs Garretson who taught me harmony, counterpoint, and orchestration. Trutner let me write for and conduct our high school orchestra. I still have an arrangement I wrote of Hoagy Carmichael's Star Dust that was played by the Symphony in Oakland when I was 13. It has some good ideas in it, but like every inexperienced arranger, I put in too many ideas. Experience teaches you to not throw in everything you know, and to build out of fewer ideas.

Our first job with our little band was in the Santa Cruz Mountains south of San Francisco, at a ballroom near the famous Brookdale Lodge with its stream flowing down through the dining room. A beautiful setting. We had just started our first set in the ballroom and the police came in and closed the place down. They said neighbors complained of the noise. We wondered if the lodge up the road didn't want any competition. We kids were able to stay in the old house they had put us in, so we had a month holiday. My first job had lasted 10 minutes. We pooled our money and parents sent care packages, so we had a great holiday in the beautiful Redwood Forest of the Santa Cruz Mountains. At the swimming hole, I made friends with the kids of the Capwell family that owned the biggest department store in Oakland. Their 12 year old girl insisted I go horseback riding. I think I was about 14 then and had never been on a horse. She galloped all over those mountain trails and of course I had to keep up. I was so raw I couldn't sit down for a couple of days.

In 1929, along came the Great Depression caused by corporate and individual greed, just as is happening in 2008-9. (*When will we ever learn?*) We have to change, people. Government legislation can't solve it.

Luckily, while still in high school, I was playing 5 nights a week with a band in an Oakland Ballroom and started to earn more than my father who was Credit Manager in a large department store. Even during a depression, people still managed to find the money for an evening out dancing.

When finally getting to S.F. State University, the teachers at that time couldn't compose or arrange, they had learned out of the books. And, teachers might not like it if you corrected them or suggested better ways of doing things. I was already a professional so didn't learn much there. I left after one year and worked in bands in San Francisco Hotels and Clubs. I married a nice looking intelligent girl, but I was too immature to realize she could be insanely jealous, and completely unforgiving over any real or imagined slight. Being one of five boys, never having a sister, I unfortunately knew almost nothing about girls. (*Does anyone?*)

Jealousy creates a life of hell for the jealous person as well as those around them. But we had all been taught, "For better or worse." so I stayed with the marriage even though it was a hell at times.

Soon, I was on the road with bands. Style bands and later with big bands that were just starting to get popular. I played 3rd or 4th trumpet with some because they wanted my arranging. It was exciting for a young kid like me.

My first job out of California was in Dallas. A friend and I were walking on the sidewalk and when a black-skinned man got off and stood in the

Russ playing the trumpet

gutter till we walked by, I said to my friend, "Do I smell bad? Maybe I should have my yearly bath before Xmas." He explained about prejudice in the South. I was shocked. In California, this didn't exist. I was so happy to go to Dallas a few years later and see this nonsense was largely cured.

Sometimes, it was a month at a hotel and sometimes killer one nighters with long drives or bus rides in between jobs. Once, with several days to drive to Dallas from Memphis, I drove up into the Ozarks near Hot Springs, Arkansas and got talking to a real hillbilly in a little town. Instead of standing and talking to each other, they would squat and talk on the sidewalk. Comical to me. But you wouldn't dare laugh. One friendly old boy and his wife insisted I come to their house up in the hills and spend a couple of nights. Their homemade house was built out of large stones with no windows, just big open holes. I'm glad it was summer. His wife showed me what a crack shot she was knocking tin cans off a stump with a pistol. They made their own "likker" in a hollowed out tree stump they had charcoaled. When we went down to collect his mail, he kept his rifle next to him on the old auto seat in case we ran into one of the families they were feuding with. It was hard to believe. I felt like I was in a Lil' Abner cartoon. But, it was an experience to remember.

After three years or so, I decided to get off the road and went to Hollywood to "make good" (*And whadda you know, I did*). I studied composition privately with the best teachers I could find, Edmund Ross, Ernst Toch, Castelnuovo Todesco, plus the conducting lessons with Sir Albert Coates.

During this time, I was composing and having a few chamber music and symphonic things played, but was still playing trumpet in a band at a beach ballroom. As it happened, the conductor-composer on a radio show that featured film stars in a drama each week became ill and they said, in a panic, "The show is on in three days. Who can write the music and conduct?" I had a friend, working on the show who recommended me highly.

I apparently did a good job. When the next series of 13 radio shows started, they hired me instead of the other composer-conductor. The director of the show was Ronald Reagan. (*Even at that time, he thought there was a Communist hiding behind every bush waiting to subvert us*). I never dreamt that one day he would be President of America. He was married to the famous, and lovely actress, Jane Wyman, then.

When that show finished, Jane Wyman sent me to NBC. She said, "Talk to the conductor, Bud Dant. He'll be nice to you. I gave him a horse a couple weeks ago." So, at the Artist's Entrance of NBC I asked on the phone for Bud Dant, and they said, "He has just left this job. Would you like to talk to the new conductor, Tom Peluso?" (*Of course I would*). Peluso said, "Write me one original and one standard," and told me how many strings, brass etc. in the staff orchestra. "Leave the scores at the artist entrance. I'll have them copied and play them. If I like them, maybe I can give you some work." I was soon staff composer-arranger at NBC.

My marriage had blown up just before this because of extreme insane jealousy. If some girl smiled at me and said, "Hi, Russ," it would start, "Who was that? How do you know her?" and a five-day nag would begin. I was playing trumpet at night in a beach ballroom. One night, I came home to find my record collection of solo trumpeters Bix Beiderbeck, Louie Armstrong, Bobby Hacket, Harry James, Bunny Berrigan, etc... smashed all over the floor. Another night, I came home and found every page of the score of my just completed First Symphony smeared with ink. (*It was a difficult time*). But I stuck thru it all for my two kids' sake. Now, I can forgive her for ruining the lives of so many people, including her own, because I know it was the fault of her living in a very dysfunctional family in her early childhood. She showed our daughter, Judy, love, but showed no love at all to our son David. I was away in the war for three years and unable to help the kids, except that my army pay all went to support them.

To escape the constant nag, I would take my horn and music pad each morning and walk up to the wilds of nearby Griffith park, practicing my horn and writing music, and get back to the house just in time to grab a bite to eat and go to work.

One day in the park, I walked up to the Observatory and met a fellow with his wife and mother in law. He saw my music pad and asked if I could write down music. I said, "Of course." His mother in law said, "Write it down for him and charge him whatever. He thinks he can write songs." His reply was, "There you go again, discouraging me." He sang his song to me and I jotted it down, then I went home and inked a neat lead sheet for him, and delivered it, on my way to work, to his mother in law's beautiful home in Beverly Hills. *And* it became a very popular song with two hit records. The song was "It's Been A Long, Long Time" and Jules Stein soon became a well-known songwriter in spite of his mother in law's discouragement. (*I'm sure she then bragged about her son in-law and said, "I always told you he had talent."*)

One time, when I was extremely sick, feverish and coughing up phlegm, the nagging got so bad, that to save my sanity, I grabbed a few things, got out of the house and drove all the way up to the mountains of Sequoia National Park and camped amidst the soothing quiet of the giant redwoods. After a few days, my flu got so bad I drove down the mountains to the nearest tiny town called Woodlake. The doctor gave me a shot and when he saw my name said, "Are you any relation to Russ Garcia who is a teller in the bank here?" I said, "No. I don't think so." As I started driving out of town, I turned around and went back. I just had to see if this Russ G. looked like me. I had an uncashed check and thought I'd go up to him and present my check and see his reaction. At the bank, they told me it was his day off, but were trusting enough to give me his address.

I went by and met him and his family, had dinner and a night's sleep, but couldn't find any relationship. The doctor's shot helped me greatly, so back to my camp in the mountains. The next night I was in my sleeping bag about twenty meters from my auto, and heard a big bear come busting through the bushes. It was April and they were coming out of hibernation and VERY hungry. He must have smelled the butter in the boot of my car and couldn't get to it, so with his paw, smashed a front side window. These plexiglas windows are tough, but bears pack a monstrous wallop. He crawled in and tore at the back seat but couldn't get to the butter and luckily went out thru the same window. Then he came over to check me out. PANIC! (*These mountain bears can be almost as dangerous as the Las Vegas bares.*) I didn't breathe or move a muscle when he sniffed at me. One swat from the paw of a startled bear could kill you. Then he gave a loud snort and lumbered off into the bushes. I still have the miniature score of Soshtakovich's Fifth Symphony that was on the car seat, with a muddy bear paw print on the cover. The second night after that, at dawn, I suddenly awakened from a dream of something crawling in my sleeping bag. It was so real; I lifted the covers, and there saw a big scorpion in the sleeping bag with me. (*Did I get out in a hurry?*) I caught him in a large glass jar. Enough! It was time to leave. On the way out of Sequoia National Park, I showed the ugly looking scorpion to the Ranger. He said, as he crushed this horrid looking creature under his boot, "It probably wouldn't have killed you, but you would have been mighty sick for a week."

When I took the NBC job, my marriage had blown up. So I rented a room in Peluso's house and became part of their family. Their first son A.J. showed musical talent from a very early age. His mother was an opera singer and his father an excellent pianist and conductor. When little A.J. was 4 or 5, I said to him across the room, "A.J., this is C, and I played middle C. Now, What is this?" and I played another note. He then identified every note I played. When his father came home I told him, and he said, "Impossible. A kid that age could never do that. So, I demonstrated. Daddy was SO proud.

That evening the owner of a large transcription company came to the house and Peluso said, "Wait till you see what my kid can do." And he played C and then G and said, "A.J., What note is this?" The kid said, "I don't know." Tom tried other notes and the answer was always, "I don't know." He wasn't going to perform for his father. Tom's Italian temperament nearly exploded. I had to go into another room to hide my smile. A.J.'s little brother, Tony, taught himself guitar and even tuned the strings to an F major chord instead of the orthodox way. He later became lead guitarist for the Carpenters.

This same transcription company owner, Jack Richardson, made one of the first ever stereo recordings. They got me the conductor sketches from the great Disney film *The Living Desert* and had me write arrangements featuring stereo effects. He also hired me to produce (*Sit in the booth and see that balance and recording is right*) a transcription session featuring Maria Callas, Thomas Meighan, Emily Hardy and a few other Grand Opera stars, whose names I don't recall now.

One afternoon, I was writing in my office at NBC and someone came in and said, "Come quick. One trumpet player hasn't shown up for the "Tums" Radio Show. So I sat in and played fourth trumpet with the Horace Heidt Big Band. Heidt wasn't much of a musician. He had someone else conduct for him.

Before we went on the air, he would stand on his head for a few minutes and then stand upright and close one nostril and sing six or eight times, "No Nay Noony Nah," a vocal warm up. All he did on the show was walk to the microphone and say, "Tums for the tummy" and into the show we'd go. I played several Saturday nights with the band at civic auditoriums around L.A. He had several good arrangements in the library written by Billy Finnegan, which were fun for all these great musicians to play. And, he had lots of novelty numbers where each of us had to stand and play a note at the right time blowing across the top of a tuned coke bottle or ringing a bell. Fellows in the band told me he had them once all learn to juggle three balls. The first time they did this in a theatre, the spotlights came on blinding their eyes and balls were bouncing all over the stage and into the audience. And, that was the last time they tried that act.

Quite often when some band needed a trumpet player for a few gigs I'd work with them. Alvino Rey, Pinky Tomlin, Al Donahue, the Orpheum Theater.

World War Two

NBC kept me out of the war by writing letters to the Draft Board telling them I was essential to the network. But, when the Draft Board found that my marriage had blown up, I was called.

They asked if I wanted to go to Officers Training School in Georgia, (*because my IQ was high enough*) and I refused. I knew requests would be coming in, as soon as I finished Basic Training camp, from Army Bands, and Motion Picture Units in California. What I didn't know was, they were planning the invasion of Normandy in France and orders were that anyone who could stand up and hold a rifle was to be put in the Infantry and shipped to England immediately. So I ran up on Omaha beach in France. Luckily, it was seven days after the initial invasion, or I probably wouldn't be sitting here typing this.

Russell in the US Infantry

I went thru France, Belgium, the southern tip of Holland and into Germany, doing my job but never trying to be a hero. I erased the horrid memories, but remember making a few G.I.s laugh when shells were coming in and everyone was in panic mode, by telling the guys, "This is peaceful. I could be back in California with my wife." I think trying to laugh once in a while helps to keep you half sane in such horrible conditions, but sometimes I felt ashamed to admit I was a member of the inhuman race. You develop calluses on your soul to get thru it all. Seeing young boys dying for such idiocy made me think, "If I ever get out of this alive and half sane I've got to try to do something about it." (*I did get out alive*).

Patriotism to anything less than *all* of mankind is an evil that has to go. And greed for power or money is an insanity. There's plenty for all if we could learn to co-operate. All war is sheer stupidity and completely idiotic. Can't help but wonder if there are two types of people. The macho warrior type, who make the best soldiers (*and rugby players*), and the creative thinking type (*Me, who can't kill an ant without apologizing*) and should never be put in a war.

When we first advanced into Germany just south of Aachen, the enemy broke thru south of us and pushed all the way to Dunkirk leaving us isolated. They later called this the Battle of the Bulge. On Christmas day, our own airplanes seeking 'targets of opportunity', and not realizing U.S. troops could be inside Germany, bombed and strafed us so mercilessly our artillery shot down two of our own planes. What horrible Christmas news for some families in America. When we started moving forward again, I went over the famous Remagen railroad bridge the first night, stumbling over the ties. The German army neglected to blow up the bridge in the rush before retreating. Later, I read that Hitler had several officers executed for that mistake. I did guard duty on the enemy side of the Rhine for several days. Saw a jeep blown to Hell the 2nd day with some famous war correspondent in it. A mortar shell landed right in it. Never did know his name. The Germans would send a jet plane over low and while our artillery was firing at it and missing by a mile, they'd send a slower bomber who'd drop one on the bridge. (*They had jet planes before we did*). I was shouting at our artillery, "Wait for the bomber, you idiots." (*Of course, they couldn't hear me*). Three bombs were dropped right on the bridge before our anti-aircraft gunners cottoned on to the idea. That was the end of the bridge. Our people immediately started building a pontoon bridge that was broken up twice with shells. They'd bring it back in place with inflatable dinghies with outboards on them, and finally got it secure. It was discovered that a very young kid in Remagen with a radio, was guiding the enemy artillery that were on the hills above.

I guess you can see why I say, "War is stupid. Nobody wins a war."

One pushes a lot of the horrid happenings to the back of the Albert Einstein mind's filing system and remembers a few of the comic things. (*It helps you retain your sanity*).

Every three months or so, they sent an Infantry person back to a rest camp for a week. When I was In Belgium, they sent me back to a village called Spa. A lieutenant there offered to request I be kept there as his "orderly." But his mannerisms looked a little too feminine so I quickly turned that down. Then, a lucky break, a little entertainment group came there, a comedian, a singer, and piano, bass and drums. I was surprised to see the pianist was a good friend of mine, Mike Cahn, from S.F. University days. After the show, I went up to say hello. He reacted, "Russ! What are you doing here?" (*The answer was kind of obvious*). He was not normally doing this piano thing, he was writing the history of the war from way back of the lines. When he got back to headquarters, he looked thru the records and found the 78th division was just coming up into the war and their band was short one man, a trumpet player. He asked for me to be transferred to this unit. The reply was, "Can't do. The 78th was just transferred from 2nd Army to 7th yesterday." Mike said, "Try it anyway." Back at the rest camp two days later, I was issued ammo and on the truck to go back to the front and someone shouted, "Anyone on this truck named Garcia?" I shouted, "Yo." "Get Off," was his cry, and the very next day, I was transported to the 78th Band. Almost everyone in my old unit was either wounded or killed. So, I kinda figure, Mike saved my life. (*I did take him out to dinner after the war to repay him*).

There was no music connected to the band. We had all the dirty jobs to do. Following the tanks and infantry into a town and cleaning out a tower or pillbox for communications to direct the taking of the next village. (*And, a lot of other jobs one would rather forget*).

At the end of the war, I won a pass that gave me two weeks break in Switzerland. It was heaven. Berlin, in fact all of Germany, was in ruins. No lights. Nothing in shop windows, just rubble. Still, the industrious Germans were already stacking bricks in neat piles to start rebuilding again.

All of a sudden I'm in Switzerland, bright lights, stores full of goodies, chocolate, ice cream, Swiss cheese, clean hotels, comfortable beds, hot showers, wonderful meals, Heaven on earth. When I crossed the border into Switzerland on the train, I had a drawstring bag with a series of little batteries and wire connections I had rigged up to give me 110 Volts to run my electric razor. I hadn't realized this looked just like a bomb. When they saw this, did they haul me out of line quickly and rush me into a room for interrogation. When I showed them how it ran an electric razor, we had a good laugh and they sent me on through.

Lucerne, Zurich, Locarno. It was glorious. The only drawback, was the first four days, sharing a room with a G.I. they had let out of Joliet Illinois Prison, on the condition that he join the Para-troops. He was so proud that he was a friend of Dutch Nelson and other (in) famous gangsters and he bragged about raping German girls during the war. He never could figure why I got up early and disappeared every morning and didn't hang out with him.

In Zurich one late afternoon, I wandered into the old section and into a pub called Mary's Old Time American Bar. I found it was a hangout for U.S. pilots whose planes had come down in Switzerland and who had been interned for the duration of the war. They were drawing U.S. flight pay and going to University and were out of the war. What a life! Old grey haired Mary was like a mother to them all.

After drinking a few beers, (*I hadn't learned yet that "Booze Burns Brain cells" and, I have none to spare*) I said, "Mary, I'm going to write you a song." So I scribbled some lines for a music staff and wrote down a little song. She didn't have a piano so she closed up her bar, called for taxis and took everyone to another bar that had a pianist, and she shed tears when she heard her song. Next time, I went to her place; my song was in a frame up on the wall. Years later, I found her place but she had died and there was only a Plaque on the building wall saying, 'This was the site of Mary's Old Time American Bar'. In 2008, when Gina and I went back again, we found nothing there but a new building.

To the U.S. After the War

After winning that war single-handed, I went back to work at NBC, but a few weeks later Tom Peluso, who was still music director there, went upstairs to the office of lots of Vice Presidents (*Sitting behind desks with nothing to do*) and he said, "Would you musical morons stop sending these stupid directives down to the music department?" Even though true, better left unsaid. AND swoosh! He was fired along with the whole orchestra, plus me and the two copyists. I picked up the odd arranging or playing job and went through a brief one-year marriage to a girl that did bit parts in films.

Then I took a job for a month playing trumpet in a ballroom. One evening, a fellow I had met briefly brought a gorgeous girl in to dance. I nearly fell off my chair when I saw her. At intermission, I went over to talk to him. And he made a wonderful, beautiful mistake. He went to the toilet. I had learned that this gorgeous girl was going to university night school, so I said:

"What if we had dinner together tomorrow? Then I can drop you off

Gina Garcia

at school and I can go on to work." I could hardly believe it when she gave me a happy little, "O.K."

We had a couple of double dates with friends, and in a few weeks, when I asked, "How old are you?" she said, "I'll be twenty on December fourth." She didn't say what year. (*If I'd known she was only seventeen I would have run like a scared rabbit. Seventeen is just a child.*) She did look much older. On what I thought was her twentieth birthday, I brought her twenty long-stemmed roses. And it was then she felt she had to tell me this was her eighteenth birthday. Imagine when I came to dinner to meet her parents. First of all, I wasn't a good Italian Catholic boy. That's three strikes against me already. Second, third and fourth, I was sixteen years older than their child, I had been married twice before and I had complete custody of two children. If I was her father, I would have killed me. I'm sure he wanted to. BUT, we were right for each other, and when she was twenty-one, my Gina and I married; and have had, so far, fifty-seven gloriously happy years together.

Your life depends on so many little incidents. Just think, if that fellow hadn't gone to the toilet, I wouldn't have the perfect wife and life today. I'm sure everyone has stories about little things that saved their life or changed it completely. Once, when we were driving in Italy we detoured seventy miles out of our way to have dinner in Venice and then set off north in a downpour. The rain started coming down so hard we had to drive very slowly and decided to stop for the night in a village, at the bottom of a deep canyon, called Longarone. It was ten at night and all lights were out in the village. After driving around a few streets and not seeing a hotel open, I said, "Let's drive on to Cortina." The next day, the news reported, "A dam broke and a 400 foot wall of water came down the canyon and wiped out the whole village of Longarone."

Gina wanted to get married on Xmas eve at midnight, (*and whatever Gina wants, Gina gets*).

I had complete custody of my two kids and had my son, David, in a boarding school. The same one in which a little orphan, Marilyn Monroe lived. Originally, I had both my children in this school but their birth mother had kidnapped the little girl and I hadn't known where she was for many years. Two weeks before Gina and I were to be married, I received a phone call from the Van Nuys police asking if I had a daughter named Judy Ann. This little ten-year-old girl had never gone to school. One day, the teacher at a local school was surprised to see a strange little girl playing with the others at recess time. The teacher found out where she was living and the Truant Officer was sent to see the mother. He went back and told the principal, "You can fire me if you want, but I'm never going back and face that insane woman again." I showed the police my custody papers and they gave me the address. When I asked them to send a few cops with me, they said, "We can only send police out if a disturbance is reported." So off I went on my own determined to rescue my little girl and give her a decent life. I knocked on the door. When my ex-wife saw me she slammed the door and started screaming at me. I went around the back while she was still screaming at the door. I picked up my little girl, went around outside the house with dogs snapping at my legs. I was ecstatically relieved to see a police car parked a few doors down. As I was rushing little Judy Ann to my car, her mother saw me and came running out of the house screaming. Two policemen came up and held her till I drove off. What a scene! I thank God those police were there. It would have been a horrific ordeal.

I immediately drove down to Hollywood and picked up her brother, David, and took them both for a walk in Fern Dell in Griffith Park, a beautiful valley with ferns and waterfalls. Gina was at work and wouldn't be back to her apartment till late afternoon. I rang her and told her what was happening and brought the kids when she got home.

If Gina had wanted to call the whole marriage off, I would have completely understood. (*She had agreed to marry me, not a whole family*). I was so thankful that little Judy took to Gina's kind loving manner immediately because Judy was still not sure about me. Her mother had told her I didn't want to come back and live with them because I was shell-shocked during the war and insane. Gina and I gave the kids a good meal and took Judy to buy some pretty little dresses. All she had on was a little one-piece gym-suit. Astoundingly, Gina was still willing to marry a whole family on that Christmas Eve. We bought a house from Bob Hope's brother. A house could be purchased for only $16,000 then, and every time I got a job, we'd buy another piece of furniture. We cooked in the fireplace and sat on apple boxes for a while. It was a very happy time even with so little. Both kids went to a public school and Judy learned extremely rapidly.

Judy Ann, not having gone to school could only write her name and the word "cat." So, in the evenings Gina would work with her, teaching her to read and write, and add and subtract, and the "gazintas." (*Two gazinta four two times*). And, being very intelligent, it wasn't long before Judy was

David Russell Garcia – son (died of cancer in 2007)

equal in education to all her classmates. She also became an excellent dancer but wasn't tall enough to become a professional ballet dancer. However, she became a successful accountant and provided us with four wonderful and very successful grandchildren, and six gorgeous great grandkids. First granddaughter Kristy designs window displays for Santa Monica Mall and has a Wellness Center. Her husband, Rob Dupont, designs and builds very creative furniture for Hollywood people. They have two beautiful talented children, Curtis and Capri. Grandson Sean Lurie is a Film Producer for Disney. He and wife, Jen, have blessed us with two gorgeous boys, Kaden and Collis. Third grandchild, Donny Kulp, has a pop band, 27 Miles (*the length of Malibu*) that does very well in southern California. He has a gorgeous child called Ginger. Fourth grandchild Melody, while going to University, invented an extremely successful velcro hair ornament business. She is now, with her husband, David Reinstein, designing and manufacturing teen clothing. They have James, a fabulous baby boy, and a little girl in the oven, who will be our seventh great grandchild.

We thank you, Judy, for all this joy.

Our son David turned into a genius in pure mathematics and is a scientific writer. He did work as a professional exotic drummer for a couple of years with the Mary Kaye Trio who worked steadily between Las Vegas, Los Angeles and Reno. Gina and I were in Reno, where I was teaching a week long master class in arranging and composing at the University, and of course, we went in to catch one of the Trio's shows. I had formerly done two CDs with the Mary Kaye "Trio" *(which consisted of 6 or 7 musicians)* and of course during intermission, they all came over and greeted us with big hugs. Our son also did this, and when they got back on the stand, Mary said, "David, how do you know Gina and Russ?" He replied, "They are my parents." He had taken the professional name "David Costa" because he didn't want anyone thinking, "You got work just because of your father's connections."

I was soon offered a job at Westlake College of Music. I had to plan how to teach arranging and composing to all these high-powered musicians. Because of the G.I. Bill, the government was paying tuition for ex-service men, and I had most of Stan Kenton's

Daughter Judy Ann and husband Hank Kulp

Band and Les Brown's Band plus some of the best Hollywood studio musicians in my three-hour classes. I made a four-page outline and then wrote musical examples to illustrate. This became a book we called *The Professional Arranger-Composer*. Gina and I ran 70 copies off on an old Gestetner machine, *(No computers then)* getting ink all over us. They all sold in two days. So, thinking, "Maybe we've got something here," we rented an electric typewriter and pasted up a nicer version. Two adverts in *Downbeat* magazine brought in orders. Each time one book sold to a University or High School, an order would come in for 50 or a 100. There were no books of this type then. Now there are a few dozen. *(I wonder if it sold so well because it was full of sax and violins?)* But it soon got too much for Gina

Granddaughter Kristy and husband Robert Dupont and children Curtis and Capri

Grandson Sean Lurie and wife Jennifer and children Kaden and Collis

Grandson Donald Kulp with daughter Ginger

Granddaughter Melody Reinstein with husband David and children James and Lila

to pack and mail plus all the correspondence and bookkeeping, etc. so we gave it to Criterion Music to publish. It is now in six languages and still selling all over the world after over fifty years.

My arranging classes at Westlake were a joy. I'd talk and discuss for an hour or more. Then the students would each write 8 or 16 bars, which we would play. Several students also were, at the government's expense, studying privately with me. I had the wonderful honor of helping many young musicians who later became tops in their field: Bill Holman, Bob Graetinger, Gene Puerling, Harry Betts, Ian Frasier, Willi Maiden, and many others.

The owner of the school told me one day, seriously, (I thought at first, he had to be kidding), "I heard that some students are arriving late to class. I want you to give each of them a silver star if they come every day on time, and then, if they are punctual for a whole week, we will give them a gold star." (*Did he think I was teaching kindergarten?*) I had a class full of high-powered musicians, the best in town. When I told the class about this, we were roaring with laughter. When the owner came in to see what was going on, I didn't dare tell him what was so funny. Next, he got an efficiency expert in, who had him route all the government money for private lessons directly to the school, not the teachers, and put us all on a much smaller salary. Of course, he lost every one of his good teachers and this wonderful school went right down the sewer.

Efficiency experts have ruined many a good business: Get greedy. Lower the quality. Lower the quantity. Raise the prices. Boom! Close the doors.

Sometimes there was work "sweetening" albums for pop groups. They go into a studio with an idea for a song and work for days or weeks or months getting what they want recorded with their bass, drums, guitars, keyboards and voices. A lot of them can't read or write music, but can play like virtuosos on their instruments. When they have ten or twelve songs ready, they feel the tracks may need something more, so they call in this old craftsman, and together we decide that some tracks need strings, or brass, or flute or whatever. They would give me a cassette, which I would take home, and write down what they had done, and then write the needed parts for the "sweetening." The musicians are called in and record all the added parts we need. All these players read their parts right off, of course, so we only hire them for three or four hours to sweeten a whole album. Jimmy Seals of the famous Seals and Crofts group said, "Wow, Russ, You did as much in three hours as we did in eight or nine months."

In Hawaii, I trained a large choir of youth. They sing like angels because of the ah, ay, eee, oh, uuu, vowel sounds of their native language. We toured the Islands with Seals and Crofts, and England Dan and John Ford Coley. At the end of the tour, the youth gave me a beautiful kaikui nut pendant, which I still often wear to this day, (*because I think neckties are one of the sillier inventions of mankind.*) When I want to feel dressed up, I wear a loose pendant instead.

Many times I've sworn off sending arrangements away to be recorded. Judith Durham of the big selling Seekers group had me send arrangements to Australia. These people have their young "record producers" with their own ideas, and the result can be very unrelated to what you envisioned.

RCA Victor used to have me send arrangements to N.Y. for their big pop stars to record. They were happy with the results, but I never was. Music notation just doesn't tell the whole story of what you intend, so it's much better if you are there to explain and demonstrate.

I did several recordings with April Stevens, who had a low sexy voice. Sometimes I used her brother, Nino Tempo, a tenor sax player who had a warm rich tone. Sinatra used him in Vegas and on some of his recordings. April got a lot of play on radio, especially for a song I wrote called "Soft Warm Lips."

April Stevens and Nino Tempo

Into the Recording Biz

My first lucky break at this time was getting to do a CD for Verve Records with Oscar Peterson and Buddy De Franco, with a big orchestra, of all Gershwin songs. This led to lots of work for Verve and Bethlehem jazz labels plus Trend and Liberty, RCA, Columbia, etc. etc.

Around this time, our doorbell rang and here's a young boy with his guitar and his lovely blonde wife just in from Oklahoma. Someone had told him to contact me for advice. He came in and played and sang with a very nice voice, a big range soaring way up high when necessary.

I sent him to Sy Waronker at Liberty Records who told him, "Very nice, but it's not what we're looking for at the moment." Then I sent him to another company, who recorded him and sold millions of records. His name? Jimmy Rodgers.

Whenever I saw Sy, I'd say, "Very nice, but not what we're looking for at the moment" and then get ready to run.

Oscar Peterson was such a wonderful person. He was BIG in every way: in height, width, heart, gentleness *and* the greatest jazz pianist of all.

When we were making a CD with his Trio and big brass section at Capitol Studios, we were rehearsing an arrangement before recording it. Oscar had just started into a jazz solo when Nat Cole walked in. Oscar was shaking hands with Nat and carrying on a conversation and unconsciously continued improvising his jazz solo with just his left hand. When he reached the end of the chorus the whole big orchestra applauded and Oscar looked up surprised like, "What happened?"

He gave us two books of several of his solos written down, plus photos. They included a DVD of him playing and talking. Wonderful... A form of immortality. So sad they couldn't do this in the day of Bach, Beethoven Bartok, Shoshtakovich and Stravinski. (This list could go on and on.)

Once, when Oscar had a trio with Ray Brown on bass and Herb Ellis on guitar, they were playing "How High The Moon" at a slow tempo, and Oscar

Oscar Peterson and Russ Garcia

played a gorgeous little phrase. Later, I said, "Os, can I make a tune out of that?" He said, "Go." So I did. For its first recording Bob Russell wrote a nice lyric "I Lead A Charmed Life" (*which, incidentally, I do.*) Our song has been recorded at least twenty times now as instrumentals or vocals, in many different styles.

When we did the album *In A Romantic Mood* with Oscar's trio and strings, the first arrangement started with a big string intro, and I turned to cue Herb who was to play the first chorus as guitar solo, he was staring at the string section with his mouth open. He was really "whelmed" hearing a beautiful live string section play. Guess he'd never worked with strings before. We had a good laugh and started over. I was also fortunate enough to be able to record Oscar's Trio with Ray Brown, bass, Ed Thigpen, drums and a big brass section. Later, they combined the two Albums in one CD called the *Oscar Peterson Collection*. Oscar became a wonderful friend, and we'd often meet and eat together when we were in Europe. Through Oscar, we got to meet and spend time with a lot of the greats, Stephan Grapelli, Miles Davis, Coltrane, etc... Once in Europe, we were backstage and Miles would play the first chorus and walk off stage, letting Coltrane play for 8 or 10 minutes and then Miles would walk on and play the last chorus. Oscar said, "Come on, Miles. These people didn't pay 60 dollars just for a quick glimpse of your new Italian suit. Get out there and play for them."

I was so lucky to often enjoy Oscar's company and we kept the emails going till the sad time of his passing on. They've got to have at least one Bosendorfer piano in Heaven for him to play. (*I can't imagine him sitting on a cloud playing a harp*).

Norman Granz was owner of Verve Records and manager for Oscar, Ella, and lots more. The Afro-Americans (*as they're called now*) loved Norman. He insisted on top treatment for them all, even in the bad days in the South. Charlie Parker once relieved himself of some urine in the aisle of a train in the South. (*It's a wonder this genius didn't get lynched*). Norman flew down immediately and paid off all the right people and got him out of jail. It must have cost him a lot. And, once Ella came out of a hotel and was going to get in a taxi cab and the doorman said, "No, you don't," and was going to give the cab to some white folk who just came out the door. Norman said, "Get in the cab, Ella." The doorman put a pistol in Norman's belly, and Norman said again, "Get in the cab, Ella." and she did. Luckily, nothing happened, but you can see why he was loved and respected.

Oscar, Ella. Ray Brown, and Norman Granz were all like family. During a 'Jazz at the Philharmonic' tour when we were with them in Europe, Ella got peeved at Norman and threatened to catch the next plane to the States. He immediately went down and tipped the hotel desk clerk and got her passport to insure she couldn't. Granz and Oscar and Ray loved to play practical jokes on each other. They all talked about buying a certain type of light meter when they were coming to Zurich. Norman got to the store ahead of them and bought three of them and had the store tell Os and Ray they were all sold out. Then at the hotel they found the light meters in their room. Ray did the same to Norman and Ella buying all the little onion pies their mouths were watering for on arrival in another town.

I went in to Verve Records in Beverly Hills with an idea for a CD and after I talked for one minute, Granz said, "Would you like a job?" When I asked, "What do you mean?" he said, "I would like you to be A and R man for Verve Records. (*A and R stands for "Artists and Repertoire"*). It entails planning, supervising, all CDs, signing artists, seeing that the CD covers and liner notes are good. It's actually being in charge of the whole artistic side of the company.

Granz wanted to live in Switzerland because he loved it and, I think, maybe for tax purposes. When he drove across the border, just before his midnight deadline New Year's Eve, he had a painting on the back seat. The customs man saw the painting and said, "My kid could do better than that," and Norman got through without paying duty on an original Picasso.

Anyway, he said to me, "I feel you have integrity, I can trust you." And he offered me so much money and asked me to try it for six months, so I did. (*He had to be seeing my Baha'i beliefs, not me*).

Having had no business experience at all, and suddenly having to make contracts with high-powered agents used to fighting for more money for their artists, I thought, "How can I handle this?" My beautiful Baha'i Faith stresses justice, so I would say to an agent, "Let's find a deal that's fair to you and your client, and fair to our company. Then we'll both profit and can do further business happily together." One agent said, "Man, you've got the smoothest line I ever heard."

At Verve, besides all our greatest of jazz stars, we had big success with comedy CDs. Jonathan Winters, Shelly Berman, Mort Sahl, etc. One day, Eddie Cantor came in with transcriptions of some of his radio shows under his arm. When I was a kid, neighbors used to come to our house to listen to Eddie Cantor's Sunday evening radio show. (*There was no TV then*). He was the most famous comedian of that time. I was so sad to discover the jokes that were so funny then, were just not funny anymore. And I had to tell him that, 'the committee' (me) was very sorry but we couldn't put out his records.

One day in my office at Verve, Jonathon Winters came in and seeing a monster goblet that was on my desk containing a few pencils and other things, he picked it up and using it like an echo chamber, went into an impromptu 'mine shaft' rescue, doing all the different voices and sound effects: the trapped miner, the rescuers, the sobbing mother, someone pouring him down some hot soup, the explosion, the Irish priest starting his last rites. Our engineer, Val and I were laughing so hard soon the whole staff from all the other offices were in there enjoying a hilarious impromptu performance. On his stage shows a heckler would inspire new "funnies" from Jonathon, but Shelly Berman, who sold a million records, memorized every eyebrow lift and gesture and inflection, so he could be thrown completely by a heckler.

Jonathon said to me, "They put me in the zoo (*mental hospital*) every once in a while, but I confuse the psychiatrists so much they throw me out." He loved owls and knew all about them, and he could tell you the history of every battle in the U.S. civil war. How any war could be called "civil" I don't know.

The only other comedian I worked with (*though he never knew it*) was Stan Freeburg. George Fields was in charge of music for his TV show. Would you believe the orchestra was harmonica, marimba, and bass? George, an excellent harmonica player, and close friend of mine, would phone in a panic every Thursday morning and plead, "Russ, can you come over? I haven't written the music yet and rehearsal is late this afternoon." So I wrote the Freeburg Show music without him ever knowing it.

When I was ready to leave the job at Verve at the end of six months Granz said, "You have so many projects in the works, stay till the end of the year," and he raised my salary. Finally, after almost two years, I said, "I just want to arrange and compose and not think about the business end of this profession, and I must leave at the end of the year." Granz soon sold Verve to MGM Records. They wanted our whole staff, but only Val Valentine, our Recording Engineer, wanted to live in New York. Then, Sinatra's Record Company Reprise wanted our whole staff. Mo Ostin, our Verve accountant, had never attended a recording session, even though I urged him to come and see the other side of the business. He went to Sinatra's Company and told them he was an A and R man with Granz's Company. He was hired and was smart enough to get some young producers that made him a couple of CDs that sold. Soon I heard, he had become A and R for Warner Brothers Records, and before long, became President of Warner Brothers Records. Astounding for a person who was not at all musical.

But, back to Verve recording stars: Stan Getz was another great musician. No matter what chords you wrote he would immediately hear them and play beautiful phrases over them. One CD called "Cool Velvet," (*which nicely describes his sound*) we recorded in a studio just north of Baden Baden in the Black Forest in Germany. We used the local symphony, and in the rhythm section, we had several U.S. musicians Eddie Sauter had brought to Baden Radio where he was working at the time: Sperie Karas on drums, Blanche Birdsong on harp, Dave Hilldinger on percussion. Getz, like Anita O'Day, could dissipate half the night and come in the next day looking the picture of health. He said he was the only jazz saxophone player in the Swedish Royalty Book. He had married a Swedish Countess.

Verve hired me to do a CD with the great Lester Young, a tenor sax player everyone learned from. But, even though the arrangements were all written and the orchestra hired, we had to cancel the session. The old booze bottle again. This fabulous musician was so far gone he just couldn't play anymore. The orchestra musicians had to be paid even though not playing. Whenever this happened, I didn't bill Norman Granz, and hoped I could use the ideas in later arrangements.

Art Pepper, who played such great jazz alto sax, was another who ended a wonderful career way too soon. He phoned the day he was supposed to work with me on a session, saying, "Russ, I just can't make it. I don't have to tell you why." So, I was able to get a replacement for him. At least, he realized he wasn't going to make it.

I was never involved with drugs and quit alcohol many, many years ago. (Could that be why I'm still healthy and working at 93?)

In Europe one day I ran into Count Bill Basie in a hotel lobby. He said, "Hey, Russ, it's my birthday. Why don't you write me something for the Band?" When I went back to my room, out of my pencil flowed an exciting original I called "Flyin' Free." It was hardly in that wonderful simple swinging Basie ensemble style. I doubt that he ever played or recorded it, but I've used it dozens of times for a "Knock their socks off" opener at concerts. When Shaynee Rainbolt wanted to include it in her CD, Gina wrote a lyric, and it opens her live show, and ended up in second spot on her CD.

Neal Hefti, who wrote one of Basie's best albums, became a good friend when they asked me to do a short film combining cartoon characters with Herb Jeffries and Neal's wife, Frances Wayne, a fabulous singer with a very low voice. I asked, "Why are you calling me when she's married to one of the best jazz writers around?" But they insisted on me. Maybe cause I had done several projects with Herb before, or maybe they thought I had more film experience. But it didn't seem to bother Neil, and both he and Frances became my very good friends.

The tragic combination of Frances passing away at much too young an age, and an auto accident taking their daughter not long after, were two terrible shocks to Neal, and took away a lot of his zest for writing music. (*Why do bad things happen to the good-guys, instead of the bad-guys?*)

The first arrangements I did for Johnny Hodges, Ellington's lead alto sax, was for (*You're not going to believe this*), the Lawrence Welk Orchestra. I don't know how it came about, but Dot Records called in eight west coast arrangers. We each did two arrangements for Johnny and big orchestra with strings and brass. Each of us conducted our own work. Of course, none of us wrote in the Welk style and we never saw Welk. One of my arrangements was Errol Garner's "Misty." I've used a very similar arrangement to feature a sax player many times for symphony concerts. Of course, you wouldn't dare use the same arrangement when recording with someone else.

Later, for Verve, I did a whole CD with Hodges and strings, and soon after, for Roy Eldridge, the little giant of the trumpet, and strings. Then, two albums for Buddy DeFranco with orchestra.

Bud Shank, another great alto sax and flute player, and friend, who was my first call on many a CD date, was nice enough to get up and say nice things about me at a tribute dinner and Jazz Festival. He offered to come up and play the solos in a piece I had written that he had formerly featured on a few years before on a Stan Kenton Capitol Records CD.

(*These tribute dinners are like being at your own funeral where everybody is obliged to stand up and say nice things about you, while you try to put on your shy "aw shucks" mask*).

Another joy around this time was doing an album with happy, charming, swinging Nellie Lutcher, whose big hit was "Hurry On Down To My House, Baby, Nobody Home But Me." This was that wonderful bass player Red Mitchell's last job before he went to live in Sweden.

Way back, when I was a young musician on the road with bands, I loaned a tenor sax player, Billy Binford, 75 dollars to get married. He never paid me back and I eventually forgot all about it. On their 50th wedding anniversary, I received a card with a picture of his family and a check for $300. It must have been nagging his conscience all this time so he added fifty years of interest.

Another tenor player on the same band, Ford Martin from Duncan, Oklahoma, was a bit of a con man, but a happy, likeable friend. He hung out in a very posh Dallas club, hoping to meet a rich chick. He did meet a gorgeous girl and they got married. And then, found they were both playing the same game. (*Poetic Justice?*) When I was overseas in the war, I happened to be in my "silly" mode and sent him an Air gram addressed only to, "Fibber Martin, Dunkin', Okla." and I could hardly believe it when I found out it had reached him.

When I was recording for Hamburg NDR Radio, they asked me to do an extra job. They had agreed with BBC to prepare a program each for the other. NDR asked me to write a thirteen-minute "Beatles Medley" for BBC. (*Kinda strange, an American hired by German Radio to arrange Beatle's tunes for an English radio show*).

The Fabulous Fifties and Sixties

What a great musical era it was with gorgeous melodies, beautiful harmonies, and poetic lyrics. *And* more film work and recording work than one needed. I had agreed to do a Music Festival in Stuttgart. They had given Michel LeGrand from Paris, Georg Haentzshel from Berlin, and me from the U.S., the same three folk songs, and one from each country, from which we were to write three pieces each for big orchestra. We were to come to Stuttgart and conduct our own things.

I had been working on a Hollywood film and had done two albums in the week before I got on the airplane from L.A. to Stuttgart. I had had only two or three hours of sleep each night, so, hadn't written one note of this music yet, even though they had been saying the copyists needed the scores, to be ready for first rehearsal coming up in three days. On the plane, I started to jot down a few bars of each theme in as many ways as I could think of, but next to me sat a woman who thought it was so glamorous to sit next to a real live composer, and wouldn't shut up. So I just went to sleep. When I arrived at Radio Stuttgart and told them I still hadn't quite finished my pieces, (*You have to stretch the truth a little, sometimes*) they set me up in a room and I wrote all afternoon and till 3:30 a.m. the next morning. Leaving my three scores on the desk, I rushed to my hotel and told them to wake me at seven so I could get to rehearsal that morn. They woke me at 7 p.m. Luckily, we had a good rehearsal the next day, and a run through before the concert the following day. It all must have come through fine 'cause the critics gave me superlative reviews.' The great contrapuntal Swingle Singers were on the same program and Michel LeGrand's sister sang lead in the group. He said, "I have a beautiful house on the Seine River. Why don't you come down and spend a few weeks? We can have a great time writing music and having fun." But I had to say,

"If I phoned my wife in Hollywood and told her I was going to Paris to have fun for a while, she might not understand."

Every time I went to Europe, I was asked by Sam Spence, a student of mine when he was a young lad, to work with him on the NFL Film music. He was supplying all their music for many years. Sam, and his lovely mountain climbing Austrian wife, Friedl, lived in Munich but also had a condo in the ski paradise, Davos, Switzerland, that they kindly let us use whenever we needed a few days ski break.

Another joyful outfit to work for was Bethlehem Records. They had lots of good jazz players and their A & R man, Red Clyde, was not afraid to experiment with new ideas. Though, a jealous A & R man in NY tried hard to sabotage Red by using wrong takes from the master tapes he sent back from California, and misspelling artists names and giving wrong info about composers and publishers.

Lud Gluskin, head of music for CBS TV had me write music for the Laredo TV pilot film. When they were planning a series they often made a pilot film to sell the idea. Also he had me write the music for the pilot of "Mr. Distrct Attorney" and we flew to London and used the Ted Heath Band to record this "Detective Story Jazz" type music. They were a great sounding happy friendly lot of wonderful musicians. When Dizzy Gillespie showed up at the recording session I had to help translate some of his Be Bop English that had them baffled completely.

The English Musicians Union welcomed this, but when Mort Lindsey asked me to do the arranging on a Judy Garland Film in London Offering Gina and I all expenses plus double scale for arranging, their union demanded a London arranger be paid the exact amount I would be getting. It made the cost prohibitive, so, of course they used an English arranger.

While in London Gluskin had his friend, Rudolph Friml and one of his lovely Chinese wives come to dinner with us at the hotel. Years before, Friml had bought two Chinese girls and brought them to America as unofficial wives. I had heard (*Which means, I don't know if it's true*) that when a male friend would visit he would often send one of his beautiful Chinese girls to keep them warm. When I first went to Hollywood, Friml's son, Rudy Jr., hired the "sideline" musicians at Universal Studio. These musicians pretend to play as they are filming. The music has already been recorded by the big studio orchestra. I never imagined then that one day I would be first call arranger writing for this magnificent 65 piece recording orchestra.

As a sideline musician, I was in *Rhapsody In Blue* and *Phantom Of The Opera* plus several others. Years later, at the end of the war in Europe, they were going to show us a double feature. When I told my buddies, "I'm in both these films." They had a big laugh and accused me of hallucinating, but there I was in both films on the screen pretending to play my trumpet.

When Trend Records hired me to do the album of Johnny Green songs, Albert Marx had already hired a girl singer but left it to me to choose the male voice. Gina and I had planned a holiday in Mexico and had hired a driver to take us from Mexico City to Taxco, Cuernavaca, and Acapulco. One evening, we were walking down a narrow cobble stone street in the quaint little village of Taxco when a young couple were coming up the hill. And here was Eddie Robertson, a wonderful singer I hadn't seen or thought of for several years, so I hired him right on the spot for the Johnny Green Album. (*Small world? Or fate??*)

Europe Again

During the sixties, we attended a big Baha'i Conference in London and I said to Gina, "Let's go over to Europe and if I can pick up a little work we'll stay a couple of months." In Germany, every big city radio station and the two big TV networks as well as Zurich and Lugano Radio in Switzerland loaded me with work. We stayed almost two years.

During this time at a Baha'i Summer Conference, near Frankfurt, Martin Visser, a friend from New Zealand, showed up. He was laughing and crying and saying ridiculous things like he was someone on narcotics. He had been to Maastricht, Holland to check on the inheritance he was supposed to be receiving. I wondered if his strange behavior might be jet lag. On the train going back to Holland, he remembered that his brother, who never lifted a finger in the house, had served him coffee and then washed the cup and saucer and put them away. His brother had been forging Martin's signature and collecting his share of the inheritance. He had given him a monster dose of Angel Dust or "P" or some other strong dope, thinking they would find him dead on the train and think, "Here's another foreign junkie died on the train from Holland."

Martin, a strong farmer, became sober enough on the way back to Maastricht to figure out what had happened. He arrived in the evening but didn't want to go back to his brother's so he went to the police. They thought he was just another junkie and walked him up and down all night and turned him loose in the morning. He was a strong Rotarian so he contacted the Rotary Club of Maastricht, and someone took him immediately to a hospital for addicts and insane people. By a stroke of luck, a nurse there who knew us, saw his Baha'i book, and tried to phone us. I was conducting the symphony in Hannover for a Hamburg Radio Recording and kept getting messages that a friend of mine was in the hospital in Maastricht. The minute I was thru this job we drove the hundreds of miles to Maastricht and found Martin sometimes coherent and sometimes not. This stuff must stay in your system a long time and flare up at intervals. Luckily, Martin was heavily insured to cover all costs.

Before we had left for Europe, we took Martin and his wife at that time, Wies, to see *One Flew Over The Cuckoo's Nest*, that classic Jack Nicholson film. The Maastricht hospital had the same blonde tough receptionist as the film, and the big silent Indian standing arms akimbo in the corner. Martin said in his strong voice, "This is not real. We're in a movie." We had left our VW 'Rabbit' auto in a shed garage at their NZ home, and Martin said, "When you come home, R and G, I'll wash your Rabbit and bring it down to Auckland to meet the airplane." I said, "Martin, be careful what you say. They'll think you're completely insane and never let you out of here." (*They did keep him, of course, till his insurance ran out*).

We phoned Wies and said, "You better fly over right away. We think Martin's brother tried to poison him and he's in the hospital." It took some convincing to assure her we were not joking with her.

When she arrived, she wanted to go to the police, and hire a lawyer to see that they got their rightful share of the inheritance. We cautioned her to wait because Martin was still not wholly rid of the drugs in his system.

Another kooky thing happened while we were at that hospital; a woman patient decided I was her American soldier lover who came through their town in WWII. (*Coincidentally, I did go thru Maastricht in the U.S. Infantry, but I assure you, I'm innocent*).

On their way home to NZ, the Vissers tried to telephone home from Sydney, to tell their kids they would be home the following day. The NZ operator told them, "I'm sorry I can't connect you. That house burned down yesterday," but she did assure them that their kids all escaped uninjured.

During the fire, a neighbor, meaning well, tried to take our VW Rabbit out of the shed. Having no key, he tried to drag it out with his tractor and did 1500 dollars damage to it; and then the fire never touched that building. Quite an eventful trip for that family. They did eventually get some portion of the inheritance money and thankfully, Martin recovered completely from his ordeal.

During this European time, Willie Bogner, Olympic champion downhill skier was making a film in St. Moritz using all champion Olympic Skiers. He asked me to write the music. So we had all expenses paid at the Palace Hotel and free skiing every day. How good can it get? When I'd come down the slopes in my new Bogner black ski outfit, (*I was always last of course. All the others were world champs*) they'd say, "Hier kommt der schwarze blitz" (Here comes the "black lightning").

It was fabulous until my birthday, April 12th. I overslept and as I was coming up to the ski field on the funicular, an avalanche came down one side of the valley. The skiers tried to outrun it; but then another avalanche from the other side of the valley came down and caught them all. They all escaped but two, Bogner's lovely fiancee Barbi Henneberger, the German champion, and Bud Werner the U.S. champ. They were beautiful people and fabulous skiers and were always at the front of the big ski ballet scene. Since music couldn't be done till scenes were finished and edited, I was always at the end of the scene in the bottom of the valley, with my Rolleiflex taking photos for possible publicity use. If I hadn't overslept, I would have been gone, too. Another example of one small event that changes your whole life.

Film cameras on both mountain sides had filmed the whole tragedy. The next day, the Swiss Government asked for the film, they don't want the public to think skiing is dangerous in St. Moritz. Willi Bogner said, "G and R, you have international plates on your Porsche and U.S. passports; please take this film out of Switzerland. Bring it back to Munich, and don't give it to anyone but a Bogner."

At the border, they searched everyone connected to the Ski Film, but, thinking we were just tourists, we went right on through with no trouble. We heard the news media were offering many thousands of dollars for this film. As it happened, I had to get up to Berlin right away because I was working on another film there.

In Munich, Gina got a phone call from the cameraman asking to pick up the two cans of film. To keep our promise to Bogner, and to get out of giving it to the cameraman, she said, "Russ has it with him in Berlin." Then he warned, "The police might be tapping your phone. The Swiss Government doesn't want that film to be shown." They put out the news that the avalanche had happened in Samaden, a little town in the next valley, instead of the truth that it happened above St. Moritz. Gina then hid the film cans in the attic. The Bogners got worried and thought I was probably going to sell the film in Berlin. But when I got back to Munich, I delivered them and everyone heaved a sigh of relief.

Europe was great fun for a while. Lugano, one of the most beautiful mountain lake towns in southern Switzerland had a radio station with a concert orchestra that would buy any arrangement or composition that I wrote. So whenever Gina and I had an unbusy week, we would drive to no, check into a hotel, have a beautiful holiday and the last day I would an orchestra piece or two and this would pay for our holiday. What a wonderful bounty. In Lugano we met and became good friends with Willi Ruff. Thelonius Monk had brought him to Europe as his bass player. Willi also played great jazz French horn. We decided to do an album in which I'd write six or eight horn parts that Willi would multi track. When we went to the studio, we found they only had a four-track recorder. We should have walked right out, but the owner swore he could do it. Disaster. The sound quality after three or four overdubs was so bad it was worthless. Willi was living in NY then, and I was jumping back and forth from Hollywood to Europe, we never did do anything with it. I would have loved to record it properly.

Then, we were offered four days at a modern music festival in Donau Eschingen... all expenses paid: hotel, food, tickets to all concerts—too good to pass up. All this was the gift of Hans Georg Brunner-Schwer, a large manufacturer of TVs, refrigerators, stoves, radios etc. etc. in Germany. Four days of Stockhausen and his cronies, who write with no melody, no rhythmic feel, and no human emotion, is a bit much for me. They can talk endlessly about it being mathematically perfect, but can you trust anyone who takes four pages of fine print to explain a three-minute piece of music? You come out of these concerts cross-eyed and ear-frazzled.

I'm still a lover of the three basic ingredients in music... melody, rhythm and human emotion. In writing even dissonant music, if I can't sing it easily, I don't write it down.

Brunner-Schwer had a recording studio in his home that Columbia or Capitol records would have been proud of. He often would hire people like the Oscar Peterson Trio and Ella Fitzgerald and other jazz stars working in Europe to come and record for his private collection.

He couldn't sell any of these because these famous people were all signed to record labels. He *did* record Gene Peurling's fabulous Singers Unlimited "A Cappella" CD to release under his own label. Gene, while a student at Westlake College of Music, formed the Hi-Los, which later graduated into the Singers Unlimited with the wonderful talented Bonnie Herman singing lead.

Another time, Brunner-Schwer had me write arrangements for 8 Saxes and Rhythm bringing in Hans Koller from Vienna, and Ronnie Scott on tenor sax, Tubby Hayes, baritone sax, Al Gaynly, drums, all from England, plus some of the finest musicians in Europe. This was a fun project.

One day in Europe, I received a message to phone a Dr. Erich Kleinschuster. I was prepared to speak to a pedantic professor, and on the phone comes the Dr. speaking Be Bop jargon like a hip jazz musician, which turned out to be what he was. This was a most enjoyable job writing for and conducting the Osterreichischer Rundfunk (Austrian Radio) Symphony combined with their wonderful Big Band. Several great U.S. musicians including Benny Bailey and Art Farmer were in the Band. Writing twenty, or more, thirty minute symphonic jazz shows for them was wonderful fun.

Every time I worked for Austrian radio in Vienna, the Baha'i's would ask us to travel into iron curtain countries when I finished my recording. So we went many times to visit Baha'is in East Germany, Czechoslovakia, now the Czech and Slovak Republics, Russia, Hungary, Rumania and Yugoslavia. We wanted to let them know they were still part of a beautiful worldwide Faith, with plans for a world with no prejudice, no oppression, plentiful food and shelter, and a happy peaceful life full of love.

It was always painful to see these people in communist countries living unhappily in fear and having so little of the human comforts and plentiful food we take for granted. Both Communism and Capitalism have failed because of greed for power and wealth. It seems governments can't solve the problems. We have to change the way individual people think and act.

Wouldn't it be wonderful if each country chose their most intelligent, most moral, mature citizens to have a big consultation on their cultural habits and decide which are Synergic (jargon for "constructive") and which are non-Synergic ("destructive")? And then use the media to help the public see that it's to their advantage to discard their habit of clinging to old unworkable behavior habits and replace them with new habits.

SYNERGIC.. No prejudice... Unity + Diversity... Co-operation.. Compassion...

Since I'm up on my soapbox, can I name a few of what I think are destructive (Non-Synergic) cultural habits?
1. An archaic Education System creating memorizing machines to pass exams, instead of creative minds. And good moral teaching that will help them to mature.

2. Dishonest Advertising. Can you find one honest advert? I don't think it exists. 50% off of what? "You have just won".... Scratch here... and on and on...

3. Elected Politicians that think they are Rulers and forget they are hired as Servants. We form Governments to help make life safe and to improve conditions. Then they grow extremely BIG and EXPENSIVE and too POWERFUL. We create a Frankenstein monster that becomes a threat and a terrible tax burden.

4. TV sending wrong messages to our youth. Role models that are brutal. TV could be the greatest Force for Good ever invented, OR, the greatest Force for Evil. It seems to be going the wrong direction now.

5. The popular Adam Smith and Ayn Rand belief that greed will keep the economy flowing. The grocery monopolies, oil companies, power companies and stores keep raising prices, so workers and unions demand more money. Up, up, up it goes causing INFLATION, which eventually explodes into DEPRESSION. Government legislation and spending billions to bail out poorly managed greedy businesses, to solve the resultant unemployment problem, can't solve this dilemma. One way I can see to change this is to use TV to convince people that greed backfires on all parties involved and co-operation pays off.

6. Fanaticism of any kind is a horrible thing. Prejudice, whether Religious or Patriotic or Racial or Class has got to be eliminated if we are to survive.

7. Emotional Fanatic vs. Logical Protest Groups.

8. Goals. Any goal that is not serving all humanity won't bring happiness or prosperity.

(O.K., *Time to get off my soapbox*).

As more success came to me, I'm sure all the folks who used to say, "That kid sits around writing music all day. Why doesn't he get out and get a job like a man?" were now saying, "I always told you the kid would make it."

Back to the U.S. Again

In Europe, we were getting tired of speaking foreign languages and living in Germany, so I wrote to Universal Studio saying, "I'm ready to come back if there is any work available for me." Immediately, a telegram arrived saying, "Be here Tuesday." So, forfeiting a month's rent and a load of coal in our Munich house, back we went to Hollywood to work on Feature Films and TV's *Rawhide*, and *New Addams Family* also, arrangements for The Dinah Shore, David Rose and Andy Williams TV series as well as a Vic Damone TV Special. And, the honor of conducting the Symphony for Louis Armstrong's Hollywood Bowl Concert plus three CDs with Louis.

In the forties and fifties, recording companies sent me several times to Stuttgart where they could do a whole album with a Symphony for $2000. The same would cost at least 20 or 22,000 in Los Angeles. I felt bad about not using L.A. musicians but could easily understand why record companies would do this. The first time I went to Stuttgart, I picked up a new Porsche at the factory for $3000. We drove it all over Europe, shipped it back to the States, and next time I was sent to Europe, sold this beautiful auto for a few hundred dollars more than I had paid, and picked up a new one at the factory. All in all, we had nine different Porsches for very little more than the original $3000. If I had them now they would be worth a fortune as collectors' items. Several musician friends are still driving our old autos.

Laguna Beach, California, each year put on a marvelous show. *Pageant of the Masters*. They would build sets and dress up town folk in costumes and re-create famous paintings and sculptures. Even the town dogs were used when the painting required it. Gene Ober, their conductor, had me write music for their big orchestra that played under the dialogue and for the curtain openings and backgrounds for the magnificent staging of the many different works of art, and / or architectural masterpieces.

In Hollywood, I was part of the committee that started ASMAC (American Society of Music Arrangers and Composers), and also NARAS (National Academy of Recording Arts and Sciences) that gives out the recording industry awards.

At one evening meeting of the L.A. Bohemian Club, one member came rushing in shouting, "My Stradivarius has been stolen out of the boot of my car." Years later, the insurance company he had collected over a million dollars from phoned me, because I happened to be the President of the Bohemians the year the Strad went missing, and quizzed me thoroughly on the whole story of that evening. They suspected he had faked the theft to collect from them. I never heard the outcome of this.

In the year 2003, at the eleventh international Thinkers Conference, held in Phoenix, Arizona, they put Gina and me in charge of music. Brilliant people from all over the world came and consulted on how to build a better world. A highlight for me was one exciting thinker from Japan showing

Poster of Russell Garcia at Summer Cultural Festival in Austria

Russell conducting the Choir in Austria

through a microscope how our emotions and thoughts can affect the forms of water crystals. It proves again the Quantum theory that every happening affects everything else in the whole universe. WE ARE ONE, and the Creator IS the Central Source of all energy.

For this conference, we put together a Power Point production based on the nine main points, from the Baha'i "Promise of World Peace" Message, that the world needs to bring peace to this insane planet. We used pictures and quotes from Albert Einstein, Anita Kidd Stout, Bertrand Russell, Martin Luther King, Helen Keller and others with readers, on and off stage, plus a large Choir and the Symphony. It was a big hit.
Recently, we did this same show to a very large audience in Ried, Austria with great success.

In Hollywood, when Mark Warnow had the weekly "Hit Parade" radio show, Gus Levine, Lyn Murray and I were the arrangers. Before one show, during the audience warm up, Mark had two minutes to kill before airtime. So he said, "We are honored to have Fred Wakeman the author of the current bestselling book, *The Hucksters* with us in the audience tonight." Mark looked at me and motioned for me to stand up. No one near me stood up so I stood up and took a bow to thunderous applause.

After the show, when I went to the Artist's Entrance, here was a huge group wanting an autograph. I couldn't give them the autograph because I couldn't remember the author's name. I'm sure they thought, "What a conceited snob this Wakeman is."

Sailing Away

I had always had a desire (*I think every man who reads National Geographic must have this yen*) to buy a sailboat and cruise the South Pacific. Gina's book, the *Adventures Of Dawn-Breaker* published by Naturegraph Publishers, PO Box 1075, Happy Camp, California, 96039 tells this whole story so, no need to repeat it here.

Trimaran - DAWN-BREAKER

Our New Zealand house, was 31 miles of narrow unpaved road from the village of Kerikeri. A few times, the clay was so slippery from rain, we couldn't drive out.

Halfway to our house was Te Tii, a small Maori village, with a school at which we would stop and sing with the beautiful kids who sang like angels. We built a show based on the Maori legend of the creation of the earth called *Rangi and Papa*. Parents helped with costumes and the children built simple sets. It turned out very well. The children who were in the show, now adults, often reminisce about it and we're teaching their children now.

A while back, they needed a van to take the children to their singing and dancing and sports events. We taught them 60 minutes of songs about love, peace, and brotherhood. We brought all the kids to our house, and recorded a cassette. In the beginning, we thought they could sell some cassettes to aunty, grandma and in the village store, but it turned out so well, I phoned the owner of Ode Records, Terrance O'Neil, whom I had met some time ago, and said, "I've recorded an album with some Maori kids and he said, "I'll take it." When, in shock mode, I said, "You haven't even heard it, yet." His reply was, "I'll take it." We were amazed because it's hard to get a record company to even listen to a recording you've done. He asked, "When can you bring the multitrack tapes (*No digital CDs in those days*) down to Auckland to master it?" When the cassette came out, we sent it to several Disk Jockeys. Soon the kids from this little country school were hearing Michael Jackson or the Beatles on the radio and then themselves. They were thrilled. We received thank you notes from every kid in the school. One of them wrote, "How it feels to be a star." (*And, yes. They did get their van.*)

We noticed that the children were not getting any training in virtues (morals) at home, in school, or in their churches, so we built a course, with a workbook and two CDs. We call it "Life Skills" because it teaches virtues such as Trustworthiness, No Prejudice, Compassion, Honesty, etc, which really are the skills we need to have a good life. We teach, as a labor of love, a few hours a week at three public schools using songs, clean raps that we write, stories, games, and creative exercises, and the kids love it. No lecturing at them. They are all an active part of the class, consulting on meanings and results of living these virtues. In all the stories, some new, some borrowed from Aesop or old fables, I included a little fellow, Jonny

Twigg, 20 centimeters tall, 2000 years old and very wise. When animals or people get into terrible trouble, Jonny Twigg suddenly appears and we ask the kids, "What do you think Jonny told them to get out of trouble?" And they all have a go at creative thinking before we go on with the story. They love Jonny Twigg.

Gina and Russ with children of TE TII School

We're teaching them to be happy, productive, well-adjusted citizens. It should be in school curriculums all over the world. J. K. Stout said, (*And I agree with her*), "A person educated in mind and not in morals is a menace to society." We feel morals are as important as any other subject in the schools. But it is not easy to change the bureaucratic habits of a few hundred years, even when these habits have outgrown their usefulness. "We get trapped in the claws of tradition."

One headmaster said, "I knew you were having an effect when I saw the school bully say to another kid, "I'm sorry. That was rude of me." We had just done Courtesy that week. In N. Z., it is very easy for someone to quit high school and go on the dole for the rest of his life. Some people haven't worked for years. But, I now see lots of our former students working as carpenters, barbers, driving trucks, or working in the super market and one we found managing a large pottery sales store.

Two years ago, we were asked to come to Beijing University and teach our "Life Skills" course to high school teachers that were teaching English as a second language. The government was happy that students could learn morals at the same time as a new language. Our beautiful friend

Wang Yanli translated our Life Skills Course into Chinese. We had been going to China for a month every year. I taught Modern Symphonic Composing Techniques at Changchun University to 60 or 70 eager young and talented students.

They made me an Honorary Professor of Music. I also conducted the Jilin Symphony a few times. They announced me in Chinese, of course, and as I walked on, 3000 people stood up and clapped and cheered. I was thinking to myself, "I haven't done anything yet." During intermission I asked about this and they said. "They announced your age." I guess in China they all retire at 65 or 70.

The first time I ever had a standing ovation for my age. (*It's really no mean feat to get old. It just takes time.*)

It's a joy to lecture on Modern Symphonic Composition Techniques at a University in China. Very large classes of eager students are anxious to learn all they can about our style of music, and they give you complete attention, taking notes and asking questions. A contrast to other countries where what I am telling them is related to writing exciting beautiful music, not what they must memorize to pass their exams and get those letters after their name.

In times past, it was not easy to get a Symphony Orchestra to swing. If you write eighth notes they'll play it very stiff. Though, in Latin or Boogie Woogie music straight eighths work well. Dotted eighth notes + sixteenths don't swing either. Triplets come the closest, so when I had to write a piece for the fabulous Marge and Gower Champion Dance team to be performed by the Moscow Philharmonic I wrote in twelve - eight time and they said it came off fine. Now, most Symphonies have a brass section and a drummer and at least one bass player that can swing.

I was asked to write a paper and do a 3-hour presentation at a very large conference at Victoria University in Wellington for NZ Public School Music Teachers. To better illustrate my salient points, I brought with me a few good professional musician friends so that I could convince the teachers, and more importantly the bureaucrats in the administration, of the necessity for more music in schools. It has been proven that studying music helps students in math and all their other subjects as well *and*, I wanted to convince them that music was as essential in schools as sports, and a lot of other subjects, *and* that good jazz is not evil.

Bach was the greatest jazz pianist that ever lived. Give him a few note fragments and he would sit down and compose a whole triple fugue from it right on the spot. Such creativity is the essence of jazz. Bach and jazz swing unless it's played with the stiffness of an unforgiving metronome.

When Bach would create over a bass line, it was called a Passacaglia. When he created over a chord progression, it was called a Chaccone. Jamming over the "12 Bar Blues progression" or a "Chaccone," what's the difference? I had quickly scribbled off a 16 bar melody with an interesting chord progression and had my musician friends demonstrate their creativity over it. Gina liked the melody so much she later asked me to write a bridge, a middle part, to make it into a complete song to which she wrote a lovely lyric, and it's been recorded several times by different artists. The latest CD is "Charmed Life" by singer Shaynee Rainbolt with all the songs composed and arranged by Unkl Rusl, with lyrics for half the songs written by Gina.

I hope I convinced the conference, especially the government ministers, to have more music in the schools. It will help a lot of youngsters to keep out of trouble and to have more productive, happier lives.

In our world, they allocate millions for Rugby, Cricket, and other sports, but for Education, Health, Arts, or Music, there's not much money left.

In 1974, at a big Baha'i Conference in St. Louis, more than 6000 attended, we used the musicians of the St. Louis Symphony for a concert, and included on the program a fun piece we call "Mini-Opera." I divided the audience into three sections and taught them different parts to sing. After a big orchestra intro, those on the left sing, "Green People are the best. Far better than the rest. We hate you because you're diff'rent. We love us and we hate you my friend. Then those on the right sing, "Purple people are the best etc. etc., then they both start singing their parts as a round and the middle group comes in with a broad theme that works against both, "We can build a beautiful world, When we learn that mankind is one. We can build a beautiful world, when we learn to love." Then the round again with, "Our Church superior, your church inferior, Heaven is where we go, you go to down below. etc. etc.

The next round is "Our Nation is the best, Your Nation we detest...etc."

Then: "We are the working men. We want to strike again, We hate you because you're greedy" etc. etc,

(Against) "We are employing men. Prices must go up again"... etc. etc.,

Then... 1.) "We want higher prices.." 2.) "That means higher wages.." "Higher wages.".. "Higher prices" etc. etc.. (Builds to a big CRASH)! That settles down and everyone starts singing softly and builds to a big ending... "We can build a beautiful world" ... etc. etc. "When we learn to Love... Love... Love..."

The audience enjoyed it so much they insisted we repeat the whole thing again.

We have done this production also for the Rotary Club at a Pacific Conference in Rotorua, and also, with 700 School children in Tauranga, and at other Schools in NZ. Someone translated it into German, but it bombed there. They didn't want to sing, "We hate you because you're diff'rent." (*I'm sure you can figure out why*).

One day in NZ, a phone caller said, "My name is Friedensreich Hundertwasser. I am a painter." I replied, "I know. We just saw your exhibition in Wellington last week." He added, "We have several mutual friends that say we should meet. Would it be O.K. if I came by your house for a couple of hours?" Of course it was. We both live in the beautiful Bay of Islands area.

Instead of two hours, he stayed two weeks and we became very good friends. Whenever Gina would set the table, he would move the knives and forks. He couldn't stand parallel lines. His agent Harel, whom we got to know when I worked in Vienna, told us about Hundertwasser's first big opening exhibition. Viennese society was there all dressed beautifully, cocktails in hand. They announced Hundertwasser and he walked in wearing nothing but a necktie, and started to explain his paintings to people. Of course, this got international publicity, helping him to become world famous.

These days Promotion & Publicity is everything. Also, Friedensreich was all for ecology and designed buildings with grass growing on the roof. He designed clever camouflage for the ugly smoke towers in Vienna. His design for a very unique toilet facility and his Vienna house have become very big tourist attractions.

In spite of his unashamed nudity, at his NZ property, you might walk in to find both he and his current young French girlfriend in the yard without clothes on, he was a very shy person that didn't enjoy large groups of people. If we were at some big picnic on one of the islands in the Bay of Islands, he would say, "Russ and Gina, why don't we go for a walk" and we would go off and admire the jagged cliffs and crashing surf and nature on the island. He would often sail into our bay in his sailboat *Regentag*, which had grass growing on the cabin top, no two port holes the same shape—circular, square, diamond, or polygon, a compost toilet aboard, plus an old fashioned sailing rig. She didn't sail worth a damn, but she sure was colorful. He would always bring an autographed catalogue book of his paintings with their metallic silver and gold bits.

If his fame keeps growing, these autographed books could be quite valuable one day. At his instigation, we all signed a petition to save the colorful old Kawakawa wooden post office in New Zealand. I guess we caused such a worry, they had someone burn it down in the night. (*We think*) So, no more argument possible there.

He offered to redesign the whole town but they refused his offer. They are sad now because their claim to fame is just the kooky toilet he designed and built there. It has made their town a tourist attraction. Now Kawakawa is talking about a big Hundertwasser Museum Park displaying his sailboat *Regentag* and prints of his paintings. It's ironic that his last work of art is a toilet. He passed away of a heart attack in 1999 on an ocean liner on his way to Europe.

Barry Crump, the most famous storywriter in NZ, became a good friend, through our Baha'i Faith, often visiting us for a few days at a time at our 28-acre paradise on Tangitu Bay. In the past, he had a reputation as a heavy drinking, rough, tough, Kiwi bloke. He could also be a very kind loving friend. While Gina was shopping in Kaikohe one day, Barry and I went into the pub, which was full of Maori timber mill workers just through work on a late Friday afternoon. Because of his former reputation, everyone thought there might be a big brawl. They nearly fell over when he went to the bar and ordered us each a lemonade. They were shocked. We won a few games of pool but we didn't bother collecting the money we won from them.

On my 90th birthday, Gina took me to a nice restaurant for an early dinner because we had to attend a committee meeting at 8 p.m. to discuss programs for our Concert Centre at Kerikeri. When I opened the door... No committee but 160 people singing 'Happy Birthday' in two keys at once. I never dreamed my wife could fool me so completely. Three days later in Auckland, we were to meet with the museum directors, (*I thought*), and the same thing happened. She fooled me again. (*I must be very gullible*).

Bob Harvey, now mayor of Waitakere, a beautiful mountain community near Auckland, used to own an advertising agency. He had a great idea for a TV series, featuring our most famous Kiwi, the very likeable Sir Edmund Hillary, the first man to climb Mount Everest. Hillary would be the host, ala Jaques Cousteau, for adventure expeditions: climbing sheer face mountains, sailing around the Horn in a small sail boat, difficult rapid river running, all the sorts of adventures which Kiwis (New Zealanders) so love.

Because of Hillary's wonderful loving personality, it looked to me like a sure winner. Harvey hired two young fellows from England, who claimed to have edited a film for the Beatles. A professional film editor could have done this job in four or five days. These kids were working on it almost a year. When they told me Bob Harvey said I must use themes their father had written, I should have quit right then. I wasn't the one to work with them. This project never got off the ground. Harvey lost 50,000 of his own money on it. What a great TV series it could have been. I always thought Bob Harvey was popular enough to eventually run for Prime Minister of N.Z.

Gina and I wrote an Opera that maybe should be called a Musical Drama because we don't use any of the customary silly sounding (to me) recitatives. We felt the real cruel "heavies" would be more realistic if they didn't sing and just acted. *The Unquenchable Flame* is based on the story of Tahirih, a young beautiful poet who defied the fanatic religious leaders in the mid-1800s in old Persia. She became educated, spoke out in front of men and took off her veil in public, all things forbidden to females.

The mullahs demanded that women be in the harem as "baby makers" or "husband pleasers," so her life was always in peril from the fanatic religious leaders.

Once they were about to brand her with red-hot irons to force her to confess to a murder she was not guilty of. The real murderer confessed just in time and saved her. With a short life full of crisis like this, it makes the ideal libretto for a dramatic opera.

We have performed some of the arias with narration in California and Florida but it would be such a joy to perform the whole opera on stage. Our CD that we made using lots of friends has all the beautiful melodies but doesn't capture the exciting drama of a live performance with cast and orchestra in the theatre.

I would be so happy if it could be performed before my hundredth birthday, or at least while I'm still a resident on earth.

We have dedicated our lives to Building a Better World, so one way is to write books, but maybe I don't have the right talent for this. (*Perhaps I should stick to music.*) I wrote *Wake Up World* and *Malice In Blunderland* which are full of serious solutions to the present problems of the world. Maybe my mistake is, they are expressed in a humorous style. Hopefully, my great grandkids will appreciate them.

The QSM, Queens Service Medal, has just been awarded to Gina and I in the 2009 New Year's Honors for service to music. We don't know who recommended us or why. Possibly it's for our work in the schools.

Queens Service Medal For Services To Music Awarded to Russell Garcia in 2009

Queens Service Medal For Services To Music Awarded to Gina Garcia in 2009

Our village, Kerikeri, has built a multi-million dollar Concert Centre. A miracle for a village our size. They asked me to do the opening concert with choir and orchestra and featuring two show stopping entertainers: Tim Beveridge, a wonderful singer in the Sinatra - Sammy Davis style, and Joanna Foote, a beautiful Kerikeri young lady with a natural great voice. She is a student of our stellar Kerikeri voice teacher, Carol Maher, and is now attending UCLA with a scholarship, and we expect she will be a big star before too long. We first came in contact with Joanna when she was 14 years old. A talented friend, Brenda Delamain, had written a libretto called *Through the Looking Glass*. Brenda asked me to write the music

Tim Beveridge with Russ

for the show, which I did, and Joanna played the lead. She had never sung on stage before and she did a fantastic performance.

Tim Beveridge, one of NZ's best singers. I met when he was recording with the Symphony in Wellington.

Later he gave me a chance to write and conduct for him on a wonderful swinging CD we recorded in Hollywood. We used the musicians from the Buddy Childers Big Band. They were nice enough to give us a free 3-hour rehearsal the day before our session.

Tim and his producer friend of Major Tom Productions were eating with us in a Mexican restaurant that was decorated for the festival, "Cinco De Mayo" (Fifth of May). They asked what the festival was. I didn't know, but in my silly mode, I told them that was the one-day in the year when all the old men were able to make love to their wives. They gave me a bad time a month later when they found out my story wasn't true. Then they wouldn't believe me when I told them the holiday was really celebrating a day when the British sent a big shipment of mayonnaise to Mexico and the ship sank so they called it "The Sinko Da Mayo." The holiday really was about a big battle the Mexicans won against the French. I've had the pleasure of working with Tim several times since in his wonderful productions.

Tim Beveridge CD cover - "COME RAIN, COME SHINE"

Also, had the joy of working with NZ jazz pianists Julie Mason, Phil Broadhurst, Stephan Small and Tom Rainey and the tastiest drummer, Frank Gibson.

Malvina Major, our renowned New Zealand Opera singer, honored me by having me arrange songs she did with the Mormon Tabernacle Symphony recently.

Just this minute, I received an email request to write arrangements for this year's Hollywood Academy Awards Ceremony. For some reason, I am still working all over this silly world, in NZ, China, and getting standing ovations for concerts in Europe and the U.S.

And then I... *(Please don't count the number of "I's")*.

Have you ever wondered why so many people that are loaded with talent don't get to the top in their professions? I'm convinced some of them have programmed themselves for failure. One wonderful, extremely talented creative friend of ours had an opportunity to make a pilot film of a game show he had created, for a TV network. The actors, the orchestra were brought in and he got deathly sick and couldn't appear. A very costly exercise. The second time this happened the network didn't want to hear his name ever again. This same wonderful friend wrote a stage show also which could have been a good one. I helped with the music and even recorded music backgrounds for all the songs and incidental music for him to add singers and choir and actors to for a demonstration recording, which he could use to sell the show. But he went into a young kid's four-track recording studio and let the kid make new tracks at wrong tempos, moods, and poor sound quality. Another disaster. (*What cha gonna do?*)

Many times we've tried to help talented friends and seen them blow the opportunity completely. What causes this I don't know? Some people can't help but bring about their own failure. Is it because parents convinced them when they were kids that they couldn't succeed? Or are they punishing themselves for some imaginary guilt? Our education system doesn't include the most important things all people should be taught: how to choose a mate, how to raise children, how to have good self-esteem and how to live a mature, happy, stress free, productive and moral life.

One more story? I had made a friend of one of the finest Japanese composers, Koichi Sugiyama, who instigated a big dinner party for us, and the best of the Japanese composers, at the Tokyo Playboy Club. They all appreciated my two textbooks and called me, "Sensei" (Master). (*Gina didn't think it was wise for me to take home a couple of the cute, little 'Bunnies' even just to put on the mantel piece*).

In Nagasaki, I was walking in town and feeling a bit guilty about the atom bomb. At a busy intersection, a policeman was out in the middle directing the frantic traffic. He saw me, looking obviously like an American, sport shirt, sandals, with a camera around my neck. He walked over and welcomed me to his city, asking questions while traffic was turning into a loud tangled mess, and then walked back and took over again. The next day, Gina was walking with me on the same street and as I am telling her about the policeman, he saw us and did the exact same thing again. (*Maybe, he was feeling a bit guilty about Pearl Harbor.*)

In southern Japan, where our son, David, was teaching, friends of ours had an adorable two-year-old blonde, blue-eyed daughter. When we walked down the sidewalk all the locals wanted to pick her up and admire her. In a restaurant, at a table near us, was a gorgeous tiny Japanese girl. The two little ones got up and stood three feet apart and just studied each other for a couple of minutes. All eyes were on them. Then they came close and gave each other a big loving hug. I think there was not a dry eye in the house. This proved to us that a child doesn't hate anyone of different race or religion or country unless they are "carefully taught." Unless we brainwash parents all over this planet to teach their children to love ALL mankind, I am afraid that our planet is in deep trouble.

I forgot to tell you how we ended up in NZ. Two friends of ours each built trimarans, (A sailboat with 3 hulls). This sparked our interest in trimarans. Each foolishly started a trip in very rough weather and wives said, "Enuf. It's me or the boat." One chose the boat, the other chose the wife. But, with an open mind (*and an empty head*), I took Gina to Ipswich and we went out into the rough North Sea and she liked it. We put a deposit down with Knobby Clarke, an ex-British Air force man, now a trimaran builder. When he later learned we had no sailing experience he refused to build it for us and returned our large deposit. What integrity. A year later, I sent him a post card from Tahiti to prove we could do it. (*When you tell someone they can't do something, they're gonna do it*).

If you want to hear about our hitting a hurricane the first night out off of Florida, where our yacht was finally built, you'll have to read Gina's book.

In Suva, Fiji, a cruise ship came in with some of the best musicians in NZ playing on it; Murray Tanner, Bernie Allen, Tony Baker, Merv Thomas. They heard we were there and came to our yacht to meet us. When they asked if we would like to do concerts, speak at universities, plus radio and TV in NZ, we readily agreed and forgot about it. We were used to Hollywood; "We must do lunch next week." "The check is in the mail." You smile to yourself and think, "Yes, yes," and forget about it, but, this really happened.

When we arrived in NZ, they had big posters, saying, "The Immortal Russ Garcia." (*I asked if they didn't know how to spell Immoral*)? We worked for six or seven weeks all over the country.

On our last few days in Auckland a musician friend said, "You've covered the whole country except north of Auckland. Why don't you take one of our autos and drive up to the Bay Of Islands, being yachties, you'll love it." It was cool and drizzly in Auckland. Four hours north, we came to a hilltop above Opua, and saw sun sparkling on the water, dozens of islands, fjords branching off in many directions. I said to Gina, "Let's look around for a piece of property. (*She says I'm "impulsive." Hope she doesn't spell it 're'*). We had a realtor in Kerikeri show us around and didn't find anything suitable. We should have bought a dozen waterfront lots at Opito Bay selling for 1,000 each. They are now worth close to a million.

From the top of one hill, we saw way across an inlet, an ideal bay with a red roof house, sandy beach, a jetty, and a boat swinging on a mooring. The realtor said, "Forget that. It belongs to an Aucklander named Harnish, who loves it." Our last night in Auckland we were having a cup of tea with a friend, Beryl Van der Vaart, who said, "Did you like the Bay of Islands? My brother is going to sell his place up there. He bought a business in Rarotonga." And it turned out his name was Bob Harnish. One in a million. We phoned. The price was fair, and here we are in NZ.

Last Chapter in a Charmed Life

How lucky can you get? I've earned my living doing what I love to do. (*I've always written music even when it wasn't for money.*) I have a gorgeous young Italian wife. (*She's 78 now.*) We don't owe anyone a penny. There are enough royalties coming in to keep us eating if we live sensibly. I'm still working all over the world. Of course, travel, hotel, food eats up most of these profits. We now have a nice house on the top of a hill overlooking the Kerikeri Inlet. We decided to scale down as it became too much to look after 28 acres, a boat and an old house. I am in good health. Creativity seems as good as ever. What more could a person need?

BUT, if you could give me a magic wish, I would wish for the world: 1.) A cure for its insanity, 2.) A return to an appreciation for beauty in music, art, fashions, language, attitudes, morals, 3.) To stop it's clinging to old unworkable cultural habits.

I guess I did pay my dues when I was younger, two unfortunate marriages, plus a horrible war. But, since I found the perfect mate, prepared myself to be ready when a few lucky breaks came along, and discovered my beautiful Baha'i Faith, life has been a heaven on earth. Also, my body and mind staying healthy into my nineties; what more can you ask?

- Russell G.

A PARTIAL LIST OF R.G. CDS - ALBUMS

(FILM SCORE MONTHLY) CDs
The Time Machine - MGM
Atlantis The Lost Continent -MGM

(VERVE) Louis Armstrong
Got The World On A String
Louis Under the Stars
Porgy & Bess with Ella Fitzgerald

Anita O'Day
Waiter Make Mine Blues
Anita Sings The Winners

Mel Torme
Swingin' On The Moon
Broadway Right Now with
    Margaret Whiting

Margaret Whiting
Sings Jerome Kern
Past Midnight on (MGM)
MW's Great Hits on (DOT)

Oscar Peterson
In a Romantic Mood- OP & Strings
Oscar and Brass
Oscar Peterson Collection
George Gershwin Song Book with
    Buddy DeFranco

Buddy DeFranco
Broadway Showcase

Stan Getz
Cool Velvet

(VERVE)
Frances Faye in Frenzy

Blossom Dearie
soubrette Sings Broadway Hits

Mary Kaye Trio
Up Front
Music on a Silver Platter (DECCA)

Elsa Lanchester
Cockney London

Roy Eldridge
That Warm Feeling

Charlie Barnett
Lonely Street

Jorge Sevilla Incredible Guitar of

Hollywood Sax Quartet
French Impressions

Frances Faye In Frenzy

Mitzi Gaynor

(CAPITOL) RG
Variations on a 5 Note Theme for
    10 French Horns
Adventure In Emotions with
    Stan Kenton Neophonic

(KING) April Stevens
Soft Warm Lips

(BETHLEHEM) Frances Faye
I'm Wild Again
Frances Faye Sings Folk Songs
Porgy & Bess with Mel Torme

RG
Wigville
Four Horns and a Lush life
Sounds In The Night
I'll Never Forget What's Her Name
LA River
Herbie Mann-Sam Most Quintet

Peggy Connelly

(LIBERTY) **RG**
Fantastica - Outer Space Music
Hi Fi for Kids from 2 to 92

Julie London
Make Love To Me
About The Blues

Nellie Lutcher - Our New Nellie

Joe Greene - Enchantment

Si Zentner - Sleepy Lagoon

Bobby Troup - Here's To My Lady

(ABC PARAMOUNT) **Walter Gross**
Plays His Own Great Hits

The Axidentals
Hello We're The Axidentals!

(VIC) **Helen Grayco**
After Midnight

(RCA VICTOR) **RG**
Carioca

(KAPP) **RG**
Listen to the Music of RG
Modern Jazz Gallery

(TREND) **RG**
Variations for Flugelhorn, String
    Quartet, Bass & Drums

(LOXIE)
Buddy Childers with RG
Come Home Again

(SONY) **Tim Beveridge**
Come Rain Come Shine
Singer

RG
Kaleidoscope - Munich Symphony
Dungeon Chal - NZ Symphony
Vienna Symphony + Big Band
Unquenchable Flame Opera
Variations - Little Big Band
A Girl In Every Port
RG with NZ Symphony Orchestra
Stuttgart Music Festival
Saxophony
Hollywood Sax Quartet
All The Sax You've Ever Dreamed Of

Shaynee Rainbolt with RG
Charmed Life

Alan Kaplan - Ebb Tide
Johnny Hodges and Lawrence Welk
    Orchestra

ABOUT THE AUTHOR

"If you have read any of this book, you can see that Russell Garcia has had a wonderful career. He attributes the wonderful life and sensational good luck he and his wife Gina have had because of their goal: "Dedicating their life to trying to do their share in building a beautiful, happy, peaceful, world for the people of every race, religion, and country.

Everyone should read this book. It has, as well as fabulous stories about so many famous stars, the answers to a lot of the problems we have in today's insane, mixed up world."

- *Larson Craig, writer*

"What a great book. Russ's stories of his 70 years in the Music Business are personal, unique, very interesting, full of laughs and certainly worth reading."

- *Quincy Jones,*
  Composer, Producer, Arranger, Conductor

"What a life! Russ gives us a condensed account of his life, his work, and his beliefs. He manages to find humor in some unlikely situations, and his music and lovable personality endeared him to many."

- *Bill Holman, Leader of the Bill Holman Band*

Gina and Russell Garcia

You Won't Believe Your Eyes!

PHOTOGRAPHY CREDITS

Cover photo: Reynold Brown's, movie poster of the MGM film, The Time Machine, – copyright Reynold Brown/ARS.Licensed by Viscopy, 2013

Page iii: Russell Garcia – photograph supplied courtesy of Adrian Malloch

Page xvi: Gravestone for Russ Garcia – photographer Deb Green

Page 1: 4 Bars Musical Example written by RG of song NIGHT TRAIN. Music by Jimmy Forrest Copyright © 1952 (Renewed) by Embassy Music Corporation (BMI)International Copyright Secured. All Rights Reserved. Used by Permission.

Page 2: Sophia Loren and Jane Mansfield provided by Photofest, NY

Page 3: Zsa Zsa Gabor provided by Photofest, NY

Page 7: Louis Armstrong, Ella Fitzgerald, Russell Garcia - family album

Page 9: Cyd Charisse provided by Photofest, NY

Page 13: Russell Garcia, Charlie Chaplin – family album

Page 16: Rainbow House photograph courtesy of Francois Dischinger

Page 17: Whare Koa private etching by Natalie Ward – family album

Page 19: Anita O'Day –Album with RG, "Anita Sings the Winners" – original cover photo of Anita by Ken Veedor – enhanced by photographer, Peter Green - album available world-wide (Verve 837 939-2 and POCJ-2616)]

Page 21: Margaret Whiting – photograph courtesy Debbi Whiting

Page 22: Shaynee Rainbolt – cover of CD Charmed Life courtesy of photographer John Abbott

Page 23: Tierney Sutton – courtesy of photographer Pamela Springsteen

Page 25: Frances Faye with RG – photo retouched by photographer Peter Green from back of original album "I'm Wild Again"

Page 28: CD cover "Come Home Again" – photographer Buddy Childers

Page 29: Diane Varga – family album

Page 29: Diane Varga and Buddy Childers with G and R – family album – photo retouched by photographer Peter Green

Page 32: Dizzy Gillespie – courtesy photographer Tom Meeks

Page 33: Gina and Russ in front of Rudolfinum – family album

Page 36: RG conducting in Auckland during his 95th Birthday Concert – family album – photographer Diane Miller

Page 39: RG conducting, New Zealand Symphony Orchestra - family album

Page 49: Russ as a toddler – family album

Page 52: Russ playing trumpet – family album

Page 57: Russ in the U.S. Infantry – family album

Page 59: Albert Einstein provided by Photofest, NY

Page 63: Gina Garcia – family album

Page 66: Son David Garcia – family album

Page 67: Daughter Judy and husband Hank Kulp - family album

Page 68: Grand-daughter Kristy with husband Rob Dupont and children Curtis and Capri – family album

Page 68: Grandson Sean Lurie with wife Jen and sons Kaden and Collis – family album

Page 69: Grandson Donald Kulp with daughter Ginger – family album

Page 69: Grand-daughter Melody Reinstein with husband David and children James and Lila – family album

Page 72: April Stevens and Nino Tempo – courtesy of Jim Chaffin

Page 74: Oscar Peterson and RG - family album

Page 94: Poster of Ried Cultural Festival, Austria, Europe - family album

Page 95: RG conducting choir in Ried, Austria (Bahaiblog: In Memory of Russ Garcia)

Page 97: Photo of Yacht "Dawn Breaker" – family album

Page 99: G and R at Te Tii School, Bay of Islands, New Zealand Copyright New Zealand Herald

Page 105: Queen's Service Medal for Services to Music – Russell Garcia 2009 – family album

Page 105: Queen's Service Medal for Services to Music – Gina Garcia 2009 – family album

Page 106: Tim Beveridge and RG – photograph courtesy of Cate Rainbow

Page 107: Tim Beveridge CD cover "Come Rain Come Shine" photograph supplied courtesy of Andrew White

Page 115: G and R – family album

Lightning Source UK Ltd.
Milton Keynes UK
UKOW03f1654040813

214850UK00018B/1213/P